Jesse H. Shera
THE FOUNDATIONS OF EDUCATION FOR LIBRARIANSHIP

Charles T. Meadow
THE ANALYSIS OF INFORMATION SYSTEMS, Second Edition

Stanley J. Swihart and Beryl F. Hefley
COMPUTER SYSTEMS IN THE LIBRARY

F. W. Lancaster and E. G. Fayen
INFORMATION RETRIEVAL ON-LINE

Richard A. Kaimann
STRUCTURED INFORMATION FILES

Thelma Freides
LITERATURE AND BIBLIOGRAPHY OF THE SOCIAL SCIENCES

Manfred Kochen
PRINCIPLES OF INFORMATION RETRIEVAL

Dagobert Soergel
INDEXING LANGUAGES AND THESAURI: CONSTRUCTION AND MAINTENANCE

Robert M. Hayes and Joseph Becker
HANDBOOK OF DATA PROCESSING FOR LIBRARIES, Second Edition

Andrew E. Wessel
COMPUTER-AIDED INFORMATION RETRIEVAL

Lauren Doyle
INFORMATION RETRIEVAL AND PROCESSING

Charles T. Meadow
APPLIED DATA MANAGEMENT

Andrew E. Wessel
THE SOCIAL USE OF INFORMATION: OWNERSHIP AND ACCESS

Hans H. Wellisch
THE CONVERSION OF SCRIPTS: ITS NATURE, HISTORY, AND UTILIZATION

Eugene Garfield
CITATION INDEXING: ITS THEORY AND APPLICATION IN SCIENCE, TECHNOLOGY, AND HUMANITIES

Frederick W. Lancaster
INFORMATION RETRIEVAL SYSTEMS: CHARACTERISTICS, TESTING, AND EVALUATION, Second Edition

Information Retrieval Systems

Information Retrieval Systems: Characteristics, Testing and Evaluation

SECOND EDITION

F. Wilfrid Lancaster

A WILEY-INTERSCIENCE PUBLICATION

JOHN WILEY & SONS
New York / Chichester / Brisbane / Toronto

Copyright © 1968, 1979 by John Wiley & Sons, Inc.

All rights reserved. Published simultaneously in Canada.

Reproduction or translation of any part of this work beyond that permitted by Sections 107 and 108 of the 1976 United States Copyright Act without the permission of the copyright owner is unlawful. Requests for permission or further information should be addressed to the Permissions Department, John Wiley & Sons, Inc.

Library of Congress Cataloging in Publication Data:

Lancaster, Frederick Wilfrid, 1933–
   Information retrieval systems.

  (Information sciences series)
  "A Wiley-Interscience publication."
  Bibliography: p.
  Includes index.
  1. Information storage and retrieval systems.
I. Title.

Z699.L35 1978   029.7   78-11078
ISBN 0-471-04673-6

Printed in the United States of America

10 9 8 7 6 5 4

To Vilma

Information Sciences Series

Information is the essential ingredient in decision making. The need for improved information systems in recent years has been made critical by the steady growth in size and complexity of organizations and data.

This series is designed to include books that are concerned with various aspects of communicating, utilizing, and storing digital and graphic information. It will embrace a broad spectrum of topics, such as information system theory and design, man-machine relationships, language data processing, artificial intelligence, mechanization of library processes, non-numerical applications of digital computers, storage and retrieval, automatic publishing, command and control, information display, and so on.

Information science may someday be a profession in its own right. The aim of this series is to bring together the interdisciplinary core of knowledge that is apt to form its foundation. Through this consolidation, it is expected that the series will grow to become the focal point for professional education in this field.

Preface

The first edition of this book appeared in 1968. I am happy to say that it was well accepted, got favorable reviews, and received in 1970 the "best book in information science" award from the American Society for Information Science. It has since been translated into Japanese and Russian.

I was never completely satisfied with the first edition, however, mostly because it was not sufficiently broad in its coverage to be suitable for use as a text for an introductory course in information storage and retrieval. The present edition has grown out of such a course as I have presented it in the past eight years at the Graduate School of Library Science of the University of Illinois.

It is a greatly expanded version of the original, and it has been completely rewritten. Nevertheless, it is still no more than an introductory text. Many of the chapters could be expanded into books in their own right. I have already treated some of these subjects—for example, those dealt with in Chapters 4, 12, and 25—in much greater detail in other books.

In working on this revision, during 1977, I discovered that some parts of what I wanted to cover had already been covered in other papers, articles, or reports that I have published elsewhere. I have not hesitated to draw on these sources, some passages retained virtually intact, for the present work. In particular, Chapter 3 draws heavily on a report, *Principles of Medlars*, prepared under contract for the National Library of Medicine in 1969. Chapters 4 and 18 are based largely on two articles prepared for the *Encyclopedia of Library and Information Science*. Chapter 15 is a modified version of a paper that appeared in *Evaluation and Scientific Management of Libraries and Information Centres* (edited by F. W. Lancaster and C. W. Cleverdon), published in 1977 by Noordhoff. Chapter 16 is a much modified and expanded version of an article, "The Cost-Effectiveness Analysis of Information Retrieval and Dissemination Systems," published in the *Journal of the American Society for*

Information Science in 1971. In addition, Chapter 12 draws heavily on my review "Vocabulary Control in Information Retrieval Systems" published in *Advances in Librarianship*, vol. 7, 1977 (Academic Press); Chapter 17 on my *Guidelines for the Evaluation of Information Systems and Services* (UNESCO, 1978), and Chapter 25 on an article, "Whither Libraries? or Wither Libraries," published in *College and Research Libraries* in 1978. Appendixes 1 and 2 are drawn from O. A. Badran, et al., *Report on the Independent Appraisal of AGRIS* (UNESCO, April 1977). My thanks go to the National Library of Medicine; Marcel Dekker, Inc.; Sijthoff & Noordhoff International Publishers; Knowledge Industry Publications; Academic Press, Inc.; UNESCO; and the American Library Association for permission to reproduce these materials.

I would also like to thank Dianne McCutcheon and Billie Mann, my graduate assistants in 1977–1978, for helping with the bibliography and with the proofreading of this edition.

Although the book is intended primarily as an introductory text for teaching information storage and retrieval in schools of library or information science, I hope that it may also have some interest and value to the information science community at large.

F. Wilfrid Lancaster

Urbana, Illinois
December 1978

Contents

Chapter One
The Functions of Information Retrieval Systems   1

Chapter Two
The Matching Subsystem   15

Chapter Three
The Application of Computers to Information Retrieval:
Off-Line Batch Processing Systems   35

Chapter Four
On-Line Information Retrieval   69

Chapter Five
The Growth of Machine-Readable Data Bases   78

Chapter Six
Microforms and Microform Retrieval Systems   90

Chapter Seven
Information Centers and Information Services   95

xii   Contents

Chapter Eight
Criteria by Which Information Services May Be Evaluated 108

Chapter Nine
Evaluating the Effectiveness of Information Services 121

Chapter Ten
Latent Needs and Expressed Needs 140

Chapter Eleven
Selecting a Data Base and Searching It 154

Chapter Twelve
Vocabulary Control 178

Chapter Thirteen
The Indexing Subsystem 192

Chapter Fourteen
Improving the Performance of an Information Service on the Basis of Evaluation Results 199

Chapter Fifteen
The Evaluation of Machine-Readable Data Bases and Information Services Derived from Them 204

Chapter Sixteen
Cost-Effectiveness and Cost-Benefit Evaluation 218

Chapter Seventeen
Evaluation of a National Information System   250

Chapter Eighteen
Pertinence and Relevance   256

Chapter Nineteen
A Brief History of Evaluation   273

Chapter Twenty
Natural Language in Information Retrieval   279

Chapter Twenty-One
Automatic Systems   293

Chapter Twenty-Two
The Role of Informal Communication   300

Chapter Twenty-Three
Users and User Needs   312

Chapter Twenty-Four
The Design of Information Services   319

Chapter Twenty-Five
The Future: Paperless Information Systems   326

Appendix One
Interview Guide Used in Evaluation of AGRIS   335

Appendix Two
Conclusions and Recommendations from the AGRIS Evaluation 344

Appendix Three
Questionnaire Used in the Evaluation of a Current Awareness Publication 351

Bibliography 359

Index 375

Acronyms and Abbreviations

AGRINDEX—The printed index produced by AGRIS.

AGRIS—International Information System for the Agricultural Sciences and Technology.

ASTIA—Armed Services Technical Information Agency, known now as DDC.

BA—*Biogenic Amines and Transmitters in the Nervous System.*

BASIS—Battelle Automated Search Information System.

BIOSIS—BioSciences Information Service.

BROWSER—Browsing On-Line with Selective Retrieval.

BRS—Bibliographic Retrieval Services.

CAIN—Cataloging and Indexing data base (produced by the National Agricultural Library).

CHEMCON—Chemical Condensates data base.

CIJE—*Current Index to Journals in Education.*

CIRC—Central Information Reference and Control.

COMPENDEX—The machine readable version of *Engineering Index.*

CP—Consistency pair.

CRT—Cathode ray tube.

DDC—Defense Documentation Center.

DIALOG—Set of computer programs for on-line information retrieval produced by Lockheed Information Systems.

DSFR—Demand Search Formulation Record.

ERIC—Educational Resources Information Center.

ESANET—The on-line retrieval network of the European Space Agency.

EURONET—The on-line retrieval network organized by the Commission of the European Communities.

FAO—Food and Agriculture Organization of the United Nations.

GRACE—Graphic Arts Composing Equipment.

IAC—Information analysis center.

IAEA—International Atomic Energy Agency.

IICA–CIDIA—Instituto Interamericano de Ciencías Agrícolas, Centro Interamericano de Documentación e Información Agrícola.

IM—*Index Medicus*.

INFORM—A business data base produced by Data Courier Inc.

INIS—International Nuclear Information System.

INQUIRE—Set of computer programs for on-line information retrieval produced by Infodata Systems, Inc.

INSPEC—International Information Services in Physics, Electrotechnology, Computers and Control.

ISI—Institute for Scientific Information.

KLIC—Key letter in context.

LEADERMART—Full scale implementation of the experimental LEADER (Lehigh Automatic Device for Efficient Retrieval) system.

LEXIS—On-line natural language information retrieval system designed by Mead Data Central.

LITE—Legal Information through Electronics.

MEDLARS—Medical Literature Analysis and Retrieval System.

MEDLINE—MEDLARS On-Line.

MeSH—*Medical Subject Headings*.

MR—Machine-readable.

NAL—National Agricultural Library.

NASA—National Aeronautic and Space Administration.

NIH—National Institutes of Health.

NIM terms—Non-*Index Medicus* terms (nonprint terms).

NINDS—National Institute of Neurological Diseases and Stroke.

NLM—National Library of Medicine.

NSF—National Science Foundation.

NTIS—National Technical Information Service.

OBAR—Ohio Bar Automated Research.

ORBIT—On-Line Retrieval of Bibliographic Information Time-Shared (on-line retrieval software produced by System Development Corporation).

PASCAL—A multidisciplinary information service operated by the Centre National de Recherche Scientifique.

PD—*Parkinson's Disease and Related Disorders: Citations from the Literature.*

RECON—Remote Console (on-line retrieval system of NASA).

SCAN—Selected Current Aerospace Notices.

SCANNET—An on-line network linking the Scandinavian countries organized under the aegis of NORDFORSK.

SCI—*Science Citation Index.*

SDC—System Development Corporation.

SLIC—Selected Listing in Combination.

SDI—Selective dissemination of information.

SDS—Space Documentation Service (of European Space Agency).

SIDC—Scientific information dissemination center.

SHARP—Ships Analysis and Retrieval Project.

SMART—Set of experimental retrieval programs developed by Salton and now implemented at Cornell University.

SRIM—Selected Research in Microfiche.

SSIE—Smithsonian Science Information Exchange.

STAIRS—Set of computer programs for on-line information retrieval produced by International Business Machines (IBM) Corporation.

TELENET—A time-shared communications network operated by the Telenet Communications Corporation.

TIP—Technical Information Project.

TYMNET—A time-shared communications network operated by Tymnet Inc.

UNESCO—United Nations Educational, Scientific and Cultural Organization.

UNISIST—World Science Information System (a program of UNESCO).

Chapter One

The Functions of Information Retrieval Systems

This book is concerned with "information services," "information centers," and, most particularly, "information retrieval," and this chapter attempts to define or illustrate the scope of these terms as they are used throughout the text.

The important functions performed by information centers are perhaps best understood when viewed in the broader context of the complete cycle by which information is transferred through formal channels. The major elements of the cycle are depicted in Figure 1. The "user community" is simply the community of individuals working in a particular subject area. Some of them are involved in "research and development activities" and some in a variety of other activities loosely referred to as "application activities" in the diagram. All of them are, in some sense, users of information, and some are also creators of information products. This means that some people, whose activities are pre-

The Functions of Information Retrieval Systems

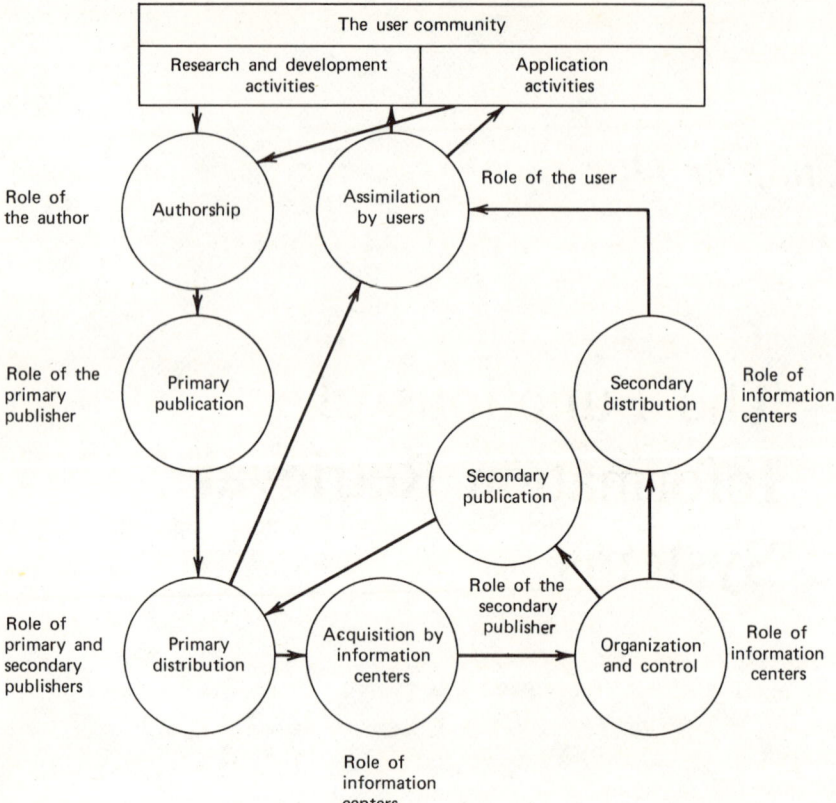

Figure 1 The information transfer cycle.

sumed to be of interest to others in the community, describe their experiences, research, or opinions in some form of report. This is the "role of the author" in the communication cycle. But authorship is not in itself a form of communication. The work of an author has little or no impact on the professional community until it has been reproduced in multiple copies and distributed in a formal manner, that is, published, which is the "role of the primary publisher" in the communication cycle. A primary publication may be a book, a journal, a technical report, a dissertation, a patent, and so on.

In the diagram, primary publications are shown to be distributed in two ways:

1. Directly to the user community through subscription and purchase by individuals.

2. Indirectly to the user community through subscription and purchase by information centers.

Information centers—this term is used generically in the diagram to represent libraries, other kinds of information centers, and the publishers of secondary services—have very important roles to play in the information transfer cycle. Through their acquisition and storage policies, libraries provide a permanent archive of professional achievement and a guaranteed source of access to this record. In addition, libraries and other information centers organize and control the literature by means of cataloging, classification, indexing, and related procedures. Another major role in organization and control is played by indexing and abstracting services and publishers of national bibliographies. These organizations are responsible for the publication and distribution of "secondary publications." Some secondary publications may go directly to the user community. The great majority, however, go to institutional subscribers, that is, information centers, rather than to individuals.

Information centers also perform important "presentation and dissemination" functions in the cycle. These activities, which constitute a form of secondary distribution of publications and information about publications, include circulation of materials as well as various types of current awareness, reference, and literature searching services. In the 1970s, the machine-readable data bases of the secondary publishers are playing an increasingly important role in the provision of various types of information service.

The final stage in the cycle, as shown in Figure 1, is "assimilation." This, the least tangible, is the stage at which information is absorbed by the user community. Here a distinction is made between "document transfer" and "information transfer." The latter occurs only if a document is studied by a user and its contents are assimilated to the point at which the reader is informed by it, that is, his state of knowledge on its subject matter is altered. Assimilation of information by the professional community may occur through primary or secondary distribution. Different documents have different levels and speeds of assimilation associated with them, and the contents of some may never be assimilated at all because they are never used.

The processes of formal communication are presented as a cycle because they are continuous and regenerative. Through the process of assimilation a reader may gain information that he can use in his own research and development activities, which, in turn, generate new writing and publication, and the cycle continues.

The diagram is oversimplified in one important respect. It shows the dissemination of information through formal channels but does not explicitly illustrate the processes of informal communication. But the informal channels do not generally disseminate different information from that disseminated through the formal channels. Both disseminate the results of the same experience or research. The informal channels differ from the formal channels in that they disseminate information in a different format or in the same format but at a much earlier time, as, for example, in the distribution of drafts or preprints. The informal channels are important because they disseminate information more rapidly than the formal channels, at least to those well integrated in a professional community, and because they disseminate information to some individuals who, for one reason or another, choose not to use the formal channels.

This brief discussion of the information transfer cycle is presented in order to clarify the role played by information centers and services in the complete cycle. The present text is mainly concerned with this role as depicted in the diagram by the circles captioned "Acquisition by information centers," "Organization and control," and "Secondary distribution." Because some information centers also create secondary data bases, which may be used in the provision of various kinds of information services, the activities of "Secondary publication" and "Primary distribution," of secondary publications, also fall, at least in part, within its scope. The other activities depicted, relating to authorship, primary publication and distribution, and the assimilation of information by users, are outside the direct control of information centers and services. Although these activities may be touched on at various points, they are not dealt with in any detail in this text.

THE ROLE OF INFORMATION SERVICES

The major function of any information service is to act as an interface (Figure 2) between a particular population of users and the universe of information resources in printed or other form. The user community is usually defined by geographic area, institutional affiliation, subject interest, or some combination of these. In the case of a national information system, the user population is the community of scientists and other professionals working in the country as a whole. The other universe dealt with is one of information resources. The most important type of information resource for most information centers is in documentary form, using the term "document" in its widest sense. It is the function of the information service to bring together ("interface") these two populations as efficiently and economically as possible; that is, in a somewhat passive

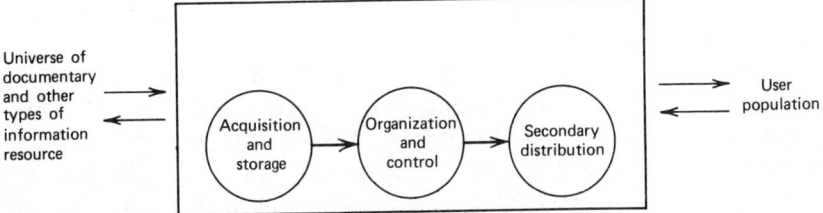

Figure 2 The interface role of an information service.

role, its function is to ensure that any document or information needed by a member of the user community should be made available to him, as far as possible, at the time that he needs it. In its more active role, it is the function of the information service to bring documents or data to the attention of the user community through searches of the literature conducted on demand to meet the problem-solving or decision-making needs of members and by notifying the members of the community, on a continuous basis, of newly published literature in their areas of interest ("current awareness").

An efficient, modern information service should be able to guarantee that virtually any document in the universe of available literature, or any data contained in documents, should be accessible to any member of the user community served. This implies that the "universe of document resources" should be available to the user population at different levels of accessibility. Since no library or information center can own everything, it is important that the documents that it does add to its collection have the greatest probability of being of value to its own users. It is also important, however, that the information center should be able to acquire, as rapidly as possible, any other document for which there is a legitimate need in the user community, through purchase, photocopying, or interlibrary loan. Moreover, in the center's own collections, documents need to be organized according to expected levels of demand, those most likely to be used being most accessible. Thus, it would be possible to say that the universe of document resources is made available to the users of an information center according to tiers of accessibility that might, for certain institutions, be as follows:

1. Documents in the center's collections and on open shelves.
2. Documents in the center's collections but in controlled-access stacks.
3. Documents in off-site storage areas.
4. Documents not in the center's collections.

This sequence is, in general, one of decreasing accessibility. However, this is an oversimplification in that a copy of a document not owned by the center may be more accessible than one that is, but mislaid, at the bindery, or out on loan. Moreover, all items not in the center's collections are not equally accessible, or inaccessible, because, presumably, geographic distance from the center has some effect on their accessibility. So do certain other factors, including whether or not the publication is still in print, whether it is included in some union catalog, the reliability and speed of the postal service, and so on.

To fulfill its interface role, an information service is engaged in three major activities (Figures 1 and 2): the acquisition and storage of documents, their organization and control, and their distribution, or distribution of information concerning them, to users by means of various kinds of services: circulation, literature searching, photocopying, and so on.

TYPES OF INFORMATION NEED

The principal needs, and demands, of users of information services really fall into two broad categories:

1. The need to locate and obtain a copy of a particular document for which the author or title is known.
2. The need to locate documents dealing with a particular subject or capable of answering a particular question.

The first of these may be referred to as a "known item need" and the second, obviously, as a "subject need." The ability of the information center to supply known items when needed is its "document delivery capability." The ability of the center to retrieve documents on a particular subject, or provide the answer to a specific question, is its "information retrieval capability." These two functions, document delivery and information retrieval, are the major activities engaged in by information services. The functions are quite closely related in that many requests for known documents are likely to stem directly from information retrieval activities conducted at an earlier time.

Subject needs also fall fairly clearly into two main types:

1. The need for information to aid in the solution of a particular problem or to facilitate the making of a particular decision.
2. Information on new developments in a particular field of specialization.

The latter is usually referred to as a current awareness need, but there is no single term that is generally accepted to describe the first type of information need. It can only be referred to as the need for problem-solving information. In practice this type of need is usually satisfied through a search of the past literature conducted by an information service in response to a specific demand from a user. This type of search, then, is usually referred to as a "retrospective search" or sometimes a "demand search."

The problem-solving search differs from the current awareness search in a number of ways. It is more purposive—the user must initiate the action whereas, in the current awareness situation, the information service may take the initiative—it tends to be more specific, it may need to cover a much greater volume of literature—that is, going back many years—and the results of this search are likely to be judged more stringently by the user than those of the current awareness search.

Problem-solving information needs may themselves be divided into a number of types:

1. The need for a single item of factual data. This is the typical "quick reference" inquiry handled by libraries. Although documents are usually involved in satisfying such a need, the requester does not necessarily have to receive any document—that is, the answer to the question can be given by telephone.
2. The need to have one or more documents discussing a particular subject, but less than the total literature published or available from a particular center. This is a typical library situation as exemplified by a request for a few recent papers discussing ultrasonic welding. A special category is the type of need that is completely satisfied when the first document of a particular type is found. As an example, a patent examiner may need only one case of a previous application in the literature in order to disallow a patent claim.
3. The need for a comprehensive search, one that retrieves as much as possible of the literature published on a particular subject in a particular time period. Such a comprehensive search might be needed by someone writing a book or a review article or by a scientist beginning a new research project. A special category is the search that is conducted to confirm that nothing exists in the literature on a particular topic; that is, the requester thinks that nothing has been published and sets out to prove it. The obvious case is that of the inventor who wants to confirm the patentability of his invention.

INFORMATION RETRIEVAL SYSTEMS

The major activities of many types of information systems are presented in a somewhat simplified form in Figure 3. The system input consists of

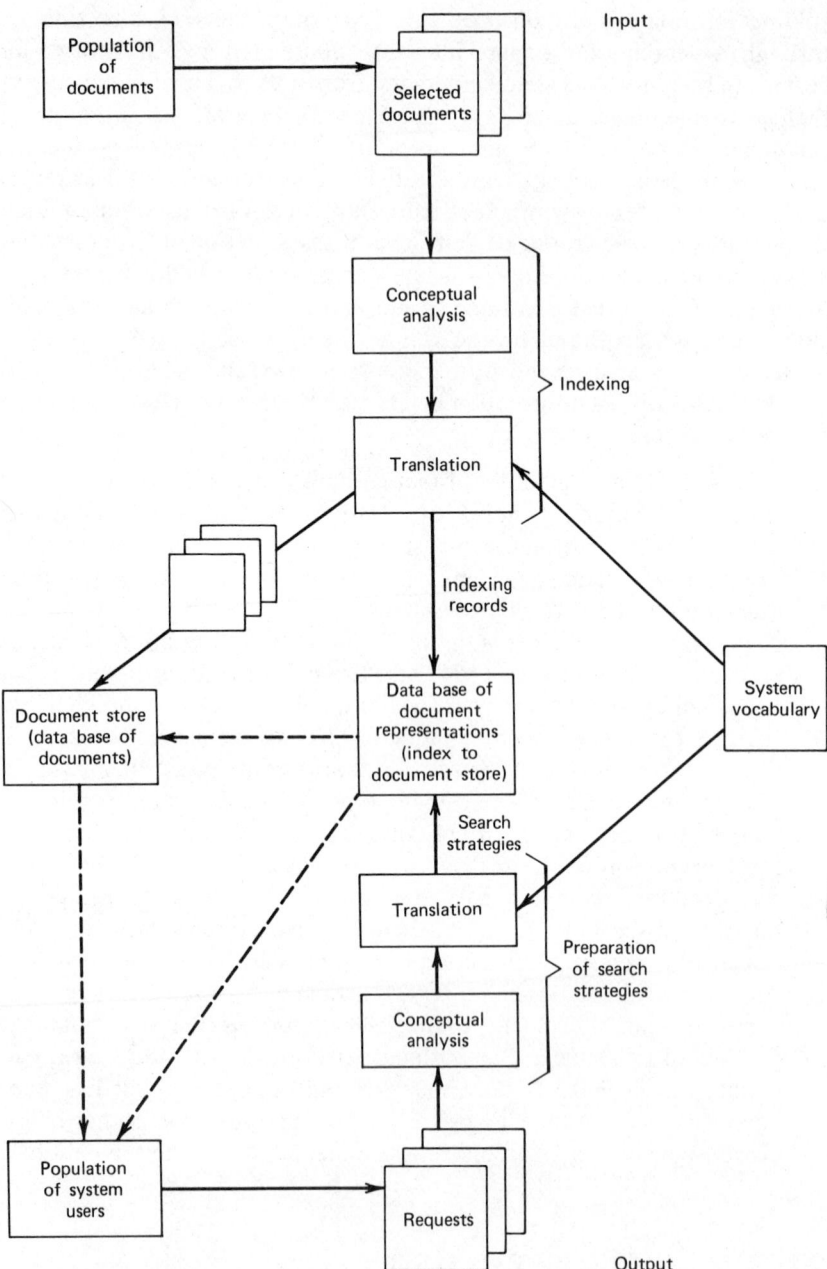

Figure 3 The major functions performed in many types of information centers.

documents; that is, certain documents are acquired by the information center. This implies the existence of selection criteria and policies, which, in turn, implies a detailed and accurate knowledge of the information needs of the community to be served. Once the documents are acquired, they need to be "organized and controlled" so that they can be identified and located in response to various types of user demand. Organization and control activities include classification, cataloging, subject indexing, and abstracting. As depicted in Figure 3, the subject indexing process involves two quite distinct intellectual steps: the "conceptual analysis"—we might also call it "content analysis"—of a document and the "translation" of the conceptual analysis into a particular vocabulary. It is rare that the two steps are clearly distinguished. This is a pity because each step offers different constraints and brings in different factors affecting the performance of the system. For efficient conceptual analysis the indexer needs both an understanding of what the document is about, that is, some comprehension of its subject matter, and a good knowledge of the needs of the users of the system. The recognition of what the document is about and why users may be interested in it, that is, what aspects of the document are of most concern, is what constitutes conceptual analysis. The conceptual analysis of a document may be recorded on paper. It is more likely, however, that it exists only in the mind of the indexer.

The second step in the indexing process is the translation of the conceptual analysis into some vocabulary or "index language." In the majority of systems this involves the use of a "controlled vocabulary," that is, a limited set of terms that must be used to represent the subject matter of documents. Such a vocabulary might be a list of subject headings, a classification scheme, a thesaurus, or simply a list of "approved" key words or phrases. An "uncontrolled vocabulary," quite obviously, places no restrictions on the terms the indexer may use. The uncontrolled vocabulary usually implies the use of words or phrases occurring in the document being indexed. The terms used by an indexer to represent the subject content of documents, whether from a controlled or an uncontrolled vocabulary, are referred to generically in this book as "index terms."

Once the indexing process has been completed, the documents go into some form of document store (data base), and the indexing records go into a second data base, where they are organized in such a way that they can conveniently be searched in response to various types of subject, and other, requests. The data base of indexing records, or "document representations," may be as simple as a card file or an index in printed form. In a modern system, however, it is more likely to be a machine-readable file on magnetic tape or disk. The data base may be termed the "index" to the document store.

The steps involved at the output side of the system are, in fact, very similar to those involved at input. The user population to be served submits various requests to the information center, and members of the staff prepare search strategies for the requests. It is convenient to consider the preparation of search strategies as also involving the two steps of conceptual analysis and translation. The first step involves an analysis of the request to determine what the user is really looking for, and the second involves the translation of the conceptual analysis into the vocabulary of the system. The conceptual analysis of the request, translated into the language of the system, is the "search strategy," which may be regarded as a "request representation" in the same way that an indexing record may be regarded as a document representation. The only real difference between the two is that the former usually contains "logic," that is, a certain set of logical relationships among the index terms is specified; and the latter is usually without logic, that is, logical relationships among index terms are not explicitly stated.

Once the search strategy has been prepared, it is "matched" in some way against the data base of document representations. This could involve a search of card files, printed indexes, microfilm, or magnetic tape or disk. Document representations that match the search strategy, that is, satisfy the logical requirements of the search, are retrieved from the data base and delivered to the requester. The process, which may be iterative, is completed when the requester is satisfied with the results of the search, which may, in some cases, mean that he is satisfied that nothing in the data base is exactly relevant to his needs.

The steps depicted in Figure 3 illustrate a "delegated search" situation, that is, one in which the person with the information need delegates the responsibility for searching the data base to some information specialist. In the "nondelegated search" situation the process is somewhat simplified by the fact that the user goes directly to the data base. Even in this situation, however, the user must conceptually analyze his own information need and translate his analysis into the language of the system. In searching many kinds of systems, of course, the search strategy is not constructed away from the data base and separately from the searching operation itself. In searching a card catalog, a printed index, or an on-line system, the search strategy is likely to be developed interactively and heuristically; that is, the conceptual analysis and translation activities are more or less concurrent with the file searching activities. Nevertheless, some form of conceptual analysis–translation activity is needed even in this situation. The only real difference between a retrospective search service and a current awareness—for example, selective dissemination of information—service is that in the latter the search strategies, or "user interest profiles," represent the current research interests of system users; they are matched against the representations of incoming documents on a regular basis, that is, every time the data base is updated; and the results of this match are delivered to the users at the same regular intervals.

Of course, some of the requests made to the information service are for specific documents, for which the author or title is known, rather than requests for information or documents on a particular subject. In the case of these known item requests, the request (see Figure 3) is made to the document store via author or title access points in the indexes or catalogs of the collection, or possibly by some other approach such as that of report number or patent number. The ability of the center to supply needed documents may be referred to as its document delivery capability.

So far, no attempt has been made to give a precise definition of information retrieval system, although the scope of this term was certainly implied in the previous discussion. As it is most commonly used, the term information retrieval is really synonymous with literature searching. Information retrieval is the process of searching some collection of documents, using the term document in its widest sense, in order to identify those documents which deal with a particular subject. Any system that is designed to facilitate this literature searching activity may legitimately be called an information retrieval system. The subject catalog of a library is one type. So is a printed subject index.

The output of an information retrieval system usually consists of one or more bibliographic references, perhaps with some added information such as an abstract or a list of the terms under which the document has been indexed. These document representations are usually delivered to the person who requested the search. The "requester" may then ask the information center, or some other center, to deliver to him some or all of the documents referred to in the output of the literature search. In some cases an information center eliminates the intermediate step and delivers the documents themselves, or perhaps a sample that members of the staff judge most likely to be relevant, directly to the requester. Occasionally the information retrieval function and the document delivery function are combined in a single system. For example, a microfilm retrieval system or a computer-based system might include the full text of short documents—for example, cables or newspaper articles—and the output of the search is a printout of the documents themselves rather than their representations. Most information retrieval systems, however, stop at the delivery of document representations. The delivery of the documents themselves is a completely separate activity that may or may not be provided by the organizations conducting literature searches.

It should be clear from the discussion above that information retrieval is not a particularly satisfactory term to describe the type of activity to which it is usually applied. An information retrieval system does not retrieve information. Indeed, information is something quite intangible; it is not possible to see, hear, or feel it. We are "informed" on a subject if our state of knowledge on it is somehow changed. Giving a requester a document on lasers, or a reference to such a document, does not inform him on the subject of lasers. Information transfer can only take place if the user reads the document and understands it. Information, then, is something that changes a person's state of knowledge on a subject. This may not be a very precise definition but it is perhaps the best we can do. It is at least an adequate definition for our present purposes.

The inappropriateness of the term is further emphasized by a reconsideration of Figure 1. The activities of information retrieval systems end with the circle captioned "Secondary distribution," the items distributed being documents or their representations. But information transfer, if it takes place at all, occurs only in the circle captioned "Assimilation by users." The assimilation stage of the information transfer cycle is not directly under the control of information centers.

Despite its inappropriateness, information retrieval is the term commonly used to refer to the types of literature searching activities described earlier, and it is used with this scope in the present book.

An information center activity sometimes referred to as "question answering" can also be regarded as a form of information retrieval. A question-answering service attempts to produce the direct answer to a particular question—for example, what is the height of . . . , what is the melting point of . . . , what is the address of?—rather than simply referring to documents that might provide the answer to the question. Many libraries and other types of information center provide a question-answering service of this kind. Sometimes it is referred to as a "quick reference" or a "factual reference" service. Clearly, question answering may be a second stage in a larger information activity. The first stage involves the use of some information retrieval system, perhaps a library subject catalog, a printed index, or even a "back of the book" index, in order to identify documents likely to provide the answer to a question posed by a user. The second stage involves the extraction of the answer from the document and the transmission of the answer to the user.

Some computer-based question-answering systems have been developed. Such systems accept a question in natural language, although a prescribed syntactic structure may be required, and produce the answer, printed out or displayed on a screen, directly. Because of the complexity involved in the design of systems of this type, those which have been developed are restricted to rather limited bodies of knowledge—for example, baseball results or the highway code of a particular state. A system that stores physical, chemical, or other types of data, and answers questions from the stored data, may be referred to as a "data retrieval system." The stored data may be referred to as a "data bank." Examples are census data, thermophysical properties data, or data on interatomic potentials.

Another type of information retrieval system, which may be termed a "passage retrieval system," is intermediate between a system that retrieves documents or their representations and one that attempts to answer questions directly. A passage retrieval system is one that stores a body of text in some subject area and can retrieve a passage of text—for example, a paragraph—when it matches a search strategy representing some information need. A computer-based system may store a body of legal text—for example, the statutes of a particular state—and allow the retrieval of paragraphs of text in which particular word combinations occur—for example, a word indicating child and a word indicating physical cruelty.

Question-answering systems, data retrieval systems, and passage retrieval systems are all legitimate forms of information retrieval systems. Although such systems may sometimes be referred to, they are not the major emphasis of the present book, which is primarily concerned with systems retrieving references to documents in response to subject requests.

THE COMPONENTS OF INFORMATION RETRIEVAL SYSTEMS

The major components of an information retrieval system are evident in Figure 3. The system may be considered to comprise six major subsystems:

1. The document selection subsystem.
2. The indexing subsystem.
3. The vocabulary subsystem.
4. The searching subsystem.
5. The subsystem of interaction between the user and the system (user-system inferface).
6. The matching subsystem, that is, the subsystem that actually matches document representations against request representations.

In some ways the matching subsystem must be considered the least important of the six, for it has no direct influence on the effectiveness of the complete system, that is, on whether or not it can retrieve items that satisfy the information needs of users, although, clearly, the efficiency of the matching subsystem exerts a rather great influence on system economics and overall system efficiency, measured, for example, in response time. In a "conventional" computer-based system the computer contributes directly only to the matching operation. It acts as a giant matching device. But, in most systems at least, it contributes nothing directly to the selection of documents, the indexing of documents, the control of the vocabulary used in indexing and searching, the preparation of search strategies, or the interaction with system users—for example, for the purpose of "request negotiation." These are all intellectual activities, performed by humans in most existing systems, and these intellectual activities govern the effectiveness of the system.

The most important factors controlling the effectiveness of a retrieval system may be separated into two groups:

1. Data base factors.
2. Factors associated with the exploitation of the data base.

The major data base factors, which can also be regarded as "input factors," are three:

1. What documents are included.
2. How completely and accurately the subject matter of these documents is recognized and represented in the indexing operation.
3. How adequate is the vocabulary of the system to represent the subject matter of these documents.

There are also three "exploitation" or output factors:

1. How well the staff of the information center is able to understand the information needs of the users (user-system interaction).
2. How well they can transform these needs into searching strategies.
3. How adequate is the vocabulary of the system to represent the subject interests of system users.

The intellectual components of information systems, and the influence of these on system performance, are the major themes of this book.

Chapter Two

The Matching Subsystem

The history of methods for the physical implementation of information retrieval systems falls into several periods that are fairly clearly defined:

Pre-1940	Precoordinate indexes, completely manual, in printed book or card form
1940s	The first postcoordinate indexes; manual
1950s	Punched card systems; microfilm retrieval systems
1960s	Computer-based systems operating via magnetic tape in an off-line batch processing mode; improved microfilm systems
1970s	Computer-based systems operating on-line
1990s	Completely paperless systems

These eras should not, of course, be considered watertight compartments. The list indicates only the decades in which the major development in a particular type of system occurred. The first computer-based systems were introduced in the 1950s, but off-line batch processing systems only began to have a significant impact on information services in the 1960s. Experimentation with on-line retrieval dates back at least to 1964, but on-line systems really only came into their own in the 1970s. The developments of the 1990s, of course, are purely speculative, but, as shown later, there is much evidence to suggest that paperless, that is, fully electronic, systems are rapidly approaching and will indeed be here before the end of the century.

THE LIMITATIONS OF PRECOORDINATE SYSTEMS

A major distinction to be made here is between precoordinate and postcoordinate systems. To allow a particular document to be retrieved from a collection according to its subject matter, the subject matter must be described in some way, and the description thus generated must be in a form suitable for storage in a file that can conveniently be searched by man or machine. The description of the subject matter of documents is the process of subject indexing. To say that a particular document has been indexed under the terms LUBRICANTS, COLD ROLLING, and ALUMINUM ALLOYS implies that an indexer has examined the document and decided that it deals with the subjects represented by these three index terms. The subject representation of this document may consist of the terms

    LUBRICANTS
    COLD ROLLING
    ALUMINUM ALLOYS

The indexing of the document goes only part of the way toward making it retrievable. In practice, the representation created by the process of indexing must be placed in some file, and the file must be organized in a way that permits the retrieval of documents by whichever index term, or combination of index terms, they may be asked for. Thus, the document mentioned above is probably relevant to requests for information on

1. Aluminum alloys
2. Cold rolling
3. Lubricants
4. Cold rolling of aluminum alloys
5. Lubricants for cold rolling
6. Lubricants for aluminum alloys
7. Lubricants for cold rolling of aluminum alloys

and it should be retrievable in a search on any of these topics. A kind of multidimensional network exists among all the topics discussed in a document, and all the terms used to represent them, in the form where A, B, C, and D represent topics discussed in a document and the arrows indicate the possible relationships among them. Thus, the document may be of interest to someone who needs information on a general topic, such as B; to someone who needs information on a more specific topic, such as the relationship between B and D; or to someone who needs information on something highly specific, such as the relationship of A, B, C, and D. An information retrieval system must be capable of retrieving this document at any of the levels of complexity of subject matter represented in the relationships of the network. Indexes printed on paper or catalog cards are somewhat limited in their search and retrieval capabilities by the fact that the entries made in such indexes must follow a linear sequence, one term filing before another, as in the example

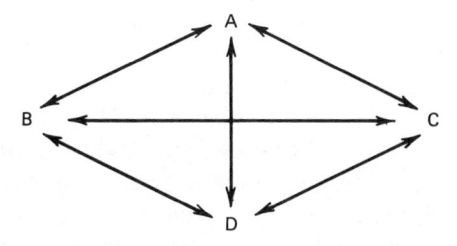

ALUMINUM ALLOYS, COLD ROLLING, LUBRICANTS

This entry, filed under the first term, permits the document represented to be retrieved by someone interested in aluminum alloys but does not allow it to be found easily in a search on cold rolling or lubricants. The multidimensional character of the subject matter has been forced into a one-dimensional representation. To make the document more accessible, it is necessary to repeat the index entry in some way—for example, by rotation of the terms—so that it becomes retrievable under cold rolling and lubricants as well as aluminum alloys.

This type of index, as exemplified by the subject catalogs of most libraries and most printed indexes—for example, the subject index to *Chemical Abstracts*—is now frequently referred to as a "precoordinate" index. Precoordinate in this context means that important relationships among topics discussed in a document must be recognized by the indexer and explicitly brought together (coordinated) in the index entries used to represent the document in the data base. In a precoordinate system, then, relationships among topics are built, once and for all, into the system vocabulary or index entries formed from its components by the indexer. The relationships are fixed at the time of indexing and cannot conveniently be varied or augmented at the time that subject searches are

18   The Matching Subsystem

conducted. Another way of saying this is that precoordinate indexes are "nonmanipulative."

To illustrate further the distinctions between these systems and postcoordinate systems, let us take another example. Suppose we are indexing documents in the field of library science and encounter one that deals with the subject of cooperation in the acquisition of phonograph records in public libraries. If the controlled vocabulary used in indexing is a list of subject headings, we might decide that four such headings are potentially applicable to describe the subject matter of this document:

LIBRARY COOPERATION
ACQUISITIONS
PHONOGRAPH RECORDS
PUBLIC LIBRARIES

Likewise, if the controlled vocabulary is a classification scheme, we might find four class numbers that relate to the subject matter:

Ey	Loe
Ge	Vv

where Ey represents library cooperation; Ge, acquisitions; Loe, phonograph records; and Vv, public libraries.

It is important to recognize that all subject indexing is a classification process. When we assign the subject heading LIBRARY COOPERATION to a document, we assign the document to the class library cooperation along with other related documents to which this term has been assigned. The assignment of subject headings, key words, or descriptors to documents is just as much a classification process as the assignment of numbers from a classification scheme. By labeling a document LIBRARY COOPERATION, we classify it just as surely as if we had labeled it with the notation Ey. Moreover, once we have identified a set of documents that we recognize as dealing with library cooperation, it makes not the slightest difference, for purposes of information retrieval, whether we label the set LIBRARY COOPERATION or Ey. The class remains the same and has the same characteristics for retrieval purposes in either case. It is what we decide to put into a class, that is, the definition of its scope, not what we name or label the class, that is important for purposes of information retrieval.

Having decided that the document legitimately belongs to four classes, the least we could do to represent its subject matter in some index is to enter it under one of the four classes only. For example, we might enter it under the heading LIBRARY COOPERATION in an alphabetical subject catalog or printed subject index or under the notation Ey in a classified catalog. The limitations of this are obvious; a user can retrieve this document only by the cooperation approach. It will not be retrieved in a search relating to acquisition procedures, phonograph records, or public libraries, although it presumably has some relevance to all three of these topics.

A multiple access approach is possible if we enter the document several times in the index. We could, for example, duplicate the citation under all four subject headings or all four class numbers, whether the index is on cards or in printed book form. This has the obvious advantage that it provides access to the document from four different approaches, any one of which may represent the interest of a particular user in the document. It has the obvious disadvantage that duplication of entries in this way greatly increases the size and cost of the index.

Even the extensive duplication of entries in a precoordinate index does not provide the true multidimensional retrieval capability that is needed. Suppose, for example, we were looking for documents relating to cooperation in library acquisition procedures. Since, in the example we are using, there is no subject heading that exactly fits our information need, we must look under all the entries under LIBRARY COOPERATION to try to identify documents that relate to acquisition procedures or all the entries under ACQUISITIONS to try to identify those which relate to cooperation. This is a rather inefficient approach to the retrieval of information on this subject. It is possible that there are 60 entries under LIBRARY COOPERATION but only 2 of these refer to documents discussing cooperation in acquisition. We must look at 29 irrelevant entries for every relevant one we find. Moreover, there is no guarantee that the entries provided will allow us to recognize which documents under LIBRARY COOPERATION deal with acquisition procedures. In fact, in the subject catalogs of libraries, and in most printed indexes, we will recognize these documents only if the acquisition concept is explicitly represented in their titles.

It is clear, then, that the duplication of entries in a precoordinate index does not solve the problem of providing an efficient multidimensional access to multidimensional subject matter. Another possibility, however, is the use of some type of "synthesis" in the creation of index entries. Subject headings or class numbers may be combined to create new headings or class numbers that are more specific.

A limited level of synthesis, common in alphabetical subject catalogs, can be achieved by the joint use of main subject headings and subheadings. Thus, if ACQUISITIONS were designated as a subheading, we could combine this with an appropriate main heading to form a new index entry such as PUBLIC LIBRARIES—ACQUISITIONS or PHONOGRAPH RECORDS—ACQUISITIONS.

But the principle of synthesis does not need to be thus restricted. Indeed, we could build a single index entry that is more or less coextensive with the major subject matter of a document by combining subject headings, phrases, or class numbers in a single string, as follows:

PUBLIC LIBRARIES, ACQUISITIONS, PHONOGRAPH RECORDS, COOPERATION

or

Phonograph records, cooperation in acquisition of, among public libraries

or

Vv Loe Ge Ey

The first two are examples of entries that might appear in a printed alphabetical index, and the third is an example of an entry as it might appear in a catalog or index based on an analyticosynthetic classification.

Synthesis of this type, then, allows the formation of single index entries that are quite specific statements of the subject matter covered in documents. But, as in an earlier example, even this is not enough. The entry PUBLIC LIBRARIES, ACQUISITIONS, PHONOGRAPH RECORDS, COOPERATION provides access to the document represented only to the user who seeks the document from the public library aspect. But what of users who are looking for documents on library acquisition policies, or acquisition of phonograph records, or cooperation among libraries, or cooperation in acquisition procedures, or cooperation in the acquisition of phonograph records? They would be rather unlikely to find the document, although it seems to be relevant to all these information needs.

The problem is that efficient approaches to information retrieval demand systems that permit the free "combination" of classes and the terms representing them—for example, all four terms, any three out of four, any two out of four, any one—and precoordinate indexes based on linear index entries do not permit the combination of terms. They permit only term "permutation." But full permutation (all possible sequences) of four subject headings or four class numbers would require 24 entries in a card catalog or a printed index and, as we add further subject headings or class numbers, the permutations needed increase dramatically. For example, we would need no less than 40,320 entries to provide every possible permutation of eight subject headings or class numbers.

It is true, of course, that there are ways of providing multiple approaches to retrieval in precoordinate indexes without complete permutation of index terms. In an alphabetical subject index, one may construct a single index entry by combining terms or phrases according to a strict, preestablished sequence—for example, thing, part, material, action, property. Additional retrieval approaches may then be made by means of cross-references instead of duplicate entries; for example,

COOPERATION See also PUBLIC LIBRARIES, ACQUISITIONS, PHONOGRAPH RECORDS, COOPERATION

An excellent discussion on the construction of alphabetical subject indexes of this general type is given by Coates (1960).

Sharp (1966) has shown that complete permutation is unnecessary in precoordinate alphabetical indexes. By following a strict alphabetical sequence in the construction of index entries—for example, ACQUISITIONS, COOPERATION, PHONOGRAPH RECORDS, PUBLIC LIBRARIES—and by eliminating redundant combinations—for example, the combination ACQUISITIONS, COOPERATION is unnecessary because it was already provided for in the earlier entry—it is possible to produce a multiaccess printed index with many fewer entries than the number needed in an index based on permutation. Sharp's SLIC index (selected listing in combination) requires 2^{n-1} entries per document, where n is the number of elements—for example, subject headings—in an index entry.

In a SLIC index, then, all useful approaches to a four-element heading would require only 8 entries (2^3) whereas complete permutation would require 24. For a five-element heading the SLIC index requires only 16 entries, as opposed to 120 in one based on complete permutation.

A subject catalog based on an analyticosynthetic classification may also avoid complete permutation of entries. This is usually accomplished by building an index entry through the synthesis of class numbers according to a strict and predetermined sequence of facets ("citation order" or "preferred order") in much the same way that "tailor-made" index entries are constructed in an alphabetical index. Thus, to return to the example used earlier, the entry Vv Loe Ge Ey reflects the facet sequence type of library, library material, library activity. In the classified part of the catalog only one index entry occurs, in this case filed under Vv, which represents public libraries. Additional access points are provided in the alphabetical index to the classified file. To ensure completeness and consistency in the construction of the alphabetical index, a procedure known as "chain indexing" is frequently followed. Chain procedure involves the systematic indexing of each step in the chain by which a class number is built up, from the most specific to the most generic, as in the example

> Cooperation, Acquisition, Phonograph Records, Public Libraries VvLoeGeEy
> Acquisition, Phonograph Records, Public Libraries VvLoeGe
> Phonograph Records, Public Libraries VvLoe
> Public Libraries　　　　　　　　Vv

A more complete discussion of analyticosynthetic classification and the principles of chain indexing is given by Vickery (1960), Mills (1960), and Foskett (1977). Campey (1972, 1973) provides a useful discussion of the use of computers in the generation and printing of precoordinate indexes in general. Further discussion of the differences between precoordinate and postcoordinate systems may be found in an earlier book by Lancaster (1972).

POSTCOORDINATE SYSTEMS

As indicated in the previous section, various methods can be used to produce a precoordinate index in which multiple access points can be provided. But precoordinate indexes are inherently inflexible because entries in such indexes must follow a linear sequence. The complex relationships among topics discussed in documents are not one-dimensional and are not readily reduced to a linear method of representation. When an indexer assigns four terms to a document he places it in four classes:

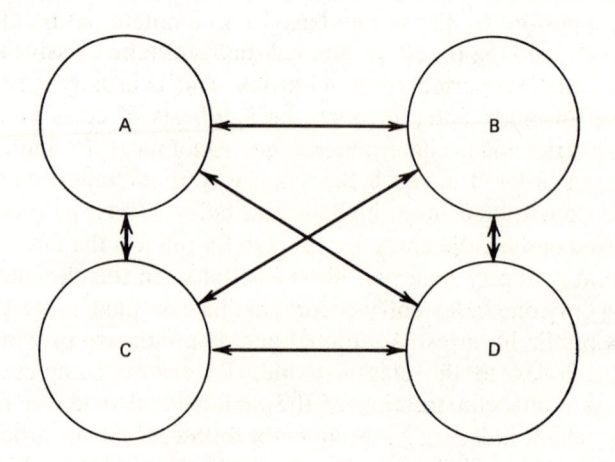

For efficient retrieval we need a system that permits the recovery of the document for any possible combination of these classes—for example, BC or ABD. In the relationship among these classes linear sequence has no significance; ABD, for example, is identical with BDA. But a precoordinate index cannot escape the limitations of a linear sequence. When we construct an index entry by putting together ("precoordinating") the four terms representing the four classes we construct an index entry in which a linear sequence of classes is implied:

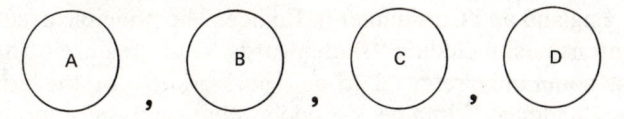

$$\text{A} \quad , \quad \text{B} \quad , \quad \text{C} \quad , \quad \text{D}$$

It is true that this type of entry can be made to represent highly specific subject matter. The entry above can be considered to represent the "logical product" of the four classes A, B, C, and D:

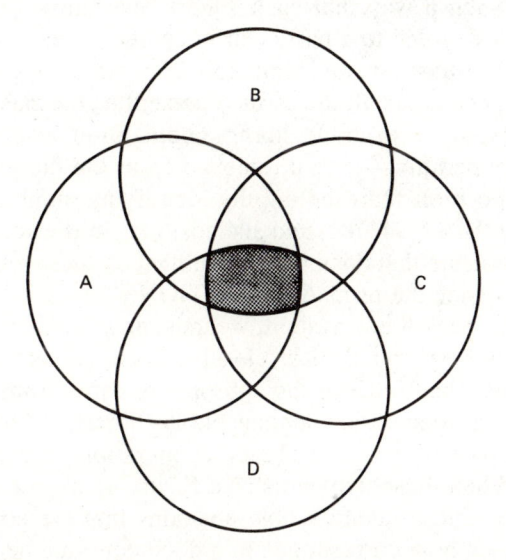

But this is not in itself a solution to the information retrieval problem. The multidimensional relationships implied in this diagram cannot be reduced to a single entry in a precoordinate index. In fact, they are not susceptible to reduction to a linear form. It is just not economically attractive to construct precoordinate indexes that attempt to provide access to a document from every possible combination of even a small number of classes. When we increase the number of terms assigned to a document, that is, increase the number of classes to which it has been assigned, say, to an average of 10 or 15 per document, the situation becomes completely impossible to handle in a precoordinate system.

What is needed for efficient retrieval is a system in which all document classes formed during the subject indexing process are equally accessible, no "sequence" of classes is implied, and it is easy to compare the contents of the various classes—for example, to find which documents belong to both class A and class B. To satisfy these requirements, we need "postcoordinate" retrieval systems.

The first true postcoordinate systems were introduced in the 1940s by Batten in England and Cordonnier in France. The principle used has been given many names, including "Batten cards" and "feature cards," but is now most commonly referred to as "peek-a-boo" or the principle of "optical coincidence." In a peek-a-boo system each class, formed by the process of subject indexing, is represented by a single card. The name given to this class—for example, subject heading—the "index term," is recorded at the top of the card. The remaining surface of the card is divided up in such a way that each square, assuming a matrix type of arrangement, is devoted to a particular document number—that is, there is an identifiable 8 position, an identifiable 23 position, and so on. When a document has been indexed, the cards representing the classes to which it has been assigned—for example, library cooperation, acquisitions, public library, and cooperation—are all removed from the file and punched or drilled in the position representing the identifying number of the document. Holes in the 12, 94, 182, and 304 positions in the acquisitions card, for example, indicate that documents identified by these numbers have all been indexed under the term ACQUISITIONS.

To search a peek-a-boo system, we must first decide which combinations of classes correspond most closely to the subject matter we are interested in and then retrieve the appropriate cards from the file. If we are interested in cooperation among public libraries, for example, we would presumably remove the library cooperation card and the public library card. When these two cards (see Figure 4) are correctly superimposed, it is possible to identify hole positions that are common to both cards. Since each hole corresponds to a document number, it is possible to identify which documents have been indexed under both PUBLIC LIBRARIES and LIBRARY COOPERATION and which presumably have something to say about the subject we are interested in.

It is clear that the peek-a-boo principle is capable of satisfying all the requirements of a retrieval system that were previously identified. Any possible combination of classes can be searched for; it is just as easy to combine three or four classes as it is to combine two. Each class carries equal weight in the system; no sequence of classes is involved. A com-

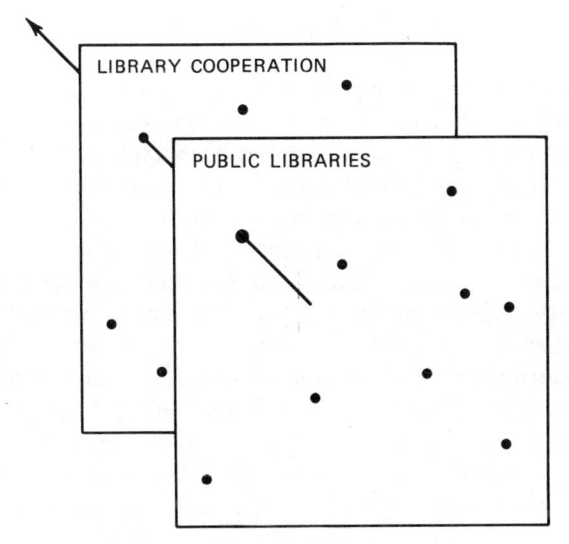

Figure 4 Peek-a-boo principle. A hole in an identical position on the two cards, represented by the arrow, identifies the number of a document common to both cards.

pletely multidimensional approach to the representation and retrieval of subject matter can be achieved very economically. If we index a document under 10 terms, this merely means that we must enter its identifying number on 10 cards in the file. Any possible combination of the 10 terms can then be searched on, which is roughly equivalent to having 3.5 million permuted entries for the document in a precoordinate index.

In its simplest form, a peek-a-boo system can be implemented with IBM "port-a-punch" cards, which are standard size data processing cards preprinted with document numbers and preperforated in the document number position. Document numbers can be punched out with the point of a pen and can be read off simply by holding the superimposed cards up to the light. The capacity of such a simple system is less than 1000 document numbers. In a more sophisticated modern peek-a-boo system a card of approximately 10 by 11 inches may have 10,000 dedicated positions. Document numbers are entered through the use of a high-precision drill—a hole can be drilled in all the necessary cards at once—and they are read off by means of a transparent grid used in association with a light box.

A somewhat different approach to the implementation of a postcoordinate system was the Uniterm system of Taube, which dates from about 1951. As originally described, the Uniterm system involves the indexing

26 The Matching Subsystem

of documents under single words (Uniterms) extracted from the document itself.

Each Uniterm used to index documents appears as the heading on a separate 5- by 8-inch Uniterm card, and the accession numbers of all documents to which a particular term has been applied are "posted," that is, written or typed, on the card for the term. A search is conducted (see Figure 5) by withdrawing from the file the cards representing classes that collectively express the subject sought and comparing the columns of document numbers posted on the cards. Numbers that are common to all selected cards identify documents that are common to all the sought classes and therefore are presumed to deal with the precise subject of the inquiry. As an example, if we are seeking information on boiler feed pumps, we examine the Uniterm cards for boiler, feed, and pump and read off those document numbers which are posted on all three cards. We now go to a secondary file to locate the actual documents referred to, which, since they are common to the classes boiler, feed, and pump,

BOILER									
0	1	2	3	4	5	6	7	8	9
20	11	22	13	14	25	36	7	18	29
60	31	62	63	74	85	66	57	48	59
80	81		83	104	125	116	97	88	99
	101		93		135	156	127		119
	131						147		
							167		

PUMP									
0	1	2	3	4	5	6	7	8	9
10	31	2	43	24	15	16	37	18	39
40	71	52	73	54	65	26	87	98	89
110	81	72	123	84	105	66	137	118	159
	111	102		124		136	177	148	
		152		134					
				164					
				174					

Figure 5 Uniterm type of card. Document numbers are written or typed on the card in columns corresponding to their terminal digit.

should deal with boiler feed pumps. With respect to the physical implementation of the file, the Uniterm system was actually a step backward from the peek-a-boo principle, since it requires much more effort to compare columns of document numbers on, say, four cards than it does to read off the numbers common to four cards in a peek-a-boo file.

The peek-a-boo and Uniterm systems have one important thing in common: they both operate on the principle of one card per class, or index term, existing in the system. Such systems are frequently referred to as "term entry" systems or "item-on-term" systems, because the representation of an item, that is, a document, is entered on a term card. They are also known now as "inverted file" systems (see Figure 6) because the relationship between terms and item, as existing on an indexer's worksheet, has been inverted in the file organization.

There is another, completely different way of organizing a file for the purposes of information retrieval. Instead of inverting the item-term relationship represented by an indexing worksheet, we can transfer the relationship directly to some form of searchable file. The system thus implemented would be an "item entry" or "term-on-item" system. A single entry in such a system represents a bibliographic item. On the entry all the index terms assigned to the item are listed.

The first item entry systems, as exemplified by the Mooers Zator system (1947–1948), were implemented by means of "edge-notched cards." The principle is illustrated in Figure 7. Holes occur close to the edge of one or more sides of the card. Each hole can represent a class existing in the system. The bibliographic citation for the item itself, and

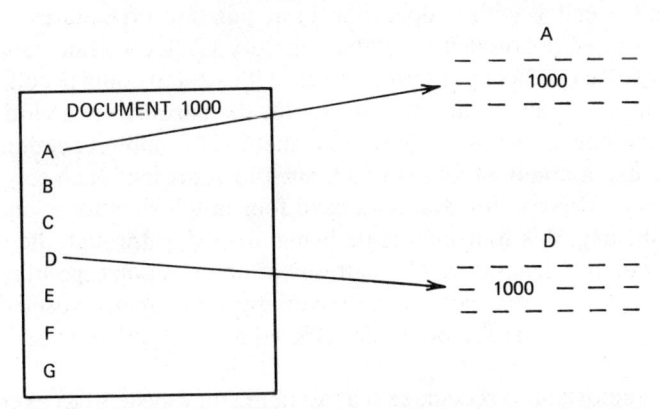

Figure 6 The meaning of "inverted file." The rectangle represents an indexer's worksheet for document 1000. The document has been indexed under seven terms. When the relationship represented by the worksheet (term on item) is inverted in a file organization, so that item numbers are listed under terms, an item-on-term or inverted file results.

The Matching Subsystem

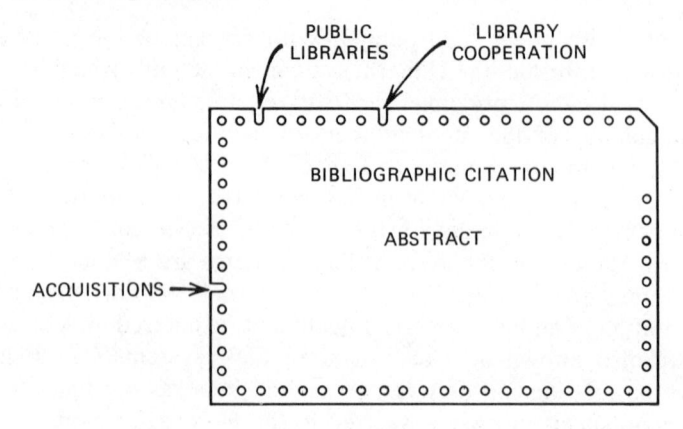

Figure 7 Principle of the edge-notched card with direct coding.

perhaps an abstract, is typed on the face of the card. Holes corresponding to the index terms assigned to the item are notched on the edge of the card. In Figure 7, the document represented has been indexed under three terms. Suppose we want to find all documents indexed under LIBRARY COOPERATION and also under ACQUISITIONS. We insert a rod, or "needle," through the library cooperation hole in the entire deck of cards. When the rod is lifted up, the cards notched in this position fall from the deck. We now take these cards and insert the rod again, this time in the acquisitions position. Any cards that fall from the deck in this operation have been notched in both of the sought positions and presumably refer to documents dealing with cooperation in acquisition procedures.

Clearly, edge-notched cards have a very limited coding capacity as long as we use one hole per term. The card illustrated could accommodate only 64 index terms by direct coding. But the capacity of a card can be greatly extended if we use instead some method of "indirect coding," that is, if we use a combination of notch sites to represent each term in the vocabulary. Mooers, for example, used four notch sites for each term in his vocabulary, this four-digit code being arrived at through the use of a random number generator. The patterns of notches corresponding to the terms assigned to a document are all overlapped or superimposed over the coding area of the card, a principle referred to as "random superimposed coding."

It is important to recognize that an item entry system, as exemplified by edge-notched cards, has a retrieval capability identical with that of a term entry system such as peek-a-boo. If we index a collection of documents and correctly enter the resulting document term relationships into a term entry system, and also into an item entry system, the two systems will have an identical retrieval capability if properly used; that is, a search on a particular combination of classes will retrieve the same set of documents whichever system is used.

The forms of file organization—term entry and item entry—developed by Batten and Mooers in the late 1940s remain the basic forms of file organization used in modern computer-based systems for information retrieval. Indeed, all systems developed since the 1940s can be regarded simply as increasingly sophisticated automated versions of the Mooers and Batten systems (see Table 1).

Although they have the same inherent retrieval capabilities, term entry and item entry systems differ in a number of significant ways. Item entry systems must be searched in their entirety; every item must be examined to determine whether or not it satisfies the requirements of the search; item entry involves a "serial search" or "sequential search" system. Since the entire file must be searched anyway, there is no need to keep an item entry system in any logical order; new items can simply be added at the end of the file. Term entry systems do not need to be searched in their entirety. Only the terms corresponding to the classes we

Table 1 Development of Term Entry and Item Entry Systems

Term Entry (Item-on-term, inverted files; one card or record per term)	Item Entry (Term-on-item; one card or record per item)
Batten Cordonnier { Peek-a-boo, peephole, optical coincidence 1940–1944	
Taube; 1951; uniterm	Mooers; edge-notched cards; Zator, Zatocoding, 1947
Punched card systems using a collator (1950s)	Microfilm retrieval (the Rapid Selector) 1940s
Computer-based systems, off-line, using random access devices (e.g., *discs*)	Punched card systems using a sorter (1950s)
	Computer-based, off-line, magnetic tape, batch-processing (late 1950s, early 1960s)
On-line systems	More sophisticated microfilm retrieval

choose to search on need be looked at. This implies, however, that the file of term entries must be maintained in some logical—for example, alphabetical—order. It also implies that rather than using some form of serially searched file, a term entry system must use a method of file organization that allows us to go directly to the terms we are interested in. In other words, it must use some form of direct access, or, as it is more commonly referred to now, "random access," device.

A more complete discussion of the characteristics and use of manual postcoordinate systems can be found in volumes by Foskett (1970), Jahoda (1970), and Simonton (1963). Systems based on edge-notched cards are dealt with comprehensively by Casey et al. (1958).

The entirely manual era of postcoordinate information retrieval was followed by a more automated period. As data processing equipment became more readily available, it was natural that this equipment should be applied to information retrieval. Moreover, both the Mooers and Batten-Taube systems were readily convertible to punched card operation, the former using a standard card sorter and the latter a collating device. Consequently, a number of retrieval systems using punched cards were developed in the 1950s, some of them of respectable size, and they were the immediate antecedents of our present mechanized systems. Although most of the activity in the application of punched cards to information retrieval took place in the 1950s, systems of this type were still being put into operation in the late 1960s, and some were still in use in the 1970s—for example, special-purpose systems at the U.S. Patent Office. Because punched card systems have now only a historical interest, they are not discussed here. A rather complete description of information retrieval through punched card data processing equipment can be found in Bourne (1963).

THE DOCUMENT–TERM MATRIX

The subsystem that we have referred to as the matching subsystem can be considered to have two major components:

1. A data base of records that tie identifications of documents to index terms assigned to the documents to represent their subject matter. The data base may be referred to as the index of the system.
2. A device to allow the data base to be searched, that is, to allow the terms associated with documents to be matched against those of some search strategy. The device can be as simple as a card file, arranged in alphabetical order and visually scanned by humans, or as sophisticated as a file on magnetic disks, searched by computer.

	Documents									
	1	2	3	4	5	6	7	8	9	10
A	X				X		X	X		
B		X						X		X
C						X				
D	X	X		X		X			X	X
E									X	X
F	X		X			X		X		X
G								X		
H			X				X			
I					X	X				
J	X			X			X			

Terms (representing classes)

Figure 8 The document–term matrix.

Conceptually, the data base itself can be regarded as a document-term matrix, as shown in Figure 8.

In this diagram the letters A to J represent a vocabulary of index terms, and the numerals 1 to 10 represent documents indexed into the data base. To enter a document, we assign it to classes, on the basis of its subject matter, by tagging it with the appropriate index terms. This assignment is indicated by the presence or absence of an X in each cell of the matrix. Thus document 1 has been assigned to class A, class D, class F, and class J, document 2 to class B and class D, and so on. Reading in the reverse direction, we can say that term A has been assigned to documents 1, 5, 7, and 8 or that the class A contains documents 1, 5, 7, and 8.

The data base (index), then, is essentially a document-term matrix, indicating which documents have been assigned to which classes. The vertical columns are document descriptions or index term profiles of the documents, whereas the horizontal rows are class descriptions, that is, they define the membership of each of the document classes. It is obvious, from a brief consideration of this matrix, that an index must be organized by one of the two basic methods mentioned earlier. Either it must list all the classes having membership, indicating for each one the documents that belong to it (term entry), or it must list all the documents in the collection, indicating for each one the classes to which it has been assigned (item entry).*

---

*Some alternative methods of file organization are possible, but we need not be concerned with these in the present discussion.

32   The Matching Subsystem

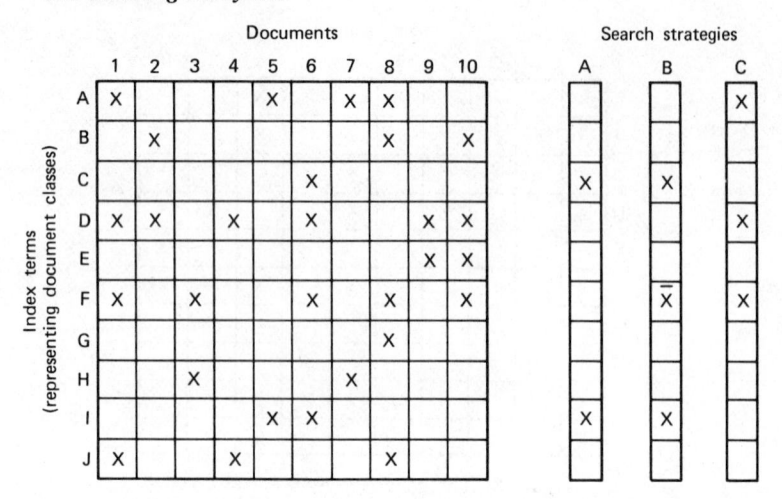

Figure 9   Matching request profile against document file.

Figure 9 illustrates how a subject search is conducted in an index to a document collection. A subject request, translated into the language of the system to allow it to be searched against the index, can be referred to as a "search strategy." Strategy A represents a simple two-concept request for retrieval of documents that belong to class C and also to class I. The searching operation consists in matching the search strategy against the document-term matrix in order to identify documents whose index term profiles satisfy the logical requirements of the strategy.

It can be seen that only document 6 will be retrieved in this case, since it is the sole document in the collection that has been assigned to both class C and class I. Note that this search strategy asks only for documents that are common to both C and I but does not otherwise restrict class membership of acceptable items. Thus, document 6 is acceptable, even though it belongs to class D and class F as well as to C and I. Suppose the request is for documents that belong to class C and class I, but not class F, represented by search strategy B. In this case, there is no match between the search strategy and the document-term matrix, and the index correctly delivers a null response.

It is obvious that the mode of searching an item-on-term index differs from that of searching a term-on-item system; in the latter, we must examine serially all the columns of the matrix, that is, document unit records or index term profiles, in order to identify columns (documents) whose term-assignment pattern includes that of the search strategy. We can readily see that document 1 is the only item whose profile includes that of search strategy C. To conduct the same search in an item-on-term file, however, we scan row by row rather than column by column. We look in turn at each of the rows corresponding to the terms or classes demanded in the search. For economy in searching, it is convenient to scan the least heavily posted row (class) first. If we examine row A, we find that the class has four members, documents 1, 5, 7, and 8. We record this information and move to the next indicated row or class, in this case, row F, which is less heavily posted than row D. We are no longer interested in all the cells in this row, but only in cells F1, F5, F7, and F8. F5 and F7 are empty, so that we know that neither document 5 nor document 7 can satisfy the search requirements. When we move to the final row, D, we are interested solely in two cells, the D1 cell and the D8 cell, since postings in these cells are necessary to match the search strategy. Cell D8 is empty but D1 is not; thus, document 1 is the only item in the collection that matches the search formulation. Although the method of searching differs, the result of the two searching methods remains the same. Given the assignment of certain documents to certain classes, the method of file organization adopted has no effect on what is retrieved in a particular search.

From this example, it can be seen that to search a term-on-item file we must examine every unit record, that is, column of the matrix, if we want to identify all items in the collection that meet the search requirements. Of course, if we are seeking only a selection of the acceptable items, we can stop the search at the point at which a sufficient number of them have been identified. On the other hand, as we have seen, when we search an item-on-term index, whether we want complete or partial retrieval, we need not examine every row of the matrix, but only the rows corresponding to the classes demanded in the formulation.

It is useful to regard any type of index as a form of document-term matrix. In a very large system the matrix must also be very large—perhaps 1 million document numbers on one axis and 10,000 terms on the other.

The matrix also illustrates another very important point: the performance capabilities of a retrieval system are very largely fixed once a particular document collection has been indexed in a particular way, that is, the documents have been assigned to a particular group of classes defined by a particular index language.

The document-term matrix illustrates the major data base characteristics affecting the performance of a retrieval system: indexing policy and practice, on the one hand, and the characteristics of the index language, most notably its specificity, on the other. To return to Figure 9, document 5 is unlikely to be retrieved in a search on topic C, even though many people might consider it relevant to the subject, if the indexer has not assigned term C to the document. How much precision can be achieved in a search, that is, the proportion of the items retrieved that are judged relevant by the requester, is largely dependent on how many classes exist in the system, which tends to reflect the size of the index language. A system with a very large vocabulary (many rows in the matrix) is one in which subject matter is indexed at a high level of precision. Conversely, a system with a small vocabulary implies a more general level of indexing—larger classes of documents are formed—and lower precision on the average.

The characteristics of the document-term matrix formed by the indexing process—which documents are assigned to which classes and how large the classes are—then, very largely determines the capabilities of the system. These are data base or input variables affecting performance. As suggested in Chapter 1, the only other major variables are the output variables of quality of the requests made to the system and quality of the search strategies derived from the requests.

Information retrieval is very much dependent on classification. Subject indexing, as pointed out before, is a classification process; the index language is a set of labels that identify the classes existing in a particular system; a search strategy is nothing more than a "class membership statement," that is, a statement of what class or classes a document must belong to in order to be considered relevant and in order, therefore, to be retrieved.

Chapter Three

The Application of Computers to Information Retrieval: Off-Line Batch Processing Systems

The early history of information retrieval by computer has never been well documented. In fact, it is not altogether clear as to which system can legitimately be regarded as the first computer-based system for information retrieval. Among the earliest true computer-based systems were those established at the Naval Ordnance Laboratory, Silver Spring, Maryland, in 1959, and the system put into operation by Western Reserve University for the American Society for Metals, apparently in 1960.

It is probably safe to say, however, that the really major information retrieval systems in the United States emerged in the federal government in the early 1960s. Perhaps the most important were the services initiated by the Armed Services Technical Information Agency, later the Defense

Documentation Center, in the period 1959–1963, the National Aeronautics and Space Administration in 1962, and the National Library of Medicine, whose MEDLARS service was launched in 1963. These agencies must be regarded as the pioneers of large-scale bibliographic processing by computer, although many other organizations have followed in their footsteps. Although all three of these agencies have been important and influential in the development of information retrieval in the United States, the National Library of Medicine has perhaps been most influential of all. This is due to a combination of several factors: MEDLARS (Medical Literature Analysis and Retrieval System) was the first large system to be made widely available without security or other restrictions, the system is still in many respects the largest information retrieval system on a worldwide basis, and it has generated more literature than any other system of its type.

The characteristics of MEDLARS, as the system existed in 1970, are presented in some detail as an example of a large bibliographic processing system operated in an off-line batch processing mode. It is important to recognize that ten years ago, and even, for that matter, today, it may have been difficult to justify economically the dedication of a computerized system solely to the purpose of retrospective searching of bibliographic records. Most of the very large bibliographic systems have been justified by their virtuosity. They tend to be multipurpose, generating from a single input operation a range of products or services. MEDLARS itself is an excellent example of such a multipurpose system. It was in fact developed primarily as a publishing system, the computer being used to manipulate citations in machine-readable form—that is, the operations of error checking, sorting, formatting—and to interface directly with a "computer typesetting" operation (the Photon photocomposition equipment, designed to NLM specifications, was the first equipment of its type in regular production use). Through the computer-controlled publication programs, the monthly *Index Medicus* is produced. The machine-readable tapes generated as a result of this activity can then be used to generate additional publications and to offer further services. The additional publications include the annual *Cumulated Index Medicus* and a wide range of more specialized recurring bibliographies. The major service allowed by the existence of the machine-readable data base is a retrospective search service on demand ("demand search service"), although some use is also being made of the data base in current awareness activities (Selective Dissemination of Information).

The operational computer-based retrieval systems of the 1960s were mostly very similar in characteristics. They were off-line batch processing systems, using magnetic tape as the storage medium, and, by and large, they were serially searched.

Although some experimental on-line systems were in use in the early 1960s and a few major on-line systems were operational in the late 1960s, on-line information retrieval really came into its own in the 1970s.

Many of the major operating systems of the 1960s were multipurpose, at least to the extent of offering both retrospective search and Selective Dissemination of Information (SDI) services. Almost all were based on human indexing and the use of humanly prepared searching strategies, both activities being aided by a controlled vocabulary, usually a "thesaurus."

MEDLARS AS AN EXAMPLE OF AN OFF-LINE SYSTEM (STATUS AS OF 1970).
MEDLARS INDEXING

Approximately 18,000 separate journals are received at the National Library of Medicine. In 1970, about 2300 were indexed into MEDLARS. These 2300 were selected as an optimum set of biomedical journals, in all languages, to satisfy the interests of the majority of MEDLARS users. An effort was made to maintain a reasonable balance among the various subject areas. In the selection of journals to be included in MEDLARS, the library is advised by a Committee on Selection of Literature for MEDLARS, composed of leading physicians, medical librarians, and editors of medical journals. The committee constantly evaluates new journals being published for possible inclusion in *Index Medicus*. It also evaluates the status of journals already being indexed and considers suggestions about candidates for inclusion in the system.

Most journals are indexed cover to cover. Original articles are indexed, as well as those editorials, biographies, and obituaries which have substantive content. The designation "selective" is applied to those journals which are not exclusively medical. General scientific journals, such as *Science* and *Nature*, frequently contain biomedical articles. These journals are selectively indexed for their biomedical coverage only.

As of March 1970, the MEDLARS data base comprised over 1 million citations to biomedical articles input to the January 1964 and subsequent issues of the monthly *Index Medicus*. The data base was growing at the rate of about 200,000 citations annually. The great majority of the citations are to articles from journals and other serial publications—for example, annual reviews—but some refer to the technical report literature. Approximately 50% of the articles cited are written in languages other than English.

The indexing process involves the careful analysis of articles and description of the contents of each by the use of specific subject headings selected from a controlled list. High-quality articles are indexed with as many terms (subject headings) as are needed to describe fully the subject matter discussed. Although there is no ceiling placed on the number of headings, in practice, between 10 and 20 terms are assigned for these types of articles on the average. They tend to be long and are often research-oriented.

Shorter articles, and those which contain less substantive information, are usually indexed with enough subject headings to describe the principal points or highlights of the article. Indexing in 1970 was performed by a group of approximately 50 highly trained medical literature analysts, located at the National Library of Medicine and at MEDLARS Service Centers throughout the United States and abroad.

Figure 10 depicts, side by side, completed indexer data forms for two journal articles, one of which required more subject headings than the other to describe its content. Any given citation is published in *Index Medicus* under only a limited number of the subject headings assigned to it. Such headings, which are known as "print terms" or "*Index Medicus* terms" (IM terms), are those which, in the indexer's judgment, cover the

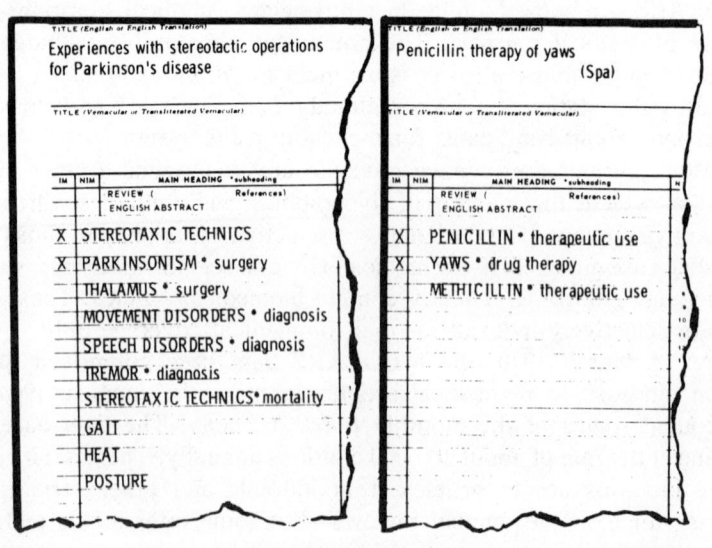

IM	NIM	MAIN HEADING *subheading
		TITLE: Experiences with stereotactic operations for Parkinson's disease
X		STEREOTAXIC TECHNICS
X		PARKINSONISM * surgery
	—	THALAMUS * surgery
	—	MOVEMENT DISORDERS * diagnosis
	—	SPEECH DISORDERS * diagnosis
	—	TREMOR * diagnosis
	—	STEREOTAXIC TECHNICS * mortality
	—	GAIT
	—	HEAT
	—	POSTURE

IM	NIM	MAIN HEADING *subheading
		TITLE: Penicillin therapy of yaws (Spa)
X		PENICILLIN * therapeutic use
X		YAWS * drug therapy
	—	METHICILLIN * therapeutic use

Figure 10 The difference between depth and nondepth indexing in MEDLARS.

principal points of the article. An X on the left of the data form under the IM column designates those IM terms under which the citation will be printed in *Index Medicus*. The remaining headings assigned, "nonprint terms" or "non-*Index Medicus* terms" (NIM terms), represent data or discussions, contained in the article, that are worth bringing out in the indexing but are not the central points of the article. All headings are recorded on the citation file (magnetic tape) and are used in machine search and retrieval operations.

In describing the contents of an article, an indexer must use only the subject headings appearing in a list of accepted subject headings. This list, *Medical Subject Headings,* is published annually and is generally referred to as MeSH. In 1970 the published MeSH contained about 8000 subject headings.

In addition to the subject headings, MEDLARS makes use of about 60 subheadings. Subheadings are general-concept terms that enrich the vocabulary considerably. They are used only in combination with main headings to show a particular attribute or effect of the concept expressed by the main heading. For example, a user of *Index Medicus* may want to locate articles on the liver, but from the anatomical point of view rather than that of physiology or metabolism. He does not need to look at all citations under LIVER but only at those under LIVER with the subheading anatomy & histology.

Every day, each MEDLARS indexer is assigned a pile of journals to be indexed. This assignment is in keeping with his or her experience or level of training, language abilities, and subject knowledge. Most analysts are able to read at least one foreign tongue, and many are able to index literature in four or five languages.

The high production demanded by MEDLARS (about 200,000 citations annually) precludes the possibility of an indexer's reading every word of an article. With practice, one can index efficiently without the perusal of every single word of a text. Analysts use a read-scan method based on the following instructions:

1. Read and understand the title.
2. Read the text down to the point at which the author states the purpose of his paper.
3. Scan the text, reading chapter headings, section headings, boldface, italics, charts, plates, X-rays, etc.
4. Read every word of the summary.
5. Closely scan the abstract.
6. Scan the bibliographic references.

This stage of the indexing operation is "conceptual analysis" or "content analysis," that is, deciding what the article is about. The next stage involves the transformation of the conceptual analysis into the most appropriate set of subject headings and subheadings, which are then recorded on the indexer's data form. This form is the official worksheet of the analyst. A data form accompanies each article indexed in each journal from the point of indexing until the indexed citation has been input to the computer.

A blank data form is shown in Figure 11. The upper part is used to record a full bibliographic description of the article, and this forms the basis of the printed citation in *Index Medicus* or in a MEDLARS search printout. Some of the items—for example, translation and transliteration of foreign titles—are always supplied on the data form by the indexer or an indexing clerk. The language of a foreign article is always indicated. This appears as an abbreviation in *Index Medicus* and can be used as a search parameter in retrieval operations.

Before describing the contents of the article in MeSH terms, the indexer turns his attention to a set of routine items that must be accounted for in the indexing of every article. These items are known as "check tags," and they are preprinted on the data form so that the analyst can check off all appropriate terms. For example, the indexer must account for the age of any person discussed in the article, for whether the study is performed on humans or animals, and for the sex of the person or animal.

The remaining space on the data form is reserved for the description of the article in terms of *Medical Subject Headings*. Here the indexer types all the headings, with subheadings whenever appropriate, necessary to describe the content of the article. MEDLARS indexing is "postcoordinate" indexing. This means that complex concepts may be expressed by combinations of two or more terms. We have already seen how we can combine a main heading with a subheading to express a more complex (specific) concept as HEPATITIS* prevention & control. We can also express a complex concept by the joint use of two or more main headings. For example, an article discussing community health services under regional medical programs might be indexed with the main headings COMMUNITY HEALTH SERVICES and REGIONAL MEDICAL PROGRAMS. Coordination may also be achieved by the joint use of a main heading and a check tag. Thus, HEPATITIS in females may be expressed by assigning the term HEPATITIS and checking the tag FEMALE.

Some coordination already exists in the characteristics of certain main headings themselves. Thus, LIVER GLYCOGEN represents a precoordination of the concept liver and the concept glycogen. Likewise, DIABETES MELLITUS, JUVENILE is a precoordination of the concept diabetes mellitus and the concept child.

A cardinal rule of indexing in MEDLARS is that a topic is always indexed under the most specific available term. An article on sunburn is indexed under SUNBURN and not under BURNS, and an article on eye burns under EYE BURNS and not under BURNS. An article on friction burns, however, would be indexed under BURNS because no specific term for friction burns exists in MeSH. The work of trainees and junior indexers is subjected to a checking operation conducted by a fully experienced indexer, known as a "reviser." The reviser rapidly scans the bibliographic description and then concentrates on the assigned subject headings, asking the following questions:

Do the main headings reflect the true content of the article?
Do the *Index Medicus* (print) headings cover the central points of the article?
Are the headings spelled correctly, in exactly the form appearing in MeSH?
Are the correct subheadings used?
Are all necessary check tags present and have they been used correctly?
Are the relationships expressed (by the subheadings, for example) correct? Did disease X lead to Y or did Y cause X?
Are the headings at the correct level of specificity for the article?

To illustrate the MEDLARS indexing process further, it may be useful to look over the shoulder of an indexer, as it were, to see the steps involved in subject-indexing a typical article. The sample article is entitled "Positive Sputum Cytologic Tests for Five Years before Specific Detection of Bronchial Carcinoma."

After reading key portions of the article and scanning the remaining text, the indexer decides that the article deals primarily with the diagnosis of pulmonary and bronchial neoplasms by means of cytological tests of the sputum. He therefore assigns the following main heading–subheading combinations:

X SPUTUM*cytology
X CARCINOMA, BRONCHOGENIC*diagnosis
X BRONCHIAL NEOPLASMS*diagnosis
X LUNG NEOPLASMS*diagnosis

indicating by the X that these are print terms, representing headings under which the citation should be printed in *Index Medicus*. This is also a study, by cytological methods, of the pathology of various types of tumors, and this leads him to assign the additional terms

① ⑧ PAGINATION	⑨ LANGUAGE ENG.	⑪ ANONYMOUS A☐	⑰ REFS	⑬ SUBJECT NAME
C				

⑩ AUTHOR DATA

⑮ TITLE (Eng or Transl)

⑭ TITLE (Vernac or Translit)

⑲	⑳					
A ☐ HIST ART	A ☐ PREGN	J ☐ CATS	T ☐ RATS	c ☐ ANCIENT	I ☐ NIH SUP	
B ☐ HIST BIOG	B ☐ INF NEW (to 1 mo)	K ☐ CATTLE	U ☐ ANIMAL	d ☐ MEDIEVAL	m ☐ NON NIH SUP	
C ☐ BIOG-OBIT	C ☐ INF (1–23 mo)	L ☐ CHICK EMBRYO	V ☐ HUMAN	e ☐ MODERN		⑫ AUTHOR
D ☐ SYMPOS	D ☐ CHILD PRE (2–5)	M ☐ DOGS	W ☐ MALE	f ☐ 15th CENT		☐ AFFIL
E ☐ PROCEED	E ☐ CHILD (6–12)	N ☐ FROGS	X ☐ FEMALE	g ☐ 16th CENT		
F ☐ TECH REPT	F ☐ ADOLESC (13–18)	O ☐ GUINEA PIGS	Y ☐ IN VITRO	h ☐ 17th CENT		㉒ AUTHOR
G ☐ MONOGR	G ☐ ADULT (19–44)	P ☐ HAMSTERS	Z ☐ CASE REPT	i ☐ 18th CENT		☐ ABST
H ☐ ENG ABST	H ☐ MID AGE (45–64)	Q ☐ MICE	a ☐ CLIN RES	j ☐ 19th CENT		
	I ☐ AGED (65 +)	R ☐ MONKEYS	b ☐ COMP STUDY	k ☐ 20th CENT		
		S ☐ RABBITS				

㉑

1		1
2		2
3		3
4		4
5		5
6		6
7		7

8		8
9		9
10		10
11		11
12		12
13		13
14		14
15		15
16		16
17		17
18		18
19		19
20		20
21		21
22		22
23		23
24		24
25		25
26		26
27		27
28		28
29		29
30		30
31		31
32		32
33		33
34		34
35		35

NIH–1416
(Rev. 3–75)

INDEXED CITATION FORM

☆ GPO : 1976 O - 217-796

Figure 11 MEDLARS indexing form.

BRONCHIAL NEOPLASMS*pathology
CARCINOMA, EPIDERMOID*pathology
CARCINOMA, BRONCHOGENIC*pathology
ADENOCARCINOMA*pathology
CYTODIAGNOSIS

The patient discussed in the article, a 72-year-old man, was subjected to various diagnostic procedures, including radiography, bronchoscopy, and biopsy. The following terms were therefore assigned:

BRONCHIAL NEOPLASMS*radiography
CARCINOMA, BRONCHOGENIC*radiography
BRONCHOSCOPY
BIOPSY

and the following check tags were marked:

AGED
HUMAN
MALE

In addition, the provisional heading* TIME FACTORS was assigned to account for the time period (five years) over which the cytologic tests were conducted. The completed data form is shown as Figure 12.

PROCESSING THE CITATIONS

The monthly output of completed indexer data forms (about 20,000 monthly in 1970) is used as input to procedures that generate the machine-readable data base. The subject headings assigned to a particular journal article, together with the full bibliographic citation for the article, were put into machine-readable form by input typists using paper tape typewriters. These machines simultaneously produce a punched paper tape and a proof paper copy. After proofreading, the input paper tapes and correction tapes go through a computer input procedure that transfers the input data for each article (bibliographic citation plus index terms) to magnetic tape (see Figure 13).

The magnetic tapes produced by these input procedures contain unit records for each citation, arranged sequentially in order of accession, that is, in citation-number order. For each citation, the following data are recorded: citation number, author and title of article (including English translation of foreign titles), journal reference, language abbreviation for

---

* A provisional heading is one that can be used in indexing and searching but has not yet been approved for inclusion in the printed *Medical Subject Headings*.

languages other than English, all the subject headings assigned by the indexer, and other pertinent information such as place of publication. For review articles, the number of references is also recorded. The contents of the tape are shown in simplified form in Figure 14.

The magnetic tape containing one month's input of indexed citations is processed to generate the next monthly issue of *Index Medicus*. The computer programs used to generate this publication are rather complex. Essentially, however, they accomplish the following tasks (Figure 15):

1. *Replication and Sorting*. A citation is replicated and sorted under all the headings under which it is to be printed, that is, all the headings marked as print headings by the indexer, plus author headings and cross-references for the author section.
2. *Formatting*. A series of programs transforms each citation into standard print formats, arranges the citations in the columnar form in which they will appear in the final publication, and handles such additional items as page headings, column headings, and page numbers.
3. *Photocomposing*. The correctly formatted tapes are processed by a photocomposing machine known as GRACE (Graphic Arts Composing Equipment). The final product of GRACE is a roll of exposed paper, each roll containing about 120 pages for publication (Figure 15).

The exposed paper is developed by an automatic processor. The developed paper is inspected, cut into page-size sheets, and packaged for delivery to a commercial printer. Offset printing and binding complete the publication cycle (Figure 16). Figure 17 shows part of a sample page from a monthly issue of *Index Medicus*. Note how the subheadings, as assigned by the indexers, are used to subdivide the entries under a main subject heading. After paper tape input, all sorting, formatting, and composing functions are computer-controlled. Identical procedures are followed in the production of the annual *Cumulated Index Medicus*, although processing time for the annual publication is obviously much greater.

RETROSPECTIVE SEARCHING ON DEMAND

A MEDLARS search request asks for the conduct of a retrospective search, through the indexed citations in the MEDLARS data base, in order to retrieve citations that deal with a particular item of subject matter. These requests are made by medical educators, practitioners, researchers, and other health professionals. Searches are requested for a variety of purposes: for example, to determine the state of research in a

① ⓒ ⑧ PAGINATION | ⑨ LANGUAGE ENG. | ⑪ ANONYMOUS A☐ | ⑰ REFS | ⑬ SUBJECT NAME

⑩ AUTHOR DATA

⑬ TITLE (Eng or Transl)

⑭ TITLE (Vernac or Translit)

⑲
A ☐ HIST ART
B ☐ HIST BIOG
C ☐ BIOG-OBIT
D ☐ SYMPOS
E ☐ PROCEED
F ☐ TECH REPT
G ☐ MONOGR
H ☐ ENG ABST

⑳
A ☐ PREGN
B ☐ INF NEW (to 1 mo)
C ☐ INF (1–23 mo)
D ☐ CHILD PRE (2–5)
E ☐ CHILD (6–12)
F ☐ ADOLESC (13–18)
G ☐ ADULT (19–44)
H ☐ MID AGE (45–64)
I ☒ AGED (65 +)

J ☐ CATS
K ☐ CATTLE
L ☐ CHICK EMBRYO
M ☐ DOGS
N ☐ FROGS
O ☐ GUINEA PIGS
P ☐ HAMSTERS
Q ☐ MICE
R ☐ MONKEYS
S ☐ RABBITS

T ☐ RATS
U ☐ ANIMAL
V ☒ HUMAN
W ☒ MALE
X ☐ FEMALE
Y ☐ IN VITRO
Z ☐ CASE REPT
a ☐ CLIN RES
b ☐ COMP STUDY

c ☐ ANCIENT
d ☐ MEDIEVAL
e ☐ MODERN
f ☐ 15th CENT
g ☐ 16th CENT
h ☐ 17th CENT
i ☐ 18th CENT
j ☐ 19th CENT
k ☐ 20th CENT

l ☐ NIH SUP
m ☐ NON NIH SUP

⑫ AUTHOR ☐ AFFIL
㉒ AUTHOR ☐ ABST

㉑
1	SPUTUM/*cytology
2	CARCINOMA, BRONCHOGENIC/*diagnosis
3	BRONCHIAL NEOPLASMS/radiography
4	BRONCHIAL NEOPLASMS/*diagnosis
5	CARCINOMA, BRONCHOGENIC/*radiography
6	CYTODIAGNOSIS
7	BRONCHIAL NEOPLASMS/*pathology

8	BRONCHOSCOPY
9	CARCINOMA, EPIDERMOID/pathology
10	LUNG NEOPLASMS/*diagnosis
11	ADENOCARCINOMA/pathology
12	CARCINOMA, BRONCHOGENIC/pathology
13	BIOPSY
14	TIME FACTORS
15	
16	
17	
18	
19	
20	
21	
22	
23	
24	
25	
26	
27	
28	
29	
30	
31	
32	
33	
34	
35	

NIH-1416
(Rev. 3-75)

INDEXED CITATION FORM

☆ GPO : 1976 O - 217-796

Figure 12 Partially completed MEDLARS indexing form.

47

48   The Application of Computers to Information Retrieval

Figure 13   Bibliographic records transferred from paper tape to magnetic tape.

particular field, to assist in the preparation of a review article, or to help solve a clinical problem. About 20,000 MEDLARS searches were completed in the United States in the year 1970.

In indexing an article for input to MEDLARS, the indexer goes through a two-stage process:

1. Deciding what the article is about.
2. Describing the contents of the article by means of MeSH terms.

A search analyst goes through the same two-stage process. First, he must decide what the request is about, that is, what kinds of articles the requester really wants to see. Second, he must translate his interpretation of the request into a search statement, in MeSH terms, that can be processed against the citation file.

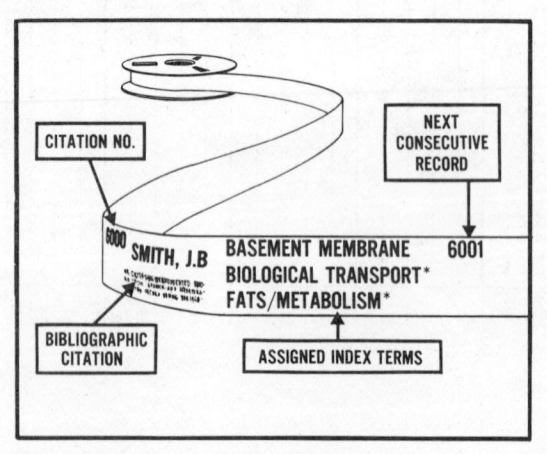

Figure 14   Conceptualization of a single bibliographic record on magnetic tape.

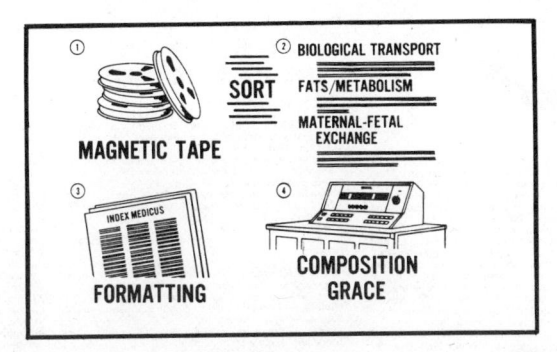

Figure 15 In MEDLARS, computer programs sort citations and produce a formatted tape from which *Index Medicus* will be photocomposed.

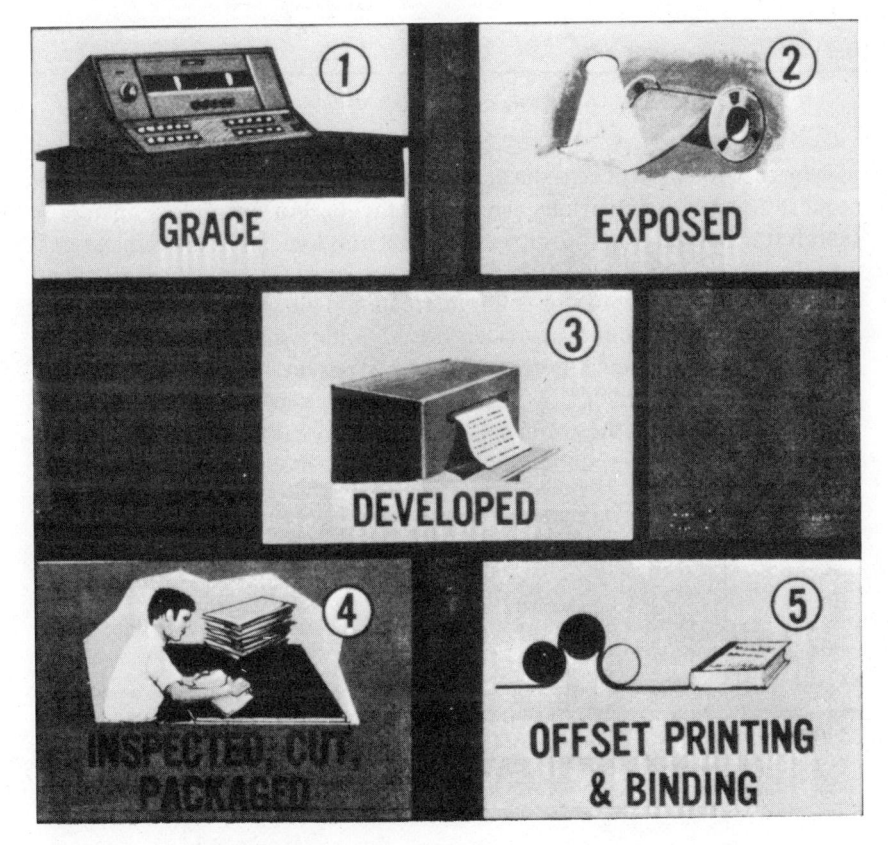

Figure 16 Steps in the production of *Index Medicus* from photocomposition to binding.

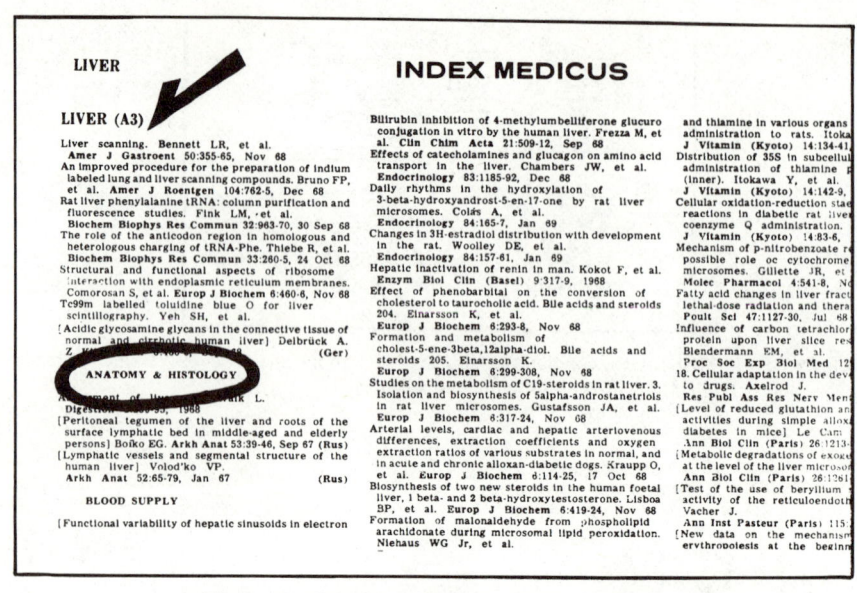

50   The Application of Computers to Information Retrieval

Figure 17   Sample of the *Index Medicus* format.

In the analysis of a request, it is logical to begin by breaking the request down into its various aspects, or facets. For example, consider a search for literature on the subject of renal amyloidosis. This request has two facets: (1) the organ facet (kidney) and (2) the disease facet (amyloidosis). The requester is not interested in all articles on the kidney, and he is not interested in all articles on amyloidosis. He is interested only in articles which discuss both facets of his request, that is, kidney and amyloidosis, and which presumably deal with renal amyloidosis. This relationship between the two facets may conveniently be represented by a Venn diagram of overlapping circles, as shown below:

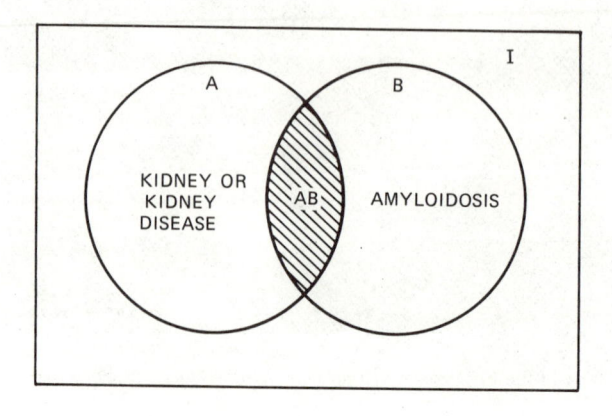

The rectangle I represents the entire MEDLARS collection. For this particular request we are interested in two classes of articles: the class A, dealing with the kidney, and the class B, dealing with amyloidosis. Specifically, we are interested only in the intersection or overlap of these two classes, namely, the subclass AB that deals with both kidney and amyloidosis. The overlap of classes is also known as the product or intersection of these classes. The relationship between these classes is an AND relationship. In the above example, both classes must be present in order for an article to be of interest, that is, KIDNEY *and* AMYLOIDOSIS.

Having conceptually analyzed a request into its component facets, the next step involves translating this conceptual analysis into MeSH terms. There is no single MeSH term covering renal amyloidosis. We must therefore search for articles that are indexed under terms indicating kidney and under terms indicating amyloidosis. We make use of MeSH to arrive at lists of terms indicating, on the one hand, kidney and, on the other, amyloidosis as follows:

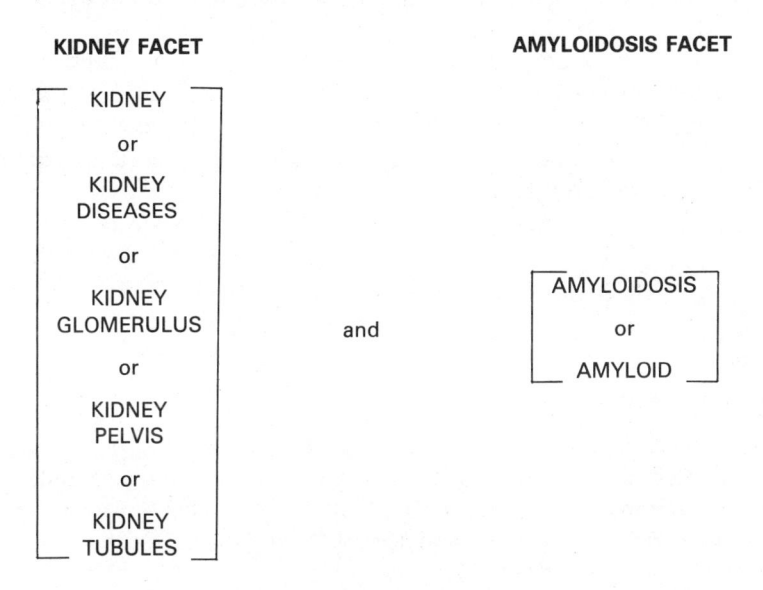

KIDNEY FACET **AMYLOIDOSIS FACET**

[KIDNEY or KIDNEY DISEASES or KIDNEY GLOMERULUS or KIDNEY PELVIS or KIDNEY TUBULES]   and   [AMYLOIDOSIS or AMYLOID]

Note that we accept any of the selected terms indicating kidney and any indicating amyloidosis. Thus, the terms in the kidney facet are all alternatives (substitutes) for one another. The relationship between these terms is therefore an OR relationship. We will accept KIDNEY GLOMERULUS or KIDNEY TUBULES. A list of alternative terms, that is, terms in an OR relationship, is called a sum of these terms.

Summations of classes can also be represented diagrammatically. For example, we can depict the sum of the class amyloid and the class amyloidosis as follows:

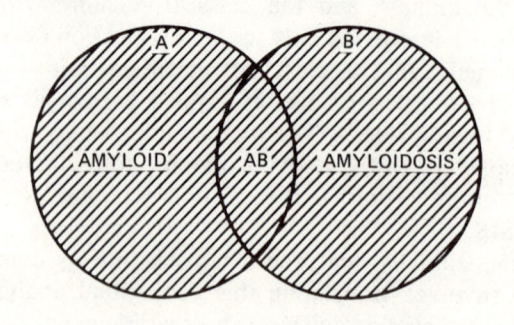

Thus, in a MEDLARS search strategy, when we say AMYLOID or AMYLOIDOSIS, we accept any citation indexed under the term AMYLOID (Class A) or any citation indexed under AMYLOIDOSIS (Class B) or any citation indexed under both the term AMYLOID and the term AMYLOIDOSIS (AB).

Above we have graphically represented a very simple search strategy for a request on renal amyloidosis. By giving each term in this strategy a unique identifying number and by using symbols that are recognized by the MEDLARS computer, we can reduce this strategy to a simple algebraic search equation. Consider the following:

M_1 KIDNEY
M_2 KIDNEY GLOMERULUS
M_3 KIDNEY PELVIS
M_4 KIDNEY TUBULES
M_8 AMYLOID
M_9 AMYLOIDOSIS

In our search equation we want to specify that we accept any article indexed under any one of the kidney terms, M_1 to M_4, and also under one of the amyloidosis terms, M_8 to M_9; that is, we want the intersection or product of the class kidney and the class amyloidosis. This could be represented as follows:

$$(M_1 \text{ or } M_2 \text{ or } M_3 \text{ or } M_4) \text{ and } (M_8 \text{ or } M_9)$$

However, in the search equation the OR relationship is represented by a plus (+) sign, and the AND relationship is represented by an asterisk (*). We could therefore rewrite the above equation as follows:

$$(M_1 + M_2 + M_3 + M_4) * (M_8 + M_9)$$

In actual practice, we can compress this equation even further by assigning identifying numbers to sums of terms. Thus, we could say that M_5 = the sum of M_1 to M_4, that is, M_1 or M_2 or M_3 or M_4, and that M_{10} = the sum of M_8 to M_9. By adopting these further abbreviations, the whole search equation can now be reduced to

$$(M_5) * (M_{10})$$

or, because, as we will explain later, the parentheses now become redundant, to

$$M_5 * M_{10}$$

Using a very simple example, we have now gone through the entire search formulation process:

1. Analysis of the request and identification of the facets involved.
2. Selection of MeSH terms appropriate to each facet.
3. Assignment of identifying numbers to the terms selected.
4. Preparing summations of terms and a search equation that specifies which combinations of index terms must be present in order to cause a citation to be retrieved.

It is important to recognize that a search strategy is really a condensed statement of all the possible term combinations that could cause a citation to be retrieved. $M_5 * M_{10}$ means that we accept any citation indexed under a term represented by M_5, that is, M_1 to M_4, so long as a term represented by M_{10}, that is, M_8 to M_9, is also present. In other words, going back to the terms selected above, we want to retrieve only those articles which have been indexed under one of the following term combinations:

KIDNEY and AMYLOID
KIDNEY and AMYLOIDOSIS
KIDNEY GLOMERULUS and AMYLOID
KIDNEY GLOMERULUS and AMYLOIDOSIS
KIDNEY PELVIS and AMYLOID
KIDNEY PELVIS and AMYLOIDOSIS
KIDNEY TUBULES and AMYLOID
KIDNEY TUBULES and AMYLOIDOSIS

By assigning identifying numbers to each term, and by using the standard symbols, we have reduced this statement of acceptable term combinations to the very concise search equation $M_5 * M_{10}$.

It is also important to note that, in the above example, we have not placed any other restrictions on the citations that may be retrieved; that is, we accept citations to any articles indexed under any of the term combinations listed above no matter what other terms have also been used in indexing. Thus, we are equally happy to retrieve any of the following articles:

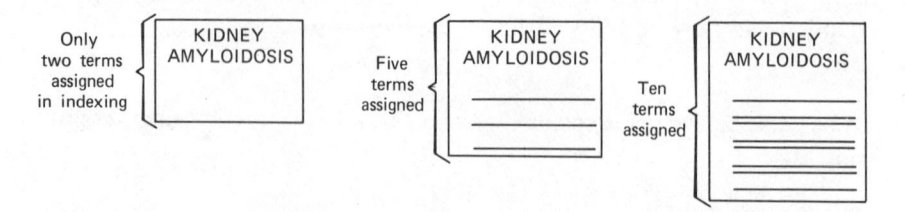

Only two terms assigned in indexing { KIDNEY AMYLOIDOSIS }   Five terms assigned { KIDNEY AMYLOIDOSIS }   Ten terms assigned { KIDNEY AMYLOIDOSIS }

Many of the requests made to information systems are more complex than the simple two-faceted request used as an illustration above. For example, the requester might have asked for renal amyloidosis as a complication of tuberculosis or for the effect of prednisone on this condition. The former request is three-faceted, and the latter involves four facets: kidney, amyloidosis, tuberculosis, and drug therapy (specifically, prednisone therapy). These requests are represented diagrammatically below:

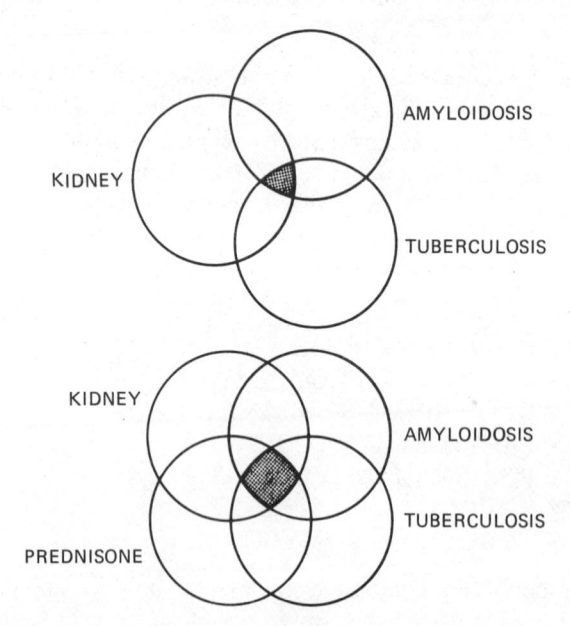

In the former case we are looking for the intersection of three classes; that is, we are seeking articles indexed under a kidney term and an amyloidosis term and a tuberculosis term. In the latter, we are demanding a fourth intersection: in addition to the above, a term indicating prednisone involvement must also be present.

As the requests get more precise, and we demand that more terms must co-occur in order to cause retrieval, the volume of literature retrieved becomes less. Thus, we expect more citations to be retrieved for a search on renal amyloidosis than we do for a search on renal amyloidosis as a complication of tuberculosis, and we expect more on the latter topic than we do on effect of prednisone in cases of renal amyloidosis complicating tuberculosis.

However complex the request, we can still reduce it to the type of search equation illustrated earlier. For example, the search equation

$$M_5 * M_{10} * M_{20} * M_{25}$$

might be used to express the most complex request mentioned, where M_5 represents a list (sum) of the kidney terms, M_{10} the sum of the amyloidosis terms, M_{20} the sum of the tuberculosis terms, and M_{25} the term PREDNISONE.

Terms may be assigned to an article to describe aspects other than purely subject aspects. These parameters can also be incorporated in search strategies. For example, we can search for review articles on amyloidosis, amyloidosis articles written in French, or for articles on amyloidosis from a particular journal:

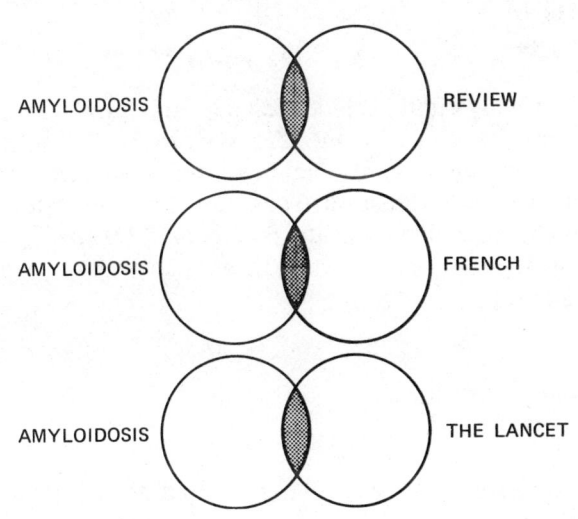

We have already mentioned that the logical *or* (sum) can be used to indicate terms that are accepted as equivalent (substitutable) for search purposes—that is, AMYLOIDOSIS or AMYLOID. We can also use logical sums to incorporate alternative search strategies into a complete search formulation. Consider a request for literature on the effect of cortisone on the choroid or the retina. This may be represented as follows:

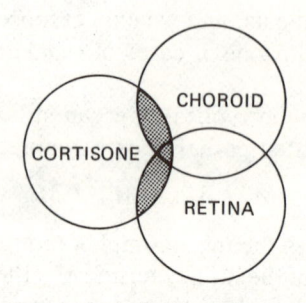

Here we are interested in any articles indexed under a term indicating cortisone and also a term indicating choroid or retina. We can reduce this to a simple strategy as follows:

M_1 CORTISONE
M_4 CHOROID
M_5 RETINA

$$M_1 * (M_4 + M_5)$$

That is, retrieve any citations indexed under the term CORTISONE and either the term CHOROID or the term RETINA.

A search equation is an algebraic expression with the characteristics of any other algebraic expression. Thus, the terms inside the parentheses are governed by everything outside; that is, $M_1 * (M_4 + M_5)$ is equivalent to $M_1 * M_4 + M_1 * M_5$, which would be another way of writing the same search equation.

$$M_1 * (M_4 + M_5)$$

is not the same expression as

$$M_1 * M_4 + M_5$$

which means anything indexed under M_1 and M_4 or anything indexed under M_5 (alone). Note that the *or* (+) has here introduced an alternative search expression.

In addition to using the logical *and* and the logical *or*, we can also "negate" terms by use of the logical *not*. Consider a request for literature on the effect of cortisone on the retina but not where the retina is detached:

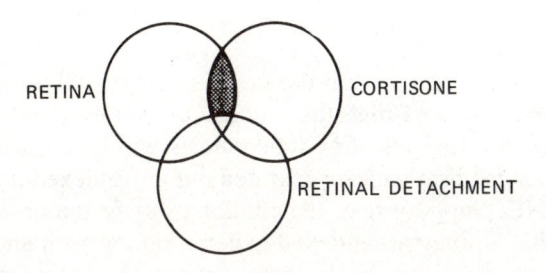

RETINA   CORTISONE

RETINAL DETACHMENT

Here we are interested in any article indexed under RETINA and under CORTISONE but not if also indexed under RETINAL DETACHMENT; that is, we specifically wish to exclude articles with the term RETINAL DETACHMENT. The negation (*not*) is expressed by the use of a minus sign ($-$). In this case we are saying *and not* ($* \ -$) and the search equation can be derived as follows:

M_1 RETINA
M_2 CORTISONE
M_3 RETINAL DETACHMENT
$M_1 * M_2 * - M_3$

The MEDLARS search programs, as used in the United States in 1970, allowed up to three subsearches of increasing specificity to be combined in a single search strategy. Consider again the request for literature on renal amyloidosis as a complication of tuberculosis and the effect of prednisone on this condition. Perhaps the requester indicates that he is generally interested in all renal amyloidosis, particularly when it is a complication of tuberculosis. His most particular interest is in the effects of prednisone on this condition. For this request we can create a three-tiered strategy of increasing specificity:

4   all articles on renal amyloidosis
5   renal amyloidosis as a complication of tuberculosis
6   the effects of prednisone on this condition

In MEDLARS the numbers 4,5,6 were used to indicate subsearches of increasing specificity in a complete search formulation. Reduced to a search equation, this appears as follows:

M_5 terms indicating kidney
M_{10} terms indicating amyloidosis
M_{15} terms indicating tuberculosis

M_{30} the term PREDNISONE
4 $M_5 * M_{10}$
5 M_{15}
6 M_{30}

What we are saying here is that the broad strategy will retrieve anything on renal amyloidosis. From this subset of retrieved citations, those indexed under a term indicating tuberculosis will be separated out, and from this second subset will be separated out any indexed under the term PREDNISONE. Suppose that 100 citations satisfy the broad search requirement, that is, they are indexed under a kidney term and also a term for amyloidosis. Of these, 20 also have a tuberculosis term present, and, of these, 2 have been indexed under the term PREDNISONE. A total of 100 citations will be retrieved by this strategy, but when these citations are printed out by the computer, those most specifically related to the requester's need (Section 6 of the bibliography) will appear first, followed by the next most closely related (Section 5), and finally by the residue of citations that satisfy the most general search requirement only, as follows:

Section 6	2 citations
Section 5	18 citations
Section 4	80 citations

for a total of 100 citations satisfying the search logic. All relationships among document classes (or the terms representing these classes) may be expressed in terms of the relations of Boolean algebra: logical sums (*ors*), logical products (*ands*), and logical differences (*nots* or *negations*). When reduced to a search equation, these relationships may be expressed by symbols such as +, *, and −. For purposes of illustration, we have drawn our examples from fairly simple requests involving relatively straightforward strategies. However, complex requests, involving many more terms, may be reduced to search equations in the same way.

The MEDLARS search analyst prepared a strategy on a special form known as the Demand Search Formulation Record (DSFR). An example is shown in Figure 18. This particular request is for articles on tissue culture studies of human breast cancer. It has three facets:

1. Breast cancer
2. Human
3. Tissue culture

Note how the searcher has divided up his list of terms into separate lists for each facet. The breast cancer terms are two: BREAST NEOPLASMS and CARCINOMA, DUCTAL. To arrive at the requirement for human,

REQUEST NO. 194249

DEMAND SEARCH FORMULATION RECORD

DATE 2 Aug 1969

TITLE Tissue culture studies of human breast cancer.

ELEM. SYMBOL (11-14)	EXPL. (17)	LEVEL (18)	CATEGORY NUMBER (19-31)	ELEMENTS	TALLY
M1				BREAST NEOPLASMS	
M2				CARCINOMA, DUCTAL	
M10				HUMAN	
M11	E		B2	VERTEBRATES	
M12				ANIMAL EXPERIMENTS	
M13				VETERINARY MEDICINE	
M14	E		C15	ANIMAL DISEASES	
M20				TISSUE CULTURE	
M21				CULTURE MEDIA	
M22				CHICK EMBRYO	
L1				ENG	
S1				Veterinary	

ELEMENTS A, J, I, N, Y, X, AND SUMMATIONS

SECT. (7 3-)	ELEM. SYMBOL (11-14)	33-36	37-40	41-44	45-48	49-56
	M3	SUM	M1	M2		
	M16	SUM	M11	M14		
	M23	SUM	M20	M22		

REQUEST STATEMENTS

SECT. (7)	ELEM. SYMBOL (9-10)	11-80 COLUMNS	FOUND
4	1	M3 * (M10 + -M16 * -S1) * M23 * L1.	11

BATCH NO.	DS MODULE	COMMENTS	RG MODULE	COMMENTS

PHS-4667-2 (4-67)

Figure 18 MEDLARS search strategy.

he searches on the term HUMAN and also negates terms indicating animal studies, including the subheading VETERINARY. There are three tissue culture terms to be searched. Finally, he indicates that the search is to be conducted on English-language material only.

Having decided on his search terms, the searcher gives them identifying numbers with the prefix *M* for main subject headings, *S* for subheadings, and *L* for language. He wants to negate all vertebrate terms and all animal disease terms; so he lists the category numbers (B2 and C15) and indicates by use of the *e* in column 17 that these terms are to be "exploded," that is, the entire group of terms in category B2 and category C15 are searched on. In the central part of the form he records his summations: M_3 for the two breast cancer terms, M_{16} for the four animal terms, and M_{23} for the three tissue culture terms. Finally, he reduces the entire strategy to a search equation ("request statement"):

$$M_3 * (M_{10} + - M_{16} * - S_1) * M_{23} * L_1$$

which translates as

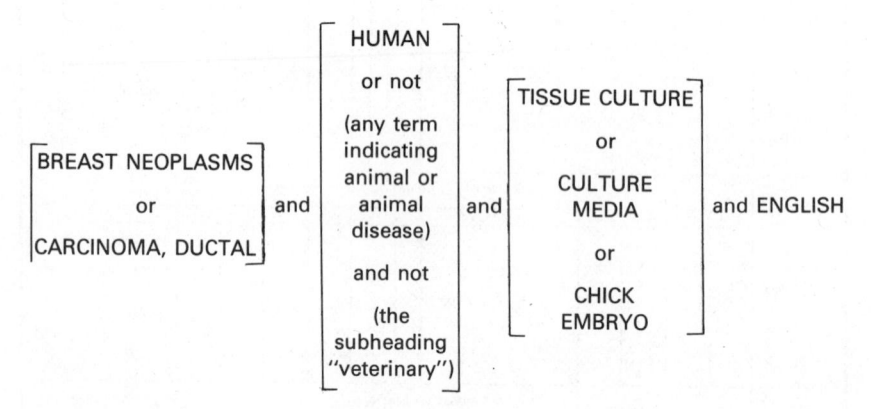

[BREAST NEOPLASMS or CARCINOMA, DUCTAL] and [HUMAN or not (any term indicating animal or animal disease) and not (the subheading "veterinary")] and [TISSUE CULTURE or CULTURE MEDIA or CHICK EMBRYO] and ENGLISH

No subsearches of increasing specificity were used in this particular strategy because only a small number of documents were expected to be retrieved. In fact, only 11 citations were found to meet the search requirements.

Once the search strategy has been reduced to an appropriate search equation, the entire formulation—terms and search equation—are put into machine-readable form—for example, by the use of punched cards. The search is now ready for processing. Several searches are batched together and processed simultaneously. A batch might typically consist of 40 to 50 searches but it could include over 100. The search strategy is matched sequentially against the complete data base of indexed citations. A citation is retrieved from the data base when its index terms match one of the combinations of index terms demanded by the search strategy. Qualifying citations are copied from the main citation file onto a "retrieved citation tape." Before the retrieved citations are printed, however, printing instructions are supplied by the search analyst who formulated the search. The following options are available:

1. The citations may be printed on 3- by 5-inch cards or on continuous computer paper (8½ by 11 inches).
2. The citations may be arranged in a number of different ways, including:
   a. Alphabetically by first author
   b. By journal title abbreviation
   c. By language

In fact, a MEDLARS search was carried out in two steps: (1) a high-speed search and (2) a "logic" search. The search programs were designed in this way to minimize the amount of machine processing needed to handle a batch of searches. Suppose that a search has three facets and that the number of documents indexed under terms appearing in each facet is as follows:

Facet A	12,000 documents
Facet B	700 documents
Facet C	124 documents

It is clear that the maximum number of documents that could possibly be retrieved is 124, and this number would be retrieved only if all the C documents were also indexed under a term from facet B and a term from facet A, a very unlikely occurrence. Facet C, thus, can be regarded as a kind of least common factor in this search strategy.

The search programs were designed in such a way that the "least common factor" in each strategy was automatically recognized by counting the number of documents indexed under the terms comprising each facet of the search strategy. The frequency with which each term has been used in indexing is recorded routinely by the programs, and these statistics are maintained as part of a machine-stored vocabulary that interfaces with the input and output modules of the system.

The high-speed search is concerned only with the least common factor of each search strategy. For the example under discussion, the entire data base is searched in order to locate the 124 documents of facet C. When found, these records are read onto an interim tape. The tape is then used as input to the logic search, which is much slower because each C record must be examined to determine if any B terms are present and, if so, if any A terms are present. The final set of documents satisfying the logic of the search (A * B * C) is then read onto the retrieved citation tape from which the search results are printed.

This division of the search into two phases optimizes the procedure because the entire data base can be searched rather rapidly on the basis of the least common element of each strategy in a batch. Only the much smaller file of citations retrieved in the high-speed search is subjected to the considerably slower logic search operations.

Illustrations of partial search printouts in paper and card formats are included in Figure 19. Notice that the printout provides, in addition to the bibliographic reference, a listing of all the headings used in indexing the article. These terms (an optional feature of a printout) may aid the user in deciding which articles he may want to read.

The searcher's final responsibility is to review the printout carefully for probable success or failure and then to take appropriate action. If the retrieved citations appear to meet the requester's need, the printout is mailed to him with an explanatory letter. If, in the searcher's estimation, the search results are poor, he may try another approach and reformulate the search, or he may contact the requester and discuss the problem with him. Adequate interaction with the user prior to initial formulation, along with careful thought during the formulation process, will usually avoid the need for reformulation.

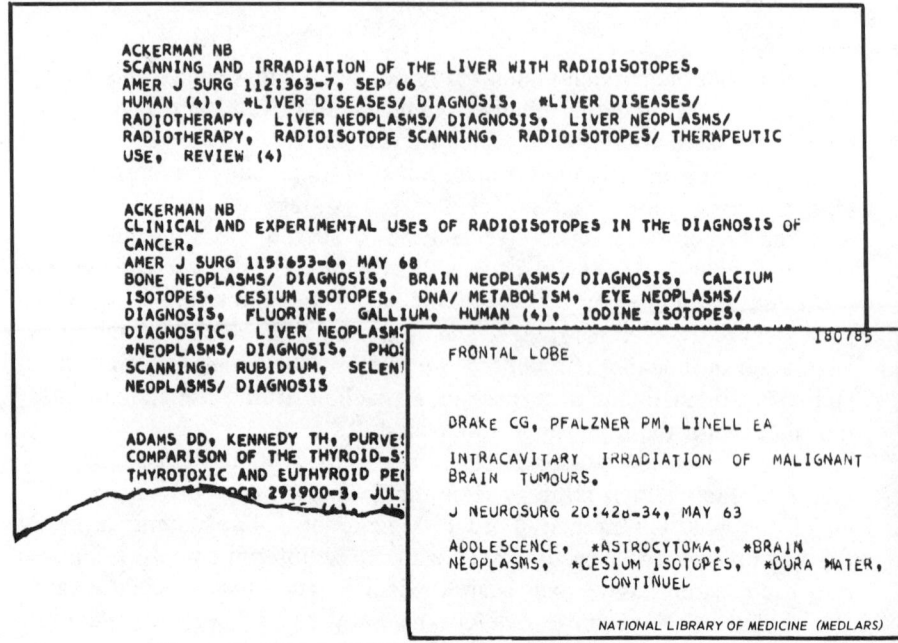

Figure 19 Sample MEDLARS output on paper and cards.

SELECTIVE DISSEMINATION OF INFORMATION

Batch processing systems can also be used in current awareness activities. In particular, it is possible to undertake selective dissemination of information (SDI) by computer. In SDI, search strategies are prepared to represent the current awareness information needs of individuals. These search strategies, usually referred to as "user interest profiles," are put into machine-readable form, stored on magnetic tape, and matched at regular intervals, perhaps monthly, against new additions to the document data base. Every month, then, a scientist, engineer, or other professional can receive a printout of references to new documents, matching his interest profile, that have been added to a particular data base. Suppose that a metallurgist is primarily interested in keeping up to date on the subject of joining processes applied to light metals. His interest profile may look something as follows:

(Joining or Welding or Brazing or Bonding) and (Light metals or Aluminum or Magnesium or Cadmium or Beryllium or Manganese or Antimony or Bismuth)

By matching this interest profile (a kind of "standing search strategy") against a data base of metals literature, the metallurgist can be kept continuously informed of newly published items relevant to his research interests.

As far as the computer system itself is concerned, there is essentially no difference between the operations involved in retrospective searching and SDI. The matching operation performed by computer is exactly the same in each case, the search strategies are of the same type, and the output—a printed list of citations—is also the same. The only real difference, a rather unimportant one, lies in what is stored permanently, that is, what constitutes the permanent data base, and what causes it to be searched. The situation is illustrated in Figure 20. In the case of retrospective searching, a data base of document representations is stored in machine-readable form. Incoming requests for information are converted into search strategies, put into machine-readable form as a batch, and matched against this data base. In the case of SDI, the "standing requests for information," in the form of user interest profiles, are stored and are matched at regular intervals against the representations of documents newly added to the system. Of course, these incoming document representations, once they have been used for SDI purposes, are likely to be added to a permanent data base, so that they can later be used in retrospective search operations. The retrospective search data base, then, is likely to grow very rapidly, and the SDI data base rather slowly. When

64   The Application of Computers to Information Retrieval

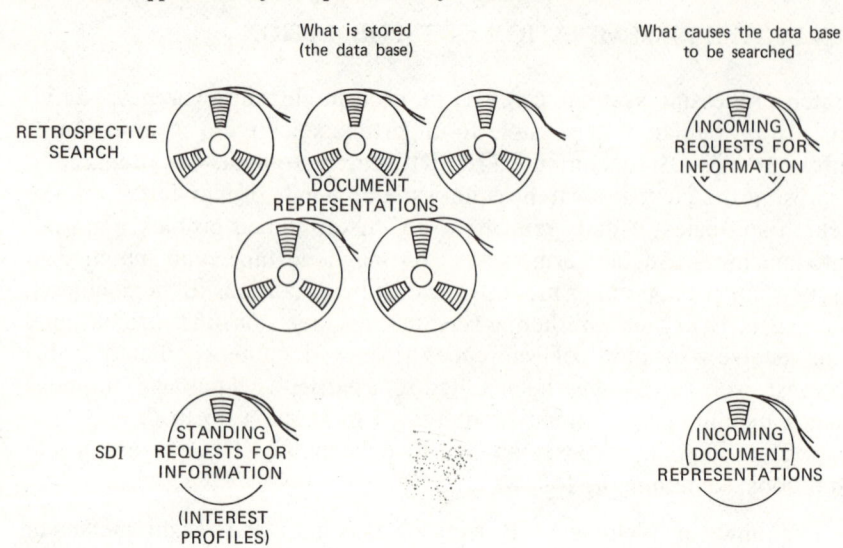

Figure 20 The difference between retrospective searching and selective dissemination of information by computer.

operating through the use of tapes that must be sequentially searched by batch processing—the entire data base, record by record, must be searched—computer systems tend to be more economically attractive for SDI than for retrospective searching. In SDI, the two files to be matched are always rather small. In the retrospective search situation, on the other hand, the document data base may grow extremely large, and the computer processing involved in a complete search of this data base will be very much greater than that involved in the SDI match. The SDI operation tends, therefore, to be a much more economical application of magnetic tape systems than the retrospective search operation. In fact, under certain circumstances it might be possible to receive a whole year of SDI service for little more than the cost of one retrospective search in a large data base. The fact is that computer systems based on the sequential searching of magnetic tapes are very efficient for SDI purposes but rather inefficient for retrospective searching. For retrospective searching we need the more rapid access that on-line systems offer, as discussed in the next chapter.

The use of computers to provide SDI service was first suggested by Luhn (1958) of IBM. In the "business intelligence system" he described, the computer would be used not only to match users with documents but to match users with other users. Luhn recognized the probability that people sharing common interests, that is, people with similar SDI profiles, could be "brought together" through a computer matching operation.

As in the retrospective search situation, the relationship between users and document classes can be represented in the form of a matrix (Figure 21).

In this matrix the columns 1 to 12 represent the interest profiles of 12 users, the rows A to L represent 12 areas of subject interest, that is, 12 document classes. An X in a user column indicates that this user is interested in any documents belonging to the class represented by the intersected row. Documents entering the system are indexed in the same way as they would be for input to a retrospective search system; that is, they are given index terms that assign them to appropriate subject classes. The document profile thus created is matched against the matrix of user interest profiles.

The input document in Figure 21 has been assigned to the classes B, F, and J. When this document profile is matched against the file of user interest profiles, it can be seen that it matches at a 100% level the interests of user 12—all three terms used to describe the document appear in the interest profile of this user—it matches at a lower level—two out of three terms—the interests of users 2, 7, and 8. It matches the interests of users 4 and 5 at a much lower level—one term out of three. There is no match at all with the interests of users 1, 3, 6, 9, 10, and 11. Where strict matching

	1	2	3	4	5	6	7	8	9	10	11	12	Input document
A	X				X	X							
B		X			X		X				X		X
C	X	X		X				X					
D		X			X			X					
E	X		X	X	X					X			
F			X			X	X				X		X
G		X	X	X					X		X		
H	X				X		X						
I	X			X	X		X	X					
J		X					X				X		X
K			X		X	X							
L			X	X		X			X	X			

Index terms (representing document classes) / User interest profiles

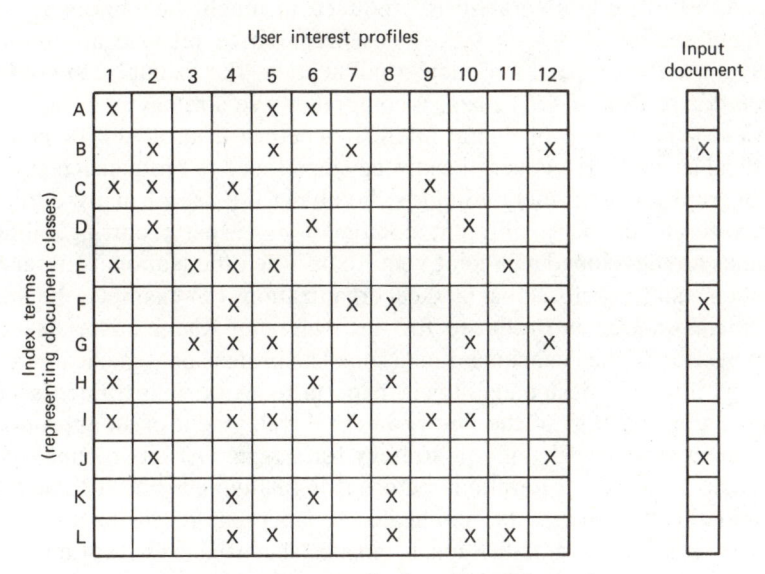

Figure 21 Conceptualization of an SDI search.

criteria are adopted, this document would be brought to the attention of only user 12. With more relaxed criteria, it would also be brought to the attention of users 2, 7, and 8.

"Group SDI" is another possible application of computers. In group SDI an attempt is made to identify a group of users having common subject interests. A group interest profile is set up and matched at regular intervals against updates of some data base. Document records matching this "standard profile" are retrieved, printed out, and delivered to the subscribers to this particular profile. Information services that offer group SDI publish a list of subjects covered by standard profiles. Individuals may then subscribe to one or more standard profiles that correspond to their areas of interest. The cost to a user of group SDI service is likely to be considerably less than the cost of completely individualized SDI. The National Aeronautics and Space Administration (NASA) has offered a group SDI service, called SCAN (Selected Current Aerospace Notices), for a number of years. The National Technical Information Service (NTIS) offers a group SDI service that delivers documents in microfiche form to subscribers to standard profiles. This service is referred to as Selected Research in Microfiche (SRIM).

The group SDI component of MEDLARS is used to generate a number of regularly published special bibliographies in various fields of medicine: dentistry, nursing, toxicology, anesthesiology, endocrinology, and other fields. These are termed "recurring bibliographies."

A recurring bibliography is produced in much the same way as a demand search. A search strategy is prepared to retrieve all citations relevant to the scope of a particular publication. For example, to produce the *Index to Dental Literature,* a comprehensive strategy is designed to retrieve all citations of dental interest, whether from dental or general medical journals. However, the strategy developed to produce a recurring bibliography is extremely complex, involving the use of many different index terms in many different combinations. Most recurring bibliographies are developed as a joint venture between the National Library of Medicine and a professional medical organization. For example, the *Index of Rheumatology* is produced for the American Rheumatism Association Section of the Arthritis Foundation. The professional medical organizations involved designate subject experts to work with trained search analysts on the staff of the library in the development of an appropriate searching strategy. Usually, a strategy for a recurring bibliography goes through a number of iterations before it is finally accepted as a suitable formulation to produce the publication concerned. It will be subject to further continuous modification to ensure that it remains optimally responsive to the needs of the specialized audience it is to serve.

The search strategy for a recurring bibliography is matched—monthly, bimonthly, or quarterly, as appropriate—against all the citations input to MEDLARS since its last issue was produced. The magnetic tape of retrieved citations is sorted, formatted, and photocomposed by procedures similar to those used in the production of *Index Medicus*. The positive camera-ready copy thus created is then delivered to the professional organization sponsoring the bibliography. This organization is responsible for publication and distribution. A major feature of the recurring bibliography program is the ability to retrieve a citation for several different bibliographies on the basis of different selection criteria. The same citation, printed in three different recurring bibliographies, may appear under different subject headings in each, these headings reflecting the interest that the target audience is likely to have in this particular article.

THE ADVANTAGES OF COMPUTER-BASED SYSTEMS

Computer retrieval systems, as developed early in the 1960s, offered many advantages over their predecessors, including

1. The possibility, through batch processing, of conducting many searches at the same time.
2. The ability to provide many access points to a document extremely economically.
3. The ability to handle very complex searches involving large numbers of terms in complex relationships.
4. The ability to generate an output in the form of a printed bibliography and even to produce a high-quality publication by interfacing the retrieval system with a photocomposition device. Output can also be made directly to microfilm (computer output microfilm or COM).
5. The ability to collect, on a regular basis and as essentially a by-product of normal system operations, management data on how and how much the system is used.
6. The ability to produce many outputs and services from a single input operation. The MEDLARS tapes, for example, although produced as a result of one indexing operation and one procedure for reducing the index records to machine-readable forms, can be used to generate a general printed index, specialized bibliographies, retrospective search, and SDI searches.
7. The data base, once captured in machine-readable form, can be duplicated simply and cheaply, it is easily shipped around and thus can be used in the provision of information services by a number of

different centers. This is perhaps the most important advantage of all. The growth of machine-readable data bases has had a dramatic impact on the provision of information services in the last fifteen years. These developments are discussed in Chapter 5.

This chapter has reviewed the general characteristics of off-line systems used for information retrieval and related processing activities. MEDLARS, as it existed in 1970, was used as an example, but the characteristics of this system are in many ways typical of all large off-line batch processing systems. For a more detailed and parallel discussion of input and output processing in another large system of this type, that of the Educational Resources Information Center (ERIC), consult Mathies and Watson (1973). Useful reviews of SDI are provided by Mauerhoff (1974) and Leggate (1975).

Chapter Four

On-Line Information Retrieval

Although the computer offered many advantages in information retrieval activities, the off-line batch processing systems also have associated disadvantages. They are essentially "one-chance" searching systems in which the searcher has to think in advance of all possible search approaches and construct a search strategy that, when matched with the data base, is likely to retrieve all the relevant literature. Put somewhat differently, an off-line system is noninteractive and nonheuristic. Neither does it provide any true browsing capability.

A second major disadvantage of the off-line system is that the search results are substantially delayed. It is not possible to get an immediate response from such a system. At best, the search results are obtained in a matter of hours; at worst, in the case of searches processed by a large national information center, the delay may involve several days or perhaps weeks.

A third disadvantage is that the search in an off-line system is generally a search of a delegated nature; that is, the individual who needs information must delegate the responsibility for preparing the searching strategy to some information specialist and has no opportunity to conduct his own search. Although nondelegated searching is not invariably better than delegated searching, the process of delegation is tricky. It is obvious that a search will produce very poor results if, in the process of delegation, the requester is unable to explain clearly what he is seeking or if the information specialist misinterprets the real needs of the user.

On-line retrieval systems have all the advantages that apply to computer-based systems in general, as listed earlier, but avoid all these major disadvantages. On-line retrieval systems are heuristic and interactive; they permit browsing, can provide rapid response, and may be used in a nondelegated search mode.

SOME CHARACTERISTICS OF ON-LINE RETRIEVAL SYSTEMS

The term on-line refers to the fact that the searcher is in direct communication ("on-line to") the data base he wishes to interrogate and to the computer on which it is loaded. A search is conducted as a two-way conversation between the searcher and the system (computer). Each takes turns in communicating with the other. For this reason the on-line system is frequently referred to as interactive or conversational. The interaction between searcher and system is effected through some form of terminal connected to the computer through communications lines.

These terminals are of two principal types: typewriter terminals and video terminals. The interactive typewriter terminal closely resembles a conventional typewriter. The searcher uses the keyboard to communicate with the system, and the system's response is also recorded on the paper output of the searcher's terminal. In the case of the video terminal the searcher also communicates by means of a keyboard. Both the searcher's messages and the system's messages are displayed on a viewing screen resembling that of a domestic television receiver. This viewing device is likely to be a conventional cathode ray tube (CRT) display. It may, however, be an alternative display device such as a plasma panel. For information retrieval purposes, it is necessary to supplement a video terminal with an adjacent printing device capable of recording on paper anything displayed on the viewing screen.

The terminal communicates with the computer, and vice versa, by means of common communications lines. There are no real restrictions to this communication in terms of distance. A terminal may be in the same building as the computer facility, or in the same complex of buildings, or it may be several hundred or several thousand miles away. A terminal in the same building or building complex may be physically connected to the computer by cable, whereas a remote terminal communicates via telephone lines or, possibly, communications satellite. In this way, it is perfectly possible for a scientist in Australia to make use of a data base loaded on a computer in the United States. A simple schematic of a computer communications network, capable of supporting an on-line retrieval system, is shown in Figure 22.

As well as being referred to as interactive, or conversational, and heuristic, an on-line system is frequently associated with the adjectives "time-shared" and "real-time." Time sharing merely means that the processing time of the computer is shared among several completely independent activities. On-line time sharing implies the sharing of machine processing time among a number of terminals. More precisely, an on-line time-shared system operates via a number of independent, concurrently usable terminals, giving each terminal user processing time when he needs it and creating the illusion, most of the time, that he is the sole user of the computer facilities. Real-time operation implies that the computer receives data, processes it, and returns results quickly enough for them to be used in some ongoing activity. Applied to information

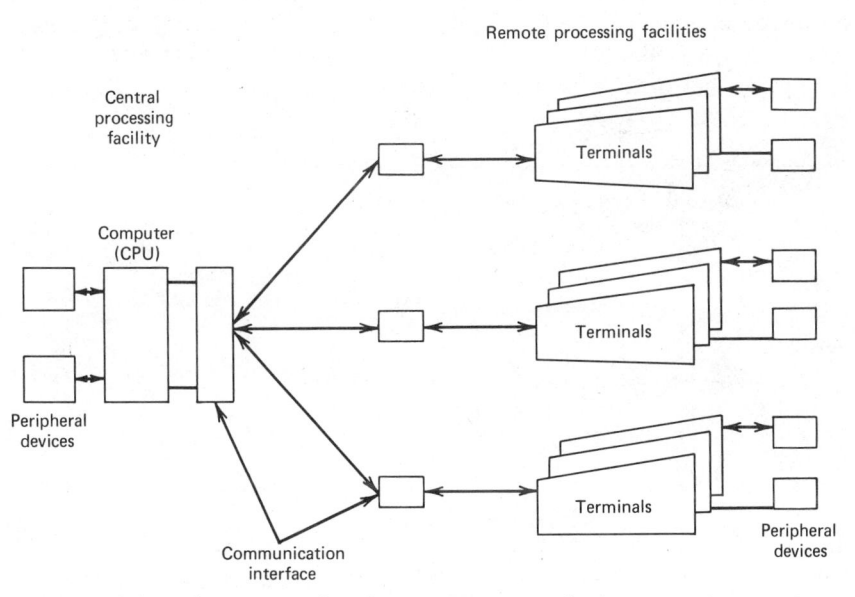

Figure 22 Schematic representation of a computer communications network. Reproduced from Lancaster and Fayen (1973).

retrieval, real-time implies that the computer responds quickly enough to interact with a user's heuristic search processes. Most of the time a well-designed on-line system responds to a query or command so rapidly, say, three to five seconds, that its response may be regarded as almost immediate.

SEARCHING PROCEDURES

A search in an on-line retrieval system normally involves four stages:

1. *Log-on procedures,* whereby the user calls the computer on which the needed data base is loaded, identifies himself as a legitimate user, and asks for access to a particular file.
2. *Search negotiation,* in which the user tries out various searching strategies, perhaps using various aids provided by the system itself.
3. *Result manipulation,* in which the user specifies how he would like the search results to be presented to him.
4. *Log-off procedures.*

In the on-line search the user communicates when prompted to do so by the system. He uses both index terms and commands. The conversation that takes place between user and system is best illustrated by an example, as shown in Figure 23. In this hypothetical dialogue, the user knows that it is his turn to communicate when the system gives him a prompt in the form of SS (for "search statement"). Each of the user's

---

SS1:	PSORIASIS	
PROG:	192	
SS2:	SWEAT OR SWEAT GLANDS OR BODY TEMPERATURE REGULATION OR THERMOGRAPHY	
PROG:	1,107	
SS3:	1 AND 2	
PROG:	45	
SS4:	3 AND ENGLISH	
PROG:	27	
SS5:	4 AND 1974	
PROG:	12	
SS6:	"PRINT"	

Figure 23 Example of a search dialogue in a hypothetical retrieval system. Although this sample dialogue is typical of a number of on-line retrieval systems, it is modeled particularly on the ORBIT software of the System Development Corporation.

search statements is also given a number by the system. The system's responses are preceded by the abbreviation PROG (for "program").

The user is looking for documents discussing some relationship between psoriasis and body temperature regulation or perspiration. He first enters the term PSORIASIS and is told, within seconds, that there are 192 documents in the data base that satisfy this requirement, that is, have been indexed under the term PSORIASIS. The searcher next enters a string of terms that represent the second facet of his request. These are entered in an OR relationship; they are logical alternates in the search. That is, the presence of any one of these terms is sufficient to indicate the relevance of the document to the subject of body temperature regulation or perspiration. The system responds, again in seconds, that the data base contains 1107 documents that satisfy this logical requirement. The searcher now asks that these two sets be combined; that is, he wants to know how many documents are in common between the psoriasis set and the body temperature set. The system indicates that there are 45 common documents, documents that presumably have something to do with the relationship between psoriasis and body temperature regulation. The searcher then restricts the search further by language and date and finally asks for the 1974 items in English to be printed out at his terminal. This simple search, including printout of the citations for 12 items, is likely to have taken five minutes or less.

The search shown, although very simple, is quite typical of the way searches are normally conducted in on-line retrieval systems. It illustrates a number of important points, including the use of Boolean logic in searching, the capability for "set building"—the first two sets defined in the search are combined, by set number, to form a third set—and the capability of searching on elements, such as language and date, other than subject terms.

The system illustrated in this example allows the searcher to enter one term at a time or to combine a whole string of terms, in AND or OR relationships, into a single search statement. Certain other systems, however, only allow the searcher to enter one term at a time. He must later combine these into a single logical statement, using AND, OR, and NOT or symbols for these logical operators (*, +, −, for example).

FILE STRUCTURE

The majority of on-line systems consist of three separate but closely related files, maintained on a disk or some other random-access storage device. These files, illustrated in Figure 24, are the index file, the inverted

74   On-Line Information Retrieval

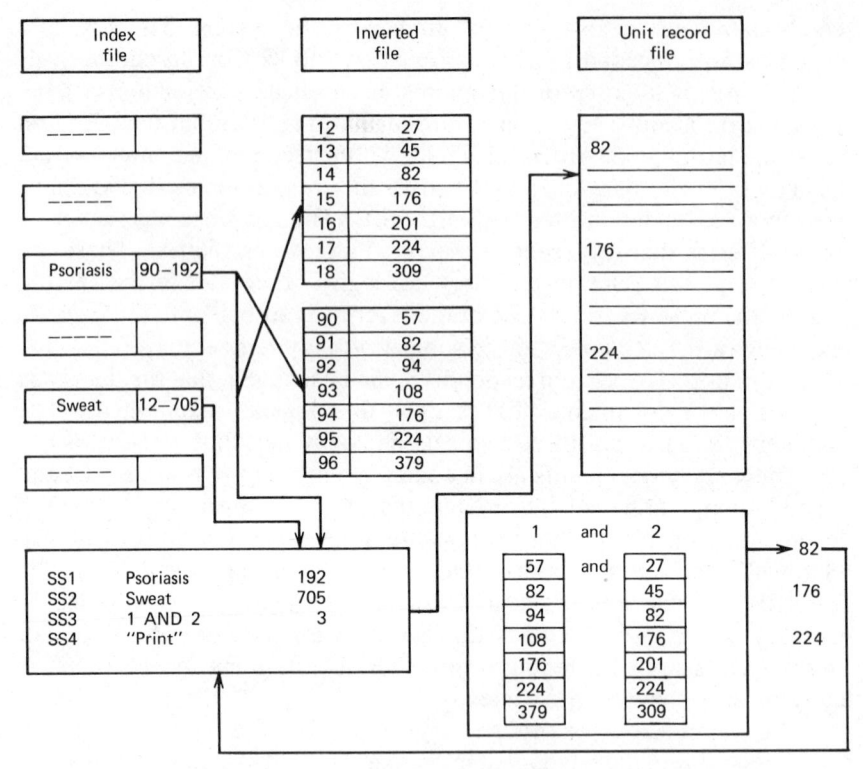

Figure 24   File structure in a typical on-line retrieval system.

file of postings, and the unit record file. The index file is an alphabetical list of the searchable terms in the data base. Associated with each term, in this file, are two items of data: (1) the address on the disk where the "postings" for this term are stored and (2) the number of postings associated with this term, that is, a count representing the number of documents to which this particular index term has been assigned. The inverted file stores, for each term appearing in the index file, a list of all the document numbers to which this term applies, that is, the list of numbers of all the documents to which this index term has been assigned. The third file, the unit record file, or linear file, is a file organized by document number. This file stores, for each document in the data base, various bibliographic data—at least a full bibliographic citation and possibly also an abstract or a list of all the index terms associated with this document.

We can now relate the file structure illustrated in Figure 24 to the type of search illustrated in Figure 23. When the searcher enters the term PSORIASIS, the system checks the index file and is able to inform the searcher, in perhaps three seconds, that 192 items satisfy his request. It responds similarly when the term SWEAT is introduced by the searcher. When the searcher asks that the two sets be combined, the system goes to the appropriate addresses for the two terms in the inverted file, reads the document numbers associated with them into core, compares the lists, and recognizes that there are three common numbers in the two lists. It reports this back to the searcher. The searcher now decides that he wants to see these three items. He therefore enters the command "PRINT," which causes the records for these items to be retrieved from the unit record file and displayed at the searcher's terminal.

Although the schematic in Figure 24 is not representative of all on-line retrieval systems, it is representative of a great many. A more complete discussion of file organization for on-line retrieval systems is given in Lancaster and Fayen (1973). The subject of file structures for on-line systems in general is discussed by Lefkovitz (1969).

SOME FURTHER FEATURES OF ON-LINE RETRIEVAL SYSTEMS

A rather complete description of the features of on-line retrieval systems is given in Lancaster and Fayen (1973) and, more concisely, in a report by Martin (1974). Only some of the major features can be mentioned here. The on-line system usually has the capability of displaying its own controlled vocabulary. In response to a particular command followed by an index term, the system displays the terms alphabetically adjacent to this index term, along with the postings for each term. The system produces this display even if the term entered by the searcher does not exist in the system. In this case the system displays the terms that are closest alphabetically to the term entered, but the term entered by the searcher has no postings against it. If the vocabulary of the system exists in systematic form, it is also capable of being displayed in systematic form; that is, the searcher can request that, for any term entered, the hierarchy in which it appears be displayed. The terms related to the entered term by means of cross-references may also be displayed. In many systems each line in a vocabulary display, alphabetic or systematic, is given a line number by which the user can incorporate a term into his strategy; that is, he may use the identifying number of the term rather than having to enter the full term itself at the keyboard. In some systems the user may incorporate a complete hierarchy of terms into his strategy by means of a single command.

The user of an on-line system is also likely to have a number of options available to him at the result manipulation stage. By varying the print commands, he may request that records of varying length—that is, bibliographic citation only, citation plus index terms, citation plus abstract—be displayed. In some systems he may specify which parts of the record are to be displayed and in what sequence. Almost certainly he has an "off-line print" capability; that is, he may request that the entire set of records satisfying his search statement be printed off-line and mailed to him.

We have so far assumed a system based on human indexing of documents by means of some type of controlled vocabulary—for example, a thesaurus. It is also possible to operate an on-line system in a natural language mode. In this case the complete text of a document collection is stored in digital form, or, alternatively, the text of abstracts may be stored. Inverted files are built for all the words appearing in the text, except that a "stop list" is applied to avoid the creation of inverted files on prepositions, conjunctions, articles, and other nonsubstantive words. There is only one major difference between an inverted file built for a controlled vocabulary system and one built for a natural language system. In the former the inverted files record only document numbers. In the latter, however, they record the document number plus an indicator of the exact position of the word in the text—that is, paragraph number, line number, word position in the line. Searching on-line in a natural language system is very similar to searching in a controlled vocabulary system, as illustrated earlier, except that additional searching features are likely to be available. The subject of natural language searching is discussed in a later chapter.

SOME HISTORY

The first significant experiments in on-line information retrieval appear to be those conducted by Kessler at M.I.T. around 1964. Kessler's experimental system in physics, known as TIP, was notable for several reasons. Not only was it the first important on-line system for bibliographic searching, but it also incorporated some "unconventional" approaches to searching. Searching could be conducted on the principles of citation indexing and bibliographic coupling as well as on key words in titles of papers.

The first large-scale on-line retrieval system was the RECON (Remote Console) system of the National Aeronautics and Space Administration (NASA). Experiments with the system began in 1965, but the system became fully operational only in 1969. RECON was designed for NASA by Lockheed Missiles and Space Company, and equivalent software is commercially available from Lockheed as DIALOG. RECON is now an international system; the NASA data base is available for on-line search in Europe through the European Space Agency.

Another important set of search programs is known as ORBIT, commercially available from the System Development Corporation. The ORBIT software is used in the MEDLINE (MEDLARS On-Line) service offered by the National Library of Medicine. The MEDLINE service, initiated in 1971, is perhaps the largest on-line retrieval network now in existence in the United States, with over 300 centers conducting in excess of 200,000 searches each year. The ORBIT software has also been adopted by the U.S. State Department and various other organizations.

The Data Central system, initiated in the 1960s, is designed for text searching (natural language) applications. It has been used with a number of important data bases, especially in the legal field. One important application is OBAR (Ohio Bar Automated Research), a legal retrieval system operated by the Ohio State Bar Association. LEXIS, a legal data base of national scope, also uses the Data Central software. Hundreds of millions of characters of legal text are now available for on-line search through this software.

The Information Bank of the *New York Times,* the most important on-line system providing access to current awareness information, became operational in the early 1970s. It provides access to newspaper clippings, from the *Times* and other selected sources, for reporters in the *Times* building and customers in remote locations up and down the country. Other software for on-line searching is available from the Battelle Memorial Institute (BASIS), IBM (STAIRS), and Infodata Systems Inc. (INQUIRE).

A development that has had significant impact on the provision of on-line information service is the emergence of time-shared data communications networks such as Tymshare and Telenet, which operate by means of leased voice-grade telephone lines. These networks of leased lines, which now span the United States and extend to Canada, Mexico, and Europe, are used to link computer facilities with each other and, more important, to give users of on-line terminals the ability to access a remote data base at communications rates that are considerably less than the rates that would be involved in the use of nondedicated lines. Communications costs are spread among many institutional customers, who, in turn, pass their costs on to their own users. Many important bibliographic data bases can now be accessed through these networks. Another important development, occurring in the 1960s, has been the emergence of the on-line retailers of bibliographic services, which make their services accessible through the data communication networks. The on-line retailers are discussed in the next chapter.

Chapter Five

The Growth of Machine-Readable Data Bases

The very rapid growth in the number of machine-readable data bases that have become available in the last twelve years, coupled with on-line facilities for making the data bases widely accessible, has created a revolution in the provision of information services. Although it was not the first machine-readable bibliographic data base, MEDLARS was probably the first to be made widely available in machine-readable (MR) form. MEDLARS tapes were made available by the National Library of Medicine for use by other libraries (MEDLARS centers) as early as 1965. Since then, we have seen a phenomenal growth in the availability of MR files. In fact, it was estimated in 1977 that over 500 such files were in routine use in the provision of information services. They span an extremely wide range from very general, covering all medicine or all chemistry, to highly specific, covering, for example, files on interatomic potentials and tall buildings. Files of numerical, statistical, physical, and chemical data

("data banks") exist in MR form as well as files that are strictly bibliographic ("data bases"). A rather complete directory of data bases has been compiled by Williams and Rouse (1976).

AVAILABILITY OF MACHINE-READABLE FILES

But the mere existence of MR files did not in itself create a revolution in the provision of information services. Just as important has been the eagerness of the producers of these data bases to make them widely available for exploitation by other institutions. These data bases have been made available in several different ways, and new developments have occurred at a furious pace over the last ten years. There appear to be seven major possible methods in the mode of access to machine-readable data bases:

1. Through a library network or similar cooperative activity established by the producer of the data base—for example, MEDLARS centers.
2. Through leasing a data base and operating it in-house.
3. Through purchase of service from a retailer, a scientific information dissemination center, providing such service in an off-line batch mode.
4. Through purchasing direct on-line access from the producer of the data base—for example, the *New York Times* Information Bank.
5. Through purchasing on-line access through an on-line service center.
6. Through some form of regional scheme for data base access.
7. Through an international network.

First, a number of data base producers have established networks or other cooperative activities, on a national or international level, in order to make service from these data bases widely available. A notable example is the international network of MEDLARS centers set up by the National Library of Medicine. This arrangement permitted medical libraries throughout the United States, and later beyond, to provide a level of literature searching service that they were completely unable to provide earlier. The MEDLARS network allowed the physician or other biomedical professional to request a comprehensive search of an extremely large national bibliographic resource through his own local medical library, possibly a small hospital library with only a single professional staff member. It also allowed certain medical libraries designated as MEDLARS centers to offer an SDI service, based on MEDLARS tapes, to keep users informed of new biomedical literature of direct concern to them. A number of centers did establish such a service, sometimes restricted to their own organization—for example, the faculty of a medical school—but sometimes offered to other organizations.

The second development is that many data bases have become available through leasing arrangements. A library—for example, an industrial library—may lease one or more data bases that are of particular interest to the organization and may offer service from these files, both retrospective search and SDI, using in-house computer facilities, to the organization's own staff of engineers, scientists, or other professionals. Unfortunately, the cost of leasing a data base can be quite high, perhaps $10,000 or more a year for very large files. It is clear that this kind of investment could be justified only if there was an extremely high level of demand for service from a particular data base in the organization, this large volume of use leading to a relatively low unit cost per retrospective search or user interest profile. The fact that few individual institutions have the level of demand to justify an in-house operation of this type led to a third major development, the emergence of the scientific information dissemination center (SIDC), which was a completely new phenomenon in the information world. The SIDC is a retailer or middleman between the producer (wholesaler) of information products and the end user. The SIDC enters into licensing agreements with one or more producers of data bases, usually the producers of printed indexes or abstracting publications, such as *Chemical Abstracts, Biological Abstracts,* and *Engineering Index.* This agreement permits the center to offer service to a wide audience of users on a fee basis. Any individual, research group or institution, including a library, can purchase service from a center of this kind. Although great emphasis is placed on SDI, some retrospective search capability is also provided. The SIDC may be operated by an academic organization, a government agency, or research institution of some type. In Canada, and in certain other countries, this role has been adopted by a national library.

The fourth development, and perhaps the most important of all, has been the emergence of on-line interactive searching capabilities. As discussed in Chapter 4, on-line bibliographic systems have existed, at least in experimental or prototype form, for about 15 years, but it was not until the late 1960s that any significant level of on-line service was provided from a large bibliographic file. A pioneer in this area was the RECON system of the National Aeronautics and Space Administration (NASA), which was made widely available to NASA facilities in the United States and subsequently, through the European Space Agency, in Europe. But RECON had limited impact on the library world, and on-line information retrieval really came into its own only in the 1970s.

The major development is again due to the National Library of Medicine, which began to move toward an on-line implementation of

MEDLARS in 1970. The result was MEDLINE (MEDLARS On-Line), a development that put a very extensive medical data base in the hands of virtually all major medical libraries in the United States and considerably beyond. We have now reached the situation in which the medical librarian is using this computer-based retrieval system routinely as just another bibliographic tool, but a tool more powerful than any previously available. As a result of the development of on-line searching, academic and other medical libraries have been able to extend their capabilities for literature searching greatly. Through MEDLINE, they can undertake comprehensive literature searches of at least the most recent medical literature at a depth and level of complexity that is quite beyond the capability of printed indexes and other manual tools.

In addition, on-line systems have greatly increased the capability of libraries to respond to the user who does not need a comprehensive search but needs a few relevant references and needs them right away. As one example of this, the use of MEDLARS, as an off-line batch processing system, was largely restricted to biomedical professionals working on relatively long-term research projects. Because of its often poor response time, the system was not particularly suitable for satisfying the clinician who needed information to use in immediate problems of patient care. The on-line version of the system, MEDLINE, can satisfy such needs, and, in fact, the system has been found to attract to the medical library people who were not previously library users. Moreover, by decentralizing the actual searching process, on-line systems have extended by orders of magnitude the volume of machine literature searches that can be conducted in a particular data base.

Although medical libraries, through the National Library of Medicine, were at the forefront in the use of on-line systems for information retrieval, important data bases in many other areas are now being exploited by libraries through remote access via on-line terminals. Moreover, not all these data bases are scientific. A very important data base on current affairs exists in the shape of the Information Bank of the *New York Times*, and other files cover the literature of education, business, law, and several other fields.

The fifth development of importance is the emergence of the on-line service center. Like the scientific information dissemination center, this organization offers service on a retail basis. But it differs from the SIDC in that the service is offered on-line and the emphasis is on retrospective searching rather than current awareness (SDI). The on-line service center also enters into licensing agreements with data base producers. These agreements allow the center to load these data bases on its own computer facilities and to offer on-line access to various subscribers, including libraries. Any library can now subscribe to on-line service from a growing array of files made available in this way by the System Development Corporation, Lockheed Information Systems, and Bibliographic Retrieval Services. Among data bases thus available for on-line access are Chemical Condensates (CHEMCON), the ERIC files (Educational Resources Information Center), the INSPEC files of the Institution of Electrical Engineers, INFORM (in the field of business), the National Technical Information Service (NTIS) files, and data bases from the Institute for Scientific Information and the American Psychological Association. The use of these data bases via on-line access is growing, especially among industrial libraries and specialized information centers. But use of such systems is not restricted to industrial and other special libraries. Academic libraries are also making use of these important resources. So are some public libraries.

It may be worthwhile to look at one of these centers in more detail, particularly with regard to the costs of the services provided. The newest of the major on-line retailers is Bibliographic Retrieval Services, Inc., which began operation in 1977. In 1977, BRS was offering access to 11 different data bases: MEDLARS, BIOSIS Previews, Chemical Abstracts Condensates, Psychological Abstracts, CAIN (in agriculture), ERIC (in education), the National Technical Information Service (NTIS), INSPEC (in physics, electronics, and related sciences), Pollution Abstracts, Pharmaceutical News Index, and INFORM (in the field of business). A BRS customer, then, can access any one of these data bases and can switch a search from one data base to another in a single terminal session.

Excluding the cost of the searcher's time, the total cost of conducting a search in one of these data bases through BRS is the sum of the following component costs:

1. The BRS charge per connect hour. This is dependent on total use made of BRS services by the customer. A high-use customer, using BRS facilities for 80 hours per month, may pay as little as $10 for each hour connected to the BRS computer. A low-use customer, 5 hours per month, will pay $25 per connect hour.
2. The cost of the communications connection. Assuming that the customer is accessing the BRS services through TELENET (see Chapter 4), the communications cost could be as little as $3 per hour.
3. A royalty charged by the producer of the data base. This varies rather considerably from one data base to another. There is no royalty charge for the ERIC, CAIN, and MEDLARS data bases. For Chemical Abstracts Condensates the royalty charge is $4 per connect hour, plus 2 cents per citation; for Psychological Abstracts it is $20 per connect hour.

4. If citations are printed off-line, at the BRS computer facility, and mailed to the searcher, there is a charge of 15 cents per page of printout (10 cents per page for MEDLARS).
5. The cost of purchase or rental of the terminal used to conduct the search, this cost being amortized over a particular time period.

We can now put these component costs together to derive a hypothetical, but realistic, cost for a single search, assuming a certain set of conditions:

1. The customer is an information center using BRS resources at a level of 20 hours per month. BRS charges this customer $16 per connect hour.
2. Terminal rental is at the rate of $150 per month.
3. The center conducts approximately 75 on-line searches per month, most, but not all, through BRS.
4. A search in the MEDLARS data base is conducted through a TELENET connection and is completed in 20 minutes.
5. A 10-page off-line printout is generated as a result of this search.

The total cost of this search, exclusive of staff time, is estimated to be $9.33, of which $5.33 is the BRS connect hour charge, $1 is the cost of using TELENET, $2 is that part of the cost of the terminal which is allocated to this search, and $1 is the cost of the off-line printout. There is no royalty charge for this particular data base.

It can be seen, then, that the cost of one on-line search in a very large data base can be quite low, perhaps less than $10. Given the use of a data base with royalty charges of, say, $20 per connect hour, the cost of the aforementioned search would be about $17. But the costs of either of these hypothetical searches would be reduced if the monthly volume of searches in BRS was increased, for this would lower both the connect costs per search and the amount to be charged against the search for terminal rental ($2 per search, assuming 75 searches per month and a rental fee of $150 per month). The cost would also decline, of course, if a cheaper terminal were used or, conceivably, if the terminal were purchased outright.

The sixth development is the gradual recognition that any scientist or other professional should have the capability of accessing any MR data base that he needs, for retrospective search or current awareness purposes, at the time that he needs it. Data files as well as bibliographic files should be available to him. To achieve this goal the scientist needs to know (1) what data bases are available, (2) which one is most likely to be relevant to his information needs, and (3) how to obtain service from these files. The obvious place for him to go for this information, and for this service, is to some accessible library, academic, industrial, governmental, possibly even a public library. In other words, the library, especially, perhaps, academic and special libraries of various types, should be able to provide access, in some way, to any available MR file that exists, just as these libraries provide access to printed indexes and claim the capability of getting virtually any book to any reader, if not from their own collections, then from some outside source. One possibility for guaranteeing such access is through some form of regional cooperation among groups of libraries or information centers, with each center having guaranteed access, at various levels, to a large number of data bases.

Working through "information services librarians" in member institutions, various modes and levels of service can be provided by a regional cooperative:

1. Some major data bases, for which there is likely to be a high level of demand, can be acquired by licensing agreements, brought into the region and operated on computer facilities in the region itself. On-line service, off-line service, retrospective search, and SDI could all be provided.
2. For certain other data bases, arrangements for a batch processing service can be made either with the producer of the data base or with an existing information center, that is, a scientific information dissemination center. Both SDI and retrospective search on demand can be provided in this way. Because of the volume of demand in the area as a whole, a regional center may be able to negotiate particularly favorable rates for service of this kind, thus keeping the unit costs per search or user interest profile relatively low.
3. On-line access to various data bases, for the region as a whole, may be provided through terminals at the regional headquarters or at one or more large libraries within the region. For example, the headquarters may use on-line terminals to access the *New York Times* Information Bank, MEDLINE, and a range of data bases available through one or more of the existing on-line service centers. The regional center will then accept requests for on-line searches from libraries in the region, by telephone or possibly telex. Where the projected demand seems to warrant it, some of the larger libraries in a region are likely to have their own on-line terminals to provide more direct, interactive access to those files of greatest interest.
4. The use of any other data base within a particular region is likely to be infrequent and irregular. Nevertheless, service from these data bases should be rapidly available when the need for this service arises. It will be important, therefore, for the regional center to enter into agreements, with the producer or some other information center, to

obtain such service for any member library at the time it is needed—with the minimum of delay and inconvenience to the user. This situation is likely to pertain to the many quite specialized data bases that are now available in machine-readable form. Demand for use of the tall buildings file at Lehigh University or the data base on interatomic potentials at the University of Belfast may not be very great, even within a region, but these files should, nevertheless, be readily available when they are needed.

Various characteristics of a regional center of this kind are worth special emphasis:

1. The regional center may largely operate through existing centers and is likely to buy service from such centers—data base producers or information retailers—when it is more economical to do so.
2. The long-range goal of such a regional center should be to guarantee access, at some level, to any machine-readable file that exists.
3. An important role is played by the information services librarians in member institutions. This role is that of an interface between a particular user population and a large and growing array of files—bibliographic, chemical, physical, numerical, statistical—in machine-readable form.

In Europe international on-line networks exist, or are planned, to provide access to machine-readable resources. ESANET is at present the most widespread on-line network for information retrieval in Europe. ESANET is operated by the Space Documentation Service (SDS) of the European Space Agency. More than a dozen data bases are loaded on the SDS computer facility at Frascati, Italy, including Chemical Abstracts Condensates, COMPENDEX, INSPEC, the NASA files, the data base of the *Science Citation Index,* and the PASCAL data base of the Centre National de Recherche Scientifique. ESANET serves information centers in Belgium, Denmark, France, Ireland, Italy, the Netherlands, Spain, Sweden, Switzerland, the United Kingdom, and West Germany.

Two other on-line networks are truly international cooperative networks in that member nations each load a certain number of data bases on national computer facilities and provide access to the data bases to users in all cooperating countries. One of these, SCANNET, is already operational, at least on a limited scale, and serving information centers in Denmark, Finland, Norway, and Sweden. A network serving a much larger community of users—all members of the Commission of the European Communities—is planned. The first phase of EURONET, with 21 host computers providing access to over 80 data bases, was expected to be operational in 1977.

The Growth of Machine-Readable Data Bases

The growth of the use of machine-readable data bases in Europe has been spectacular, as indeed it has been in the United States. Figure 25 shows the rate of growth of on-line searching in Europe for the period 1976–1978 with projections to 1983. The European networking developments are well covered in a review chapter by Tomberg (1977).

The growth of machine-readable data bases, coupled with networking arrangements for making them accessible, has greatly increased the availability of information services. This can be demonstrated by using the National Library of Medicine example once more. In 1965, when the MEDLARS retrospective search service was just beginning, virtually all the expertise in searching this data base was concentrated in a handful of

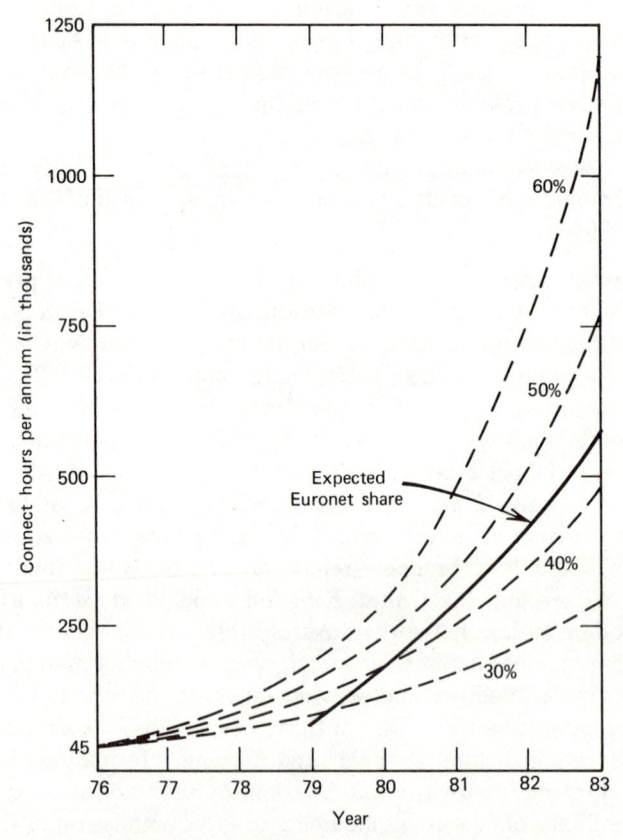

Figure 25 On-line searching in Europe based on assumed annual growth rates of 30, 40, 50, and 60%. Prepared by H. Ungerer, Commission of the European Communities, and reproduced with his permission.

search analysts on the staff of NLM itself, and the volume of searches that could be conducted in the United States was severely limited, perhaps to something on the order of 3000 a year. When the MEDLARS off-line network was fully developed, at the end of the decade, the situation had considerably improved. Through the establishment of a network of regional MEDLARS centers and the training of information specialists on the staff of the centers, the number of qualified MEDLARS analysts increased considerably, to perhaps 50 active searchers, and the number of searches handled in the United States rose to about 20,000 a year. The move to on-line processing, in the 1970s, improved the situation considerably further. In 1975 there were about 300 MEDLINE centers operating in the United States, the number of trained searchers had increased to perhaps 500, and the number of searches conducted had grown to about 20,000 each month in the United States alone, with many additional searches occurring elsewhere in the world.

The increasing accessibility of information services, as demonstrated in the MEDLARS example, has a very favorable effect on their economics, since the economics of information services is very volume-dependent. In 1967 a realistic estimate of the cost of one MEDLARS search was $150 when personnel costs, machine costs, and a part of the costs of creating the data base, the remainder being allocated to the published indexes, were allocated to the retrospective search function (Cummings, 1967). In 1977, less than ten years later, a typical cost of a single search of this data base on-line, as demonstrated earlier, can be less than one-tenth of this. Thus, in the case of this data base, at least, the cost per machine search has come down dramatically in less than ten years.

Another aspect of the economics of information services is worth mentioning. On-line processing makes large data bases available to many organizations and individuals who could not otherwise afford convenient access. Consider the case of a small industrial library for which chemistry is a subject of peripheral rather than central interest. It would probably be uneconomical for this library to subscribe to the printed *Chemical Abstracts* at $4000 a year. At a level of demand of, say, three searches each month, "access cost" for the printed data base would work out to be more than $100 a search. It is considerably cheaper to buy on-line access when the need for a search in the data base arises. It is only when the volume of searches in *Chemical Abstracts* approaches 150 a year that the data base investment costs for the printed version begin to approach the costs of purchasing on-line access when the need arises. Moreover, the on-line search is more efficient, rapid, and thorough than a comparable search in the printed index. Some types of searches are practical only in the machine data base because they are too complex to handle manually—too many terms in too many combinations—or involve the use of access points that exist in the digital files but not in the printed indexes.

Machine-readable data bases and on-line processing have greatly improved the accessibility of information resources and have practically eliminated geographic distance as a barrier to information flow. In the world of electronic communications the small library can have access to the same range of machine-readable files as the largest information centers. A one-man hospital library in a small town can use a terminal to exploit the MEDLINE data base as well as a number of more specialized files in medicine, thus giving the doctor associated with the hospital literature searching capabilities more sophisticated and more comprehensive than he has ever had before. It would be true to say, in fact, that the accessibility of information resources in on-line machine-readable form is increasing at least as rapidly as their accessibility in printed form declines.

Machine-readable data bases also have some impact on the timeliness of secondary services, since the machine-readable version of an index is likely to be available some weeks before the printed version to which it relates. This is particularly valuable in the dissemination of information internationally. The monthly update of a machine-readable file may be flown from the United States to, say, Australia to arrive days or even hours after it is available for use in the United States and some months before the printed analog reaches Australia. International on-line connections can speed up this process even more.

It may be worthwhile now to recapitulate briefly some of the major points made in this chapter. Fifteen years ago there were no generally available machine-readable files, and the application of the computer to literature searching was literally in its infancy. Approximately ten years ago, the first steps were taken to make machine-readable data bases more widely available. But, at that time, the availability was quite limited, and very few people had any experience in searching files of this kind. Machine-readable data bases were concentrated in a few institutions: the Defense Documentation Center, NASA, the National Library of Medicine, and a few others. Now, a very wide range of such data bases are available, and they are rapidly being integrated into library service. In fact, their use in many libraries is already considered routine. They may be used by (1) bringing in-house and operating in an off-line batch processing mode, (2) accessing them remotely through on-line terminals, or (3) purchasing off-line service from the producer or some other information center.

In relation to machine-readable files, the librarian is assuming the role of a broker between library users and a wide range of bibliographic and data resources in MR form. It is clear that this role calls for a new type of librarian or, at least, a librarian with somewhat new skills. These information services librarians must

1. Be fully aware of what is available in the way of data bases and of centers providing service from them.
2. Be able to choose the data base most appropriate to any particular information need whether for current awareness or retrospective search purposes.
3. Know how to obtain service and perhaps be capable of evaluating and choosing among various suppliers of service.
4. Be able to evaluate various competing and overlapping data bases.
5. Be capable of constructing searching strategies and user interest profiles, possibly for a number of different data bases involving differences in vocabularies and searching logic.
6. Be capable of searching files in an on-line interactive mode. Again, the librarian may need to know more than one language of interrogation.
7. Know a considerable amount about indexing techniques and vocabularies (indexing languages), as well as searching strategies, in order to be able to exploit machine-readable files effectively and efficiently.
8. Be able to interact successfully with users in order to determine the precise nature of their information needs.

Chapter Six

Microforms and Microform Retrieval Systems

A reexamination of Table 1 will show that there is still one type of retrieval system that has not been mentioned. This is the microfilm retrieval system, which actually predates computer-based systems. Before we discuss the characteristics of this type of system, however, it is necessary to say a few words about microforms in general.

Microforms are generated as a result of microphotography, which is the application of photography to produce, on film or another medium, reduced images of documents; these images are too small to be read by the human eye without the aid of some magnifying device. Microphotography or, as it is now more frequently referred to, "micrographics," is not a new art. Indeed, it dates back to the first half of the nineteenth century.

There are three major types of microform:

1. *Continuous*. The continuous form is true microfilm, a series of images, or "frames," on a roll of film. The film can be manually wound onto a spool, or it can be enclosed in a "cassette" or cartridge in much the same way as audiotape is stored in a "tape cassette."

2. *Discrete.* In the discrete, or "unitized," form, each physical unit of microform stands alone. Each piece, or "chip," of film is a single document in itself. One example of a discrete microform is the so-called "aperture card," a standard data processing card with a frame of film inset as a "window" in the card. Another example is the Minicard introduced by Eastman Kodak.
3. *Matrix.* In this type of microform, the photographic images are arranged in a two-dimensional array of rows and columns. At one time the most popular form was a microopaque, known as a "microcard," but this has been replaced by the transparent "microfiche." The standard microfiche is about 4 by 6 inches, capable of storing 98 images. A special form of microfiche is ultramicrofiche, which is the product of microphotography with very great reduction ratios (150:1 or more). An ultrafiche of 4 by 6 inches can accommodate as many as 3000 page images, and an "ultrastrip" of 1.4 by 8 inches can hold images of 2000 8½- by 11-inch pages.

In this book, we are concerned only with the use of microforms in information retrieval and not with their other advantages and applications.

Applied to the area of information retrieval, microform systems fall into two quite distinct types:

1. Systems that are simply document delivery systems. The microforms are arranged in document number sequence. When a particular document is asked for, the system "finds" the appropriate image and displays it on a screen or produces an enlarged print. These can also be referred to as "addressing systems."
2. Systems in which the microforms themselves are coded to represent the subject matter covered in the documents. These codes can be scanned by some device—for example, photoelectric—in order to locate microforms that match a particular search strategy representing some subject interest. In this case, the system is a true information retrieval system with a document delivery capability built in.

DOCUMENT DELIVERY SYSTEMS

It is possible to use microform in a rapid document delivery system that can be used in conjunction with some other information retrieval system—for example, an on-line system. The subject search in the on-line system results in the retrieval of references to documents, including their identifying numbers. The numbers are then input to the microform delivery system, resulting in the recovery and display of the necessary images. One possible approach is to make each on-line search terminal self-contained by providing a complete document file in microform at the terminal itself. Adjacent to the searching terminal is a document collection on microfiche, aperture cards, or roll microfilm, along with a reader-printer. Once the searcher has identified some promising references, he pulls the necessary microforms and views them on the reader, producing hard copy of any items or parts of items he wishes to retain. A convenient alternative to a manual file of fiche would be an automated access system based on microfiche or roll microfilm stored in cassettes. Such systems will permit access to a particular document image in ten seconds or less.

A typical automated microform display system is MENTOR, a device produced by Image Systems Inc. MENTOR is a random-access address system that stores up to 780 fiche—up to 182,520 pages—in a carousel and provides access to any image in approximately 3 seconds or less. The system may be accessed by entering the desired document number into a keyboard. Other devices (ISI 5000 from the same company, for example) can be activated directly by computer through commands generated as a result of an on-line search. Such systems provide file integrity, because the fiche are not handled manually. Equipment costs per fiche are high, however, and such devices are extremely limited in capacity. Systems based on roll microfilm stored in cassettes or "magazines"—for example, Eastman Kodak's Microstar—have virtually unlimited capacities but require manual selection of the appropriate cassette and insertion into the reader.

By using ultramicrofiche, it is possible to store a very large data base at a search terminal and access it efficiently and economically. An example is the M-380 system developed by Microform Data Systems Inc. The M-380 uses Ultrastrips (about 1.4 by 8 inches), each holding up to 2000 8½- by 11-inch pages at a reduction ratio of 210×. Ultrastrips are stored in film cartridges, 50 strips to the cartridge, and the cartridges are easily plugged into the M-380 reader. Up to 100,000 pages (8½ by 11 inches) can be accessed through a single cartridge. Because the cartridges are easily interchanged, the system can provide rapid access to a very large data base. The M-380 readers are linked to an index controller that uses a minicomputer to address any page in a particular cartridge. A keyboard entry is converted to a specific film location, and the desired page is automatically accessed and displayed in an average of less than three seconds.

Another alternative is to establish one complete document collection in microform and provide a mechanism for viewing selected images remotely at the searching terminals. A number of complete systems have been designed to provide fast, remote access to a centrally stored document file. Some of these systems involve the use of a human operator to select from the microform file, and others automatically retrieve a microimage. In either case, the image is relayed to the user's terminal via closed-circuit television. The image is likely to be of low quality unless zooming is used to permit part of a page to be displayed. Equipment of this type has been described in some detail by Lancaster and Fayen (1973).

MICROFORM RETRIEVAL SYSTEMS

Of more interest to the present text, however, are systems that use microforms in true information retrieval applications. The first system of this kind, the Rapid Selector, dates from about 1938. In the Rapid Selector, documents were photographed on roll microfilm, each 2000-foot roll containing 72,000 frames. Alongside each frame the contents of the document—for example, its subject matter—could be represented in a binary coded form, the binary code being achieved through patterns of opaque and transparent markings. The user of the Rapid Selector was able to enter a search strategy into the machine. The strategy is converted by the machine into the same form of binary code used to represent the contents

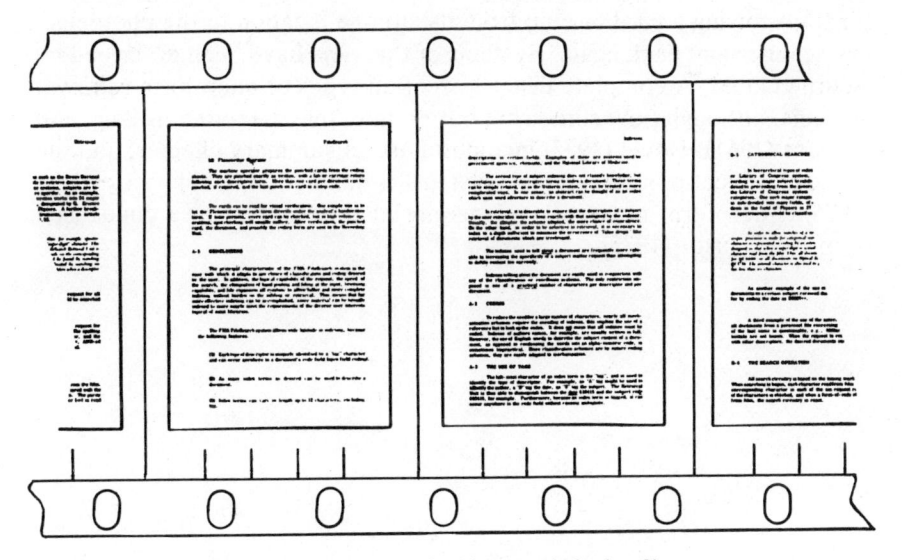

Figure 26 Example of a binary coded microfilm.

of documents. The film is passed, at up to 12½ feet per second, before a photoelectric cell that has been "programmed" to look for a particular code pattern. When a document bearing this pattern is found, the image is copied photographically "on the fly" and presented to the searcher. It is obvious that the searching of binary coded microfilm in this way is conceptually identical with the searching of binary coded magnetic tape. Microfilm retrieval systems of this type offer faster response times than those normally associated with off-line computer systems. Usually, however, they are limited to the conduct of a single search at a time.

The Rapid Selector has many descendants—modern systems that search coded microfilm in much the same way that it did. One example is Oracle, an Eastman Kodak product based on 16-millimeter microfilm stored in cassettes. Search strategies are entered at a keyboard. When a cassette is inserted into the retrieval terminal, a search can proceed at a speed of up to 280 documents per second. A typical piece of binary coded microfilm of the type used in search systems of this kind is shown in Figure 26.

It is also possible to design systems to search binary coded microfilm in discrete form. Such systems operate in a similar way to the Rapid Selector principle—discrete units of microfilm (cards or chips) are passed by a photoelectric scanner, which is programmed to look for a particular code pattern. Such systems, which include Filmorex and Minicard, have never been as widespread as those based on reel microfilm. They are generally more complex and costly because they require some mechanism for transporting a card or chip from its storage location to the photoelectric scanner and back again. Systems of this type have been described by Bourne (1963). A complete discussion of all types of microform retrieval systems, although now somewhat out of date, may be found in Bagg and Stevens (1961). Doyle (1975) includes a useful summary chapter, and the broader subject of micrographic systems is handled in detail by Costigan (1975). Microform retrieval systems are also described in a condensed form by Courtot (1975).

Chapter Seven

Information Centers and Information Services

In this chapter an attempt is made to identify some major kinds of information centers and the types of services each provides. As a point of departure we begin by considering possible components of a national information system. A complete national system for providing access to published and semipublished literature and to certain informal sources of information would probably include the following elements:

1. A referral center
2. A center maintaining an index to ongoing research
3. Several information centers that, for various types of documents, collectively provide the following services:
    a. Collection
    b. Cataloging
    c. Indexing and abstracting
    d. Announcement
    e. Literature searching, including SDI services
    f. Evaluation and synthesis

REFERRAL ACTIVITIES

As its name implies, a referral center refers a user to some other source likely to be able to answer his question or provide the service he requires. Most information centers, including libraries, provide some level of referral service; that is, it is common for these centers, when they receive questions they are unable to handle satisfactorily from their own resources, to refer the inquirer to some other, more appropriate source of information. To make this referral activity possible, they maintain a collection of published directories of information resources. Some may even create their own indexes to particular types of information resources. For example, a public library may maintain an index to local sources of legal, public health, and other types of information. Referral sources may point to individuals rather than institutions. An example of such an index is one that lists people in a particular community who are capable of translating to and from various languages. A special type of referral source, maintained by some companies and universities, is the "expertise index," an index to the specialized knowledge and interests, not necessarily job-related, of the staff of the institution. For a complete discussion of the value of expertise indexes see Hoey (1972) and Barry (1976).

A referral center is wholly concerned with referral activities. Such a center exists only to answer one type of question: "Where or who do I go to for this type of information?" Centers devoted exclusively to referral activities are rather uncommon, especially at national levels, but an outstanding example exists in the United States in the National Referral Center. The center, located in the Library of Congress, maintains very extensive indexes to information resources, both institutional and individual. As well as publishing directories of information resources of various types—for example, by subject area—the center responds, at no cost, to any inquiry of a "Where do I go?" type, received by telephone, letter, or personal visit. The source referred to may be an institution or an individual known to have expertise in a particular specialized subject. Very extensive indexes are maintained to support this referral activity.

INFORMATION ON ONGOING RESEARCH

Another type of question is the "Who's doing what?" variety, the most important of this kind being the question "Who is doing research in this particular subject area at the present time?" A center that maintains an index to ongoing research within a particular country has an extremely important role to play in the national information system. As Martyn (1964) showed clearly, there is a danger that if information services are not used properly, research projects will be duplicated and investigators will try approaches previously shown to be infeasible, or will use materials or equipment that have already been improved on in other projects. Before any significant research project is begun, it is important that the investigators conduct a thorough literature search to determine what has already been published in the area of their proposed studies. It is also important that they determine what other investigators are at present working in the same or a similar area of research. It is this information need that indexes to ongoing research are designed to satisfy. A search of such a system will yield the identity and address of people currently working in a particular area of research. An abstract describing the ongoing research may also be part of the search output.

Indexes to ongoing research in various subject areas exist, or have existed, in published form. A notable example, *Current Research and Development in Scientific Documentation,* once existed in the information science area; it was published by the National Science Foundation. More useful, perhaps, is a data base in machine-readable form, which can be kept more up-to-date and can be used in the conduct of machine literature searches.

Although a number of countries maintain systems providing access to ongoing research conducted within their own boundaries, the most complete of these is maintained in the United States by the Smithsonian Institution. It is known as the Smithsonian Science Information Exchange. SSIE is fairly complete in its coverage of research projects in the sciences, in the United States, that are supported by government agencies and the major research foundations. The data base of SSIE does not, of course, include "proprietary" research conducted within a company and supported by the company's own research funds. Nor does it include research projects of a "classified," in a security sense, nature.

Input to the SSIE data base is in the form of a Notice of Research Project (see Figure 27 for an example), completed by the investigators. The notice includes project title, names of investigators, institutional affiliation of investigators, identity of supporting agency, scheduled duration of the project, the funds committed to the project, and a summary of the proposed research. These data are put into machine-readable form, along with codes representing the subject matter of the research. All these elements can be searched on in the SSIE files. On a fee basis, SSIE conducts a complete search of the projects currently in its data base. It also offers a form of SDI service consisting of quarterly or monthly updates to a previously conducted search. A group beginning, say, a

SMITHSONIAN SCIENCE INFORMATION EXCHANGE
Room 300 • 1730 M Street, N.W. • Washington, D.C. • 20036
Telephone (202) 381-4211 • Telex 89495

NOTICE OF RESEARCH PROJECT

SSIE NUMBER: BV-495-2

SUPPORTING ORGANIZATION:
U.S. National Science Foundation
Div. of Chemistry
1800 G St. N.W.
Washington, District of Columbia 20550

SUPPORTING ORGANIZATION NUMBER(S): CHE76-05163 A02

PROJECT TITLE:
PHOTOCHEMISTRY OF LOW-VALENT TRANSITION METAL COMPLEXES

INVESTIGATOR(S): MS WRIGHTON
DEPARTMENT/SPECIALTY: CHEMISTRY

PERFORMING ORGANIZATION:
MASS. INST. OF TECHNOLOGY
SCHOOL OF SCIENCE
77 MASSACHUSETTS AVE.
CAMBRIDGE, MASSACHUSETTS 02139

PERIOD FOR THIS NRP: 11/77 TO 10/78
FY78   FUNDS $22,500

PROJECT SUMMARY:

Studies of excited-state chemistry of low-valent transition metal complexes are being carried out. Strong emphasis is placed on the study of primary photoprocesses which yield very reactive, coordinatively unsaturated species. Photoinduced cleavage of metal-metal bonds is a continuing aspect of the work, and a systematic study of metal carbonyl anions that undergo unusual oxidative addition reactions will be undertaken. It is planned to begin the first studies of the photochemistry of CO2 complexes with emphasis on photoassisting the conversion of CO2 to CO plus O2. Intraligand excited-state reactions are to be investigated to demonstrate the fact that coordination of the ligand can lead to new, highly selective chemical reactions. A final area of considerable importance concerns the chemistry of metal to ligand charge-transfer (M yields L CT) excited states. First, these states will be probed with respect to their substitution chemistry. Then, examples of bimolecular reactions of the M yields L CT excited states including electrophilic substitution reactions of L and intraligand reactivity of the L will be studied. Accompanying the photochemical studies will be electronic absorption spectral investigations to aid in characterizing the nature of the excited states. This work should add very substantially to the present understanding of the reactions of the excited metal complexes. An impact is expected in the synthesis, catalysis and photochemical energy conversion involving metal complexes. This work is a continuation of that currently supported by Foundation grant, MPS 7308670.

Figure 27 Sample of input to the SSIE data base.

two-year research project may request a search of the file and also ask for the regular updates. Thus, the investigators are made aware of others working in related research areas, including projects begun during the two years of their own studies. The data base of SSIE is also available for interrogation through one of the on-line retailers (see Chapter 5).

A recent review by Hersey (1978) describes the growth, development and characteristics of information systems on ongoing research and provides a good overview and state of the art report in this area of the information field.

CENTERS PROVIDING SERVICES RELATING TO DOCUMENTS

Table 2 illustrates, for various kinds of documents, the most important types of services to be provided in relation to these documents and the

Table 2   Major Centers, or Types of Center, Processing Various Types of Documents in the United States

Documents	Collection	Cataloging	Indexing and abstracting	Announcing	Searching	Document delivery	Evaluation and synthesis
Books and periodicals	National libraries, research libraries	National libraries, commercial publishers		National libraries, commercial publishers	National libraries, research libraries	National libraries, research libraries, publishers, booksellers, subscription agencies	Information analysis centers
Periodical articles	National libraries, research libraries			National libraries, government agencies, professional societies, commercial publishers	+ SIDC's + IAC's and research libraries	National libraries, research libraries, commercial publishers	
Technical reports	National Technical Information Service, Defense Documentation Center, Educational Resources Information Center, National Aeronautics and Space Administration				+ SIDC's + IAC's		
Patents	U.S. Patent Office			+ Commercial publishers	+ Commercial publishers	+ SIDC's + IAC's	
Translations	National Translations Center						

centers, or types of centers, that fulfill these functions in the United States. The table is intended to be illustrative rather than complete. We are concerned here with illustrating types of centers and services, not with identifying even the major examples of each type. The services identified are document collection; cataloging; indexing and abstracting; the production of various types of announcement devices; the searching of data bases in printed or machine-readable form, including searches conducted for current awareness purposes; document delivery, by means of sales and lending or photocopying procedures; and evaluation and synthesis.

It can be seen from Table 2 that the major responsibilities for collecting the book and periodical literature in the United States rest with the three national libraries—Library of Congress, National Library of Medicine, and National Agricultural Library—and with the nation's research libraries, especially those of the large academic institutions. Collectively these libraries acquire virtually everything of significance published in all fields on a worldwide basis. The national libraries, most notably the Library of Congress, play a major role in cataloging the documents acquired and announcing them through printed catalogs, printed catalog cards, and magnetic tape services. The national library of any country is quite likely to be the publisher of the national bibliography of the country. It may also be the compiler or publisher of a union catalog of the holdings of the major libraries of the country. This is the situation in the United States, where the Library of Congress is the compiler of the *National Union Catalog* and the *New Serial Titles,* the latter representing new titles recently added to the collections of the major research libraries in the United States. Commercial publishers may also play important roles in bibliographic control. For example, the H. W. Wilson Company is responsible for the *Union List of Serials* as well as the *Cumulative Book Index,* the latter being perhaps the closest approximation of a true national bibliography existing in the United States.

Responsibilities relating to making the contents of periodicals, that is, the individual articles published, accessible are shared by many organizations in the United States. Some of the indexing of this literature is handled by the national libraries. The National Library of Medicine produces, in *Index Medicus,* the major index to the periodical literature of medicine, and the National Agricultural Library performs a similar function in the compilation of the *Bibliography of Agriculture,* which includes report and other types of literature as well as periodical articles. Major indexing and abstracting services are also produced by other government agencies, professional societies, and commercial publishers. Several of the professional societies in the United States, as well as publishing primary journals, compile and publish major secondary services in printed and machine-readable form. Obvious examples are the American Chemical Society, publisher of *Chemical Abstracts,* and the American Psychological Association, publisher of *Psychological Abstracts.* As described in Chapter 5, large numbers of machine-readable data bases have emerged in the last fifteen years, and a major responsibility for searching them has been assumed by the scientific information dissemination center, abbreviated to SIDC in Table 2. I include in this group the on-line retailers. Although the latter do not necessarily provide searching services, they are certainly responsible for making data bases accessible in a searchable on-line form. Apart from the SIDC's, already described in Chapter 5, the major responsibility for providing literature searching services, using both printed tools and on-line facilities, remains with the national, academic, and industrial libraries.

Other types of information centers represented in Table 2 include centers concerned with making the technical report literature available, translations centers, and information analysis centers (IAC's). A number of agencies have responsibilities for the collection, cataloging, indexing and abstracting, announcing, and distribution of technical report literature in the United States. The Defense Documentation Center (DDC) performs these functions for reports of research supported by the Department of Defense and the armed services. The National Aeronautics and Space Administration (NASA) fulfills these roles for its own report literature and, in cooperation with the American Institute of Aeronautics and Astronautics, produces indexes and abstracts of all types of literature of relevance to the space program from all sources. In the field of education, the major role in the collection, bibliographic control, and dissemination of the report literature is played by the Educational Resources Information Center (ERIC) of the National Institute of Education.

Probably the most important of the organizations providing access to the technical report literature, however, is the National Technical Information Service (NTIS), located in the Department of Commerce. NTIS has the major responsibility for making available to industry and the general public the reports of research funded by the various agencies of the United States government. To achieve this goal, it collects these reports—at present at a rate of about 90,000 titles a year—indexes and abstracts them, and announces them through various publications, some comprehensive, some selective, as well as through a form of SDI service (Selected Research in Microfiche), by which a subscriber can receive microfiche copies of all reports falling within a prescribed area of interest.

NTIS also produces a machine-readable data base corresponding to its major announcement device, *Government Reports Announcements,* which can be accessed through the on-line retailers.

A "translations center" is not a center that undertakes translating services but one that collects translations, catalogs them, announces them, and, usually, sells copies. It can be regarded as a type of "clearinghouse" for information on the availability of translations. A substantial amount of translation into English, particularly of scientific and technical literature, is done every year, some by government agencies and some by private industry. Many of these organizations are willing to deposit translations they have undertaken or commissioned in a translation center so that the expense of duplicate translation can be avoided by other organizations. The philosophy is one of quid pro quo. Most organizations that deposit hope, in return, to receive translations prepared by other organizations, thereby avoiding needless expenses of their own. In the United States the National Translations Center is located in the John Crerar Library, Chicago. The British Library performs a similar function in England, and an International Translations Center exists in Delft, the Netherlands.

INFORMATION ANALYSIS CENTERS

There are great similarities among many of the centers represented in Table 2 in terms of the range and scope of the services they offer. Most have responsibilities for collecting a specified body of literature—in a designated subject area, of a designated document type, or a combination of these—and for cataloging, indexing, and abstracting it. Many agencies compile and maintain their own thesaurus, or other form of controlled vocabulary, to facilitate these bibliographic control activities. Many issue an indexing or abstracting service or some other announcement device to inform users of newly published material. Frequently such publications are produced under computer control, and the machine-readable data base thus derived is available for retrospective searching and SDI activities. Most of these data bases are now accessible on-line, either directly from their producer or through one of the on-line retailers. Some form of document delivery capability also exists in most centers. In fact, the activities and services illustrated for MEDLARS in Chapter 3 are fairly typical of many of the major information centers represented in Table 2.

But these typical information center activities tend to exclude evaluation and synthesis. That is, evaluation of what is to be included in the data base usually occurs at only a rather general level—for example, it may be decided that a particular periodical is to be indexed, but no choice is made among the various articles included in it—and, in some cases, there may be no evaluation at all. That is, a center may collect all materials of a specified type—for example, all technical reports issued by designated agencies—without using any qualitative selection criteria. Many information centers, too, may use little or no qualitative evaluation of output. For example, if a user requests an on-line literature search on the subject of ultrasonic welding, he is likely to receive a complete printout of all citations retrieved. The staff of the information center may attempt to eliminate obviously irrelevant items before submitting the results to the requester. It is highly unlikely, however, that they will attempt, or, for that matter, be qualified to undertake, any assessment of the quality of the items retrieved ("this is an excellent and reliable paper," "this is very superficial," and so on). Most centers, too, refrain from true synthesis activities; that is, they may create indexes to and summaries of existing literature, but they do not normally involve themselves in the production of new literature or new compilations of data.

Evaluation and synthesis activities are, however, essential elements in the philosophy of the information analysis center, and they most clearly distinguish it from other forms of information centers.

An information analysis center (IAC) tends to be restricted to a rather specialized area of study—for example, thermophysical properties of materials, early childhood education, Parkinson's disease. Within this subject field, it performs many of the functions performed by other types of information centers. It collects the relevant literature, but is likely to have much more stringent, qualitative evaluation criteria, and is likely to index and perhaps abstract or condense it. The IAC may also produce some type of announcement device. It certainly undertakes literature searches on demand. But the results of such searches are likely to be critically evaluated before they are delivered to the requester. The output of the IAC, in fact, is less likely to be a bibliographic listing than extracted data or even advice on the solution of a user's problem, this advice backed up by appropriate references to or extracts from published sources.

An IAC may also produce new publications, either on its own initiative or in response to specific demands made by members of the user population. This is its synthesis function. Such publications may include compilations of data—for example, *Thermophysical Properties of Matter*—critical reviews of the literature in particular subject areas, and reports and interpretations of papers presented at specialized conferences and symposia. Informal sources of information—for example, consultants—tend to be used much more by IAC's than by other types of information centers. In fact, the giving of technical advice based on extensive personal experience may be an important activity of many centers of this kind. It is clear, then, that the staff of an IAC must have a level of subject knowledge and experience greatly beyond that normally required of personnel in other types of information centers. Although there will still be a need for personnel with less knowledge of the subject area—for example, to perform collection, cataloging, and other basic documentation functions—those individuals who are directly involved in evaluation, critical analysis, and synthesis must be subject experts.

The term "clearinghouse" has been avoided in this chapter, although a number of information centers refer to themselves as clearinghouses. The term seems to have its origin in the field of banking, where it retains a rather precise meaning; it has no such precise connotation in the information center environment.

NETWORKS

The term "networks" should at least appear in this chapter, although a detailed discussion of networks of information services, which could occupy a whole book in itself, is well beyond the intended scope of this book. At its most general, the term refers to nothing more than a set of interconnected points. Applied in the context of information service, it is generally used to refer to a group of centers that cooperate among themselves and collectively provide various levels and types of service to a particular community of users. Usually one of the centers in the network is a "headquarter center," providing coordination, control, or management over the other elements (nodes) in the network. There are many possible configurations to information service networks; several alternatives are described by Kent (1967). Perhaps the most obvious division is into subject-oriented and geographically oriented networks. The second type is well exemplified by the network of MEDLARS centers established by the National Library of Medicine in the 1960s. Each MEDLARS center was assigned responsibilities for providing literature searching services to a designated geographic region, and each covered the entire range of subjects within the scope of the MEDLARS data base. The network of the Educational Resources Information Center (ERIC), however, is based on subject rather than geographic responsibilities. Each center in the ERIC network—they are really information analysis centers—covers a particular branch of education—for example, reading and communication skills, junior colleges, early childhood education—and has responsibilities for collecting literature in this subject field, indexing it, and providing a wide range of information analysis activities based on it. As with other information analysis centers, an attempt is made to place an ERIC center in an institution that is recognized as a "center of excellence" in the subject field covered. There is no geographic significance to this placement. For example, three ERIC centers may exist in Illinois, but they provide no more service to Illinois residents than to residents in other states.

INTERNATIONAL INFORMATION SERVICES

There are various types of information services that can be considered in some sense "international." The following sequence is one of increasing internationality:

1. A service international in coverage but national in control
2. A service international in coverage, national in control, but receiving input from a limited number of other countries
3. A truly international service, controlled by an international body, receiving input from many countries, with each country having equal rights in the partnership

The first of these is exemplified by the *Bibliography of Agriculture,* a printed index compiled by the National Agricultural Library (NAL). Although international in scope, the publication is produced entirely by NAL and receives no input from other centers. The second is exemplified by MEDLARS. Although this system is entirely under the control of the National Library of Medicine (NLM), input is received from a number of countries; that is, personnel from information centers in a limited number of countries—for example, the United Kingdom, Sweden, Japan—are trained in MEDLARS indexing procedures at NLM. These indexers then provide input from a designated group of journals—for example, indexers at the Karolinska Institute in Stockholm cover the Scandinavian medical journals. The indexing records thus created are submitted to NLM, which retains the functions of quality control and the actual production of the data base in printed and machine-readable formats. In MEDLARS these international arrangements are made on a quid pro quo basis. In return for its input, a participating country receives a set of the MEDLARS tapes, which can be used in the provision of SDI or retrospective search services within the country itself or in a larger geographical region.

As of 1977 there are two operating information services that can be regarded as international in the true sense of the word. Both are operated by agencies of the United Nations, and both involve full participation of member countries. The first is INIS, the International Nuclear Information System, operated by the International Atomic Energy Agency (IAEA), and the second is AGRIS, the International Information System for the Agricultural Sciences and Technology, operated by the Food and Agriculture Organization (FAO). The two systems are more or less identical in their mode of operation. Indeed, AGRIS was deliberately modeled on the earlier INIS program.

INIS and AGRIS both operate through input centers established in participating countries. A national input center has responsibility for identifying the current national literature that falls within the scope of the system, collecting the literature, and cataloging and indexing it according to standard procedures. The indexing records thus created are submitted to the international coordinating center. For IAEA this center is in Vienna; for FAO it is in Rome. The coordinating center has responsibility for overall quality control of the input and the actual production of the data base in printed and machine-readable versions, although, at present, all machine processing for AGRIS as well as INIS is conducted at the INIS center in Vienna. The printed version of the INIS data base is *Atomindex*; the printed version of the AGRIS data base is *Agrindex*.

The machine-readable versions of the data bases, in magnetic tape form, are made available to any of the national centers that have the necessary computer facilities available and wish to use the tapes in the provision of national SDI or retrospective search services. For "nonconventional" literature, mostly technical reports, INIS also provides a document delivery service. National centers submit one copy of all such documents to Vienna, where they are duplicated in microfiche form. Sets of microfiche may then be redistributed to national centers. In the case of AGRIS, a substantial amount of input is received from international rather than national centers. For example, most of the input for Latin America and the Caribbean is handled through the Instituto Interamericano de Ciencias Agricolas, Centro Interamericano de Documentación e Información Agricola (IICA-CIDIA), located in Costa Rica.

INIS and AGRIS are true "participatory" international systems. Each participating country has equal rights in the partnership, and it exercises some control over the system and its policies. Each country assumes financial responsibility for the input of its own literature, but, in return, it receives the input of all the other countries in the partnership.

It seems desirable to conclude this chapter with some reference to UNISIST, a program of UNESCO. UNISIST (not an acronym) is said to be a "world science information system," but this is a misnomer, since it is not restricted exclusively to science and it is not, strictly speaking, a system. It is, however, worldwide. The major purpose of the UNISIST program is to encourage and assist national governments in the establishment and maintenance of information programs, to coordinate such activities, and to promote cooperation at international levels. To put it in UNESCO's own jargon, the principal aim is to establish the necessary "infrastructure," at national and international levels, by which scientific, technical, and other types of information can be transferred efficiently from producer to consumer. UNESCO encourages the establishment of national "focal" points (foci) for UNISIST-related activities, and the UNISIST office in Paris is regarded as the international focus of all these activities. The UNISIST program has a somewhat modest budget of its own, but it has been able to attract funds from elsewhere in the United Nations and from the foreign aid programs of some member nations. The UNISIST program attempts to achieve its goals in a number of different ways:

1. By providing funds to get national or international information programs going (this may be done on the basis of a "matching fund" arrangement with a national government)
2. By providing consultants
3. By organizing training courses
4. By promoting conferences and other forums for discussion
5. By production of various guidelines (on thesaurus construction, evaluation of information services, organization of training courses, and so on)
6. By setting up various kinds of international programs or centers—for example, the International Serials Data System

Altogether, the UNISIST program has had some considerable success in promoting awareness of the importance of information services and in stimulating the strengthening of such services in many countries. A major emphasis of UNISIST is in the area of programs designed to transfer scientific and technical information from the developed to the developing countries.

An excellent review of international programs has been prepared by Tocatlian (1975). A useful summary of some major programs in the United States was made by Herner and Velluci (1972), but this is now rather outdated. More detailed information on the operations of information analysis centers can be found in a book by Weisman (1972).

Chapter Eight

Criteria by Which Information Services May Be Evaluated

The users of services of any kind usually evaluate them, consciously or unconsciously, against cost, time, and quality criteria. Thus, a tourist planning to fly from Miami to Buenos Aires is likely first to inquire if one airline operates this route at a lower cost than others. If there are no cost differences or if they are insignificant, time factors may become paramount; the traveler looks for the most direct (rapid) flight or the one that leaves at the most convenient time. If several leave at equally convenient times, the traveler's perception of the quality of the airline, based on his own experience or that of friends, influences his decision.

Users of information services also tend to judge them against cost, time, and quality criteria. The specific criteria that seem most important in the information service environment are listed below:

Level 1. Evaluation of effectiveness (considerations of user satisfaction)
    a. Cost criteria
        (1) Monetary cost to user (per search, per subscription, per document)
        (2) Other, less tangible cost considerations
            (*a*) Effort involved in learning how to use system
            (*b*) Effort involved in actual use
            (*c*) Effort involved in retrieving documents (through backup document delivery systems)
            (*d*) Form of output provided by the system
    b. Time criteria
        (1) Time elapsing from submission of request to retrieval of citations
        (2) Time elapsing from submission of request to retrieval of documents
        (3) Other time considerations—for example, waiting time to use an on-line system
    c. Quality considerations
        (1) Coverage of the data base
        (2) Completeness of output (recall)
        (3) Relevance of output (precision)
        (4) Novelty of output
        (5) Completeness and accuracy of data
Level 2. Evaluation of cost effectiveness (user satisfaction related to internal system efficiency and cost considerations)
    (1) Unit cost per relevant citation retrieved
    (2) Unit cost per new, that is, previously unknown, relevant citation retrieved
    (3) Unit cost per relevant document retrieved
Level 3. Cost-benefit evaluation (value of system balanced against costs of operating it)

Cost factors are as important in the evaluation of information services as they are in the evaluation of other services and products. The service must be provided at a cost that the user feels is reasonable in relation to the benefits associated with it. Cost to the user involves more than direct charges. It includes the cost of his own time, that is, how much effort is involved in the use of the system. Studies of the information-seeking behavior of scientists and other professionals have consistently shown that accessibility and ease of use are the prime factors influencing the choice of an information source. In general, the most convenient source of information is chosen, whether or not it is perceived by the user to be the most comprehensive, authoritative, or, in some sense, the "best." Ease of use factors include ease of interrogating the system in the first place, that is, ease of making one's needs known, and ease of use of the output provided by the system, especially the ease with which the output can predict the relevance of the documents it refers to. A very important facet of the latter is the availability of an efficient and convenient document delivery capability. A service that stops at the delivery of bibliographic citations goes only part of the way toward satisfying an individual's information needs. Such a service causes considerable frustration if the user is unable to obtain the documents cited or can do so only through procedures that he views as inconvenient and time-consuming.

As mentioned in an earlier chapter, the users of information services have various kinds of information needs, including the need for

1. A particular document whose identity is known
2. Specific factual information of the type that might come from some type of reference book or from a machine-readable data bank—for example, thermophysical property data on a particular substance
3. A few "good" articles, or references to them, on a specific topic
4. A comprehensive literature search in a particular subject area
5. A current alerting service by which the user is kept informed of new literature relevant to his current professional interests

These different needs have different response time requirements associated with them. The requirement relating to the current alerting service is that it should deliver regularly and frequently and that the information supplied should be as up-to-date as possible. The user needing a comprehensive literature search is usually engaged in a relatively long-term research project. Speed of response may not be critical to him, except that there may be some date beyond which the search results will have no value or, at least, greatly reduced value; he is willing to wait longer in order to achieve completeness, that is, completeness is more important to him than speed. For the other types of information needs, on the other hand, the user generally wants fairly rapid response.

The cost and time criteria relevant to the evaluation of information services seem fairly obvious and are relatively constant from one activity to another. But the quality criteria are perhaps less obvious and vary considerably with the particular service being evaluated. They may also vary with the kind of need that a particular user has in relation to a service.

There seem to be two major qualitative measures of success as applied to information services:

1. Does the user get what he is seeking or not?
2. How completely or accurately does he get it?

The first of these measures, which applies, for example, to the search for a particular item or the answer to a particular factual question is simple and unequivocal. The second, however, is much more difficult to apply in practice because it implies both a human value judgment and the use of some graduated scale to reflect degree of success. The second type of measure is necessary, however, in the evaluation of most types of information retrieval activity. "Recall" and "precision" are two criteria frequently used to judge the performance of a search in an information retrieval system.

RECALL AND PRECISION

The term "recall" refers to a measure of whether or not a particular item is retrieved or the extent to which the retrieval of wanted items occurs. In the case of a user seeking a particular document, the document is either retrieved from the collection, that is, recalled, at the time it is needed, or it is not. In the case of a user wanting a comprehensive search of a data base, the success of the search may be expressed in terms of the extent to which all the relevant documents, or references to them, are retrieved. This measure of the completeness of a search in a data base is frequently referred to as a "recall ratio," and the statement "80% recall" implies that 8/10 of the relevant documents, in the data base, were found. The term "precision" refers to a measure of signal-to-noise ratio in certain kinds of information systems. A literature search that retrieves 50 documents, of which 10 are judged relevant by the person requesting the search, can be said to have operated at a "precision ratio" of 10/50, or 20%.

These two measures, recall ratio and precision ratio, can be illustrated further by means of a 2 × 2 table presenting the results achieved in a particular literature search. Table 3 is a table of this type. When a search is conducted in most information retrieval systems, the system divides up the collection into two parts. The documents that match the search strategy used to interrogate the system are retrieved $(a + b)$, and all the documents that fail to match the strategy are not retrieved $(c + d)$. This dichotomous partitioning of the document collection may be regarded as a form of system relevance prediction. The system, in a sense, predicts that certain documents are likely to be relevant and others are likely not to be. It retrieves the former and holds back the latter.

In almost all situations the number of documents retrieved by a search is very small in relation to the total collection size. Put differently, in almost all searches $a + b$ is small, but $c + d$, the number of items not retrieved, is very large. A search might, for example, retrieve 80 document references from a total file of 500,000 references. In this case, $a + b = 80$, and $c + d = 499,920$.

The other dimension of the 2 × 2 table relates to the relevance decisions of the system user, that is, the person for whom the search is conducted. A perfect search retrieves all the documents in the data base that the user judges to be relevant $(a + c)$. In this case, there is perfect coincidence between the user relevance assessments and the system relevance predictions; that is, $b = 0$ and $c = O$. We say that this search has achieved 100% precision. It has also achieved 100% recall.

Recall relates to the ability of the system to retrieve relevant documents, and *precision* relates to its ability not to retrieve irrelevant documents. The degree of recall achieved in a search, and the degree of precision, may both be expressed as ratios.* The *recall ratio* is defined as

$$\frac{\text{Number of relevant documents retrieved}}{\text{Total number of relevant documents in the collection}} \times 100$$

In terms of Table 3, the recall ratio is

$$\frac{a}{a + c}$$

The *precision ratio* is defined as

$$\frac{\text{Number of relevant documents retrieved}}{\text{Total number of documents retrieved}} \times 100$$

In terms of Table 3, the precision ratio is

$$\frac{a}{a + b}$$

The precision ratio and the recall ratio, used jointly, express the filtering capacity of the system—its ability to let through what is wanted and to hold back what is not. Neither one on its own gives a complete picture of the effectiveness of a search. It is always possible to get 100% recall if we retrieve enough of the total collection; if we retrieve the entire collection $(a + b + c + d)$, we certainly achieve 100% recall. Unfortunately, however, precision would be extremely low in this situation because, for any typical request, the great majority of the items in the collection are not relevant.

The precision ratio may be viewed as a type of cost factor in user time—the time required to separate the relevant citations from the irrele-

---

* The derivation of these ratios is discussed in greater detail in Chapter 9.

Table 3   2 × 2 Table of Results of a Literature Search

		User relevance decisions		
		Relevant	Not relevant	Total
System relevance prediction	Retrieved	a (Hits)	b (Noise)	$a + b$
	Not retrieved	c (Misses)	d (Correctly rejected)	$c + d$
	Total	$a + c$	$b + d$	$a + b + c + d$ (Total collection)

vant ones in the output of a search. Consider, as an illustration, a search request for which there are 20 relevant documents in a particular data base. Suppose that three different search strategies are used to interrogate the system and that each retrieves 15 of the 20 relevant items; that is, recall is 75%. In the first search, the total number of items retrieved is 30, in the second it is 60, and in the third it is 150. The precision ratio in these three searches is 50, 25, and 10%, respectively. In the first search the user has to examine only 30 citations to find the 15 of relevance; in the second, 60; and in the third, 150. All other things being equal, it takes him longer to separate the relevant from the irrelevant in the second search than in the first, and considerably longer in the third. It is in this sense that we can regard the precision ratio as a measure of user effort or cost. A search that achieves 75% recall at 50% precision is more efficient than one that achieves 75% recall at 25% precision, and this is more efficient than one that achieves 75% recall at 10% precision.

As stated earlier, these ratios measure the degree of coincidence between the user relevance assessments and the system relevance predictions. In a perfect search these exactly coincide. Unfortunately, such perfect searches are relatively rare. We are more likely to get a situation in which there is partial coincidence between the set $a + c$ and the set $a + b$, as shown in Figure 28. This hypothetical, but very typical, search has retrieved most, but not all, of the relevant documents and avoided most, but not all, of the irrelevant.

Recall and precision tend to be related inversely. By this we mean that when we broaden a search to achieve better recall, precision tends to go down. Conversely, when we restrict the scope of a search, in order to

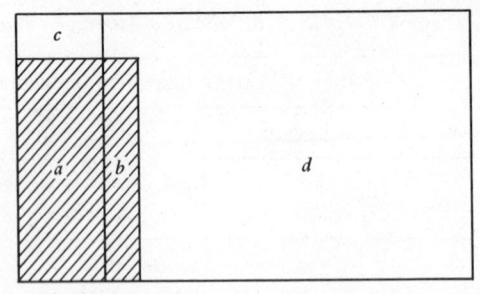

Figure 28 Typical results of a search in a retrieval system. The search has retrieved most of the relevant documents (*a*), missed some relevant (*c*), and retrieved some irrelevant (*b*). Most of the collection (*abcd*) is correctly rejected (*d*). Recall in this search appears to be about 80% and precision about 70%.

improve its precision, recall tends to deteriorate. For a particular group of, say, 50 requests, we could conduct each search at a number of different levels, from an extremely broad search designed to get high recall to an extremely narrow one designed to get high precision. If recall and precision ratios were derived for each of these search approaches and if these ratios were plotted against each other, the plot would look something like that in Figure 29. It represents the average of the recall and

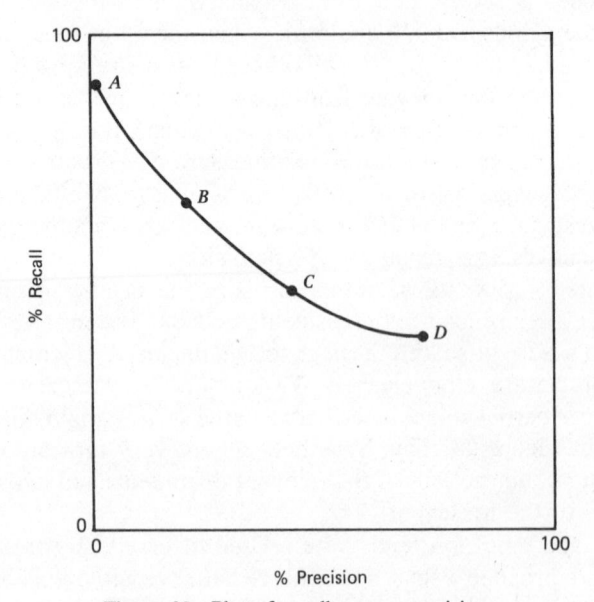

Figure 29 Plot of recall versus precision.

precision ratios for all 50 searches, with each search being conducted at four different "levels." It can be seen that when the searches are conducted very generally (point A), a very high recall of around 90% is achieved; the precision, however, is very low. When, on the other hand, the searches are made very specific, a high-precision, low-recall result (point D) is achieved. The points B and C represent compromise strategies between these two extremes.

Not everyone needs high recall all the time. Different users have different requirements for recall and precision, and a particular individual has different requirements at different times. The precision tolerance of the user is likely to be directly related to his recall requirements. At one end of the spectrum we have the individual who is writing a book, preparing a review article, or beginning a long-term research project. He is likely to want a comprehensive (high recall) search, and he may tolerate fairly low precision in order to assure himself that he has not missed anything of importance. At the other end, we have the typical user of, say, an industrial information service who needs a few recent articles on a subject and needs them right away. He does not need high recall but he expects high precision in the search results. Other individuals may prefer a compromise; they would like a "reasonable" level of recall at an "acceptable" level of precision.

It seems rather pointless to use the recall ratio as a measure of the success of a search in which high recall is unimportant. This has led some writers to suggest the use of some measure of proportional recall, or relative recall, in which the success of the search is expressed in terms of the number of relevant documents retrieved over the number of relevant documents wanted by the requester. For example, the requester specifies that he needs five relevant documents, but the search retrieves only three. The proportional recall ratio is, therefore, 3/5, or 60%. This measure, although attractive on the surface, is rather artificial in that very few requesters are able to specify in advance just how many documents they want from the system.

Another limitation of the recall ratio is that it more or less assumes that all relevant documents have approximately equal value. This is not always true. A search may retrieve 5 relevant documents and miss 10 (recall ratio = 33%), but the 5 retrieved may be much better than the 10 missed. They could, for example, be more up-to-date and might in fact make the other 10 items completely redundant. This matter is discussed further in Chapter 18. The recall ratio, although important, must therefore be used with some caution in the evaluation of information services.

The precision ratio also has its limitations. As we have already seen, it is actually an indirect measure of user time and effort spent at the output stage of the information retrieval process; that is, the higher the precision ratio, the less effort the user needs to expend in separating relevant items from those which are not. In a search of very low precision ratio in which, say, only 10 items among 80 retrieved are relevant, considerable user time and effort might be required to identify the relevant items in a printed or typed list, especially if it contains only bibliographic citations and the user must himself retrieve copies of many of the documents before he can decide which are relevant and which are not. But this measure of effort is really only appropriate to the evaluation of a delegated search—one conducted, on behalf of the requester, by an information specialist. In this situation the system is viewed as more or less a "black box," into which a request is placed and out of which comes a group of documents or references to them. The precision ratio is a valid measure of the performance of any type of delegated search in which the information seeker submits a request to some "system" and waits for the results, whether the search is manual or fully mechanized.

The precision ratio is not especially meaningful when applied to the nondelegated search. Here, the user conducts his own search and makes relevance decisions continuously as he proceeds; that is, when he consults an index term in a printed index or an on-line system, he rejects irrelevant citations and records only those which seem relevant. A precision ratio could be derived for this type of search by counting the total number of citations the user consulted and the number he judged relevant, the precision ratio being the number of relevant citations found divided by the total number of citations consulted. This is a rather artificial measurement, however, because user effort in the nondelegated search situation can be expressed more directly in terms of the time required to conduct the search, and, from this, a unit cost, in time, per relevant item found can be determined. Presumably, the higher the precision of a nondelegated search (proportion of relevant items examined to the total items examined), the less time it takes, all other things being equal.

Leaving aside direct costs, four performance criteria by which any type of literature search, manual or mechanized, may be evaluated from the viewpoint of user satisfaction have been discussed thus far: recall, precision, response time, and user effort. The salient points of these performance measures are as follows:

Recall. Important to all users of information services who are seeking bibliographic materials on a particular subject. In some cases, only a minimum level of recall is required—for example, one book or a few articles on a particular subject—and this is likely to be the most typical situation. In other cases, maximum recall is sought—for example, the user who wants a comprehensive search conducted in *Chemical Abstracts*.

Precision. A meaningful measure of the performance of a delegated search conducted in any form of system, manual or mechanized. It is an indirect measure of user time and effort and not particularly appropriate in the evaluation of nondelegated searches, including nondelegated searches in on-line retrieval systems.

User Effort. In a nondelegated search, effort is measured by the amount of time the user spends conducting the search. In a delegated search, it is measured by the amount of time the user spends negotiating his inquiry with the system and the amount of time he needs, when the search results are delivered to him, to separate the relevant from the irrelevant items, which is directly related to the precision ratio.

Response Time. In a delegated search, this represents the time elapsing between the submission of a request by the user and his receipt of the search results. In a nondelegated situation, it represents the time involved in the actual conduct of the search; in this case, it also is a measure of user effort.

All these criteria are closely related, and there are tradeoffs among all of them. For example, the user who wants a high recall usually tolerates a lower precision, is willing to put more effort of his own into the search, and perhaps is resigned to some searching delays. The user who requires a minimum level of recall, however, is likely to expect high precision and fast response time; he is probably not willing to put great effort into the search himself. It is important to recognize that response time is always secondary to recall and precision. Even in an information retrieval situation in which rapid response is essential—for example, a poison information center—the first requirement is that information should be supplied and that it should be completely accurate, that is, there must be some recall and 100% precision; response time, although extremely important, is secondary. Indeed, it is logically absurd to put response time in the first position in any ranking of performance criteria, for this would imply that requesters would put immediate access to irrelevant information sources before delayed access to relevant ones.

ALTERNATIVES TO RECALL AND PRECISION

The 2 × 2 table (Table 3) contains all the data that we really need to know about a search in a retrieval system for evaluation purposes. One way of expressing the results of the table is by the recall ratio and the precision ratio, used jointly. But there are several other measures of performance that can be derived from the table, and there are various ways in which these results can be presented.

From Table 3 all the following measures can be derived:

$a/a + c$ The recall ratio, also known as "hit rate." The measure was apparently first suggested by Kent et al. (1955), who referred to it as the "recall factor." Swets (1963) calls it the "conditional probability of a hit." Goffman and Newill (1964) have called it "sensitivity."

$c/a + c$ This is the complement of recall. Fairthorne (1965) has called it "snobbery ratio." Swets terms it "conditional probability of a miss."

$a/a + b$ This is the precision ratio, sometimes referred to as the "relevance ratio." Again, Kent et al. seem to have introduced the measure. They called it the "pertinency factor." Others have referred to it as an "acceptance rate."

$b/a + b$ This is the complement of the precision ratio, sometimes referred to as the "noise factor."

$b/b + d$ This measure seems to have been first suggested by Swets, who referred to it as the "conditional probability of a false drop." Cleverdon et al. (1966) have since named it the "fallout ratio." It has also been referred to as "discard."

$d/b + d$ The complement of fallout. Goffman and Newill have called it "specificity." Swets names it the "conditional probability of a correct rejection."

Each of these measures can be referred to a "single measure" of merit for a search. When two measures are used together, as in a plot of recall versus precision or recall versus fallout, this has been referred to as a "twin variable measure." When an attempt is made to combine two of these separate measures into a single measure—for example, one reflecting both recall and precision—the result is known as a "composite measure" or, possibly, a "single figure of merit."

These measures are appropriate for use with a retrieval system that merely divides a collection into two parts, those items retrieved and those not retrieved by a particular search. But certain systems do more than this. They generate a "ranked output" of documents in order of probable relevance to a request. Ranking systems should be evaluated in a somewhat different way because here we need an indication of the success of the ranking procedure. Various measures that have been applied to ranking systems include "rank recall," "log precision," "normalized recall," and "normalized precision." These measures, introduced by Salton (1971), essentially compare the actual ranking achieved by the system with an ideal ranking.

Rather complete discussions of evaluation measures, methods of averaging results, and methods of presenting results of retrieval tests have been provided by Keen (1966, 1971) and Robertson (1969). Recall ratios and precision ratios have been the measures most used in evaluations of information retrieval systems. These measures were popularized by Cleverdon (1962) in the ASLIB Cranfield Project. Many other writers, however, have presented reasons why other measures may be regarded as more accurate or more informative. Robertson's paper provides a useful analysis of the pros and cons of the various measures that have been proposed or used.

Another useful parameter is the "generality number," which expresses the number of documents relevant to a particular request over the total number of documents in the collection. The higher the generality number, the greater the density of relevant documents to total collection; and, generally speaking, the greater the density, the easier the search tends to be.

OTHER PERFORMANCE CRITERIA

The outline on page 109 lists some further performance criteria that may be applied in the evaluation of information retrieval systems, including "coverage" and "novelty." Coverage* actually is an extension of recall; it is expressed in terms of how much coverage of the literature on a specific subject is provided by a particular data base. Suppose, for example, that a scientist wishes to find all possible references to the use of lasers in eye surgery. An obvious source would be the printed *Index Medicus* or, even better, the computer-based MEDLINE service operated by the National Library of Medicine (NLM). Suppose also that the search in the NLM data base retrieves everything of relevance, that is, achieves 100% recall—a rather unlikely situation. Even if the search is complete, so far as the data base is concerned, the user who needs a really comprehensive search also wants to know the exact coverage of the data base, that is, what proportion of all the literature on eye surgery using lasers is contained in the data base. Searching a particular data base may result in 100% recall but may give a low overall coverage of the literature. Absolute coverage of the collection is only of direct concern to the person who

* Estimation of coverage is discussed in Chapter 9.

needs a comprehensive search. It is probable that the user whose need is satisfied by finding, on the library shelves, one or two books on a subject of interest is quite unconcerned as to how complete the library's collection may be in this subject area. At a later time, however, he may require a comprehensive search on this or some other topic, and the coverage of the collection consulted would then be important to him. Coverage, like recall and precision, can be expressed as a percentage. If, for example, the results of a search conducted in *Chemical Abstracts* were being evaluated, it could be estimated, not very easily, that the recall ratio is 75%; it could also be estimated, even less easily, that the coverage of *Chemical Abstracts* on the subject area of the search is 40%. With an estimated coverage of 40% and recall of 75% the overall estimate of the comprehensiveness of the search is 30%.

Another performance measure that may have some value is the novelty ratio, the proportion of relevant items retrieved in a search that are new to the requester, that is, brought to his attention for the first time by the search. The novelty ratio is particularly appropriate in the evaluation of literature searches conducted for current awareness purposes, that is, SDI, since, presumably, a good current awareness service brings documents to the attention of users before they learn of them by other means.

When cost criteria are related to quality criteria, cost-effectiveness criteria are derived. Some possible cost-effectiveness criteria applicable to information services (see page 109) include the unit cost per relevant item (document or document reference) retrieved and the unit cost per new relevant item retrieved. Cost can be measured directly in monetary units or in time and effort expended. Cost-effectiveness analysis is discussed in more detail in a later chapter.

There is still one further evaluation criterion listed on page 109, namely, accuracy of data. This criterion substitutes for recall and precision in the evaluation of information services designed to answer questions that have unequivocal factual answers. The answer to such a question as "What is the melting point of . . . ?" is either supplied completely and correctly or it is not. Question-answering services, whether the answer is supplied from a printed source or a machine-readable data bank, must therefore be evaluated in terms of the completeness and accuracy of the data supplied.

Chapter Nine

Evaluating the Effectiveness of Information Services

There are four possible levels at which an evaluation of an information service may be carried out:

1. Evaluation of effectiveness
2. Evaluation of benefits
3. Evaluation of cost effectiveness
4. Evaluation of the cost-benefit relationship

An evaluation of effectiveness is a study of the extent to which the service satisfies the information needs of its users. At least, this is what an evaluation of effectiveness should be. In fact, however, it is more likely to be a study of the extent to which the service meets the demands, that is, expressed needs, of its users, the unexpressed or latent needs of present users and the needs of present nonusers being largely ignored. This limitation is mentioned again later. The major criteria by which the effectiveness of an information service may be evaluated were discussed in the previous chapter.

In discussing the evaluation of effectiveness, King and Bryant (1971) draw an important distinction between "macroevaluation" and "microevaluation." The former is concerned only with determining the present level of performance of some service. The latter, on the other hand, is analytical and diagnostic. It goes beyond macroevaluation in order to discover why the service operates at its present level and what might be done to improve its performance in the future. To take a simple example, a macroevaluation might determine that the coverage of a particular data base in some specific subject field is 72%; that is, 72% of the literature published on the subject in a specified period of time has been indexed into the data base. But a microevaluation would seek to discover how this coverage could be improved; that is, it would distinguish the characteristics of the 72% covered from the 28% not covered and would generate recommendations on policies or procedures that could raise the coverage to, say, 85%.

A benefit evaluation attempts to determine what impact an information service has on its users, that is, how the users are benefited by the service. There are major differences between a study of the effectiveness of an information service and a study of the benefits of the service. It should always be possible to evaluate the effectiveness of the service in quantitative terms: the percentage of success in document delivery, the percentage of reference questions answered completely and accurately, the percentage of interlibrary loans successfully filled within x days, the recall and precision ratios of a literature search, and so on. But it is difficult and frequently impossible to express the benefits of an information service in quantitative terms. The evaluation of effectiveness can be objective, but the evaluation of benefits tends to be subjective. The effectiveness of a literature search conducted for a user can be estimated to be 80% recall and 50% precision. This is an objective expression of the performance of the system, although admittedly dependent on a subjective judgment of relevance. It is highly unlikely, however, that we can reduce to any meaningful quantitative terms any expression of the benefits of the search results to the user. Nevertheless, it seems reasonable to assume that a direct relationship exists between the effectiveness of a service and its benefits. For example, a service that is 89% successful in meeting demands may be presumed to offer greater benefits to users than one that is only 64% successful. In this sense, a quantitative measure of the effectiveness of a service can be considered to be a somewhat distant approximation of a measure of benefits.

A cost-effectiveness evaluation relates measures of effectiveness to measures of cost. For example, it may be possible to identify various methods by which the document delivery capability of a library can be raised from 72 to, say, 80%. An analysis that determines which of these methods is least expensive is a cost-effectiveness analysis. A cost-benefit study attempts to relate the costs of providing some service to the benefits of having the service available. In the information processing environment, cost-benefit analysis is unusually difficult because of the problems involved in trying to assign some actual monetary value to information.

Cost-effectiveness evaluation and cost-benefit evaluation are both discussed in a later chapter. The remainder of this chapter is devoted to the diagnostic microevaluation of the effectiveness of information service.

THE MAJOR STEPS OF AN EVALUATION

The major steps involved in the conduct of an evaluation program are the following:

1. Defining the scope of the evaluation
2. Designing the evaluation program
3. Execution of the evaluation
4. Analysis and interpretation of the results
5. Modifying the system or service on the basis of the evaluation results

The first step, the definition of scope, entails the preparation of a precise set of questions that the evaluation must be designed to answer. The purpose of an evaluation is to learn more about the capabilities and weaknesses of a system or service, and the definition of scope is really a statement of what precisely is to be learned through the study. The definition of scope must be prepared by the person requesting the evaluation, who is usually one of the managers of the system or one of those responsible for funding it. It is the responsibility of the evaluator to design a study capable of answering all the questions posed in the definition of scope. A sample work statement for an evaluation program is given in Figure 30. This statement is a list of the questions to be answered in the MEDLARS study, as reported by Lancaster (1968a). It is a rather long list because the study was a comprehensive evaluation of a very large system. Evaluation studies of more modest scope would involve fewer questions. In fact, it is quite conceivable that an evaluation might be designed to answer only one or two important questions.

Overall Performance

1. What is the overall performance level of the system in relation to user requirements? Are there significant differences for various types of request and in various broad subject areas?

Coverage and Processing

1. How sound are present policies regarding indexing coverage?
2. Is the delay between receipt of a journal and its processing in the indexing section significantly affecting performance?

Indexing

1. Are there significant variations in inter-indexer performance?
2. How far is this related to experience in indexing and to degree of "revising"?
3. Do the indexers recognize the specific concepts that are of interest to various user groups?
4. What is the effect of present policies relating to exhaustivity of indexing?

Index Language

1. Are the terms sufficiently specific?
2. Are variations in specificity of terms in different areas significantly affecting performance?
3. Is the need for additional precision devices, such as weighting, role indicators, or a form of interlocking, indicated?
4. Is the quality of term association in the thesaurus adequate?
5. Is the present entry vocabulary adequate?

Searching

1. What are the requirements of the users regarding recall and precision?
2. Can search strategies be devised to meet requirements for high recall or high precision?
3. How effectively can searchers screen output? What effect does screening have on recall and precision figures?
4. What are the most promising modes of user/system interaction?
    a. Having more liaison at the request stage.
    b. Having more liaison at the search formulation stage.
    c. An iterative search procedure that presents the user with a sample of citations retrieved by a "first approximation" search, and allows him to reformulate his request in the light of these retrieved items.
5. What is the effect on response time of these various modes of interaction?

Input and Computer Processing

1. Do input procedures, including various aspects of clerical processing, result in a significant number of errors?
2. Are computer programs flexible enough to obtain desired performance levels? Do they achieve the required checks on clerical error?
3. What part of the overall response lag can be attributed to the data processing subsystem? What are the causes of delays in this subsystem?

The second step of the evaluation involves the preparation of a plan of action that allows the gathering of data needed to answer the questions posed in the definition of scope. The designer of the study must identify what data are needed to answer each question and what procedures could be used to gather the data in the most efficient and expedient way. For each question, the evaluator must decide whether (1) it can be answered simply by collecting data from the system as it presently exists or (2) some changes in the normal functioning of the system must be made in order to collect the necessary data. For example, the question "What is the present response time of the system, expressed in ranges, means, medians, and modes?" can be answered from the system as it is now. It involves the collection of data from the existing system, on the date and time a request is received and the date and time the results are submitted to the requester, for a representative sample of transactions. To answer a question of this kind, new records may need to be created for the purpose of the study, but, apart from record keeping, the existing system is not perturbed in any way. In contrast, consider the question "What would be the effect on response time if action X were carried out?" This implies a change in the present system, and the question can be answered only by deliberately applying action X to a representative sample of transactions and comparing the response times with those of the system as it normally functions.

In some cases, then, the evaluator is primarily concerned with systematic and controlled observation of the system. In other cases, however, he needs to go beyond simple observation of this kind and into the field of experimental design. In the evaluation program it is important that well-established procedures of experimental design be followed and that appropriate statistical techniques be applied to the analysis and interpretation of the results.

The third step, execution of the evaluation, is the stage at which the data are gathered once the evaluation design has been agreed on by all the parties concerned. This stage is likely to be the longest in terms of elapsed time. It may also be the stage in which the evaluator is least directly involved and perhaps the stage over which he has the least direct control. Although the execution stage can hardly begin before the design stage is completed, the analysis and interpretation stage should certainly begin before the execution stage is concluded; that is, the evaluator must ensure that he receives data continuously from the beginning of the execution

---

Figure 30 Specimen statement of questions to be answered in the evaluation of a large system.

stage, so that they can be reduced to a form suitable for analysis and interpretation. It should be fairly obvious what is involved in the analysis and interpretation stage of an evaluation project. Here the evaluator is concerned with reducing the data and manipulating it in such a way that it can answer, or at least contribute to answering, the questions posed in the work statement. It is not possible to present any precise guidelines for analysis and interpretation because they vary considerably from one evaluation application to another. In the case of the evaluation of an information retrieval system, this stage of the study is mainly concerned with the derivation and manipulation of performance results—for example, recall and precision ratios—and with the analysis of recall and precision failures. The failure analysis itself entails an examination of each document involved, the indexing records for the documents, the requests that caused the searches to be conducted, the search strategies, the system vocabulary, and the relevance assessments of the users. Through the examination of each of these it should be possible to determine which component of the system was largely responsible for the failures occurring. In addition to the analysis of the failures occurring in particular searches, the evaluator can use the recall and precision ratios, or alternative measures of search performance, as indicators of conditions under which the system seems to perform well and under which it seems to perform badly. For example, searches can be grouped by broad subject category, and an average performance figure, or figures, can be derived for each group. It would then be possible to identify subject areas in which unusually low scores occur. Through the joint use of performance figures, in this way, and analyses of failures in particular searches, the evaluator learns a great deal about the characteristics of the system, its weaknesses and limitations as well as its strong points. The joint use of the performance figures and failure analyses should answer most of the questions identified in the work statement for the evaluation. The final element in the analysis and interpretation phase is that in which the evaluator presents his report to the managers of the system, including in his report recommendations on what might be done to improve its performance. The fifth and final step of the evaluation program is that in which some or all of the recommendations are implemented, that is, the step in which the evaluation results are applied to the improvement of the system.

Although not specifically mentioned in the discussion above, the value of a pretest should be recognized. Before the complete evaluation is carried out, it is important to follow through all the proposed procedures on a small sample of transactions, to ensure that the procedures are, in fact, viable and that they are capable of gathering the data needed to complete the study.

DERIVING PERFORMANCE FIGURES

To assess the extent to which some of the performance criteria mentioned in Chapter 8 are actually met by an information service—for example, response time, form and amount of user effort, monetary cost—it is necessary only to observe the system in operation. For the qualitative criteria, however, it is necessary to take some deliberate steps to gather the necessary performance data.

The major emphasis in designing an evaluation of an information retrieval system or service is likely to be the measurement or estimation of the recall and precision achieved in a representative sample of the searches conducted. Recall and precision ratios, or some other methods of presenting the results in the 2×2 table, are the most important measures of the quality of a delegated search in any type of system, since, together, these ratios indicate how successful the system has been in filtering the data base to retrieve the items that are relevant and avoid those which are not. If a search were perfect, it would retrieve all the relevant items in the data base without any accompanying irrelevant items: recall and precision would both be 100%. Although it is sometimes possible to achieve a perfect result in a particular search, it is very unlikely that a retrieval system will be able to achieve perfect results in a large sample of searches because this would imply that the indexing, the vocabulary, the search strategies, and the user-system interaction were all perfect throughout the system.

The way in which these performance figures may be derived is perhaps best illustrated by means of an example. Suppose that we want to evaluate the performance of a particular computer-based information service and that we decide to carry out the evaluation on a random sample of, say, 100 searches conducted in a particular period. The system operates in a delegated search mode: requests for searches are made to the information center, and the results, in the form of lists of document references retrieved, are delivered to the requesters. It is immaterial to the evaluation whether the search is conducted on-line or off-line.

We will follow one of these searches in order to identify the data we must collect, and the procedures we must adopt, to evaluate the performance of the service for this particular search. First, we must have a complete written record of the user's request for information. The request should preferably be recorded, in the user's own words, on a specially prepared form. A search strategy is prepared for the request by a member of the staff of the information service, and the strategy retrieves 25 document references from the data base. For evaluation purposes we need a copy of the search strategy, whether the search is conducted on-line or off-line. In order to derive a precision ratio for the search, it is necessary to ask the requester to judge which of the retrieved items are relevant to his information need and which are not. Preferably, these relevance assessments should be made on the basis of the complete documents. They might, however, be made on the basis of rather complete document representations—for example, abstracts. It is desirable that a "relevance assessment form" (see Figure 31 for an example as used in the evaluation of MEDLARS) be completed for each document assessed for relevance, although a composite form to collect relevance assessments for several documents can also be used. It is also desirable

---

NATIONAL LIBRARY OF MEDICINE
Bethesda, Maryland

Request No. _____
Document No. _____

MEDLARS EVALUATION PROJECT
Form For Document Evaluation

1. Were you previously aware of the existence of this article?
 Yes [ ] *How did you learn of its existence?*
 No [ ]

2. By checking the appropriate box, please evaluate this article in relation to the information need that prompted your request to MEDLARS.

 (a) Of major value to me in relation to my information need [ ]
 Please explain why:

 (b) Of minor value to me in relation to my information need [ ]
 Please explain why:

 (c) Of no value to me in relation to my information need [ ]
 Please explain why:

 Were you glad to learn of its existence because of some other need or project:
 Yes [ ] *Please explain why*:
 No [ ]

 (d) Unable to make an assessment because of language of the document [ ]

 Do you intend to take any steps to determine the contents of this foreign language document?
 Yes [ ] *Please specify what steps*:
 No [ ] *Please explain why*:

Figure 31 MEDLARS relevance assessment form.

that the requester be asked to judge relevance according to some simple scale—for example, major, minor, none—and that the reasons why certain documents are judged relevant, and others not, also be recorded. If the search retrieves a large number of documents, it is sufficient for purposes of evaluation if the requester is asked to assess the relevance of a random sample only.

Returning to the hypothetical search that retrieved 25 documents, let us suppose that the requester judges 15 to be relevant and 10 not relevant. Let us also suppose that the total data base comprises 500,000 document references. In this case, then, we are already able to place certain values into the 2×2 table of search results, as follows:

	Relevant	Not relevant	Total
Retrieved	15	10	25
Not retrieved			499,975
Total			500,000

The precision ratio of the search is 15/25, or 60%.

The major problem remaining is that of the estimation of recall. The term "estimation" is used deliberately because it is not possible to establish absolute recall for the search unless the requester is willing to look at all the 499,975 items not retrieved and to tell us, using the same criteria as before, which he considers relevant and which not. If he were willing to do this, it would be possible to put all the missing values into the table of results, but, clearly, the examination of all the items not retrieved by a search is completely impractical in any system of a realistic size. It is also impossible to arrive at the recall estimate by conventional random sampling among the items not retrieved because the set of items that are not relevant to any particular request is usually orders of magnitude greater than the set of items that are relevant. Consequently, an impossibly large random sample would need to be drawn—in this example, from the 499,975 items not retrieved—in order to have any probability of finding even one relevant document in the sample.

In the evaluation of an operating information service, then, we must give up all thoughts of arriving at "true" or "absolute" recall and concentrate instead on the derivation of the best possible recall estimate for the searches to be evaluated. One possible method of estimating recall involves the use of "parallel" searches conducted by other members of the information staff. Thus, the recall of the original search, conducted by staff member A, is expressed as

$$\frac{\text{Number of relevant items found by A}}{\text{Number of relevant items found by A + number of additional relevant items found in the data base by B, C, } \ldots, n}$$

The implication here is that any additional items found by B, C, and other searchers, but not found in the original search, must be submitted to the requester for relevance assessment.

For certain evaluation purposes, we may be perfectly satisfied with a "comparative recall" rather than a true recall. If, for example, we wanted to determine how successful chemists are in the on-line searching of a chemical data base to satisfy their own information needs, as compared with information specialists searching for information on the same subjects, it would be possible to express the recall of a chemist's search as

$$\frac{\text{Number of relevant items found by chemist}}{\text{Number of relevant items found by chemist + number of additional relevant items found by information specialist}}$$

For diagnostic microevaluation, however, the estimation of the recall ratio of a search by means of the conduct of further searches in the same system has one obvious disadvantage: it is limited in the type of recall failure it is likely to disclose. It may be perfectly possible to use the technique to identify recall failures due to poor searching strategies, vocabulary deficiencies, or inadequacies in user-system interaction. It is unlikely, however, that the technique will disclose indexing failures. If a document has something to do with topic X but topic X has not been indexed, it is unlikely that searcher A will retrieve this document in a search on X. It is equally unlikely that additional searchers B, C, and D will find it.

A better technique for estimating recall in an operating system is by the conduct of a parallel search in one or more other systems, which may be printed indexes. This is the technique used by Lancaster (1968a) in the evaluation of MEDLARS. The technique works as follows:

Suppose we want to estimate the recall ratio for a literature search conducted in a particular information system on the subject of, let us say, thermal pollution of water. We conduct the same search in other systems, mechanized or manual. Any systems can be used as long as they are completely independent of the system we have to evaluate. Suppose that the search, which does not necessarily have to be comprehensive, discloses 14 papers that appear to be relevant to the subject of thermal pollution of water. These papers are submitted to the requester of the original search, who judges 12 of them to be relevant. These 12 papers are

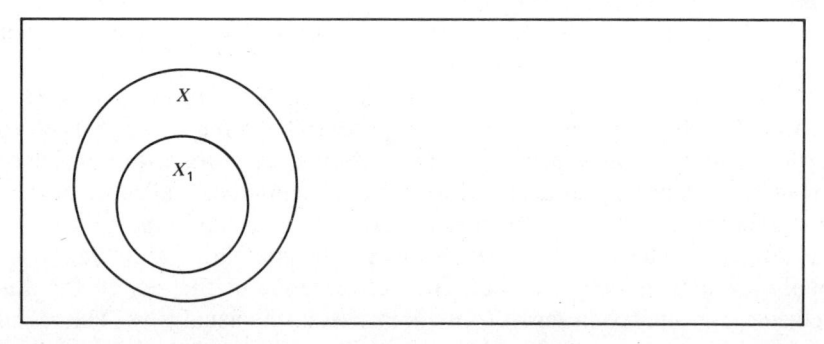

Figure 32 Estimation of recall by extrapolation of results from a known population X_1 to an unknown X.

then checked against the data base of the system we are evaluating, and 10 of them are found to be included. These 10 are then checked against the printout of the original search in the system, and 7 of them are found to be retrieved and the other 3 not retrieved. Our recall estimate for the search is, then, 7/10, or 70%.

This technique is one of extrapolating from a known population of relevant documents to an unknown population of relevant documents, as illustrated in Figure 32. For any particular request to the system, the data base, represented by the entire rectangle in Figure 32, contains a subset of documents X that the requester would judge relevant if he saw them. We do not know, however, the complete identity of this set X. The technique we used, however, identified a subset of X, namely, X_1, and the recall ratio for the subset was found to be 7/10. It is reasonable to suppose, then, that if X_1 is fully representative of X, the recall ratio for X (unknown) should approximate that for X_1 (known). The technique gives us a recall estimate for X, rather than absolute recall, but this is the best that is possible under most circumstances. The estimate can also lead to the other values of the 2×2 table of search results. Returning to the hypothetical example used earlier, our recall estimate indicates that the 15 relevant documents retrieved comprise about 70% of the total of relevant documents in the data base. If 15=70%, then 100% is approximately 21. The complete values for the table of search results thus become

	Relevant	Not relevant	Total
Retrieved	15	10	25
Not retrieved	6*	499,969*	499,975
Total	21*	499,979*	500,000

The values marked with an asterisk are estimates only, and the other values in the table are all absolutes.

There are other possible ways of estimating recall for an information retrieval system, but they are more appropriate to the evaluation of an experimental system than to a system offering an information service to an actual community of users. One of these techniques, called a "source document test," involves the fabrication of an artificial request based on the subject matter of a document known to be contained in the data base of the system to be evaluated. The performance of the search for this request is evaluated in terms of its precision in the usual way. The recall ratio merely expresses whether or not the source document, from which the request was derived, was retrieved. Recall will be 0 or 1, depending on whether or not the source document itself was retrieved. In a more refined version of this procedure, the source document itself is discarded, and the bibliographic items cited in the source document become candidate items for the estimation of recall. The recall ratio is the proportion of these items, contained in the data base to be evaluated and judged relevant according to some standard, that the system is able to retrieve.

As a result of the procedures described above, it is possible to derive performance figures for a representative sample of the searches performed by an information service. The techniques described above are as applicable to the evaluation of on-line systems, operated in a delegated search mode, as they are to the evaluation of off-line systems. In the evaluation of on-line systems, however, we must be careful to ensure that we obtain a printout of the entire dialogue between the searcher and the system, because we need this in the analysis of the search results. The evaluation of an on-line search conducted in a nondelegated mode—the person who has the information need does his own search—is a rather different situation. It is still necessary to estimate recall for such a search, using one of the techniques described earlier, but the precision ratio is a less useful measure here than some more direct measure of unit cost per relevant item retrieved. Probably the cost of the search, in dollars or in user time, rather than the precision ratio, will be balanced against the recall ratio. The evaluation of a nondelegated on-line search differs in fact very little from the evaluation on a nondelegated search in a printed index but is simpler in that the on-line system can give us a complete record of the search dialogue. We do not usually have such a record, unless we construct it somewhat artificially, in the case of a search in a printed index.

If relevance assessment forms of the type illustrated in Figure 31 are used, it is possible to derive a novelty ratio as well as a precision ratio for each search. The novelty ratio can be expressed in one of two ways:

$$\frac{\text{Number of new relevant documents retrieved}}{\text{Number of relevant documents retrieved}}$$

or

$$\frac{\text{Number of new relevant documents retrieved}}{\text{Number of documents retrieved}}$$

Measurement of the coverage of a data base requires a somewhat different evaluation procedure. One way of achieving this is through the use of specialized bibliographies in subject areas within the stated scope of the data base. Review articles are good sources of such bibliographies. Suppose one wants to determine how comprehensive *Index Medicus* is in its coverage of a particular area of medicine, say, nutrition disorders. This could be accomplished by locating several review articles covering specific aspects of the subject in the *Bibliography of Medical Reviews*. The more review articles located, and the more complete they are, the better they will fulfill this purpose. Suppose three recent review articles covering various aspects of nutrition disorders are found and that, collectively, they cite 120 unique papers in various sources. These citations are then used to assess the extent to which *Index Medicus* (IM) covers the literature of the subject; that is, each citation is checked against the author index of IM to determine which items are and which are not included until, eventually, the proportion of the 120 citations covered by the index is known.

To undertake a comprehensive evaluation of the coverage of a particular index, it is necessary to obtain several well-chosen review articles representing various facets of the subject matter under consideration. For example, a comprehensive study might be made of the coverage of the *Current Index to Journals in Education* (CIJE) through the use of, say, 12 review articles each in some specific area of education. The same technique can be used to compare the coverage of two or more indexes. Examples of the use of this procedure in the evaluation of the coverage of data bases can be found in Martyn (1967) and Martyn and Slater (1964).

ANALYSIS OF THE EVALUATION RESULTS

Having conducted an evaluation program, average recall and precision figures achieved by the system can be determined; that is, the individual performance figures of the test searches can be averaged to arrive at overall average performance figures, say, 82% recall at 14% precision or

134   Evaluating the Effectiveness of Information Services

60% recall at 35% precision.* By variations in search strategy within the group of test searches, a series of performance points can be derived to plot an average performance curve, which looks very much like that in Figure 29.

The average performance curve shows the range of system operation, on the average, at the present time. By variations in strategy, a searcher can range, on the average, up and down the performance curve. However, averages are misleading. In addition to plotting this curve, the individual performance points must also be plotted in the form of a scatter diagram, as shown in very simplified form in Figure 33. Here, curve *A* represents the present average performance curve, and each X marks an individual performance point. Note that few, if any, of the individual performance figures fall exactly on the average performance curve. In fact, the individual results scatter widely. There are some very good results (top right-hand corner), some very bad results (bottom left-hand corner), some high recall and low precision results, some high precision and low recall results, and some middle-of-the-road results. When all these various results are averaged out, average performance figures and an average performance curve can be derived.

The most important element in the evaluation program is to distinguish successes from failures. By determining what makes a good search good and what makes a bad search bad the evaluator can identify major system problems and suggest possible solutions. If, in the future, some of the searches that presently perform badly are turned into good searches, the average performance level of the system can be raised; that is, the average performance curve can be pushed up to a higher point, closer to the ideal but unattainable top right-hand corner of the plot, as illustrated by curve *B* in Figure 33.

In determining major sources of system weakness, analysis of individual failures, as described later, is used. Thorough use is also made of the performance figures. These performance figures, which should not be used to compare the performance of one system with a completely different one having different documents, requests, and users, are used to compare the performance of the system under varying conditions or modes of operation. The corpus of test searches is divided a number of

---

*It may in fact be preferable to use a recall ratio based only on documents judged of major relevance, although the precision ratio is based on documents of any degree of relevance. On the whole, it is probable that an article judged of major relevance by a requester is one that he would not want to miss, whereas a minor relevance article is one that he is quite happy to see retrieved but does not really care too strongly about. For a group of, say, 200 test searches we may be able to say that the system retrieves 81% of the major relevance documents at a precision ratio of 23%.

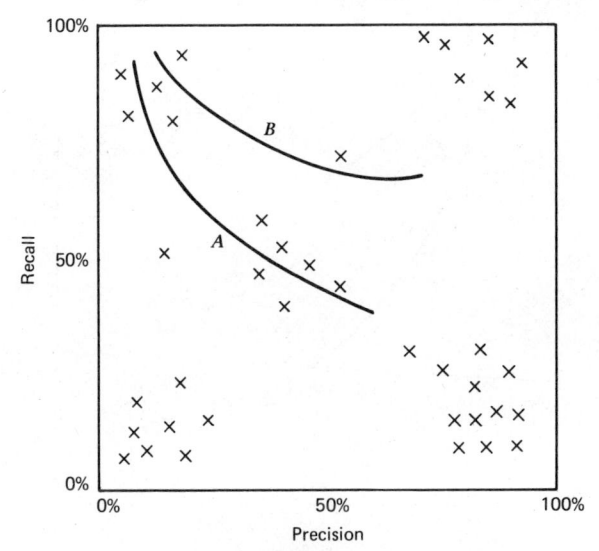

Figure 33 Scatter diagram of search results.

different ways in order that the performance figures reveal whether or not there appear to be significant differences in performance under alternative operating conditions. For example, does the system operate, on the average, better in certain subject areas than in others? Does it operate better for certain user groups than for others? Is there a particular mode of interaction in which the system appears to function most effectively—for example, personal visit of requester to center as opposed to mailing of requests? Of course, the performance figures indicate that certain things are happening in the system, but they do not indicate why they occur. This requires intellectual analysis and interpretation.

By dividing up the evaluation results in various ways, it is possible to derive a family of performance curves, each representing the performance of the system under a particular condition of use. Such a family of curves is illustrated in Figure 34.

Clearly, group 1 has produced the best results and group 3 the worst. The curves shown in Figure 34 may represent searches conducted in different subject fields, searches conducted by different processing centers, searches conducted for different types of users, searches conducted for requests arriving in various ways—by mail, by telephone, by personal visit—and so on. An analysis of this type might indicate weaknesses in the system and ways in which the performance might be improved. For example, if the group 3 curve represents searches in a particular subject

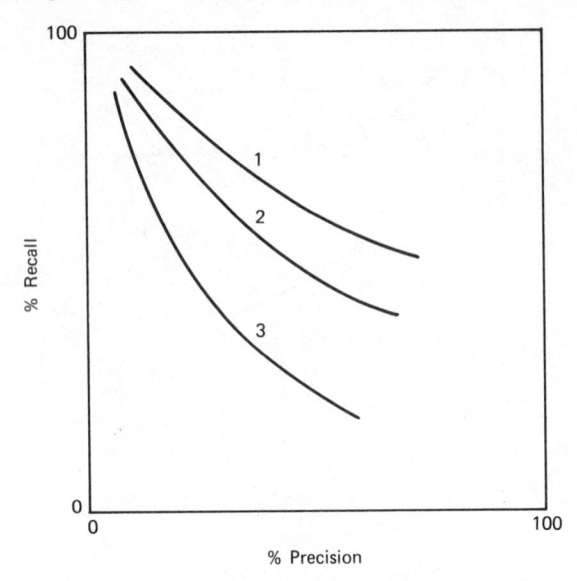

Figure 34 Recall and precision results for three groups of searches.

area, these poor results might indicate inadequacies in the vocabulary of the system in this subject field. The evaluation has pinpointed this weakness and thus allows us to take appropriate corrective action. It should be pointed out, however, that we are likely to need a fairly large number of searches to conduct, with any level of statistical confidence, the type of comparison exemplified by Figure 34.

Recall and precision ratios have another important use. Each ratio is likely to indicate a certain number of failures, and this permits us to conduct an analysis to determine why they occurred. Consider a hypothetical search in which the system retrieves 6 of the 10 "known relevant" documents and misses 4; that is, the recall ratio is 60%. The requester assesses a random sample of 25 retrieved articles, judging 10 to be of value and 15 of no value; that is, the precision ratio is 40%. In this particular search, then, we are faced with the analysis of (1) 4 recall failures and (2) 15 precision failures. It must be stressed here that the 4 recall failures and 15 precision failures are not the only failures occurring in the search. They are the only ones that we know of, and, as such, they are accepted as exemplifying the complete recall and precision failures of the search; that is, they are symptomatic of problems occurring in the search.

The hindsight analysis of a search failure is the most challenging aspect of the evaluation process. It involves, for each failure, an examination of the following:

1. The full text of the document itself.
2. The indexing record for the document, that is, the index terms assigned.
3. The request statement.
4. The search strategy on which the search was conducted.
5. The requester's completed assessment form, particularly, in a precision failure, the reason for an article being judged of no value.

On the basis of all these records, a decision is made as to the prime cause or causes of the particular failure under review. Almost all failures are attributable to some aspect of indexing, searching, the index language, or the area of interaction between the requester and the system. In a well-designed study, the attributing of precision failures, at least, is the joint decision of the requester and the evaluator, because the requester's statement of why a particular document is of no value is often a good guide to where, in fact, the system has failed. For example, suppose the requester indicates that a particular article is irrelevant because it deals with electronic noise generators whereas he wanted mechanical noise generators. When the requester gives us such a statement, we know precisely why the retrieved article fails to satisfy his information need. Now we must examine the necessary records to determine if the search was conducted too broadly; if the index language is insufficiently specific for the request, that is, it allows us to specify noise generators, but not to distinguish the electronic from the mechanical variety; if the article was incorrectly indexed; or if the request statement was inexact, that is, it did not specify an interest only in mechanical noise generators.

Whenever possible, for any one failure, a single most critical cause is isolated. In some instances, however, it is not possible to identify a single cause because two functions of the system are equally involved. For certain recall failures we can say that the article would have been retrieved if the indexer had used the additional term A_2. On the other hand, and equally important, had the searcher generalized from the adopted strategy A_1 and B and C to the reasonable approach of A and B and C, the article would also have been retrieved. In such cases, the failure must be jointly attributed to indexing and searching or whichever other elements of the system were jointly responsible.

In the MEDLARS evaluation (Lancaster, 1968a), over 302 searches, 797 recall failures, and 3038 precision failures were analyzed. These

Table 4 Major Categories of Failures Identified in the MEDLARS Evaluation

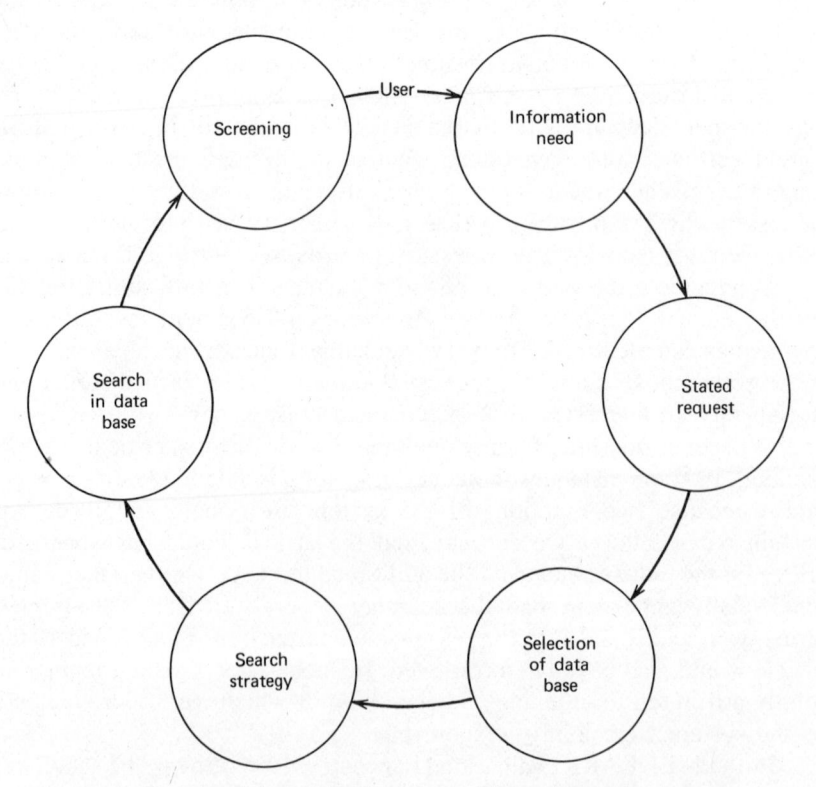

	Recall failures	Precision failures
Index language	81 (10.2%)	1094 (36.0%)
Indexing	298 (37.4%)	393 (12.9%)
Searching	279 (35.0%)	983 (32.4%)
Defective user-system interaction	199 (25.0%)	503 (16.6%)
Other	11 (1.4%)	78 (2.5%)

Figure 35 Principal steps involved in the information retrieval process.

failures were attributed to the principal system components, as shown in Table 4. Obviously, the proportions of failures, and their exact type in each category, vary from system to system. The principal types of retrieval failure, however, are common to most operating retrieval systems.

FACTORS AFFECTING THE PERFORMANCE OF INFORMATION RETRIEVAL SYSTEMS

Figure 35 depicts a sequence of actions that take place from the time that a user, needing information on some subject, comes to an information center to attempt to satisfy this need to the time that a set of search results is delivered to him. A delegated search is assumed here. The user's information need must be converted into an expressed need (stated request), the information specialist must select the most appropriate data base or data bases in which to conduct the search, he must construct an appropriate strategy, the search is conducted by matching the strategy against the data base, and the results thus achieved may be "screened" by the searcher—for example, to try to eliminate obviously irrelevant items—before being submitted to the user. Each of the steps depicted in Figure 35 introduces some potential sources of noise or information loss. Moreover, the effect is cumulative. For example, we may get some loss of information because the user's request does not accurately reflect his true information need, more loss because the data base selected is not the one most appropriate for the search, some further loss due to an inadequate search strategy, and so on. In the analysis of the results of an evaluation program, and particularly in the analysis of recall and precision failures,* the investigator attempts to determine where in the entire information service operation, as depicted in Figure 35 or, in an alternative presentation, in Figure 3, the majority of problems or failures occur. In the next four chapters the sequence of actions depicted in Figure 35 is dissected, with the object of identifying, in some detail, the factors that have greatest influence on the performance of information retrieval systems of all types.

---

*In a nondelegated search, as mentioned earlier, the precision ratio is not a very meaningful performance measure. In this situation we are probably more concerned in identifying the reasons why certain searches have involved unusually large amounts of time or have operated at very high unit costs, in time or money, per relevant item retrieved.

Chapter Ten

Latent Needs and Expressed Needs

The first steps of the information retrieval operation (see Figure 35) are those in which some individual in the community to be served by an information center recognizes a need for information and visits the center to attempt to satisfy this need.

In considering the evaluation of information services, it is important to distinguish between the information needs of the community served and the demands actually made on the service. The needs can be assumed to be more numerous than the demands (expressed needs), because not all information needs are converted into demands. The managers of information services must be concerned with identifying the information needs of the population served and with recognizing discrepancies between needs and demands. An important aspect of evaluation should be the identification of differences between needs and demands in terms of quantitative considerations—how many needs are not converted into demands—and qualitative considerations—what types of needs are not converted into demands, what factors determine whether or not a need is converted into a demand, and how well the demands of users accurately reflect their real information needs. Most evaluations of information services, unfortunately, concentrate almost exclusively on measuring the degree to which the demands of users are satisfied by the service. This is a somewhat superficial approach to evaluation in that

1. It ignores the unexpressed needs of users.
2. It assumes that the demands made by users are identical with their needs, a somewhat dangerous assumption to make.

Concentrating exclusively on the demands actually made, and accepting them at face value, is like focusing on the tip of a large iceberg and assuming that the tip is fully representative of the much greater mass that is submerged. Line (1973) has pointed out the dangers of this approach. It is obvious, of course, that demands can be recognized much more easily than needs. But an important facet of evaluation cannot be ignored simply because it is difficult.

Kochen (1975) has attempted to distinguish among "needs," "problems," and "expressions" of needs and problems. In a very simplified form the situation may be represented as follows:

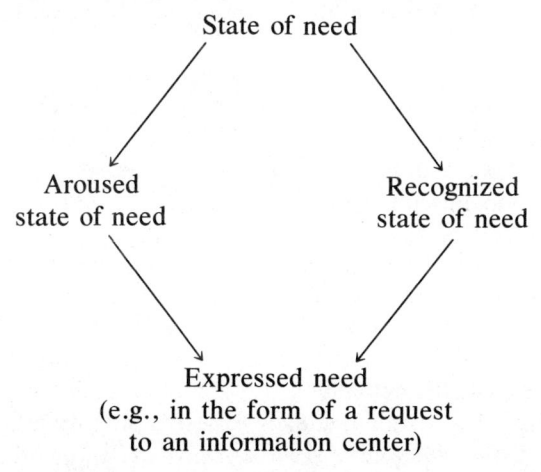

```
                    State of need
                   /            \
                  /              \
                 ↙                ↘
           Aroused            Recognized
          state of need       state of need
                 ↘                ↙
                  \              /
                   ↘            ↙
                   Expressed need
              (e.g., in the form of a request
                   to an information center)
```

Kochen distinguishes between the "need state" and its recognition or arousal. In certain states, a need may be aroused without being recognized; in others, it may be recognized without being aroused. In the context of information services, it is quite important to distinguish among information needs, their recognition, and their expression. Information systems cannot respond to information needs of individuals as such but only to expressions of their needs; that is, an individual who needs information must recognize his need for information and must, presumably, be sufficiently aroused to take some steps to satisfy it. Only after he recognizes his need and is sufficiently aroused (motivated) does he express it in the form of a "request" to an information center. The degree to which he is able to recognize the exact nature of his information need and the degree to which it is accurately reflected in its "expression," that is, in the request statement, largely determine how successful the information service is in attempting to satisfy it; that is, the information service can operate only on the basis of the stated request (expressed need) and, clearly, cannot respond to unrecognized needs or even to recognized needs that are unexpressed. One of the major problems faced by any information service operated in a delegated search mode is to ensure that expressed needs accurately reflect recognized needs. It is not always easy for the person who needs information to express his need clearly and unequivocally to the person who is to search for the information.

The distinction between needs for information services and demands for them is important because managers of information services should be as much concerned with the evaluation of the services in terms of the extent to which they match the needs of potential users as they are with their evaluation in relation to the demands made by actual users. Restricting evaluation considerations to the demands presently made on an information service ignores

1. Needs of present users that are not converted into demands for information service.
2. Needs of those within the community to be served who presently make no demands on the service.

In many situations the nonusers of a service may greatly outnumber the present users. Moreover, not all the information needs of present users are actually converted into demands. A further problem is that not all demands made on a service are perfect representations of the information need underlying the demand. Users sometimes demand less than they need. There is, in fact, some tendency for users of information services to ask for what they think the system can provide rather than what they really need. Frequently this means a demand much more general than the information need behind it.

The factors influencing needs and demands for information service are best discussed in the context of the "information service interface" diagram (Figure 2). At a general level, it can be recognized that the factors influencing the need for information service, and those influencing the extent to which these needs are converted into demands on a particular center, fall into three categories:

1. Factors relating to the universe of bibliographic and other resources.
2. Factors relating to the user population itself.
3. Factors relating to the information service interface, that is, system factors.

In Table 5 an attempt is made to arrive at a fairly comprehensive list of factors that might influence the need and the demand for formal information services. In this table, primary factors affecting needs for formal information services, both factors relating to the published literature and those relating to the population of potential users, are identified. Some secondary factors influencing the primary factors themselves are listed. Some primary and secondary factors influencing the demands for formal information services are also identified. It is important to note that the system factors themselves have no direct influence on the need for information services. They do, however, exert a strong influence on the demand for them. It is also worth noting that the "user population" factors influencing need may be considered aggregate factors, related to the population as a whole. The user population factors influencing demand, however, go beyond the aggregate factors. They include factors relating to the individual members of the population and the particular environment surrounding them.

The list of factors included in Table 5 should be regarded as tentative. It is undoubtedly incomplete. It is valuable, however, in that it shows rather clearly that needs and demands for information services are influenced by a rather complex set of variables, many of which are not under the direct control of managers of information services.

At the risk of oversimplification, an attempt has been made to reduce the complexities in Table 5 and to identify a small number of major factors that are likely to influence the need and the demand for a particular information service. Eleven such factors have been identified, as follows:

1. Growth of the literature in the field or fields covered.
2. Cost of the literature in the field or fields covered.
3. The size of the population to be served.
4. The educational level of the population to be served.
5. The accessibility—physical, intellectual, and psychological—of the information service.
6. The cost of the information service.
7. The ease of use of the service, that is, user time involved.
8. The potential user's previous experience with the service.
9. The speed of the service.
10. The value of the solution to an information problem.
11. The probability that a solution exists in the literature.

Table 5 Factors Affecting Needs and Demands for Information Services

| | FACTORS AFFECTING NEEDS ||
POPULATION OF RELEVANT LITERATURE (A)	Primary	Secondary

	Population A factors
	Growth of literature
	  a. Type of material
	  b. Subject field
		R&D expenditures (worldwide)
		Cost of publication
		Forms of publication
		Publishing delays
		Selection criteria (refereeing) and editorial standards
		Social pressures to publish
		Funds budgeted for publication

CHANNELS OF COMMUNICATION (C)		

POPULATION TO BE SERVED BY INFORMATION CENTER (B)	*Population B factors*
	Growth of population
	  a. Composition of population by educational level
	  b. Composition of population by subject area
		R&D expenditures
		Areas of emphasis in research programs

Concerns 1. Need of population B for population A 2. Demand of population B for population A 3. Factors affecting need and demand 4. Channels and systems to meet needs and demands most effectively	c. Composition of population by activity (research, development, application, etc.) d. Composition of population by age	General educational trends, especially growth of higher education in scientific and technical areas

Table 5 (Continued)

FACTORS AFFECTING DEMANDS

Primary	Secondary

Population A factors
 Cost of publication
 Form of publication
 Speed of publication
 Quality of publication
 Growth of literature
   a. type of material
   b. subject field
 Language of publication
 Method of presentation (intellectual accessibility)
	Manpower costs
	 Materials costs
	 Volume of material composed
	 Internal efficiency of editing, publishing, printing operations
	 Degree of automation
	 Editorial standards
	 Worldwide distribution of products

Population B factors
 All of the need factors, plus:
   Education in use of literature
   Knowledge of information sources
   Attitude of employer and peers toward use of literature
   Language capabilities
   Funds available for literature searching
   Adaptability to new technology
	General educational trends and policies
	 Government and institutional policies in relation to use of information
	 General economic trends

System and communication factors (C)
 Cost of information services
 Accessibility and ease of use of services
   a. Physical
   b. Intellectual
 Speed and efficiency of services, including relevance of output, etc.
 Form of output provided by system
 Flexibility of services to meet varying information needs
	Cost of communication
	 Cost of digital storage
	 Cost of computer processing
	 Development of networks
	 Cost of terminal devices
	 Growth of machine-readable data bases
	 Cost of indexing and abstracting
	 Cost of information specialists
	 Quality of indexing, abstracting
	 Number of access points per record
	 Speed of machine processing
	 Compatibility of vocabularies and query languages
	 Multilingual conversion capabilities
	 Degree of cooperation, overlap, redundancy

The factors are divided into four broad groups: those relating to the characteristics of the literature, those relating to the characteristics of the population to be served, those relating to the organization and effectiveness of the service itself, and those relating to the perceived value of the service in the eyes of the user and to the probability of success in using the service.

It seems reasonable to suppose that the need for formal information services in a subject field increases as the published literature in the field increases and that it also increases with the cost of the literature; that is, increasing publication costs force increased reliance on institutional copies rather than personal subscriptions. It also seems reasonable to expect the demand for information services to increase with the size of the population to be served and with increases in the educational level of the population.

The demand for a particular information service is likely to increase with the accessibility of the service, its ease of use, its speed, and its quality as perceived by the potential user, which is conditioned by his previous degree of success with the service. The demand can be expected to decline with increasing costs of the service.

Whether or not a particular information need is converted to a demand for information service appears very largely dependent on the value of the solution to the information problem—a solution valued at $100,000 to a particular company is more likely to be converted to a demand for information service than one valued at $500 or one perceived to have no monetary value—and the probability that a solution exists in the literature—the greater the probability, the greater the likelihood of a request for information service. Clearly, many of these factors are closely related and they trade off one against the other. The cost of the information service, for example, is likely to be a negligible consideration if the perceived value of the solution to a problem is very great.

Factors 1 to 4 and 10 to 11 are not factors under the direct control of managers of information services. Nevertheless, it is important for managers to recognize that these factors exist and that they have a significant effect on the need or the demand for information services. The system factors, of course, are more directly under the control of the managers of the service, but even these are quite heavily influenced by outside factors—for example, technological improvements and external costs—that are not directly controllable by the information service.

It is not likely that an information center can directly influence the need for information within the community served. But it can certainly influence the demand for information service through recognition of the system factors that influence demand, through the continuous evaluation of the extent to which the services provided match needs existing within the community, and through the evaluation of the extent to which demands are satisfied promptly, accurately, and completely.

USER-SYSTEM INTERACTION

So far in this chapter we have discussed some of the factors that determine whether or not an individual is likely to have a need for information and whether or not, when the need for information arises, he is likely to approach a particular information center in order to satisfy his need. Now we must consider another very important matter—the factors that influence whether or not the demand actually made on the information service, that is, the expressed need, accurately reflects the real information need of the requester.

The assumption here is that the person needing information must convey his need to a member of the staff of the information center by telephone, letter, or personal visit. This user-system interaction is clearly of the very greatest importance to the whole information retrieval process. The vocabulary of the system can be perfectly adequate to represent the concepts occurring in a request. The search strategy can be a complete and accurate representation of the request. The indexing of the data base can be complete, accurate, and consistent. But all these things are of little real value to a particular user if his request (expressed need) is an inadequate representation of his real need.

If a search in a retrieval system is to be successful, the stated request must be a reasonable approximation of the information need itself. The greater the "distance" between the stated request and the information need, the less successful the search is likely to be. Unfortunately, it is usually not at all easy for a user to describe his information need, completely and accurately, to another person. Factors that influence the success of the user-system interaction at the request stage include (1) the ability of the user to define his need in his own mind, (2) the ability of the user to express himself, (3) the user's expectations regarding the capabilities of the system—there is a strong tendency for a user to ask not for what he really wants but for what he thinks the system can give him—and (4) the amount and type of assistance given by the system. In the evaluation of MEDLARS as reported by Lancaster (1968a), a large percentage of all the failures in 300 searches was attributed to inadequate user-system interaction, resulting in verbal requests that inadequately represented the true information needs of requesters.

The usual tendency is to make requests more general than the actual

148 Latent Needs and Expressed Needs

information need, presumably because the requester suspects that the system can operate at the broader level but not at the more specific. In other words, the requester is conditioned by his expectations of the system and what he thinks it can give him. This surely is the only explanation for the nationally known cancer research scientist who asked for a search on cancer in the fetus or newborn infant, a subject on which a great deal of literature exists and for which a great deal was retrieved by the system, almost all completely irrelevant to the scientist's actual information need. In retrospect it was discovered that he was really looking for information on a very precise topic for which very little literature exists, namely, the relationship between teratogenesis and oncogenesis at the cellular level. This is a rather extreme example of the situation of a stated request very much more general than the actual information need. This relationship is represented conceptually in Figure 36. In this situation most of the documents retrieved are likely not to be relevant to the information need of the requester, although they may well match his stated request exactly.

Less frequently a request is more specific than the actual information need that brought the user to the information center. An example is the requester who asks for crossing of fatty acids through the placental barrier, and for normal fatty acid levels in the placenta or fetus. In retrospect it was discovered that this medical practitioner was interested in subject matter of somewhat broader scope, namely, crossing of lipids, that is, fatty substances in general, across the placental barrier, and normal lipid levels in placenta, fetus, or newborn infant. This situation is represented conceptually in Figure 37. The result of a request more specific than an

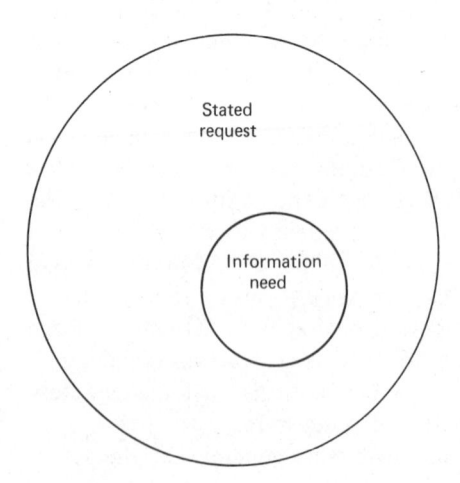

Figure 36 Request more general than information need: most documents retrieved are not relevant.

User-System Interaction   149

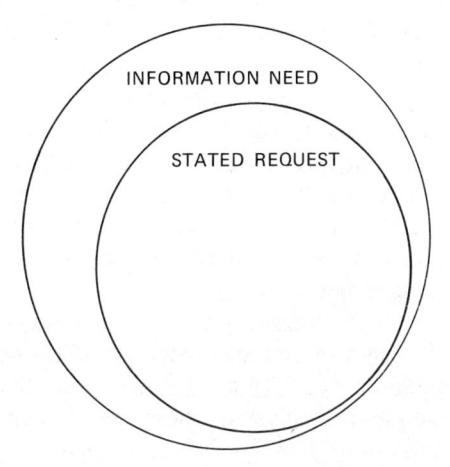

Figure 37 Request more specific than information need: documents of interest and relevance are not retrieved.

actual information need is a failure to retrieve some documents that are of relevance to the requester. This situation is rather more complex than the first simply because the expansion of the request is only likely to come as a result of a browsing, heuristic search, and not at all in the situation in which the person with the information need delegates the responsibility for the search to someone else. In the example above, the stated request represented fairly accurately what the scientist thought he wanted when he first approached the system. It was only when he saw some documents peripheral to his stated request, namely, on maternal fetal exchange of lipids and on lipid levels in the newborn, that he realized that his request was too restrictive and that these documents, outside the scope of his stated request, were in fact relevant to his current research need.

It is clear, then, that in any delegated search information system a major source of failure occurs at the user-system interface, simple failure of one human being to communicate his information needs, completely and accurately, to another.

One would suspect, however, that some modes of user-system interaction would be more effective than others. It would seem reasonable to suppose that when a scientist visits an information center directly and discusses his information need with a member of the staff, the resulting verbal statement (request statement) is a better representation of the actual information need than a request that comes to the information center by mail, without the benefit of direct face-to-face interaction between scientist and information specialist.

The evidence from the MEDLARS study does not support this hypothesis; quite the reverse, in fact. If we take the 300 searches on which the MEDLARS evaluation was based and divide them into two groups, the first consisting of searches based on requests made by personal visit to an information center and the second of searches based on requests submitted by mail, the performance on the second group is clearly superior; that is, on the average, the system was able to perform better for requests received by mail. By "better" we mean that the searches based on mailed requests were able to retrieve, on the average, more of the documents judged relevant by requesters and fewer of the documents judged irrelevant.

This discovery was unexpected and it was surprising to most people. It suggests that scientists are able to communicate their needs for information more effectively in writing than in a face-to-face situation. Subsequent analyses of these results began to reveal some reasons for this situation. It seems that, in general, the scientist who writes out his request, on a request form or in a letter, in the privacy of his own home or office, has two advantages over the scientist who makes a personal visit to an information center.

In the first place, the necessity of writing out a request statement imposes a discipline on the requester. He is forced to think about what he is really looking for and to attempt to express it clearly in writing. In the second place, he is generally uninfluenced by system constraints. Because he is physically remote from the system, he tends not to consider that the system may have limitations in its vocabulary and its search capabilities. Under these conditions the scientist tends to describe his information need in his own language and to ask for what he really wants rather than what he thinks the system can give him. Requests made to an information center in this way tend, on the whole, to be reasonably accurate descriptions of the information actually sought.

In contrast, consider the case of the scientist who makes a personal visit to an information center. In all probability he has not gone through the mental discipline of writing out a statement of his need. Consequently, it is likely that his notion of what he really wants is not completely formed in his own mind. When he comes to the information center and attempts to describe his need to a staff member, there is a very strong and definite tendency for the user to be influenced, probably unconsciously, by system constraints. Under these conditions, it seems, he is much more likely to ask for what he thinks the system is able to give him rather than for the precise information he is really seeking. This phenomenon is well known to librarians. It is exemplified by the user who comes to the library needing the address of a particular hotel in Copenhagen. Instead of asking for this, when he approaches the reference desk, he asks to see books on travel in Scandinavia.

What I claim here is that, however well intentioned the information specialist is, there is some tendency for him to influence the requester in the way the latter describes his needs. This influence may be more deleterious than beneficial when the requester has not previously thought out his information need clearly and has not stated it in writing. The likelihood of distortion is greatest when the user and the information specialist discuss the request in terms of the controlled vocabulary of the system. This immediately places an undesirable and artificial constraint on the requester. Under these conditions his information need is "forced," probably unconsciously, into the language of the system, and he may settle for something less precise or less complete than the information he really wants. This phenomenon can be illustrated by a very simple example. A user comes to an information center and indicates that he is interested in a search on the fabrication of tubes of stainless steel by means of welding processes. The user and the information specialist examine the system vocabulary together, specifically the metals terms, the welding terms, and the fabricated products terms. Because the user sees the term STAINLESS STEEL (not subdivided further) in the vocabulary, he accepts this, along with the term TUBE. In reviewing the welding terms, he sees that the specific term SHIELDED ARC WELDING exists as a subdivision of welding. He accepts the specific term. The request he leaves with the information center, then, is for a search on the subject of fabrication of stainless steel tubes by shielded arc welding processes. Unfortunately this search will not be completely satisfactory. The user is really interested in something more specific. He wants information on a stainless steel of a particular composition (chromium–nickel–vanadium), and the specific welding process he is interested in is helium arc welding. In actual fact, the system can search this specifically, by incorporating the alloy terms for chromium, nickel, and vanadium and by adding the gas term HELIUM, but the user does not realize this. Thus, he settles for a search more general than it need be in relation to his precise interest. In this he has been influenced adversely by his own interpretation of the capabilities of the system.

It should be a cardinal rule that users of information centers be required to write down a statement of their information need in their own language and that they should not attempt, initially at least, to express their need in system terms. This is important for another reason besides the matter of clarity of request. If users are asked to express their needs in terms selected from the controlled vocabulary of the system, we are never going to be able to identify areas in which the vocabulary is insufficiently specific. For example, if users are constrained to ask for shielded arc welding when they really want to search more specifically for helium arc

152   *Latent Needs and Expressed Needs*

welding or argon arc welding, we are not going to recognize the need to add these more specific terms to the vocabulary. Eventually the information center will lose many of its customers because its vocabulary has not been made sufficiently specific to keep pace with new developments in the fields covered, and consequently searches cannot be conducted with enough precision to satisfy users.

The discussion above may give the impression that any form of interaction between a requester and an information specialist, for the purpose of improving or clarifying a statement of need, is likely to degrade this statement, that is, make it further removed in some way from the actual requirement. This is not so. It appears, however, that there is an optimum stage at which this interaction process should take place. This is illustrated in Figure 38. In the sequence depicted in Figure 38*a* the request statement is the result of an interaction between requester and staff at the information center.

This interaction may cause the problems that were mentioned earlier. In the second sequence, however, the requester does not approach the information center until he has recorded his request in his own terms. The interaction between the requester and the information specialist now takes place to clarify the request. This sequence is likely to be of optimum efficiency because the staff of the information center does not step in at the request formulation stage and the system should not, therefore, adversely influence the requester in the formulation of his need.

In passing, it should be noted that the information center may be able to help its users in the formulation of adequate requests. This help can take a number of forms, from general instruction on the characteristics and capabilities of the system—by means of a user manual, for example—to the preparation of a search request form designed to help the user in stating his need precisely. Such a search request form, if well designed, can be of positive value in collecting data useful to the information staff in the interpretation of the needs of requesters. Besides a complete natural-language request statement, such a form would record details on the purpose of the search and the type of search required (comprehensive or selective). It might also present the user with a series

---

a. Requester → Information center → Request statement → Search
b. Requester → Request statement → Information center → Requester → Search

---

Figure 38 (a) Undesired, and (b) desired sequences of user–system interaction.

of check-off boxes by which the scope of his search can usefully be restricted. For example, in the field of medicine check-off boxes can be used to determine whether the requester is interested only in human studies, only in animal studies, or in both, whether he is interested only in a certain sex or age group, whether or not he is interested in case studies, in vivo studies, in vitro studies, and so on. A well-designed form can help a user to state his request explicitly and completely. In particular, it should help him to exclude various areas or aspects—for example, animal studies—that are not of interest. Probably he would not think of such exclusions without the help of the form.

Chapter Eleven

Selecting a Data Base and Searching It

Once the request has been made to the information center (see Figure 35), the next steps are for the information specialist to choose the most appropriate data base, or bases, in which to conduct the search and then to prepare an appropriate search strategy to apply to the data base selected.

The selection of the data base is relatively straightforward in the sense that this operation appears to be influenced by only three major factors:

1. Which data bases are accessible.
2. The information specialist's knowledge of the scope, coverage, and quality of available data bases.
3. His ability to match his knowledge of data bases with his understanding of the request.

The problem of selecting the most suitable data base for a particular information need is becoming more complicated, however, as more and more data bases become accessible on-line. Ten years ago, the major criterion governing the selection of a data base was its physical accessibility in the information center. The information specialist would conduct a search in those data bases—printed indexes or abstracting services—physically present in the center that seemed best to match the user's request statement. Most information centers would own a relatively small number of these printed tools, and their characteristics would be known rather thoroughly by the staff. It was therefore a rather simple matter to decide which to try first, which second, and so on. But on-line access to data bases changes all this. A small information center, instead of having access to, say, a score of printed indexes, finds itself capable of accessing over 100 data bases through an on-line terminal. Some of these data bases are highly specialized and might need to be used very infrequently by a particular information center. The staff of the center must, nevertheless, know of their existence, know how to access them, and know, or at least be able to find out rather quickly, how to search them. After all, one of these rather obscure data bases might be exactly on target for a particular request.

As more and more machine-readable data bases appear, and as more and more become readily accessible on-line, the problem of knowing which data base to try first for any particular request becomes increasingly difficult. It seems likely, in fact, that there will be a need for some kind of on-line referral center to aid in this process of data base selection.

The on-line referral data base tells an on-line user, for any preliminary inquiry he makes, which data bases have the greatest probability of satisfying his needs. In fact, the referral data base should have the capability of ranking substantive data bases according to the degree to which their characteristics match those of the preliminary inquiry. The on-line referral center would need to store, in one alphabetical sequence, the "vocabularies" of data bases accessible on-line. Any alphabetical vocabulary can be accommodated, whether in the form of thesaurus, list of subject headings, or list of key words. In principle, the referral data base stores only the following data against each term:

1. Identification of the data bases in which the term occurs.
2. The frequency with which the term occurs in each data base, where these figures are available.

The on-line user, faced with a particular information need, calls up the referral center and puts in a preliminary inquiry. Depending on the type of matching algorithm adopted in implementation of the system, the inquiry may be some form of Boolean strategy, an unweighted list of terms, a weighted list of terms, or simply a description of the information need in sentence form.

156   *Selecting a Data Base and Searching It*

The inquiry is matched against the referral data base, and the substantive data bases referenced there are given a numerical score reflecting the probability that the data base satisfies the information need. Presumably the score reflects the degree of match between the terms of the inquiry and those of the data base, taking into account also the frequency with which various terms occur in various data bases. As output, which should be generated within seconds, the referral file displays a ranked list of data bases showing, against each, its numerical score in relation to the inquiry and giving details as to how the file can be accessed, including, possibly, costs of interrogation.

A modest beginning toward such a referral data base is the issuance on microfiche, by Lockheed Information Systems, of vocabularies consolidating those of several data bases made available on-line by Lockheed. In 1976, the National Science Foundation awarded a grant to the Information Retrieval Research Laboratory, the University of Illinois, to undertake a feasibility study on an automatic data base selector. This data base selector is very similar in concept to the referral data base mentioned above. Some preliminary results of this study are presented by Williams and MacLaury (1977).

SEARCHING STRATEGIES

The construction of search strategies for computer-based retrieval systems has already been illustrated in Chapter 3 and, for on-line systems, in Chapter 4. The present discussion is more concerned with some theoretical aspects of search strategy construction and with factors that determine whether or not a particular strategy is successful.

A search strategy is essentially a statement of what classes a document should belong to before it should be retrieved. The simplest search is therefore one that involves but a single document class—for example, a search for all documents that have been assigned to the class helicopters. We can enlarge the class of acceptable documents by summing two or more classes—for example, helicopters or air cushion vehicles—which means that we are willing to accept any document that is a member of one or the other, or both, of the summed classes. We can reduce the class of acceptable documents by intersecting classes. For example, we can specify that we want documents that have been assigned to the class helicopters and also to the class aerodynamic loading. The class of acceptable documents may also be reduced by bringing Boolean complementation into play. We could, for instance, specify that we are willing to accept documents belonging to the class helicopters but not if they are also members of the class military aircraft.

A search strategy, then, is a statement of the class membership requirements of an acceptable document, expressed in terms of logical sums, products, and complements. Such a formulation can be displayed graphically, as in Figure 39, which presents part of a search formulation designed to retrieve documents on the subject of the toxicity of chlorinated hydrocarbons. This formulation demands the retrieval of any document that has been indexed by any one of the hydrocarbon terms in block 1 and also by any term indicating chlorination or halogenation (block 2) and also by a term indicating toxicity (block 3). The techniques of class intersection, summation, and complementation are used to vary the "exhaustivity" and "specificity" of the search formulation. Imagine a request for literature on oximetry applied to patients with pulmonary emphysema. This request involves only two facets or categories: the measurement technique facet and the disease facet. If we recognize both facets or categories and demand their cooccurrence, we are being exhaustive in our search strategy.

We can, however, recognize each of these facets at any of several levels, as illustrated below:

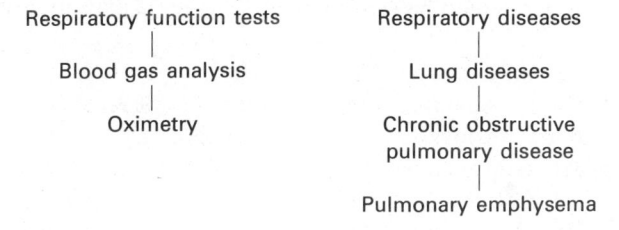

```
   Respiratory function tests           Respiratory diseases
              |                                  |
      Blood gas analysis                   Lung diseases
              |                                  |
          Oximetry                     Chronic obstructive
                                        pulmonary disease
                                                 |
                                       Pulmonary emphysema
```

If we specify that both facets occur at exactly the level of specificity demanded in the request, that is, we use terms defining precisely the classes oximetry and pulmonary emphysema, we are being fully exhaustive and fully specific in our strategy for this request. We can, therefore, expect that the group of retrieved documents will, in the main, be highly relevant to the request; that is, we will achieve a high precision.

To improve our recall for this request, by pulling in a larger class of potentially relevant documents, we can move in one of two directions. Either we can reduce the exhaustivity of the formulation or we can reduce its specificity. We usually reduce specificity by moving up in one of the hierarchies, without omitting it entirely. For example, we could move to the more generic class blood gas analysis and demand that this cooccur with a term indicating pulmonary emphysema. Or we could reduce

158   Selecting a Data Base and Searching It

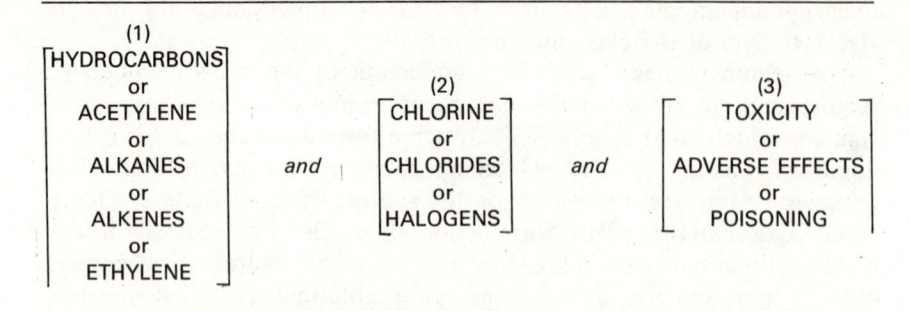

$$\begin{bmatrix} (1) \\ \text{HYDROCARBONS} \\ \text{or} \\ \text{ACETYLENE} \\ \text{or} \\ \text{ALKANES} \\ \text{or} \\ \text{ALKENES} \\ \text{or} \\ \text{ETHYLENE} \end{bmatrix} \text{ and } \begin{bmatrix} (2) \\ \text{CHLORINE} \\ \text{or} \\ \text{CHLORIDES} \\ \text{or} \\ \text{HALOGENS} \end{bmatrix} \text{ and } \begin{bmatrix} (3) \\ \text{TOXICITY} \\ \text{or} \\ \text{ADVERSE EFFECTS} \\ \text{or} \\ \text{POISONING} \end{bmatrix}$$

Figure 39 Graphic representation of a search strategy.

specificity in the disease category and ask, as an example, for the cooccurrence of the class lung diseases and the class oximetry. We can, of course, reduce specificity in more than one category simultaneously. For instance, we could demand cooccurrence of the class blood gas analysis and the class lung diseases. Alternatively, we can broaden our search, with the object of improving recall, by reducing exhaustivity in the formulation, that is, by omitting a category entirely. If we asked only for the class oximetry, we would be searching at a low exhaustivity level for the stated request.

Exhaustivity of a search strategy is obviously related to the coordination level, that is, the number of index terms required to cooccur before an article can be retrieved, but there may not be a strict one-to-one relationship between exhaustivity and coordination level. For example, PROTEIN DEFICIENCY and DYSENTERY and INTESTINAL MICROORGANISMS is a three-term coordination that is exhaustive in that it covers all the facets demanded by a particular requester, but so also does PROTEIN DEFICIENCY and DYSENTERY, BACILLARY, which is a two-term coordination. Moreover, by varying the coordination level, we may vary the specificity rather than the exhaustivity of the search. Take a request for metastatic fat necrosis as a complication of pancreatitis. The formulation PANCREATITIS and NECROSIS is exhaustive in that it asks for the cooccurrence of the two notions specified. The three-term coordination PANCREATITIS and NECROSIS and ADIPOSE TISSUE is more specific in relation to the request. Obviously, exhaustive formulations are responsible for some recall failures, and nonexhaustive formulations cause precision failures.

When we reduce the specificity of a search, we do not necessarily have to substitute for the required specific term A_1 the immediately more generic term A in the hierarchical tree. We can reduce specificity by accepting alternates for A_1—for example, its brothers in the hierarchy A_2 and A_3 and perhaps also a term B_1 from a completely different hierarchy. In other words, instead of asking only for A_1, the searcher generalizes to acceptance of A_1 or A_2 or A_3 or B_1. For example, consider a request for literature on prevalence, incidence, and epidemiology of ocular tumors. In one subsearch the searcher uses GENETICS, HUMAN as a coordinate with neoplasm terms. By doing so, he is virtually generalizing to accept prevalence, incidence, epidemiology, and genetic aspects of ocular tumors, and we must not be surprised if the search retrieves irrelevant case studies of familial gliomas, retinoblastomas, and other ocular tumors.

It is dangerous to make general statements on the matter of searching strategies. The optimum level of generality to adopt obviously varies from search to search. However, we can usefully consider some fundamentals by reference to the hierarchy below:

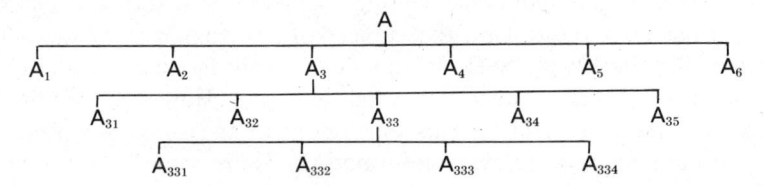

```
                          A
    ┌─────┬─────┬─────┼─────┬─────┐
   A₁    A₂    A₃    A₄    A₅    A₆
          ┌─────┬─────┼─────┬─────┐
         A₃₁   A₃₂   A₃₃   A₃₄   A₃₅
                ┌─────┬─────┼─────┐
               A₃₃₁  A₃₃₂  A₃₃₃  A₃₃₄
```

In this diagram A_{331} to A_{334} are subclasses of class A_{33}, which is itself a subclass of A_3, which is a subclass of A.

Let us assume a request for documents on the subject of sulphide inclusion content in various types of steel. This is a fairly specific request that may retrieve few documents. To generalize the search formulation, in order to optimize recall, we might legitimately decide to move up one level in the inclusion category, as from A_{33} to A_3, to pull in all nonmetallic inclusions. We are now conducting a generic search on the subject of nonmetallic inclusions; that is, we are accepting any document that belongs to the nonmetallic inclusion class A_3, including all members of the specific subclasses A_{31}, A_{32}, A_{33}, A_{34}, and A_{35}, and all members of the subclasses of these—for example, A_{332}, A_{333}, A_{334}. Of course, if we wish to generalize further, we can move up to A and undertake a generic search on the broader subject of inclusions, pulling in A, its subclasses, sub-subclasses, and so on, down to the most specific classes in the hierarchy.

Under certain circumstances we may wish to restrict the level at which a generic search is carried out. Imagine a request for general background articles on inclusions in steel. The requester may well feel that articles indexed under the term inclusions (A) or nonmetallic inclusions (A_3) would be useful but that articles indexed with more specific terms, as A_{33}, sulphide inclusions, would probably be too specialized for his interests. In this case we can undertake a first-level generic search, retrieving articles indexed A in general, or belonging to its subclasses A_1 to A_6, but not members of the more specific subclasses A_{31} to A_{35}.

In some situations we wish to search more than a single class in a hierarchical array but feel that we would be retrieving too much irrelevant material by moving up a generic level. Here a sibling search may be indicated; that is, we search selected brothers in the hierarchical tree of classes, perhaps A_{31}, A_{33}, or A_{34}, but not A_{32} or A_{35}. For example, assume a search on the subject of bending of anisotropic plates. In the deformation category, we may decide to accept the class bending and the class deflection but to reject the other siblings in this hierarchy.

A superordinate search, to be distinguished from a generic search, may be indicated in certain retrieval situations. A superordinate search is exemplified by moving from A_{33} to A_3 and accepting documents indexed with either class label, but not accepting documents indexed A_{31}, A_{32}, A_{34}, or A_{35}. Imagine a request on the subject of hemangiomas of the small intestine. Specifically we seek documents that are members of the class hemangioma and also of the class small intestine. However, we should realize that more general articles on tumors of the small intestine are likely to contain some relevant information. These may be acceptable, whereas articles on other specific tumors in the small intestine are definitely of no interest. In this case we are accepting A_{33} and A_3, but not A_{31}, A_{32}, A_{34}, or A_{35}.

Conversely, we may wish to conduct a subordinate search, exemplified by a search commencing at A_3, but later expanded to selected subclasses such as A_{31} and A_{35}. We might, for example, first specify that acceptable articles should be indexed with the term epilepsy, later elaborating to accept also items indexed with certain more specific class labels, say, photic epilepsy and reading epilepsy.

When a requester asks for a specific topic, broadening of the search to the immediate generic term, that is, a superordinate search, but not conducting a generic search on this term, may well be justified. Searching on brothers in the hierarchical tree is usually not justified. If a request relates to A_3, we would normally expect that articles indexed with the more specific terms A_{31} to A_{35} would be relevant. We might also expect that certain articles indexed under A would be relevant. We would not normally expect that articles indexed under A_1 and A_2, which are classes that should exclude A_3, would be relevant unless (1) the request statement is an imperfect representation of the actual information need, (2) the construction of the hierarchy is defective, or (3) some documents are misindexed.

Consider the previously mentioned request for literature on hemangiomas of the small intestine. The interest lies in a specific tumor (hemangioma) of the small bowel. The searcher uses the term hemangioma, A_3, and would certainly be justified in including terms A_{31} to A_{35} for kinds of hemangioma—for example, hemangioma, cavernous. Expansion to filial terms—for example, hemangiopericytoma, A_4, and hemangioendothelioma, A_5—is not justified on the basis of this request statement, because hemangiopericytomas and hemangioendotheliomas, although they are in some ways like hemangiomas, are not kinds of hemangiomas. On the other hand, expansion of the search from articles on hemangioma of the small bowel to include general articles on tumors of the small bowel, that is, moving from A_3 to search also on the general term A, seems quite desirable if we wish for high recall, because we can expect at least some of these more general articles to include discussion on hemangiomas, although, because of nonspecific indexing, the precise term hemangioma may not have been applied.

Broadening of a search strategy is usually justified when the precise topic of interest to the requester is not adequately covered by appropriate specific terms in the vocabulary. However, when the precise topic of interest is adequately covered by appropriate specific terms, broadening of the search is usually unjustified. Imagine a request for documents on analog models of inert gas exchange. The controlled vocabulary of the system does not include a generic term for the inert gases, although it does have terms for certain individual inert gases. In this situation, the searcher would probably be justified in broadening to a generic search on gases, in coordination with analog models, because no term exists to cover the inert gases as a group.

In other cases, in which a specific term is available to cover the topic specified by the requester, search generalization may not be justified. Consider a request for articles on aspergillosis of the orbit. The area of interest relates to the effect of one particular mycosis, covered precisely by the term aspergillosis, caused by one particular fungus, covered precisely by the term aspergillus. It might be unwise to generalize the search to all fungal diseases of the orbit by generic search on the terms MYCOSES and FUNGI in coordination with ORBIT, because such a strategy must inevitably result in the retrieval of many documents that can have no possible relevance to aspergillosis.

An important problem in searching is deciding which aspect of the request to generalize on. For the preceding request, we have indicated that it would be unwise to generalize in the disease category, thereby including terms for specific fungal diseases that are clearly outside the scope of the request. In this case, it might be more sensible to retain the specific terms ASPERGILLUS and ASPERGILLOSIS, but to expand in the anatomy facet by searching on terms relating to the eye in general and to adjacent anatomic structures, on the grounds that aspergillosis of the orbit may spread from elsewhere, particularly from one of the sinuses.

From the point of view of precision, it is usually disastrous to generalize in two facets of the request simultaneously; that is, given a request for A_1 in relation to B_1, under certain conditions it is reasonable to hold A_1 constant and expand to B (A_1 and B) or to hold B_1 constant and expand to A (A and B_1). However, the concurrent expansion of both categories (A and B) is rarely justified, because it almost invariably results in extremely low precision.

On certain topics, because of the characteristics of the literature or because of indexing conventions, to obtain high recall, it may be essential to expand the scope of the search. Take, for instance, the subject of tissue preservation. Much data on preservation is included in articles on transplantation—for example, heart preservation in articles on heart transplantation. Therefore, a search on preservation might need to be expanded to preservation and transplantation in order to achieve a reasonable recall.

A common failure occurs when the searcher does not list all the terms needed to complete a full generic search in a particular category. As one instance, a search on aerodynamic loading of thin wings may require that terms for specific types of loading be included with the general term AERODYNAMIC LOADING in the search formulation.

Recall failures also tend to occur when a searcher forgets that document classes may be members of several hierarchies and that a search may be generalized in a number of directions. Take a search on the subject of Reynolds stress in a two-dimensional parallel boundary layer. This may be generalized to Reynolds stress in boundary layers. It may also be generalized to Reynolds stress in parallel flow.

Some searching failures may be attributable to lack of ingenuity or persistence on the part of the searcher. Some examples will illustrate how a searcher may fail to exhaust reasonable search possibilities:

1. In a search on heat transfer between concentric cylinders, the searcher did not recognize that a concentric cylinder is a channel and that a legitimate formulation would be heat transfer in channel flow.
2. In a search on pitching moments at transonic speeds, the searcher did not try longitudinal stability as a substitute for pitching moments.
3. In a search on effects of hydrogen in metals, the searcher asked merely for the cooccurrence of the term HYDROGEN with any metal

term. No attempt was made to search on terms describing possible effects—for example, EMBRITTLEMENT.
4. In a search relating to pressurized cabins, the searcher insisted on the idea of pressurized cabins but failed to use the notion of cabin pressurization.
5. In a search on fillers suitable for use in buoyancy applications the searcher demanded the term BUOYANCY in every subsearch. No subsearches were made on terms covering obvious buoyancy applications, as buoys, lifebuoys, life preservers, and life rafts.
6. In a search on oral manifestations of neutropenia, the only terms used to express oral manifestations were ORAL MANIFESTATIONS, DIAGNOSIS, and anatomical terms relating to the oral cavity. No attempt was made to search on term combinations describing particular possible manifestations—for example, neutropenia terms and STOMATITIS.

Some searching failures may be due to lack of subject knowledge on the part of the searcher. Take, for instance, a request for literature on ignition qualities of aluminum borohydride. In error, the formulator may use the term SOLID FUELS for aluminum borohydride, when in fact it is a liquid fuel.

A rather different type of search failure occurs when the formulator tries to be too clever. For example, consider a request made to a retrieval system in the field of undersea warfare, on the subject of patch materials applied to life preserver coated fabrics. The searcher assumed that plastics were implied and asked for reports indexed with the term PLASTIC COATINGS. In fact, the relevant documents dealt with rubber coatings and adhesives.

Another threat to recall lies in the overexhaustive search formulation. Imagine a request for literature on frozen blood platelets. The search is conducted on

				FREEZING
				or
				REFRIGERATION
		BLOOD PRESERVATION		or
(platelet terms)	and	or	and	ICE
		BLOOD BANKS		or
				(other refrigeration technic terms)

In this strategy the searcher is demanding the cooccurrence of two terms relating to preservation as well as a term for blood platelets. This is overexhaustive and is likely to result in a low recall ratio.

Many requests made to an information retrieval system factor into two distinct parts: (1) the essential topic itself and (2) the point of view from which it is being regarded. A request may relate to a particular disease from the point of view of epidemiology, genetic aspects, joint involvement, or one of many other possible approaches. Likewise, a request on a particular chemical substance may be from the viewpoint of nutritional aspects, therapeutic use, and so on. Many of these aspects tend to recur frequently in requests, and it may be possible to reduce them to standard strategies, by establishing consensus among search analysts, that can be stored in machine-readable form and incorporated into a search formulation simply by citing a unique identifying number. Such preestablished strategies may not be 100% transferable from search to search, but they should have fairly general applicability. They could reduce recall failures in searching and at the same time economize on the time of search analysts.

SOME GUIDANCE IN THE CONDUCT OF AN ON-LINE SEARCH

One of the great advantages of an on-line system is that is is interactive. It is not expected that the user should have developed a search strategy, at a level of fine detail, before he sits down at the terminal. Indeed, this would be somewhat undesirable because an on-line system gives the user the capability of developing a search strategy on a trial-and-error basis. It is likely that the user will be led to new search terms or approaches as the dialogue with the system proceeds. Nevertheless, it is wise to give some thought to a particular search problem before the search is begun at the terminal. This will help to ensure that the search proceeds in a logical manner and that the time in which the user is connected to the system is used as efficiently as possible.

Basically, the search for information on a particular subject has two major components:

1. The conceptual analysis of what is really wanted.
2. The translation of the analysis into the set of terms used to represent the sought concepts in the particular data base to be searched.

It is always wise to "factor" a request for information mentally into its component facets before proceeding further with a search. Thus, a request for information on the prevention of odors in the paper industry can be recognized to have two facets: (1) odor prevention and (2) paper industry. Specifically, documents are sought on the logical product of these two facets:

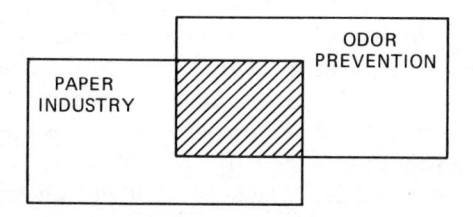

```
                    ┌──────────────────┐
                    │      ODOR        │
            ┌───────┼──┐ PREVENTION    │
            │ PAPER │▓▓│               │
            │INDUSTRY▓▓│               │
            │       │▓▓│               │
            │       └──┼───────────────┘
            │          │
            └──────────┘
```

The diagram can be considered to represent a conceptual analysis of this very simple request.

The conceptual analysis, of course, now has to be translated into the terms used to represent these concepts in the particular data base to be searched. To do this, the searcher must examine the data base, in printed form or via on-line display, in order to select the set of terms that seem most appropriate. This "term expansion" can also be represented diagrammatically:

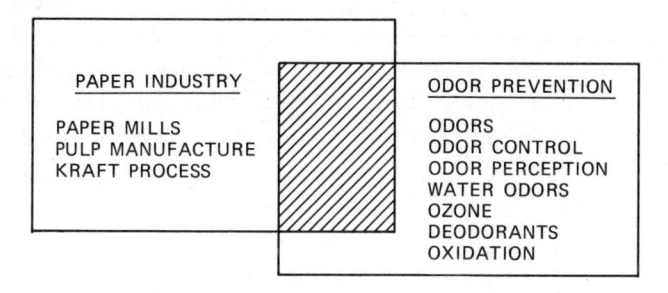

```
    ┌──────────────────┬──────────────────────┐
    │ PAPER INDUSTRY   │▓▓│ ODOR PREVENTION   │
    │                  │▓▓│                   │
    │ PAPER MILLS      │▓▓│ ODORS             │
    │ PULP MANUFACTURE │▓▓│ ODOR CONTROL      │
    │ KRAFT PROCESS    │▓▓│ ODOR PERCEPTION   │
    │                  │▓▓│ WATER ODORS       │
    │                  │▓▓│ OZONE             │
    │                  │  │ DEODORANTS        │
    │                  │  │ OXIDATION         │
    └──────────────────┴──────────────────────┘
```

Some interesting points emerge from this hypothetical example. The searcher has entered the vocabulary of the data base under ODOR PREVENTION. This term is not present, but the alphabetical display leads to ODORS, ODOR CONTROL, and ODOR PERCEPTION, which are all potentially useful search terms. Using the cross-reference structure of the thesaurus, the searcher is led from ODORS to WATER ODORS and from ODOR CONTROL to DEODORANTS. The term DEODORANTS, in turn, leads to OXIDATION and OZONE, which can be presumed to have something to do with the deodorizing process. A similar expansion of the other facet of the request leads the searcher to PAPER MILLS, PULP MANUFACTURE, and KRAFT PROCESS, which appear to be the only terms in this data base that have anything to do with the manufacture of paper. If the cross-reference structure of the thesaurus is complete, this set of terms may also be considered to be complete. If the thesaurus structure is incomplete, however, it is quite possible that additional search terms will be suggested as the on-line search proceeds.

The diagram, with index terms included, may be considered to represent a reasonable search strategy for the request. If a document has been indexed by at least one of the paper industry terms and at least one of the odor prevention terms, it can be presumed to have something to do with odor prevention in the paper industry.

It should be recognized, however, that not all the terms can be considered to carry equal weight in relation to the request. Although all the terms on the left of the diagram seem equally useful indicators of the paper industry, those on the right are not all equally relevant to odor prevention. The term ODOR CONTROL seems most relevant, with perhaps the terms that might represent particular approaches to odor control—OXIDATION, DEODORANTS, OZONE—at the next level. The terms ODORS, WATER ODORS, and ODOR PERCEPTION are lower in the ranking because the element of prevention is not directly implied by these terms. Nevertheless, a document indexed under one of these terms and also under a paper industry term may reasonably be expected to have some degree of relevance to the subject of odor prevention in the paper industry. The fact that we can rank the list of terms in a kind of sequence of "probable relevance" is quite important because this sequence represents the order in which the search should logically proceed on-line:

1. A
2. A and B
3. A and C
4. A and D

where A represents the paper industry terms and B, C, and D the odor terms in a sequence of probable relevance.

For the user who wants to locate only the most relevant documents, the search may be terminated at the second search statement, assuming that some relevant documents are found, but the user who needs a comprehensive bibliography will want to carry the search further to make sure that nothing is missed. Any information need, however complex it may seem on the surface, can be converted into a logical search strategy as long as it is "reduced" in the way illustrated above. Some examples are given below at the "conceptual" level:

Some Guidance in the Conduct of an On-Line Search   167

1. Weldability of chemically vapor deposited tungsten

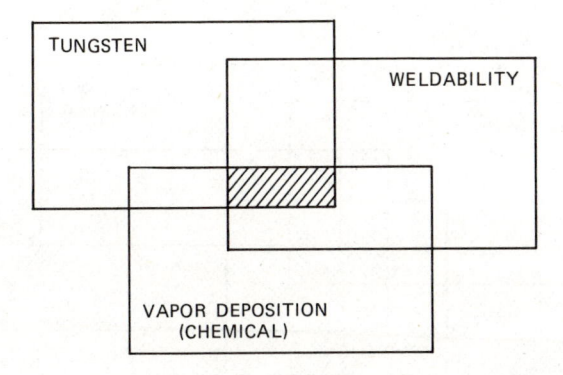

2. Deflection of square frames under distributed impulsive loads

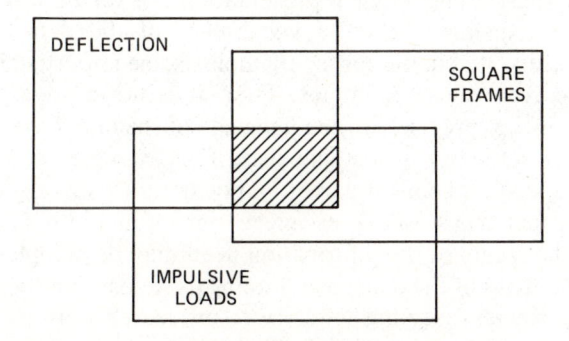

3. Measurement of the width of cracks in partially prestressed concrete beams

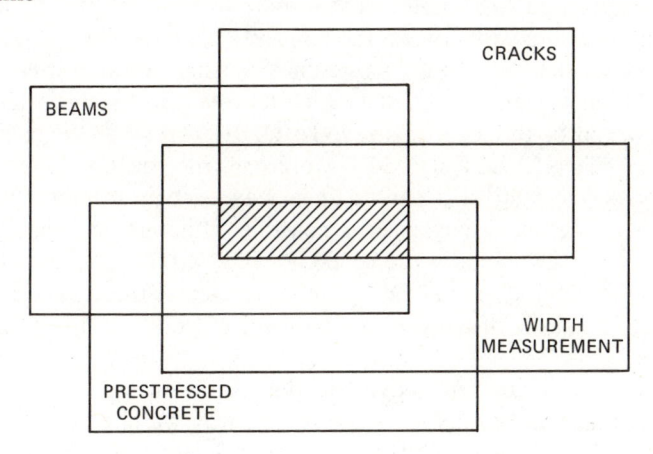

168   Selecting a Data Base and Searching It

4. Use of gauzes other than rhodium-platinum gauzes in ammonia oxidation

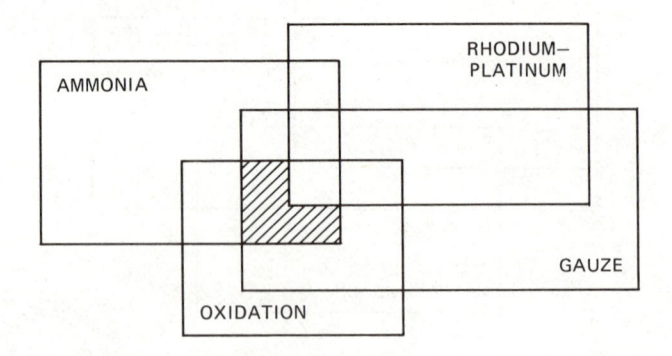

Each of these conceptual representations of an information need must now be expanded into the vocabulary of the data base to be searched, as illustrated in the earlier example. Some important lessons are to be learned from these examples. First, it is not always possible to represent a concept precisely in the language of the data base. We sometimes have to settle for something less. For example, it may not be possible to specify chemical vapor deposition, to distinguish square frames from other types, to express measurement of width, and so on. In fact, one of the facets of the information need may be completely absent from the vocabulary of the data base, forcing us to search more broadly. If there is no term representing loads, we can search only on deflection of square frames. If there is a specific load term but no deflection term, we can search only on impulsive loads on square frames. And so on.

A second point to be noted is that there may not always be a direct one-to-one relationship between the concepts we have identified and the vocabulary of the data base. Sometimes a single term present in the vocabulary may itself represent two or more facets of the search. An example would be the term AMMONIA OXIDATION or the term PRESTRESSED CONCRETE BEAMS. Moreover, the vocabulary of the data base may divide subject areas up in a way that is different from the searcher's conceptual analysis. It is possible, although perhaps unlikely, that the vocabulary includes the term CRACK WIDTH and also the term MEASUREMENT. We must be careful to recognize these possibilities in converting a search strategy from the level of concepts to the level of terms.

We do not necessarily advocate that a search strategy should be mapped out diagrammatically in exactly the way we have illustrated but merely that it is well worthwhile to adopt some systematic approach to the analysis of an information need before the search is conducted. Nevertheless, the use of diagrams of the type illustrated, which can be sketched out in a few seconds, does have value in clarifying what is wanted in a search. The technique has been found to be particularly valuable for an information specialist to use in discussing an information need with a client (see, for example, Smith, 1976).

It is important to recognize that one has considerable flexibility in the construction of a search strategy for use with an on-line retrieval system. If you need to find only a few relevant references on a subject, you use the most specific and obvious approach. But if you need a really comprehensive search, you can enlarge the scope of the strategy in order to ensure that you do not miss anything of value. It is possible to enlarge the scope of a search in one of two ways:

1. Searching one of the required facets at a more general level, that is, reducing specificity.
2. Dropping one of the required facets completely, that is, reducing exhaustivity.

There is a danger in being too precise in a search. Take, as an example, the search on measurement of the width of cracks. If you combine the four terms BEAMS, CRACKS, PRESTRESSED CONCRETE, and MEASUREMENT by means of the logical AND, any documents retrieved will almost certainly be relevant. But, with such a precise strategy, it is very likely that you will not retrieve everything of potential relevance. In fact, you may not retrieve anything at all. You are assuming that all relevant documents have been indexed in exactly the way that you visualize them to be, and this is a dangerous assumption.

The combination BEAMS and CRACKS and PRESTRESSED CONCRETE, omitting the term MEASUREMENT, may well produce something of relevance. This strategy might retrieve articles on measurement of cracks in which the term MEASUREMENT has been omitted, for some reason, in indexing. It may also retrieve more general reports on cracking of prestressed concrete beams, in which the measurement of the cracks is discussed, but this aspect has not been covered specifically in the indexing.

One must use imagination in searching. One must also avoid the assumption that the indexing of the documents in the data base completely and exactly matches one's own conception of how they should be indexed. Any of the following term combinations might reasonably be expected to produce some references relevant to the specific topic of concern:

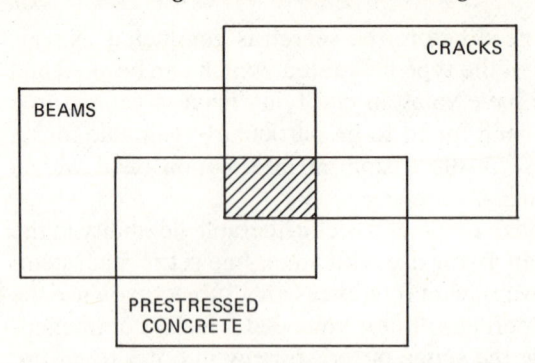

Measurement may be discussed but not specifically indexed.

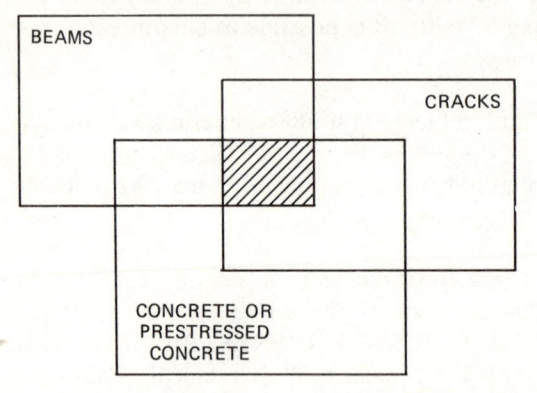

A report on cracks in concrete beams in general might have relevance to the subject of cracks in prestressed concrete beams or an article on prestressed concrete may have been erroneously indexed under the more general term CONCRETE.

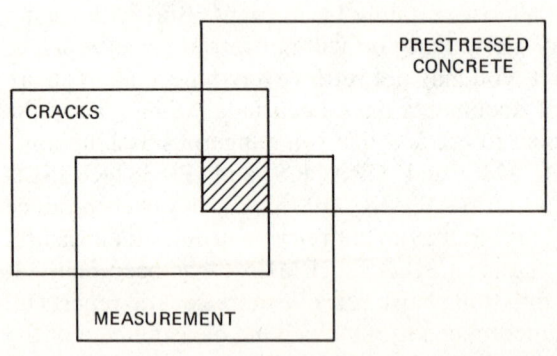

A report on measurement of cracks in prestressed concrete may be equally relevant to measurement of cracks in concrete beams.

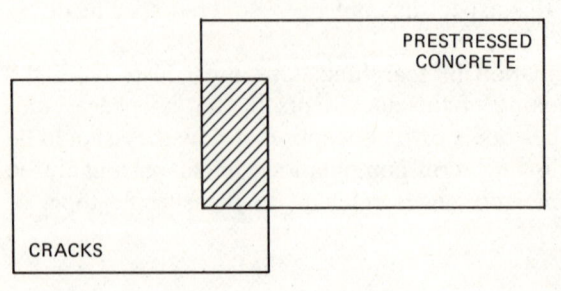

Any report on the cracking of prestressed concrete may discuss the measurement of the cracks.

The point is that it is very easy to test these various combinations at the terminal.

One can try the most precise approaches first, and if they are not successful, generalize the search in a logical manner. Even if the precise search is successful, that is, retrieves some relevant items, you will want to generalize to the other possibilities if you need a really comprehensive search on the subject.

Obviously, however, there are some penalties associated with generalization. The more a search is generalized, the more you can expect to retrieve some documents that are not relevant to your interests. The highly precise strategy BEAMS and PRESTRESSED CONCRETE and MEASUREMENT and CRACKS is unlikely to retrieve any documents that are not relevant to the current information need, but it might not retrieve any documents at all. The more you generalize from this point, the more documents you are likely to retrieve and the greater the probability that you will find some that are relevant. At the same time, however, you are increasing the possibility of retrieving irrelevant items. The combination PRESTRESSED CONCRETE and CRACKS may retrieve many items that have nothing specifically to do with the measurement of cracks, much less the measurement of cracks in beams. Nevertheless, this general combination may be the only one to retrieve documents having any relevance to the subject of interest.

You must "play it by ear" in searching an information retrieval system. Fortunately, however, an on-line system makes it very easy to search "by ear" in this way. In general, then, an on-line search is likely to be most effective, in terms of finding relevant documents, and most efficient, in terms of saving time, if it proceeds according to the following sequence:

1. Conceptual analysis of an information need into its component facets, mentally at least, but also diagrammatically if this is found to be helpful.
2. Using on-line vocabulary displays or printed displays to identify the relevant terms for each facet in the language of the data base to be searched.
3. Trying out the term combinations in a logical sequence according to the probable relevance to the request.
4. Displaying some of the retrieved references on-line to see if these records suggest additional search terms or search approaches.
5. When this iterative procedure is no longer productive, that is, when no new search terms or search approaches are suggested, printing the search results on-line or off-line.

There are ways in which searching effort or search time can be minimized in many on-line systems. A truncation feature, if used carefully, can greatly reduce the amount of typing you would otherwise need to do. For example, if a long list of paper industry terms exists in a data base, it may be possible to bring most of them into a search strategy with the simple truncation PAPER: It is also advisable to arrange a search strategy in such a way that the aspect on which the fewest documents can be expected to exist is handled first. Suppose, for example, you were looking for information on welding of chromium-nickel-vanadium steels. There may be 20 terms in the vocabulary that represent the concept of welding but only 1 term to cover the particular steel that is of interest. It is much more sensible to try the steel term first in this case. After all, there may be only a handful of documents under this term in the data base. If this is so, it would be simpler and faster to have all these displayed on-line and to select the items that deal with welding from those which are displayed. The worst approach to this requirement would be to search on all the welding terms, which might retrieve several hundred items, and then to modify this by the specific steel of interest. This is inefficient in machine time as well as your own time. So always try to identify the facet of the search that is the "least common factor," and approach the search by this facet first. It is not always possible to recognize the "least common factor" in a search, but frequently it is.

In some systems it may also be possible to "stringsearch" on the words occurring in titles or abstracts after a search has previously been narrowed down by a search of the controlled terms of the data base. This feature permits you to search more specifically than the controlled vocabulary of the data base allows. For example, the controlled terms may get you down to a set of documents that deal with cracking of prestressed concrete, but this set is found to contain a large number of items. There is no controlled term for beams, nor is there one for measurement. It may be possible, nevertheless, to narrow the search further by stringsearching the titles or abstracts of the documents in the set to see if the word BEAM or some word indicating measurement is present. But avoid asking the computer to do something that can be handled more efficiently in another way. If the set of items on cracking of prestressed concrete contains only six references, it is probably easier to have all of them displayed on-line than to try to reduce the set further by stringsearching.

Finally, some data bases may have special characteristics that can be used to improve the relevance of the search output. In particular, the indexing of documents may be "weighted" to reflect the relative importance of the terms in relation to the subjects discussed. The weighting may simply be on a scale of two: more important terms and terms of lesser importance. In such a case the weighted terms carry some special symbol, perhaps an asterisk (*), in the files. Where such an indexing device has been used, it is possible to use the device to improve the relevance of the search results. Thus

THERMAL POLLUTION*

might retrieve only documents in which the subject of thermal pollution is discussed in some detail and avoid documents in which the subject is treated only in a minor way. A weighted term can be combined with other terms to form a search strategy in the normal manner. The use of weighting, where it exists in the data base, is particularly useful in narrowing down a search that will otherwise retrieve a large number of documents.

This section of the chapter has given some general advice on the conduct of on-line searches. The use of a data base in which the vocabulary is "controlled" has been assumed. Some suggestions on the searching of natural-language data bases are presented in a later chapter. For a further discussion of searching strategies and the Boolean algebra on which they are based, see Chapters 6 and 7 of Mathies and Watson (1973).

WEIGHTED TERM SEARCHING

Some retrieval systems use weighted term searching in place of or in addition to the Boolean approach. In fact, however, the logic of the weighted term search is not different from that of Boolean algebra. Term weighting is used to simulate a Boolean strategy, and any search approach that can be achieved through the latter can also be achieved through the former.

In weighted term searching, as in other forms, the first step is the conceptual analysis of the request into its component facets and the expansion of each facet through the selection of appropriate terms from the controlled vocabulary. Each facet is then given a numerical weight, arbitrarily assigned by the searcher, and a "threshold" is established. The threshold fixes the logical requirements of the search; it is the minimum weight that a document record must "earn" before it is retrieved. Consider, as an example, the following strategy:

EVALUATION FACET 5
SEMINAR, COURSE FACET 5   THRESHOLD
INFORMATION SCIENCE FACET 5   = 15

The searcher is looking for documents discussing the evaluation of courses and seminars in the field of information science. Each facet is given a weight of 5, and a threshold of 15 is established. This means that all three facets must be represented in a document record before it will be retrieved. This is equivalent to the Boolean strategy A and B and C, where each letter represents a facet of the strategy. Note that the same weight is given to all terms in a facet and that a document can only earn the weight of a particular facet once—for example, to use the earlier example, a document can only earn five points for having the "evaluation" facet present, however many "evaluation" terms may have been assigned to it in indexing. Logical negations can be handled by assigning negative weights to facets of a strategy.

Weighted term searching has one obvious advantage over the more conventional Boolean approach: it makes it easier to produce a search output that is "ranked" in a sequence of probable interest to the requester. Take, for example, the following request:

> I am interested in amyloidosis as a complication of tuberculosis. I am especially interested in renal amyloidosis and I am most interested in the use of prednisone in the treatment of this condition.

This request factors into four facets: (1) amyloidosis, (2) tuberculosis, (3) kidney, and (4) prednisone. If these facets are weighted as follows:

AMYLOIDOSIS	5
TUBERCULOSIS	5
KIDNEY	2
PREDNISONE	1

and the threshold is set at 10, a four-level ranked output can be generated:

> Documents scoring 13 (which hopefully deal with the use of prednisone in the treatment of renal amyloidosis complicating tuberculosis)
>
> Documents scoring 12 (renal amyloidosis as a complication of tuberculosis)
>
> Documents scoring 11 (prednisone in the treatment of amyloidosis complicating tuberculosis)
>
> Documents scoring 10 (amyloidosis complicating tuberculosis)

The document records are printed out in this sequence, which should be a sequence of decreasing relevance to the interests of the requester. Even the documents in the fourth group, however, are within the scope of the request and therefore likely to be of some relevance.

It is also possible to combine the Boolean and the weighted search approaches in some systems. For example, the strategy

A and B_1 (15)
B_2 (14)
B_3 (14)
B_4 (13)
B_5 (12)

where the numbers in parentheses represent weights, specifies that a document must have both an A term and a B term present in order to be retrieved. Some of the B terms, however, are of greater interest than others, so that a document indexed under A and B_1 is ranked higher than one indexed under A and B_2, and so on. A good account of weighted term searching can be found in Sommar and Dennis (1969).

SCREENING OF OUTPUT

Figure 35 includes one further operation which may be conducted by the person who constructs the search strategy and which may have some effect on the recall and precision of the search results, namely, the screening of the output. In some systems the searcher carefully examines the output of the system before submitting the results to the user, attempting thereby to discard items that seem clearly irrelevant and thus to improve the precision ratio of the final product delivered to the user. The success of this screening operation, clearly, is directly related to the quality of the request statement, since it is on this basis that the relevance predictions are made. If the request statement is a rather imperfect representation of the user's information need, the search analyst may be as likely to discard items that the user would judge relevant as to discard items he would judge irrelevant.

The quality of the request statement and the searcher's interpretation of the needs of the user, then, are the most important factors influencing the success or failure of the screening operation. Other factors include the amount of time spent in screening and the type of document representation delivered by the system. The more complete the representation, the easier it is for the searcher to make fairly accurate relevance predictions: titles plus index terms may be more informative than titles alone, and titles plus abstracts may be more informative than titles plus index terms. The utility of a document record in the prediction of its relevance to some request statement is, in fact, likely to be directly related to the record length.

FACTORS AFFECTING THE SUCCESS OR FAILURE OF A PARTICULAR SEARCH

In this chapter various factors affecting the success of a search have been mentioned. The factors most directly related to the search subsystem itself may be summarized as follows:

1. The searcher's interpretation of the needs of the user. The prime factor is the quality of the interaction between the requester and the system. Given a request statement that inadequately represents the information requirement, there is nothing that a searcher can do, except purely by chance, to produce a good search result. Obviously, the situation is most serious when the request statement is more specific than the actual information need.
2. Given a request statement that closely matches the requester's needs, one factor that influences the search results is the complexity of the request. The "simpler" the request, that is, the fewer facets involved, the better the result is likely to be. A search that requests virtually everything on the disease of syringomyelia is single-faceted and probably involves only one index term. With such a broad request, assuming that an appropriate term exists, it should be possible to obtain high recall and high precision. Since the requester has general needs, he tends to accept as relevant any article that bears in some significant way on the subject of syringomyelia. However, consider a request on roentgenologic joint changes in syringomyelia. This is a more complex request, involving three facets—the disease facet, the diagnostic technics facet, and the anatomic facet. Many more index terms are involved, and the relationship among them becomes important. Moreover, the requester's relevance standards are likely to be much more stringent—he will probably reject any article that does not discuss the precise topic of roentgenologic changes in syringomyelia. Take a third request: spontaneous dislocation of the atlas simulating syringomyelia. This is more complex still, involving exact relationships among index terms, and the requester is likely to be very strict in his relevance standards. With this type of request we are also liable to get ambiguous and spurious relationships among terms. It is possible to get high recall on any of these three searches, but it will be achieved at a precision figure that is likely to decrease substantially with the complexity of the request.
3. Quite certainly, the performance for any request depends on the ability of the index language to express precisely the concepts involved in the request. The vocabulary of the system must be capable of expressing the subject matter of the request at a reasonable level of

specificity. This matter is discussed in more detail in the next chapter. In addition, the vocabulary should be structured in such a way, by hierarchical and associative relations, that it offers positive aid to the searcher in the construction of a strategy. In particular, it should assist him in the conduct of generic searches by drawing his attention to all the terms needed for comprehensive coverage.

4. Related to both complexity of request and adequacy of the vocabulary is the matter of the precise subject field of the request. In any particular information system, there may be certain subject areas in which the performance, on the average, is likely to be worse than that in other subject fields. In the MEDLARS evaluation, for example, it was found that searches for behavioral science requests performed noticeably worse than for other subject areas. Not only is the language of this subject somewhat imprecise, but analyses also showed the MEDLARS terminology to be weak in this area. Further, in certain subject fields, ambiguous or spurious term relationships may be more liable to occur than in other areas.

5. Indexing policies and practices affect the performance level that can be achieved in a particular search. Consider a request for articles on testicular biopsy in cases of infertility. We can only obtain high recall on this request, at least at an acceptable precision ratio, if it has been indexing policy to use the term BIOPSY whenever an article mentions that a biopsy was conducted on a patient. Likewise, we cannot conduct a comprehensive search on all applications of the Pohlhausen technique if, as a matter of policy, we do not index mathematical techniques when their use is mentioned in an article.

6. The capabilities of the searching software in use in the system also exert some influence on the performance of the search, for this governs just what the searcher is or is not able to do—for example, whether or not he can truncate terms.

7. Finally, given a request that matches the information need, appropriate specific terms in the vocabulary, and adequate indexing and searching software, a search can be ruined or substantially reduced in value by an inadequate or inaccurate strategy. As highlighted elsewhere in this chapter, the quality of the strategy is dependent on:

    a. The searcher's ability to select the correct terms to represent the subject matter sought.
    b. His ability to put them together in a way that is logically "sound."
    c. His ability to think of all "reasonable" approaches to retrieval.
    d. His ability to construct a strategy, by varying exhaustivity or specificity, that matches the recall and precision requirements or tolerances of the user.

Chapter Twelve

Vocabulary Control

Although not explicitly represented in Figure 35, the vocabulary (index language) of a retrieval system exerts a considerable influence on its performance. It greatly influences the construction of each search strategy. It also greatly influences the actual search (match with data base), since the ability of the vocabulary to describe concepts occurring in documents is obviously a major factor affecting completeness and specificity of the indexing. Although highly undesirable that it should, for reasons discussed in Chapter 10, the vocabulary may also influence the requests that users make to an information service; that is, some users may attempt to phrase their requests in what they believe to be the language of the system. It is clear, then, that the index language is very important, for it can affect, for better or worse, at least three of the steps depicted in the diagram.

The controlled vocabulary exists to facilitate communication in the information retrieval process. It does not solve all problems and may create new ones of its own. To put these problems in perspective, it is necessary to consider the major characteristics of a controlled vocabulary and the reasons why such vocabularies have been considered necessary in information retrieval systems.

Let us first consider some of the problems likely to occur in a retrieval system in which indexers use natural-language terms to describe subject matter or, in the case of a computer-based system, in which the complete text of a document, or abstract, is stored in machine-readable form. The searcher in such a system must also, of course, use natural language.

One obvious result of lack of vocabulary control is inconsistency in the representation of identical subject matter. By this we mean that a particular topic may be represented in many different ways in different documents or by different indexers. To take a very simple example, the same pathological condition may be represented by one indexer as pulmonary tuberculosis and by another as tuberculosis of the lung. To take a more complex example, the drug metharbital may be represented by this term or by any of the synonyms methylphenobarbital, Gemonil, or Endiemal (trade names). Clearly, then, in an uncontrolled vocabulary situation the searcher must think of all synonymous words or expressions in order to find all relevant literature on a particular topic. This places an additional burden on the searcher, and it is by no means certain that he will be able to come up with all synonyms. The problem is perhaps not so great at the single word level as it is when we consider synonymous phrases. For example, the concept of levels (of a chemical substance) in the blood might be variously represented in text as

blood levels
serum levels
blood concentration
serum concentration
level of . . . in the blood
level of . . . in the serum
concentration of . . . in the blood
levels in the blood, and so on

One of the major functions of the controlled vocabulary is to control synonyms, that is, to specify which of several synonymous expressions is to be used by indexers and searchers and thus to avoid the separation of identical subject matter under different terms in the system. Such control is achieved simply by choosing one of the possible alternatives, the "preferred term," and referring to it—*see* or *use*—from the variants under which certain users may be likely to approach the system. It should be obvious that the synonym selected as the preferred term, that under which documents are actually indexed and searched for, must be the one under which the majority of system users are likely to look first. Although "synonym control" is the expression most commonly used, the terms treated in this way are more likely to be near synonyms, since, apart from abbreviations, there are comparatively few words in English that are exactly synonymous.

In many systems "quasi-synonyms" are treated in the same way as synonyms. The term quasi-synonym is not very precise. It is best illustrated, in terms of its implications in information retrieval, by Mandersloot et al. (1970). As used by these authors, quasi-synonyms are antonyms that represent opposite extremes on a continuum of values. An example is the pair roughness and smoothness. Clearly, roughness may be regarded as merely the absence of smoothness, and vice versa, and an article discussing the effect of roughness on the aerodynamic properties of metal plates also deals with the aerodynamic effects of smoothness. These quasi-synonyms, and others like them, are treated in the same way as synonyms; that is, one is chosen and a reference is made from the other. Words that are synonymous in one particular subject field but not in their general usage may also be termed quasi-synonyms.

The controlled vocabulary also distinguishes among homographs, that is, words with identical spelling but different meanings, usually by means of a parenthetical qualifier or scope note. Thus MERCURY (mythology) tells us that this term is to be used exclusively for a mythological character and not for a planet, a metal, a car, or any other possible context. By controlling synonyms, near synonyms, and quasi-synonyms and distinguishing among homographs, the controlled vocabulary avoids the dispersion of like subject matter and the collocation of unlike subject matter. In this way it helps to achieve the objective of consistent representation of subject matter in indexing and searching.

Another major objective of vocabulary control is to link together terms that are semantically related in order to facilitate the conduct of comprehensive searches. It would, for example, be extremely difficult to conduct a search on cereal production in the Middle East if one had to think of all terms that might indicate cereals and all those which might indicate Middle East. A controlled vocabulary groups such related terms together, sparing the searcher from having to draw all the needed terms from his own head. If the vocabulary is well constructed, it brings together terms that are hierarchically related, in a formal genus-species relationship, and it also reveals semantic relationships across hierarchies. Gardin (1965) has referred to these two types of relationships as paradigmatic and syntagmatic. A paradigmatic relationship is invariable, one that always exists—as exemplified by the terms ALUMINUM, MAGNESIUM, and LIGHT METALS—whereas a syntagmatic relationship is transient, one that is true in certain situations only—ALUMINUM may be related to BEER BARRELS but aluminum is not always related to beer barrels and beer barrels are not always related to aluminum.

The major functions of the controlled vocabulary are summarized below:

1. To provide for consistent representation of subject matter, thereby avoiding subject dispersion, at input (indexing) and output (searching) by control of
    a. Synonyms
    b. Near-synonyms
    c. Quasi-synonyms
    and by differentiation of homographs.
2. To facilitate the conduct of broad (generic) searches by bringing together in some way terms that are semantically related, including both paradigmatic and syntagmatic relationships.

THE THESAURUS

Although there are a number of possible forms that a controlled vocabulary may take, including a list of subject headings or some form of classification scheme, modern information retrieval systems generally make use of a form of vocabulary known as a thesaurus, although the information retrieval thesaurus bears little direct resemblance to the conventional thesaurus of the Roget type.

A thesaurus is essentially a limited vocabulary of terms, in alphabetical order, that can be used in indexing and searching. It provides control over synonyms, it distinguishes homographs, and it brings related terms together. Consider the very simple example of selected thesaurus entries in Figure 40. This illustrates the major functions of the thesaurus rather clearly. Words considered sufficiently close to be synonymous are "controlled" by choosing one and referring from the other through the *use* instruction. An indexer may not use the term CEREALS but must instead use the term GRAIN, thereby avoiding separation of like subject matter. Homographs are distinguished and separated by the use of parenthetical scope notes. Semantically related terms are linked together in two ways. Words that are related in a formal genus-species way are indicated by "broader term" and "narrower term" listings. As shown in Figure 40, the term GRAIN has listed beneath it both the term immediately above it hierarchically, that is, its genus, CROPS, and the terms immediately beneath it hierarchically, that is, its species, namely, the

Barley
> Broader term: *Grain*

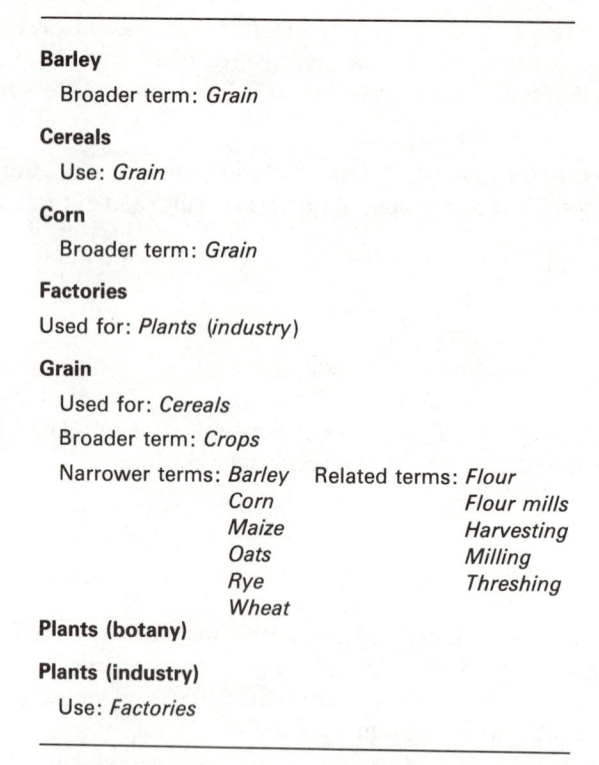

Cereals
> Use: *Grain*

Corn
> Broader term: *Grain*

Factories
> Used for: *Plants (industry)*

Grain
> Used for: *Cereals*
> Broader term: *Crops*
> Narrower terms: *Barley*   Related terms: *Flour*
>   *Corn*   *Flour mills*
>   *Maize*   *Harvesting*
>   *Oats*   *Milling*
>   *Rye*   *Threshing*
>   *Wheat*

Plants (botany)

Plants (industry)
> Use: *Factories*

Figure 40   The structure of a typical thesaurus.

individual grain terms. In addition, terms semantically related to GRAIN in other ways than a formal genus-species relation—for example, agricultural or industrial operations related to grain—are also displayed. Thus, the searcher, as well as the indexer, is given a complete picture of all terms in the vocabulary that are considered to be related to grain. This helps both indexer and searcher in selecting the terms most appropriate for a particular situation. Note also that each reference is reciprocated; that is, if A_1 shows A as a broader term, A must show A_1 as a narrower one. If B is referred to R, that is, B *use* R, R must show that it is referred to from B.

In this manner the thesaurus is able to prevent the separation of related material under synonymous terms, is able to distinguish homographs, and is able to give the searcher positive assistance in the conduct of a comprehensive search in a particular subject area.

But the thesaurus does not solve all the language problems that may occur in an information retrieval system. There are others that are essentially syntactic. Semantic and syntactic ambiguities are caused by the fact that the indexer assigns a group of index terms ("descriptors") to a document but does not, in many systems at least, indicate the relationships among them. In searching the system, this phenomenon can cause irrelevant items to be retrieved through ambiguous or spurious relationships among terms.

Consider the following group of terms, which have all been assigned in the indexing of a single report:

aluminum
copper
welding
cleaning
ultrasonic

The report discusses the manufacture of electronic components. One of the operations involves the welding of aluminum, another the cleaning of copper by means of ultrasonics. But this report would be retrieved in response to requests for information on the welding of copper, the cleaning of aluminum, and ultrasonic welding, although it is not relevant to any of them. We are getting false associations or "false coordinations" between terms; that is, a document is retrieved because it has been indexed under, or because it contains, two or more terms specified by the searcher, even though they are essentially unrelated in the document or its representation.

There is a second possible ambiguity that is frequently referred to as an "incorrect term relationship." Consider a request for literature discussing separation anxiety, that is, anxiety of a child caused by being separated from its parents. A search on this subject might retrieve a report that has been indexed as follows:

mother
child
anxiety
illness
hospital

This report does not deal with the topic required, that is, anxiety of a child separated from its parents. Instead it deals with anxiety of a mother toward a child who is ill and must be hospitalized. This is not a false coordination, since the terms anxiety, child, and mother are all directly related in the paper retrieved. Instead, it is a good example of an incorrect term relationship, a situation that occurs when the terms that caused a document to be retrieved are related in another way than that desired by the requester—in this example, it is the mother who is anxious and not the child.

These are very simple examples of the types of ambiguous and spurious relationships that can occur in an information retrieval system. This type of communication problem causes the retrieval of irrelevant documents—"noise" in the system, in the communications sense of the word. It is clear that the more terms that are used to index a document, the greater the probability of false coordinations and incorrect term relationships occurring. Since many computer-based systems routinely index at a level of 10 to 30 terms per document, these problems can theoretically be quite great.

There are ways of avoiding problems of this type. For example, false coordinations can be avoided by linking together in indexing the terms that are directly related. Terms that are unrelated do not appear in the same link. Linking is achieved by assigning a common letter or number to all related terms. Thus, in the example used earlier, aluminum and welding could be assigned the letter A, and the other three terms would be grouped under the letter B. Incorrect term relationships can be avoided by some form of role indicator or relational indicator, which is a numerical or alphabetic code showing the exact relationships that terms bear to one another. For example, we could use some form of directional code to indicate that the child rather than the parent is the object of the anxiety.

Another possible way of reducing problems of this kind is by the use of some form of subheading, that is, using one term as a subdivision of another—for example, aluminum/welding.

In general, these problems are more theoretical than actual. They are most prevalent in systems in which index terms consist of single words (Uniterms), including systems that search on complete natural-language text. When words are precombined as index terms—for example, separation anxiety; anxiety, maternal—the probability of false associations is greatly reduced, although it is certainly not eliminated entirely. Moreover, words that may be ambiguous on their own are no longer so when used in association with other words. For example, PLANT may be ambiguous, but when the word is used with the term STEEL, in searching a retrieval system, the ambiguity disappears. If a document has been indexed with both words, the assumption is that the term plant relates to an industrial plant, that is, a factory, and not some other variety. Similarly, many relationships that are theoretically ambiguous are not really ambiguous in practice. The words England, lamb, New Zealand, and export might indicate the export of lamb from England to New Zealand, but the reverse situation is much more likely to be true.

INFLUENCE OF THE VOCABULARY ON THE PERFORMANCE OF A RETRIEVAL SYSTEM

The important requirements of a controlled vocabulary are perhaps best illustrated by considering the types of failures that might occur in a search due, directly or indirectly, to defects or limitations in the vocabulary. These failures are of three major types:

1. Those due to lack of specificity in the vocabulary.
2. Those due to ambiguous or spurious relationships among terms.
3. Those due to lack of adequate "structure," causing a searcher to overlook terms that would be needed for a comprehensive search or to overlook the most appropriate terms for a particular requirement.

In a controlled vocabulary system, lack of specificity is likely to be the most important source of failure. The specificity of the vocabulary is the single most important factor influencing the precision with which a search can be conducted. Suppose, as an example, that we are looking for information on ultramicrofiche. If the system we consult includes the specific term ULTRAMICROFICHE, we can presumably conduct a search of high precision; most, if not all, of the documents retrieved should deal with the precise subject of our inquiry. But the system could conceivably have only the more generic term MICROFICHE. A search under this term, when the requirement is specifically for ultrafiche, inevitably results in low precision; most of the items retrieved are likely to be unrelated to the specific subject of the search. The situation is even worse, of course, if the most specific term available is MICROFORMS.

It is true, in fact, that the major factor controlling the level of precision that can be achieved in a retrieval system is the degree of specificity in the vocabulary. This can best be illustrated by means of an example. Consider three separate retrieval systems, A, B, and C, using controlled vocabularies of 2000, 1000, and 500 index terms, respectively. Let us suppose that we have indexed the same collection of documents on aerodynamics by each of the three systems. Some of these documents deal with the subject of slender delta wings.

When we come to index such documents into system A, having 2000 index terms, it may be possible to define their subject matter uniquely by means of the class label SLENDER DELTA WINGS. When we index the same documents into system B, with only 1000 index terms, we may not be able to define their content precisely. Perhaps we must subsume them under the more general class label DELTA WINGS. Further, in system C, the term WINGS may be the most specific we can apply to this class of

186 Vocabulary Control

document. The effect that this variation in specificity has on retrieval is illustrated in Figure 41.

When we come to put a request to system A on the subject of slender delta wings, we can express the subject precisely in our search strategy as in our indexing, and the subset of documents retrieved can be expected to be largely relevant to the request; that is, the precision ratio of the search will tend to be high. On the other hand, the recall ratio of the search will probably be low, because the system could well be holding back a number of documents that contain useful information on the subject of slender delta wings. For example, by asking precisely for the class of documents dealing with slender delta wings, we will fail to retrieve

1. Documents dealing with delta wings in general but containing substantial information on slender delta wings. These will have been indexed under delta wings.
2. Documents dealing with slender delta wings but indexed under some synonymous term or term combination, perhaps narrow delta wings.

When we put the same request to system B, our recall will tend to improve. We cannot precisely specify slender delta wings and must settle for delta wings, thereby retrieving some of the additional relevant documents missed by the search in system A. However, we may still be missing some potentially useful documents—for example, those on wings, in general, that contain information on slender delta wings, and those on delta wings that have been indexed under some synonymous term or term combination, perhaps triangular wings. These additional useful documents would be retrieved by a search in system C, in which lack of

---

High recall
Low precision
↑

Low recall
High precision

Wings
↑
General documents on wings. Documents on delta wings not indexed as "delta" (perhaps "triangular")

Delta wings
↑
General documents on delta wings. Documents on slender delta wings not indexed as "slender" (perhaps "narrow")

Slender delta wings

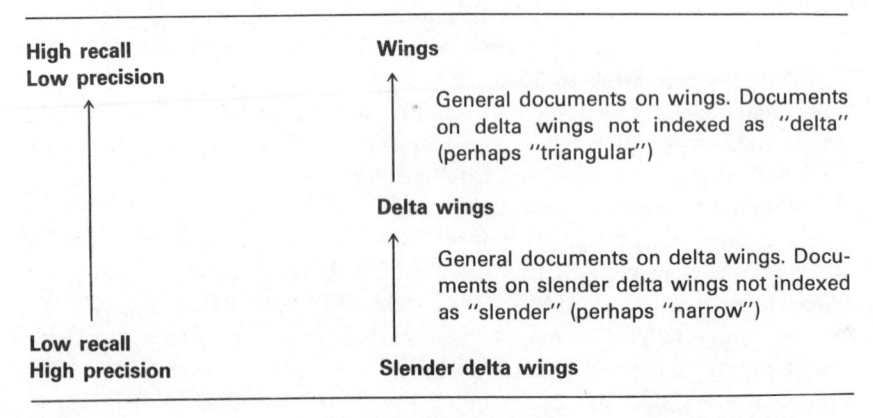

Figure 41 Effect of specificity of vocabulary on performance of a retrieval system.

specificity in the index language forces us to search under the generic class wings.

As we go from system A to system B to system C, then, because the number of distinct class labels is reduced and the size of the document classes is correspondingly increased, we tend to pull in more documents in each search and thus improve our recall performance. At the same time, our precision performance tends to deteriorate: in response to a request for documents on slender delta wings, the class precisely labeled slender delta wings should contain a higher proportion of useful documents than the class labeled delta wings, which, in turn, should contain a higher proportion of useful documents than the class labeled wings.

In other words, the greater the specificity of the index language, the more precisely we can define subject matter, and the smaller the document classes thus created; consequently, the greater the precision we can achieve in searching the system. On the other hand, in achieving precision through being able to define the class of sought documents precisely, our recall performance tends to be lower than it would be were we searching an index using a language of reduced specificity, in which the document classes defined by the system are larger in size. Put more succinctly, a highly specific index language allows high precision in searching but also tends to reduce recall. An index language of low specificity tends to produce high recall but does not allow high precision. The problem of lack of specificity is peculiar to controlled vocabulary systems. It is not true of natural-language systems, since the subject matter of a document, in such systems, can be represented as specifically as the words in the document itself. Indeed, controlled vocabulary, by definition, implies lack of complete specificity because such a vocabulary is not the complete set of terms available in a subject field but only a limited subset of them. The *Medical Subject Headings* (MeSH) used by the National Library of Medicine, for example, consists of perhaps 12,000 terms, considerably less than the number of terms in any standard medical dictionary.

An important problem faced by the managers of any information retrieval system is deciding just how specific the vocabulary needs to be. Clearly, it must be sufficiently specific to allow the great majority of searches to be conducted at an acceptable level of precision. This implies that the level of specificity varies over the vocabulary, some subject areas being developed in greater detail than others. A vocabulary developed by the National Library of Medicine would need only a few general terms in mathematics, and one developed by the American Mathematical Society would need only a few general terms of a medical nature. A second implication is that the vocabulary must constantly be adjusted to make it more specific, as more specific literature is published or more specific demands are made on the system. This, in turn, has a hidden implication. The managers of the system must have some user feedback in order to be able to recognize vocabulary inadequacies. This implies some continuous evaluation or quality control activity, which is not a routine part of many information services.

Adjusting the specificity of an existing vocabulary is somewhat easier than arriving at an appropriate level of specificity in the initial development of a thesaurus. As early as 1911, Hulme introduced an important principle known variously as "literary warrant" or "bibliographic warrant." The principle, which Hulme (1911) applied to book classification, simply states that a term is justified (warranted) if literature on the subject is known to exist; it is not warranted if no literature is known to exist. The principle can be extended to the thesaurus situation by saying that a term is warranted if enough literature on the topic is known to exist and that if the term were not introduced into the vocabulary, the literature would be hidden away in a much larger class that would not be very useful for retrieval purposes.

An important corollary principle, but one that is frequently overlooked, could be referred to as "user warrant"—a term is justified if requests for information at this level of specificity are likely to be made fairly frequently by users of the system. User warrant is even more important than bibliographic warrant in the development of efficient controlled vocabularies for information retrieval. One could probably develop a list of several hundred species of dogs, all of which names would be warranted bibliographically, but if the users of a particular system never need anything more specific than DOGS, there is no valid reason for developing this part of the vocabulary in such great detail.

The implication of this is obvious. The maker of a controlled vocabulary must know a considerable amount about the potential users of his system and about the types of requests they are likely to make, a point that is strongly emphasized in books by Soergel (1974) and Lancaster (1972).

Lack of specificity in the index language can cause either recall failures or precision failures. If we do not uniquely define a particular class of documents, but still use our entry vocabulary* to indicate how the class has been subsumed, we will get precision failures due to lack of specificity in the vocabulary, but not recall failures attributable to this

---

*The entry vocabulary (see Lancaster, 1972) is a set of terms representing concepts occurring in documents or requests that are not precisely represented by the controlled terms of the system. The entry terms are mapped to the controlled terms (A *use* B, or A *use* B *and* C) through decisions made by indexers, lexicographers, or other system personnel. Entry terms are sometimes referred to as "lead-in terms" or "nondescriptors."

cause. If we omit the notion even from our entry vocabulary, we will get both recall failures and precision failures. For example, consider the topic perceptual completion phenomena. Let us suppose that we cannot uniquely define this concept but that we decide to index it by the use of the term combination VISION and ILLUSIONS. We must now record this decision in our entry vocabulary as

Perceptual completion phenomena *use* Vision *and* Illusions

Imagine that we now have a request for articles on this subject. The topic appears in the entry vocabulary so that we know which term combination to search on. We get precision failures in this search because the product of the class labeled vision and that labeled illusions, namely, the class visual illusions, is wider than the precise class perceptual completion phenomena. Nevertheless, we should not get recall failures because the entry vocabulary allows indexers to be consistent in their treatment of the topic, and it tells the searcher how the topic has been indexed.

Suppose, however, that we have no precise term for perceptual completion phenomena and fail to include the notion in our entry vocabulary, although articles dealing with the topic have been input to the system. The results will be as follows:

1. We tend to get indexer omissions. Faced with an article that discusses perceptual completion phenomena, although the topic is not treated absolutely centrally, the indexer is more likely to omit the topic if no specific term is available in either the controlled vocabulary or the entry vocabulary.
2. Indexing inconsistencies occur. Some indexers may use VISION and ILLUSIONS, and others use different term combinations.
3. Recall failures tend to occur when we conduct a search on this topic. Some are due to indexer omissions. Others are due to inconsistencies (the searcher does not know how the required topic has been subsumed and fails to cover all the term combinations necessary to achieve high recall).
4. Additional precision failures tend to occur. Because the searcher does not know how the subject has been treated, he is forced to try a large number of alternative term combinations, some of which may be responsible for much irrelevancy.

To recapitulate on this point, a recall failure due to lack of a specific term implies that the search topic, or some aspect of it, is not even covered in the system's entry vocabulary. A precision failure due to lack of a specific term implies that the topic is not uniquely defined by the controlled terms. Obviously, therefore, to correct precision failures due to lack of specificity requires that terms or term combinations that uniquely define the notion not presently covered specifically be introduced into the vocabulary. To correct recall failures, we do not need a unique designation, but we must include the concept in our entry vocabulary.

Ambiguous and spurious relationships among terms, as discussed earlier, are another source of precision failures. Although some failures of this kind are likely to occur in any postcoordinate system, it is usually preferable to put up with them rather than taking elaborate and expensive precautions at the time of indexing—for example, through links and role indicators—to reduce the possibility of noise from this source. It is quite possible to come up with endless examples of false associations that could occur in retrieval, but the great majority, although theoretically possible, are in practice very unlikely to occur. The old classic used to be the need to distinguish between a blind Venetian and a venetian blind. But is anyone ever likely to be looking for information on blind Venetians? And if they are, would the data base they search also be likely to contain references on venetian blinds? And if it did, how difficult would it be to separate, at output, the blind Venetians from the venetian blinds? This is an absurd example, perhaps, but it illustrates a point. In practice, the context in which a term occurs—and by this I simply mean the other terms that are associated with it—removes most possible ambiguity, and, in information retrieval activities, we have both the context of the document representation and that of the search strategy. Moreover, if several possible interpretations could exist, one of them is usually more probable than the others, as in the lamb, England, New Zealand relationships mentioned earlier. The fact is that some of the literature of information retrieval has been excessively concerned with the possibilities of semantic or syntactic ambiguities that, although theoretically conceivable, have a very low probability of ever occurring in any real operating environment. Experience with even very large data bases—a million or more records—has shown that it is possible to operate a retrieval system with a very minimum of syntax or, in fact, with no real syntax at all. Moreover, as Lancaster (1968d) has pointed out elsewhere, the cost of incorporating syntactical devices—the cost in not being able to retrieve what is wanted as well as the actual cost in dollars—may far outweigh the advantage of avoiding a little irrelevancy in output.

The third possible source of failure is inadequate structure in the vocabulary. The controlled vocabulary must help the searcher by bringing to his attention all the terms that would be needed to conduct a comprehensive search in some subject area. For example, suppose that an engineer needs to conduct a search on the failure of a particular type of metal structure. When he consults the thesaurus, or other type of vocabulary, under the term FAILURE, the structure of the tool must lead him down to more specific terms indicating specific types of failure—for example, FRACTURE and RUPTURE—and from these down to terms that are still more specific—for example, BRITTLE FRACTURE and STRESS RUPTURE. It must also lead him to possibly useful terms from other hierarchies, such as terms representing conditions that could cause or contribute to failure in metal structures—CORROSION, FATIGUE, STRESS, STABILITY, HYDROGEN EMBRITTLEMENT, and so on. Unless it does this, the vocabulary does not give the searcher maximum assistance, and there is a danger that he may overlook some of the terms that would be needed to conduct a comprehensive search on this subject.

It is now possible to summarize the requirements that seem to be of most importance in a controlled vocabulary for information retrieval:

1. It should have "warrant" derived from the terminology of the literature and the information needs of the actual or potential users.
2. It must be sufficiently specific to allow the conduct of the great majority of searches at an acceptable level of precision.
3. It should be sufficiently precoordinate to avoid most problems of false coordination and incorrect term relationships. One way of achieving this, and also of economizing on the absolute size of the vocabulary, is through the use of subheadings.
4. It should promote consistency in indexing and searching by the control of synonyms, near synonyms, and quasi-synonyms.
5. It should reduce terminological ambiguity through the separation of homographs and through the definition of terms whose meaning or scope would otherwise be unclear.
6. It should assist the indexer and searcher in the selection of the most appropriate terms needed to represent a particular subject through its hierarchical and cross-reference structure.

Chapter Thirteen

The Indexing Subsystem

A reexamination of Figure 35 will reveal that there is only one step in the information retrieval process still to be discussed in terms of its potential impact on the effectiveness of the information service. This is the step in which the search strategy is actually matched against the data base, resulting in the retrieval of those document representations which match the strategy. Apart from the characteristics of the search strategy itself, a subject already examined in Chapter 11, the other major factors influencing this matching operation obviously relate to the data base. Some of these are vocabulary factors, as discussed in the previous chapter, and the others are factors relating to indexing policies and procedures adopted by the producer of the data base.

As mentioned in Chapter 1, the subject indexing process involves two quite distinct intellectual steps:

1. Conceptual analysis
2. Translation

In the first of these stages the indexer is faced with two questions:

1. What is the subject matter dealt with in the document?

2. Why is the subject matter, or some aspect of it, of interest to the users of this particular service, that is, the service for which the indexing is being performed?

To answer these questions satisfactorily, the indexer must have some understanding of the subject matter dealt with in a document, although he need not be an expert in the field, as well as a rather complete knowledge of the information needs of the community for whom the service is being provided. There is no one true indexing for any document. The same document could quite legitimately be indexed in five different ways in five different information centers. Indeed, it would be alarming if these differences were not found to exist, for this might suggest that the specialized interests of the users of each of these centers were largely being ignored.

The translation stage of the indexing operation is that in which, once he has determined which aspects of the subject matter are to be covered in the indexing, the indexer decides which terms are most appropriate to use to represent the subject matter. Usually this means the translation of the conceptual analysis into the language of a particular controlled vocabulary. This step, too, implies some familiarity with the subject matter of the document. More important, it implies a rather high level of familiarity with the particular controlled vocabulary in use.

Failures in information retrieval that may be attributed directly to the indexing process fall into two main groups:

1. Failures due to indexing policy
2. Failures due to indexing accuracy
   a. Failure to cover all concepts that should be covered
   b. Failure to use the most appropriate terms to represent the concepts chosen

EXHAUSTIVITY OF INDEXING

The most important policy decision relating to indexing regards exhaustivity, which is a measure of the extent to which all the distinct subjects discussed in a particular document are recognized in the indexing operation and translated into the language of the system. Suppose we have a document that deals with only six topics (A,B,C,D,E,F). If we recognize all six topics in the conceptual analysis stage of indexing and express them by means of appropriate combinations of index terms, we can say that we have been completely exhaustive in our indexing of this particular item. It is obvious that if all six topics are indexed, the document can be retrieved, whichever of these topics or combination of topics is requested. Thus, a high level of exhaustivity of indexing tends to ensure high recall. As the exhaustivity level is reduced, the recall capabilities are diminished. If we do not recognize concept F in our indexing of the document, we will never be able to retrieve it in response to a request for literature on F, unless the terms used to describe F happen to be related, hierarchically or in some other way, to the terms used to describe A to E. As we progressively reduce our exhaustivity level by successively omitting further topics, our recall capabilities in relation to this particular document diminish accordingly. Of course, the phenomenon applies equally to all documents indexed. If we index each document at maximum exhaustivity, we achieve a maximum recall capability for our index.

Although a high level of exhaustivity of indexing tends to ensure high recall, it also tends to reduce precision. There are basically two reasons for this; first, if, for every document input, we recognize all, or at least a substantial proportion, of the indexable topics, we will tend to index many topics that are treated in only a very minor way in the documents concerned. Consequently, they will tend to be retrieved in response to requests in relation to which they contain little information.

Let us suppose that the six-topic document previously instanced is a report describing certain aerodynamic phenomena and that a particular mathematical technique, say, the Pohlhausen technique, is mentioned as being applicable in a calculation applied to one of these phenomena. Let us also suppose that this mathematical technique has been recognized in the conceptual analysis stage of indexing and translated into appropriate index terms—in fact, this technique is topic F. For the, probably rare, request in which a researcher wants to retrieve every piece of literature indicating applications of the Pohlhausen technique, this document is relevant and should be retrieved. The high level of exhaustivity of indexing will prove useful for this high recall requirement. On the other hand, consider another, probably more common, request in which the requester wants documents describing the Pohlhausen technique and how it may be applied. He wants only substantive articles on the technique; articles which merely mention the method in passing are, to his requirement, nonrelevant. However, a search of an aerodynamics collection, indexed at a high level of exhaustivity, may tend to retrieve a large number of documents that do little more than mention the technique. In this case, the high level of exhaustivity causes a large number of unwanted items to be retrieved; that is, it reduces the precision of the search.

The second reason why a high level of exhaustivity of indexing tends to reduce precision is the simple fact that the more topics we recognize in indexing, and the more index terms we use to express them, the greater the potentiality for false coordinations in searching. Thus, in the six-topic document ABCDEF, in which, let us say, A and B are related, C and D are related, and E and F are related, we have the possibility that the document will be falsely retrieved in response to any of 12 two-topic requests—A in relation to C, A in relation to D, B in relation to C, and so on. If each of the six topics is expressed by a number of distinct unlinked index terms, the possibilities for false coordinations at the index term level are magnified exceedingly.

In view of this discussion, we reiterate that a high level of exhaustivity of indexing makes for high recall and low precision. Conversely, a low level of exhaustivity of indexing makes for low recall and high precision. Let us consider a situation in which we adopt the policy of indexing at the minimum level of exhaustivity; we index each document under a single topic only: the central topic treated in each case. Obviously, the recall potential of our index is extremely low: a document will not be retrieved in response to a request for a topic that is anything less than the core topic of discussion. On the other hand, every time a document is retrieved in a search of the index, it tends to be a wanted document, since it must deal in a substantial manner with the subject of the request. Moreover, by indexing at minimum exhaustivity—single key topics—we completely eliminate the possibility of false coordinations at the topic level and substantially reduce the possibility of false coordinations at the term level.

It must be stressed here that the level of exhaustivity applied in indexing is a policy decision established by the managers of the retrieval system. It is not dependent on the properties of the index language, since we must assume that the index language used is appropriate to handle the subject fields treated in input documents and that any topic discussed is capable of being translated into the language of the system albeit at a higher generic level. It is also a matter outside the control of the individual indexer. In establishing this policy decision, the system managers must try to determine an optimum level of exhaustivity, one that will satisfy the great majority of the requests processed by the information service. It is possible that the exhaustivity level will be related to type of document—internal technical reports being indexed more exhaustively than other types, some journal titles being indexed more exhaustively than others, and so on. Alternatively, the policy on exhaustivity can vary with the specific subject areas dealt with in the collection. In general, the exhaustivity of the indexing is the single most important factor governing the recall that can be achieved in a particular system, and the specificity of the vocabulary is the single most important factor governing its precision.

A term that is common in the literature, but is deliberately avoided in this book, is "depth." As used in the literature, depth indexing merely implies the use of more terms than in nondepth indexing. Whether the additional terms are used to cover further topics, increasing the exhaustivity, or to index a limited number of topics more exactly, increasing specificity, is rarely stated. In other words, deep indexing, or depth indexing, has been used by some authors to describe preciseness of class definition, and other authors have applied the same terminology to describe the extent to which all topics discussed in a document are recognized in its indexing.

QUALITY AND ACCURACY OF INDEXING

Although exhaustivity is beyond the control of the individual indexer, the quality and accuracy of the indexing are very much within his control. Indexer errors are of two types: (1) omission of a term or terms necessary to describe an important topic discussed in an article and (2) use of a term that appears inappropriate to the subject matter of the article. A special form of the latter is the use of a term less specific than warranted by the subject matter and allowed by the vocabulary. Omissions normally lead to recall failures, and use of an incorrect or nonspecific term can cause either a precision failure (the searcher uses the term in a strategy and retrieves an irrelevant item) or a recall failure (the searcher uses the correct terms, and a wanted document is missed because it is labeled with an incorrect term).

Recall failures due to indexer omissions must be distinguished from recall failures due to lack of exhaustivity of indexing, as follows:

1. *Indexer Omission.* A topic that appears central to the subject under discussion in the document is not covered at all in the indexing. It is felt that the omitted topic is so important that it should be covered even in nonexhaustive indexing.
2. *Lack of Exhaustivity.* An item of subject matter treated peripherally in an article is not covered in the indexing. The topic is not crucial to the article and was presumably excluded in favor of other topics because of general policy regarding the average number of terms to be assigned.

Unfortunately, if an important term is omitted from the indexing of a document, the document is likely to remain unretrieved in a number of searches to which it may be highly relevant. Moreover, this type of error, although it may come to light in an evaluation program, is likely to remain undetected in the normal operations of the system. Of course, a certain number of indexing omissions are to be expected under the pressures of tight production schedules. They are, however, likely to be greater contributors to system failures than is the use of inappropriate terms. If the work of one indexer is scanned ("revised") by a second, incorrect terms tend to stand out clearly and are thus easily corrected in the revision process. Omissions, however, are not so readily detected because this usually involves a more careful examination of the document by the reviser.

CONSISTENCY OF INDEXING

Indexing quality is not something that is readily observable. Indeed, the only true test of quality is an actual evaluation of the effectiveness of a retrieval system, including an analysis of the contribution of the indexing subsystem to recall and precision failures. But consistency of indexing is much more easily measured than quality. Consequently, there have been many more studies of consistency than of quality in indexing. Both interindexer and intraindexer consistency have been studied.

A consistency study measures the extent to which two or more indexers agree on the choice of terms needed to represent the subject matter of a particular document (interindexer consistency) or the extent to which the same indexer, at different times, agrees with himself on the choice of terms to represent the subject matter of some document (intraindexer consistency).

A number of possible measures of consistency have been tried or proposed. The most common measure, however, seems to be the "consistency pair" (CP). The CP of two indexers, A and B, is defined as

$$\frac{\text{Number of terms assigned both by A and B}}{\text{Number of terms assigned either by A or by B or both}}$$

Thus, if indexer A assigns the terms ABCDEF to a document and B assigns the terms ABCGH to the same document, the measure of consistency is

$$\frac{\text{ABC}}{\text{ABCDEFGH}} \quad \text{or} \quad \frac{3}{8} \quad \text{or } 37.5$$

The same measure can be used to express intraindexer consistency.

The consistency achieved by a group in indexing a particular collection of documents is influenced by many factors, including

1. The exhaustivity of the indexing.
2. The type of vocabulary used.

198   The Indexing Subsystem

3. The size and specificity of the vocabulary.
4. The experience and training of the indexers.
5. The subject field of the documents.
6. The types of indexing aid provided.

Studies of indexing consistency can have some value. For example, they can be used to identify types of documents—for example, by subject area—or types of terms that appear to give trouble to the indexers. But consistency studies must be treated with some caution. Consistency does not necessarily imply quality. Indeed, it is possible to be consistently bad as well as consistently good. A study may show that, in a particular group of six indexers, two individuals are more consistent with each other than any other pair of indexers in the group. One indexer in the group is the most individualistic of all; he is the least consistent on the average when his indexing is compared, in turn, with each other member of the group. The indexing of the two individuals who are most consistent with each other is not necessarily the best indexing. In fact, the individualist indexer may be the most effective in the sense that his terms best match the requests made to the system; that is, the indexing of the individualist, on the average, allows retrieval of more documents judged relevant by requesters and prevents retrieval of more judged not relevant.

A more complete discussion of consistency of indexing may be found in Cooper (1969) and Leonard (1975). A rather complete analysis of factors influencing consistency and quality of indexing is provided by Oliver et al. (1966).

Chapter Fourteen

Improving the Performance of an Information Service on the Basis of Evaluation Results

Chapters 10 to 13 have presented a rather complete analysis of factors affecting the performance of information retrieval services, based on the steps involved in the provision of such services as illustrated in Figure 35. The factors discussed importantly affect the performance of retrospective search and dissemination services of all kinds. Obviously, however, every factor identified is not equally relevant to every information system, and some factors are not relevant at all in certain situations. When one important factor is removed, however, others tend to assume greater significance. For example, in a system in which the requester conducts his own search without the use of a system intermediary—for example, an on-line system, a card catalog, or a published index—a very important source of error, the transformation of an information need into a stated request, is eliminated. However, in these situations we may get more failures due to the inability of the user to think of all possible approaches to retrieval. In a natural-language searching system, lack of specificity in the vocabulary is not a problem, but ambiguous and spurious relationships among terms certainly are. Through failure analysis in an evaluation program it is possible to determine which are the principal causes of failure in a particular system. When they are known, system modifications can be made to reduce these failures in the future.

An evaluation program is diagnostic and therapeutic. It is not conducted as an intellectual exercise. The cost of conducting an evaluation program—not negligible in the case of a large system—can only be justified in terms of improved system performance resulting from the investigation. Once an evaluation has been conducted, then, the results must be carefully analyzed and interpreted to identify steps that might be taken to improve the quality of the information service in the future. Perhaps the vocabulary of the system has been shown to be insufficient in some features—for example, it lacks adequate cross-reference structure—or in certain subject areas. It may be discovered, too, that the exhaustivity of the indexing is inadequate to satisfy a substantial number of the requests made to the system.

Elsewhere, Lancaster (1971) has reported on the results of the evaluation of MEDLARS and the recommendations made for system improvement resulting from this study. Changes made to the system included the design of a new search request form (intended to ensure that a request statement is a good reflection of the information need behind it), expansion of the entry vocabulary and improvement of its accessibility, and the adoption of an increased level of integration among personnel involved in indexing, searching, and vocabulary control activities.

The National Library of Medicine was in an unusually strong position with regard to making changes in MEDLARS as a result of the evaluation program, because, as the producer of the data base as well as its major exploiter, NLM has complete control over all stages of the information retrieval process as illustrated in Figure 35.

But only an organization that both produces and exploits a data base is in this fortunate position. In a more usual situation, an information center is merely the exploiter of a data base produced by another organization. It may also be the user of an on-line search facility that is not under its own direct control. Take, for example, the situation of an industrial information service searching a variety of on-line data bases, through an on-line service center, such as Lockheed, SDC, or Bibliographic Retrieval Services, on behalf of its users. The situation in terms of which performance factors are under the control of which organization is depicted in Table 6.

It can be seen from this table that the industrial information center has direct control of only a few of the factors that determine the effectiveness of the services it provides. It has control over the way in which it interacts with its own users. To a very large extent it has the ability to influence the quality of this interaction. It could, for example, raise the overall quality of interaction through a redesigned search request form, through improvements in the training of the information staff—for example, in the conduct of request interviews—or through insistence on a greater level of user involvement in the search process itself—for example, asking the user to be present at the terminal at the time the search is conducted. But the information center does not have absolute control over even this stage of the information retrieval process, because it does not have complete control over its own users. The staff of the information center can go only so far in leading and helping users. If a particular individual, for one reason or another, is completely unable to verbalize his information need, there may be very little that the information specialist can do to help him.

Similarly, the local center may be said to have control over its own search strategies. It does, of course, but this control is not absolute either. The characteristics of a search strategy are very largely determined by the characteristics of the software used to search on-line. The individual searcher must operate within the constraints of this software. For example, the extent to which he can use truncation in searching is obviously completely controlled by the truncation capabilities of the query language. Obviously, too, the search strategy must make use of the vocabu-

Table 6 Factors Influencing the Performance of an Information Service as Controlled by Various Types of Organization

Organization	Factors controlled
Producer of the data base	All data base factors, including coverage, indexing policy and quality, and the index language
Exploiters of the data base:	
On-line service center	Searching software and supporting hardware
Industrial information service	Interaction with the users and construction of the search strategies

lary of the data base, and it must adapt to the indexing policies in use in the data base, and these important factors affecting performance are under the control of only the data base producer.

In fact, then, a typical information center has control over only a few of the factors affecting the quality of the information services it provides. This situation, however, is not so gloomy as it first appears. The local information service has substantial control only over its approach to user-system interaction and the construction of search strategies, but these are in some ways the most important factors to control. They are most important because they are the factors that occur first in the whole operation. If a user's request statement is an inadequate representation of his real information need or if a search strategy is a very imperfect representation of a request statement, the search is virtually doomed to failure. In this case, it matters little whether the indexing is sufficiently exhaustive, whether the vocabulary is sufficiently specific, whether the query language is sufficiently flexible, and so on. Vocabulary, indexing, and other data base characteristics may be close to perfect, but this does not help if the search strategies are seeking unwanted information.

There is a second reason why control over the processes of user-system interaction and search strategy construction can be considered particularly important. Changes made to these operations can take immediate effect. If today we introduce improved methods of interacting with our users or of constructing strategies, we can expect that the overall effectiveness of our services will improve immediately. But changes to a data base tend to produce long-term rather than immediate effects, at least for the retrospective search situation. Changes made to indexing policy, or to the index language, are not going to have a very pronounced effect for some time. Consider a data base of 500,000 documents growing at the rate of 100,000 items per year. Even if sweeping changes were now made to the vocabulary or indexing policies, it would be another five years before these changes would affect even half the total data base.

Through detailed failure analysis, derived from an adequate sample of searches, the evaluator can learn a considerable amount about the problems and weaknesses of a particular system and can make recommendations on how the system may be improved in the future. This is the whole purpose of conducting the evaluation program. Evaluation is a sterile exercise unless it is conducted with the object of diagnosing existing problems and improving the performance of a system or service. The entire discussion of evaluation, presented in the last several chapters, has largely assumed the conduct of an evaluation program as a one-time study to answer various specific questions about an operating information service. Evaluation procedures are applicable, however, before the service ever becomes operational. In fact, evaluation of a service at a "conceptualization" or prototype stage is the only sensible approach to the design of information services. Evaluation at the conceptualization stage implies some type of survey of the reaction of potential users to a proposed service. Since nothing exists at this point, the "evaluation" can involve only the description of a proposed service and the solicitation of the opinions of a sample of the potential users on the service as described. At a prototype stage, an evaluation becomes more concrete. Now some specimen products can be produced on a small scale and submitted to representatives of the user population. Alternative products or services can be evaluated at the prototype stage, the object being to determine which are most acceptable to the community to be served. "Internal" evaluations can also be conducted before a service is made operational in order to test alternative indexing procedures, approaches to vocabulary control, searching strategies, and so on. In a sense, this type of evaluation is a laboratory evaluation but one to answer specific questions directly related to an actual service that is to be implemented.

Evaluation of an operating information service should not be considered as merely a one-time activity. The performance of information services should be monitored continuously in much the same way that the performance of a manufacturing plant is monitored by means of quality control procedures. It is important, then, for an information service to solicit feedback from its users on at least a sample of the services performed. Continuous quality control, applied to information services, cannot be as refined or detailed as a one-time evaluation study. Nevertheless, it can be valuable to collect evaluation data at even a relatively gross level. For example, user estimates of the number of references that are relevant in an SDI or retrospective search service give some indication of user satisfaction and allow unusually poor results to be identified and followed up with a more detailed level of analysis.

Chapter Fifteen

The Evaluation of Machine-Readable Data Bases and Information Services Derived from Them

The first problem addressed in this chapter is evaluating a data base in terms of its suitability for use in the provision of information services in a particular organization or comparing the suitability of two or more data bases dealing in approximately the same subject area. This evaluation problem applies most obviously to the situation in which an organization is considering acquiring a data base for use on its own computer facilities, with all the attendant leasing, start-up, and implementation costs. It also has some relevance, however, to any situation in which a regular information service—for example, SDI—is to be provided from one or more existing machine-readable files, including the situation in which the service is to be purchased from another organization. Even though, in the latter situation, the risks are less than in the former, one would presumably prefer to implement an information service that has continuity; that is, an organization should endeavor to ensure that any service implemented is well suited to the needs of the people it is to serve. From a cost-effectiveness viewpoint, it should endeavor to ensure that the service provided is the best that can be provided within the budget that is available. The evaluation of machine-readable data bases has, therefore, effectiveness and cost-effectiveness facets.

The following criteria appear to be those that most importantly affect the selection of a data base for use in the provision of a particular information service:

1. Subject matter
2. Cost factors
3. Qualitative considerations
   a. Coverage
   b. Time factors
   c. Indexing and vocabulary factors
4. Implementation factors

The first of these is so self-evident that it seems almost superfluous to mention it. The subject matter of the data base must be that which best matches the information needs of the user community to be served. This implies, of course, that the operators of the information service must have a detailed knowledge of the needs of its users as well as a knowledge of the subject coverage of available machine-readable files. The second of these is likely to be considerably easier than the first. The identification of the most appropriate data base to meet user needs may, however, be rather more difficult that it appears at first sight. The problems are less great if the information service is entirely discipline-oriented. The choice may be quite clear. In fact, there may be no real choice involved because only one reasonably comprehensive data base is available in the particular discipline. In the case of a mission-oriented information service, on the other hand, the situation may be much more difficult. There may be no one data base that comprehensively covers the mission-oriented needs of a particular organization—for example, an industrial corporation. Instead, there may be several candidates, one satisfying part of the requirements, a second some other part, and so on. This situation may mean that more than one data base must be selected for use and that priorities for their implementation must be established.

Given the existence of several competing and partially overlapping data bases in a particular subject field, or given the need to establish priorities for the implementation of several data bases, other considerations must be taken into account. The most obvious cost factors are those listed below:

1. Cost of acquiring the data base—for example, by leasing—or of purchasing service from it.
2. Cost of implementing the data base—start-up and running costs—assuming that it is used on in-house computer facilities.
3. Cost in relation to quantitative data base characteristics:
   Unit cost per record
   Cost in relation to the number of access points provided.
4. Cost in relation to qualitative data base characteristics.
5. Cost in relation to volume of demand for service:
   Unit cost per user interest profile
   Unit cost per group profile
   Unit cost per retrospective search.

The cost of information service is highly volume-dependent. For this reason it is extremely important that careful market analysis be applied to determine the potential level of use for any particular data base. Projected level of use, when related to cost of acquiring the data base and of implementing a service based on it, yields an estimate of the costs of units of service—cost per retrospective search, cost per user interest profile per year, and so on. In certain environments at least, data bases are implemented in an order of priority that reflects the anticipated unit costs of service.

Another way of looking at costs is from the viewpoint of how many searchable records are purchased for how much money invested. The cost of leasing several United States data bases seems to fall in the general range of 5 to 10 cents per record per year. In general, the larger data bases seem to lease at a lower unit cost per record than the smaller. But, from the point of view of return on investment, unit cost per record is not enough. The records must also be retrievable. We might also, therefore, consider the number of access points provided, on the average, per record as another useful evaluation criterion. We can refer to the accessibility of bibliographic records in terms of the exhaustivity of the indexing. The more exhaustive the indexing, that is, the more index terms or other access points provided, the more accessible the record becomes. A data base having nonexhaustive representations of documents—for example, titles only—allows only very limited access (retrieval) capabilities, whereas a data base containing searchable abstracts, or one in which each record is indexed with 10 or more descriptors, provides a much higher level of access; that is, these data bases allow the retrieval of bibliographic records from a much greater range of approaches. As one example, the printed *Index Medicus* allows a very limited access to journal articles in medicine, perhaps two or three subject access point per article, but the machine-readable version of this data base, as used in MEDLINE, provides a much higher level of access. In comparing two or more data bases, covering roughly the same subject matter, it is therefore appropriate to consider how much access each one provides. Types of access point—by subject, author, language, date, and so on—as well as number of access points, should also be considered. Level of access can then be related to the cost of acquiring the data base.

So far we have considered only quantitative aspects of data bases, and the relationship between the quantitative aspects and costs. Quality, however, is more difficult to measure than quantity, in data bases as in other things. Some major criteria by which the quality of a data base may be evaluated are listed in Table 7. Some of these qualitative criteria—for example, number of items, exhaustivity of indexing—are also quantitative criteria and have already been mentioned; that is, certain qualitative measures must be based on quantitative considerations.

Three major types of qualitative criteria are identified in Table 7: those relating to coverage, those relating to time, and those relating to indexing and vocabulary factors. The coverage criteria are concerned with the completeness of a data base, the relative completeness of two or more data bases, and the extent to which two or more data bases overlap or complement each other. Completeness may be considered in terms of

Table 7 Some Major Qualitative Aspects of Machine-Readable Data Bases

Coverage factors	Time factors	Indexing and vocabulary factors
Number of sources	Time lag	Degree of vocabulary control
Type of source	Frequency of update	Specificity of the vocabulary
Number of items		Searching aids provided
Time span		Semantic and syntactic ambiguity
Completeness in relation to user needs		Exhaustivity (number and variety of access points)
Uniqueness and overlap		Accuracy and consistency (observed error)

the absolute number of items indexed or abstracted a year, the number of sources—for example, journals—covered, the type of source—for example, whether technical reports and patents are included—and the time span for which the data base is available. The last consideration relates only to the value of the data base for retrospective search purposes. A data base is of very limited value for retrospective searching until it covers at least three years of the literature and begins to approach a high level of value when it reaches, say, five years of coverage. A longer span of coverage is likely to be more important in the social sciences and the humanities than it is in science and technology because it is probable that the rate of obsolescence is greater in the scientific and technical areas.

It is impossible, unfortunately, to measure the absolute coverage of a data base in some specialized area simply by counting the number of items or the number of sources covered. An estimate of the degree of coverage of a data base in some specialized area requires the conduct of a controlled evaluation. The appropriate technique, first referred to in Chapter 9, is to assemble a random sample of relevant articles—review articles are particularly valuable for this purpose—and use the references included in these papers as a "citation pool" for testing the coverage of a particular data base. This would be the technique to use if, for example, we wished to assess the coverage of *Index Medicus* in some specialized field such as parasitic diseases. Martyn (1967) and Martyn and Slater (1964) have used this technique effectively. It would be wrong to assume that even the great discipline-oriented data bases are complete, or close to complete, in some specialized area. Davison and Matthews (1969), using a bibliography of 183 references on the subject of computers in mass spectrometry discovered that, among 12 data bases, no one covered more than 40% of this literature and the coverage of *Chemical Abstracts* was only 24%. As another example, Bourne (1969a) estimated that the *Bibliography of Agriculture* covered only 50 to 60% of the literature relevant to agricultural research.

Indeed, it would be unusual if we did find that any one secondary source was completely comprehensive in its coverage of the literature of some area because we know from the work of Bradford, and later bibliometric analyses, that a very large number of primary sources are likely to contribute to the literature of any particular subject field, although a very high percentage of all this literature may in fact come from quite a small number of sources. The fact is that if we seek really comprehensive coverage of the literature of some area, we may have to make use of several data bases. Montgomery (1973), for example, used a sample of the toxicology literature of 1968 to evaluate the coverage of four different data bases. It was found that the four files, collectively, gave a 98% coverage of the literature but that no one of them covered more than 85%.

Some further aspects of coverage are also worth mentioning. We must have some idea of the degree of reliability with which sources are covered by the service. Clearly, a service must consistently scan all issues of the journals it claims to cover. It is also important to distinguish among journals covered completely and those covered selectively. The MEDLARS indexers include every substantive article from the majority of medical journals but index general science journals such as *Nature* and *Science* only selectively, extracting those items of a medical nature. Where a selection is made from various sources, it would also be important to assess how consistent and reliable the selection process is. Again, this type of evaluation could not be achieved by observation alone, but only through the use of some form of test.

Another important consideration in the selection of data bases relates to the local availability of the sources covered. The list of sources covered by a particular data base should be compared with the list of sources available locally. The use of SDI or retrospective search services in a particular community creates a demand for a document delivery system, and it is necessary to look ahead in order to assess the impact of these information services on other services—for example, interlibrary loan—provided by the organization. The impact of the use of machine-readable data bases on the demand for document delivery systems is frequently overlooked. If SDI services are introduced into a developing country, for example, a demand for document delivery may be created that the national resources may be incapable of responding to effectively. A major consideration should be the availability of a guaranteed source of document delivery from the producer of the data base, which is true of the data bases of the Institute for Scientific Information (ISI), the National Technical Information Service (NTIS), the International Nuclear Information System (INIS), and a few others.

Time factors should also be considered in the evaluation of machine-readable files. The most obvious time factor relates to the degree to which the file is up-to-date. Time lag between publication of an item and its appearance in the file affects the value of the data base for current awareness purposes. A good SDI service should presumably operate at a high novelty ratio; that is, the majority of items delivered to the users should not only be relevant to their interests but should also be new to them—items they have not seen before. A current awareness service can hardly be considered very successful if many of the items delivered were known to the users, from other sources, at an earlier time. The novelty ratio is obviously greatly influenced by the speed with which items are processed into the data base.

In general it is likely that data bases in which human intellectual processing is minimized—for example, those of the Institute for Scientific Information—are more current and that the more intellectual processing, such as the writing of abstracts, is involved, the less current the data base. Ashmole (1973), in evaluating data bases in terms of their value to the pharmaceutical industry, found that the *Science Citation Index* (SCI) file included items between zero and three weeks after publication on the average, and most other services averaged between two and six months, and *Biological Abstracts* fell between four and twelve months.

A closely related matter is the frequency with which the data base is updated. If tied to a publication cycle, frequency of update is likely to correspond to the frequency of publication—biweekly, monthly, and so on. In the case of some services, the leasing costs vary with the frequency with which the customer needs to have the file updated.

The indexing and vocabulary factors, listed in Table 7, also require some explanation. A major factor affecting the precision of an information service is the specificity of the vocabulary used. Natural-language data bases are almost always more specific than controlled vocabulary data bases. But natural-language systems present other problems to those constructing search strategies or user interest profiles. A controlled vocabulary reduces the problems of synonymy and near-synonymy and, by linking terms that are related by means of a hierarchical or cross-reference structure, provides definite aids to the searcher. The quality of the searching aids available to the user should, then, be another point worth considering in the evaluation of data bases. This is a significant economic consideration that is frequently overlooked. How much help is given to the searcher, and how much he is left to his own resources, has some definite effects on the cost, as well as the quality, of searching.

The exhaustivity of the indexing in a particular file was discussed earlier. Another matter is the degree to which the data base creates problems of syntactic and semantic ambiguity—problems of false coordinations and incorrect term relationships. With an exhaustive natural-language data base, such as one using searchable abstracts, these types of problem are likely to be particularly prevalent. They may also be prevalent, however, in data bases using controlled vocabularies in which the indexing is exhaustive, unless some deliberate attempt is made to avoid problems of this kind through the use of links, role indicators, subheadings, or similar devices. Finally we come to the matter of consistency and accuracy of indexing. The quality of the indexing applied to any data base may be measured in terms of inaccuracy (use of incorrect terms) and omission (failure to use a term that should have been applied). Unfortunately, it is not possible to judge the quality of indexing simply by a superficial examination. We can judge the quality of indexing only by undertaking a controlled evaluative study, which should be the responsibility of the producer of the data base rather than the user, or through experience in use of the data base over a period of time. Through its own experience in using a data base, an organization should be able to judge the quality of the indexing and might be able to identify certain types of errors or idiosyncrasies that occur. It may then be able to compensate for some of them in the construction of searching strategies. One possible way of learning more about the quality of a data base is by discussing these matters with others who have gained some experience in using it.

A final group of evaluation criteria relates to ease of implementation of an information service based on a particular data base. This situation, of course, applies only to the case in which an organization considers acquiring a data base for use on its own computer facilities. In this situation the following evaluation criteria may have some relevance:

1. Assurance of the continuity of the data base.
2. The capabilities of the searching software assuming that such software is also made available by the producer of the data base.
3. Compatibility of search programs with existing software and hardware.
4. The characteristics of the data base that determine how easy or difficult it is to exploit in the local environment. This includes the "cleanliness" of the data base—for example, the extent to which it contains superfluous elements required only for publishing and printing purposes—and its general "integratibility" with other files that may already be in use. In short, how much preprocessing will be needed to make use of the data base in the environment that already exists in the organization?

THE EVALUATION OF SERVICE CENTERS

This section of the chapter is concerned with the evaluation of centers through which information services from machine-readable files can be purchased. It is most applicable to the situation in which a contract for service must be signed for a specified period of time with a particular center. Thus, the evaluation criteria would apply in the case in which SDI service could be purchased, from a particular data base, through two or more competing centers, and an organization is faced with the decision as to which center to select. The evaluation criteria are less applicable, because less important, to the situation in which use of a particular center can be discontinued at any time—for example, the usual situation in the case of the purchase of on-line service or in which single retrospective searches are purchased when the need for them arises. All the evaluation criteria identified in the outline on page 109 are applicable in this situation.

All these user criteria must be borne in mind in planning any information services and operations. It is clear that these criteria influence many decisions that must be taken. Some of them are related primarily to data base characteristics and influence choice of data base, as discussed earlier. Others relate to the information center's own organization and facilities—for example, ease of use, document delivery backup—and yet other performance factors influence choice of outside centers from which to purchase service. It is these which we are primarily concerned with at this point.

In choosing service centers, we must seek to identify those delivering the highest quality of product with the least processing delay and at the least cost. Unfortunately, these requirements tend to be conflicting. We must usually pay a higher price for quality, and we may have to wait longer to achieve it.

One decision that might be faced for several data bases is the decision as to whether to access the data base through a center offering off-line batch processing services or through a service organization making the data base available for direct on-line interrogation from remote sites. For some data bases there is no choice available. The *New York Times* Information Bank, for example, can be accessed only on-line, and the off-line MEDLARS operations are now phased out in favor of MEDLINE. The current awareness activity is probably handled most effectively by off-line batch processing, except that the construction of user interest profiles is probably best handled by heuristic interaction with an on-line system. The comprehensive literature search may best be handled in the off-line mode, when no stringent deadlines are imposed by the user, although again there are obvious advantages associated with being able to test out a strategy on-line on part of a data base before committing the strategy to the more expensive search of the complete file. For other types of information needs, however, the response time requirements of the user are likely to be such that only rapid, direct access to the on-line data base is acceptable.

Let us now give some further consideration to the user-oriented performance criteria in the outline on page 109 and their implications for the selection of service centers. Since many information services are intended to be self-supporting operations, cost considerations are of major importance. Centers must be evaluated in terms of the cost of their services, and, because costs of information services tend to be volume-dependent, we must endeavor to negotiate the best possible terms for the projected volume of business that will be generated on a particular data base. For retrospective search purposes, the cost of dealing with a particular center operating in the off-line mode must be compared with that of accessing data bases through on-line terminals. In fact, this cost analysis may well be the most important one. The difference in charges among the various off-line centers is usually not very great, at least for several of the data bases.

The response time requirement relates only to retrospective searches. In assessing this feature of the various centers, we need to contact a representative group of existing customers of these organizations. Some processing centers operate with a short turnaround time in the range of one to five days, and others offer a service much less satisfactory, up to twenty days in some cases. In a study by O'Donohue (1973), seven centers were compared on processing time for retrospective searches. Only three of them routinely processed searches in a time that O'Donohue regards as "prompt," namely, less than two weeks. Although analyses of this type are difficult to find in published form, other customers undoubtedly have made their own comparisons, and data of this type may be available on request. Somewhat related to the response time for retrospective searches is the time it takes a service center to get an SDI profile "up and running." O'Donohue quotes a range of 2 to 6½ weeks, from initial inquiry to first machine printout, for five processing centers from which SDI service was received. Before leaving the subject of response time, it is worth noting that we may also want to identify centers that are willing and able to handle certain requests in a "special processing" mode; that is, they should be capable of handling a special request on a "rush" basis when necessary.

Although it is easy to compare centers in terms of their charges, and relatively easy to compare them from the viewpoint of response time, it is not at all easy to make this comparison in terms of the quality of the product provided, the major qualitative considerations that are at least partly controllable by a service center being the recall and precision of search results. This statement needs qualification, however. It is relatively easy to judge the performance of a center, at least in terms of the precision of its searching, through a period of experience with the center. It is difficult, however, to compare centers in terms of what their service is likely to be, that is, before a contract is actually initiated. However, it seems reasonable that we should be able to negotiate a trial period for a number of profiles, with one or more service centers, before a formal subscription is placed. In fact, we might consider developing a small group of "test searches," that is, searches for which a known set of relevant documents is identified in a particular data base, and use the test searches to evaluate various processing centers in terms of both the recall and precision of the search results, as well as response time. O'Donohue quotes some precision figures ("percent relevant"), for SDI service from several centers and based on several data bases, that range from a low of 4% to a high of 54%. It should be noted, however, that although there is likely to be a certain minimum level of precision that is acceptable to a particular user, an extremely high level of precision would suggest that the profile is missing many of the relevant documents, that is, recall is low, because there tends to be an inverse relationship between recall and precision in searching. For example, if a user interest profile consistently operates at 80% precision, we can be almost certain that it is also running at a very low rate of recall. For both the current awareness need and the "comprehensive search" need, high recall is likely to be more important to the user than high precision, although precision below a certain level may be intolerable. It must also be recognized, however, that although a user is able to judge the precision of a search, that is, determine what proportion of all citations delivered are relevant to his interests, he is usually in no position to be able to judge its recall because he does not know what the search may have missed. The recall ratio achieved for a particular SDI profile or a particular retrospective search can usually be estimated only by a specially devised test and analysis. As discussed in the preceding chapter, several of the factors affecting the performance of an information service are only under the control of the producer of the data base and are essentially outside the control of the service center processing the data base. However, two very important factors influencing performance are under the control of the center, namely, the quality of the interaction with the user—procedures by which his information need is "negotiated" with the system—and the quality of the searching strategies used, whether for SDI or retrospective search.

These performance factors are closely related to the precise modes of operation adopted. Three broad modes of operation appear possible:

1. The user to be served is put into contact with the service center. Staff at the service center clarify his needs and prepare the user interest profile or strategy for a retrospective search.
2. The user discusses his need with an information specialist in his own organization (local representative) who then relays his interpretation of the need to the service center, where a search strategy or profile is constructed.

3. The user discusses his need with the local representative, who converts the need into a searching strategy or user interest profile that is then run at a service center.

In general, the second of these alternatives is the least desirable, since the more intermediaries placed between a user and a data base, the less successful the search is likely to be. It is well known that when a message is relayed through a chain of people, the possibility of distortion ("noise" in a communication sense) exists at each step in the chain. The first alternative is likely to produce the best results initially because of the experience that personnel at a service center have accumulated in use of a particular data base. However, this mode of operation provides no training possibilities for local staff. In the long run, the third alternative may be the best mode to adopt. Once local staff have been trained to construct searching strategies or user interest profiles for a particular data base and set of searching programs, the fact that the staff members are "closer" to the user community, physically if nothing else, may result in improved user-system interaction and improved information products as a result.

Of course, this presupposes that the service center dealt with will allow us to operate in this way. If the third of the alternatives is the one that is organizationally most acceptable to our own institutions, an important selection criterion will obviously be whether or not the service center will permit a mode of operation in which search strategies or interest profiles are prepared by our own staff and simply "run," in a machine sense, at the center. This mode of operation also presupposes that the center has available adequate facilities and materials for training people in search techniques. A center that has no training program and no adequate search manuals, which should be data-base related, will be unacceptable if the third of the processing alternatives is the preferred one. It should be pointed out that some processing centers have produced very excellent searching guides and searching tools, both of a general nature and related to particular data bases.

As far as the on-line approach to data bases is concerned, our assumption is that information specialists will search these data bases for users by means of terminals located in a local information center. In this case it is clearly imperative that the staff members be well trained in the search procedures associated with a particular system and the search techniques needed to exploit a particular data base effectively. If an on-line service center is used to gain access to various data bases, it should be capable of providing the necessary training, as well as appropriate searching aids.

As previously mentioned, the factors affecting performance of an information service that are not primarily input-related—indexing and vocabulary factors—and thus outside the direct control of the local center or of any service center, relate to interaction with the user and the quality of searching strategies. In other words, the quality of the service is heavily dependent on the quality of the information staff who are interacting with the users and the quality of the information staff preparing search strategies or interest profiles, whether these be staff members of a local center or personnel associated with a processing center, the training of the staff members, and their degree of experience with particular data bases and searching software.

Clearly, however, we have just identified another important variable affecting the performance of an information service, and thus the choice of a processing center, namely, the capabilities of the searching software. In general, different service centers, both those operating on-line and those operating off-line, use different searching software. In assessing the capabilities of a processing center, we need to assess the capabilities of the search programs in use by the center as well as the output options available from the programs. Although all such programs have the same general objectives and capabilities, there are differences among them at the specific feature level. The off-line search programs, particularly those searching text, must go beyond simple Boolean AND, OR, and NOT capabilities. Weighted term searching, permitting the ranking of output, is an important capability, and nested search logic is an essential requirement for systems operating exclusively in a Boolean search mode. For text searching, word truncation capabilities, both left and right truncation, are essential, and word proximity operators, that is, the ability to specify how close two words should be in text before they are considered to be related, are highly desirable. A number of output formats should also be available, in terms of what is printed—citation, abstract, etc.—in what sequence it is printed, that is, sorting options, and on what it is printed, that is, the output medium.

In the evaluation of on-line searching systems, additional requirements become important. These requirements include the capability of displaying term lists, thesauri, or other searching aids, and the capability of providing various tutorial and "help" features to the searcher.

Before leaving this subject of service centers and their selection, some additional comments need to be made. Selection of a service center also involves considerations of experience, proven reliability, flexibility of operation—for example, the ability to accommodate high priority searches on a "rush" basis—as well as general attitude and "customer orientation" (the "personal element" in O'Donohue's evaluation). The experience of the information center is important, especially its experience with particular data bases. Experience is related to years of operation and volume of profiles or searches handled. Clearly we should deal only with centers that appear to be stable and whose continuity appears to be assured. Another element to be considered is the degree of interest that the center exhibits toward the quality control and improvement of its products. One form of evidence of this is the amount of interaction and iteration a center undertakes before it "stabilizes" a profile. Another form of evidence is the amount and type of feedback and evaluation solicited from users, and the degree to which the center attempts to improve its performance on the basis of such feedback and evaluation. O'Donohue's survey is a useful summary of experience with a small number of centers. It is important to note that some centers satisfied the evaluation criteria of this study very well, although one or two others were highly unsatisfactory. O'Donohue concluded that "great care is required in the selection of commercial information services. The spectrum of potential satisfaction is wide and the user must analyze his needs and his suppliers' capabilities carefully to optimize results."

Ultimately a user judges an information service on cost-effectiveness grounds, relating the cost of using the service to the quality of the product provided by the service. The most useful cost-effectiveness measure to use in the evaluation of information services is the cost per relevant citation obtained from the service. If a user subscribes to an SDI service, at an annual cost of $150, and is supplied with 75 relevant citations in a particular year, the cost per relevant citation is $2. When fully operational, an information service must develop quality control and monitoring operations that permit the cost-effectiveness evaluation of data bases, and services from them, in terms of this important measure. This requires the development of procedures for obtaining regular and precise feedback from users. Perhaps the most complete evaluation of data bases and services yet conducted, although restricted to drug-related information, is that reported by Ashmole et al. (1973). These investigators compared various approaches to locating information on a particular drug in terms of the yield of each source, the number of unique references supplied by each source, the source that disclosed a particular reference for the first time (novelty), and cost per relevant citation.

This chapter has presented a discussion of criteria by which an organization might evaluate data bases and service centers in relation to its own information requirements and programs. With the rapid growth in the availability and use of machine-readable files, these types of evaluation are becoming increasingly important and are likely to assume even greater importance in the future.

Chapter Sixteen

Cost-Effectiveness and Cost-Benefit Evaluation

Several possible levels of evaluation were identified in Chapter 9: effectiveness, benefit, cost effectiveness, and cost benefit. Only the evaluation of effectiveness has been discussed thus far. The other aspects are covered in this chapter.

Cost effectiveness is the relationship between level of performance (effectiveness) and the costs involved in achieving it. There may be several alternative methods that could be used to obtain a particular performance level, and these can be costed. Cost benefit refers to the relationship between the benefits of a particular product or service and the costs of providing it. Generally speaking, benefits are more difficult to measure than performance (effectiveness) except that, in a commercial sense, benefits equate with return on investment. The expression cost-performance-benefits relates to the entire relationship among costs, performance (level of effectiveness), and benefits.

The cost of an information service can be measured in terms of input of resources (funds). Under costs we need to consider both the costs that are relatively fixed—for example, equipment purchase or rental, developmental costs, costs involved in acquisition and indexing of the present data base—and the costs that are relatively variable. Variable costs are of two kinds:

1. The variable cost that is a function of the number of transactions. For example, if we increase the number of retrospective searches conducted from 1000 to 1500 per year, the cost per search may be reduced by x dollars.
2. The variable cost that is a function of alternative modes of operating the system. For example, we could vary the cost of retrospective searching by varying the mode of interaction with the user—personal visit, mail, telephone—by varying the mode of interaction with the data base—for example, from off-line batch processing to on-line interactive search—by adding or eliminating a screening operation, or by changing the professional level of the personnel conducting the searches.

In considering an information system, various levels of benefits are evident. For example, a society or institution may, quite properly, measure the benefits of its information program in terms of income from sale of publications or services and balance this income against production costs, that is, calculate return on investment. Here we are weighing costs against income benefits. On the other hand, a government agency may be partially subsidizing the information program and may adopt a broader view of its benefits in terms of much less tangible factors. Moreover, in the environment of an information system, the relationship between cost and effectiveness may be somewhat difficult to distinguish from that between cost and benefits. Suppose, for example, we reduce the average number of terms assigned in indexing, and thereby reduce the average indexing time per item. We could say that an immediate benefit of this action is to reduce input costs. On the other hand, such an action is likely to have a very definite influence on the effectiveness of the system; the average precision of the system may increase—and this in itself may be regarded as a form of benefit—and the average recall will almost certainly decrease. In other words, this action has had immediate observable benefits, in terms of cost saving at input, it will have a long-range influence on the effectiveness of the system, and it may have an even longer-range influence on the benefits of the system's products to the end user. Obviously, then, cost, performance, and benefits are very closely related and cannot be completely separated.

An evaluation of cost effectiveness is a study of the extent to which available resources are so allocated that the maximum possible return—

for example, in information service—is achieved for the investment made. The ultimate cost-effectiveness goal would be a state in which it could be said that each $1 worth of resources allocated in a particular way could not give a better return—for example, in more or better service—if it were allocated in some other manner. Usually, a cost-effectiveness analysis is conducted to determine which is the least expensive of several alternative methods for achieving a particular level of service. The cost effectiveness of a service can be improved either by

1. Maintaining the present level of performance but reducing the cost of achieving it.
2. Keeping costs constant but raising the level of performance.

Obviously, the cost effectiveness of an activity would also improve if it were possible to raise the level of performance while reducing the costs. Unless we begin with an unusually bad situation, however, this type of improvement is rarely possible.

According to Hitch and McKean (1960), there are five basic steps involved in a cost-effectiveness analysis:

1. Definition of the objectives that must be attained.
2. Identification of alternative methods of meeting them.
3. Determination of the costs of the various alternatives.
4. Establishing one or more models that relate the costs of each alternative to an assessment of the extent to which each could assist in attaining the objectives. The model used may take the form of mathematical equations, a computer program, or merely a complete verbal description of the situation.
5. Establishing a criterion for ranking the alternatives in order of desirability and choosing the most promising. The criterion provides a method of weighing estimated costs against estimated effectiveness. The structure of the cost-effective analysis program is illustrated in Figure 42, which is an adaptation of a figure presented in another context by Quade (1966).

The cost-effectiveness analysis of an information system involves a study of payoff factors, tradeoffs, break-even points, and diminishing returns. Let us now consider some of these factors in relation to the performance of an information retrieval and dissemination system, with particular reference to the intellectual aspects as opposed to the machine aspects. Figure 43 illustrates cost-performance-benefits relationships relevant to the three major components of an information retrieval or dissemination system: the acquisition and storage subsystem, the identification and location subsystem, and the presentation subsystem.

Cost-Effectiveness and Cost-Benefit Evaluation

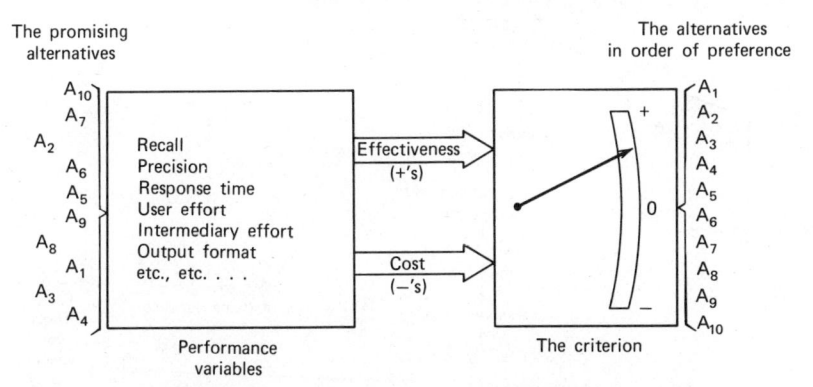

Figure 42 Structure of the cost-effectiveness analysis program.

Costs of acquisition and storage are dependent on such factors as the number of items acquired; the expected demand, which determines the number of copies and possibly the form in which the item is stored; the average cost of purchasing an item; and document size, which affects storage and duplication costs. The efficiency of this subsystem may be measured in terms of coverage and document delivery time.

Costs of identification and location are dependent on factors such as document size and complexity, which affects indexing time; the type and size of the vocabulary used for indexing; the exhaustivity of the indexing, which relates to the number of index terms used; the professional and salary level of personnel used in indexing and searching; the productivity of these individuals; whether or not their work is reviewed or revised; the number of searches conducted in a specified period; and the average time involved in conducting the search. The performance of the identification and location subsystem may be measured in terms of such factors as recall, precision, response time, and the effort involved on the part of the user, in making his needs known to the system, and the information staff.

Costs of presentation are affected by the total size of the file, which, in turn, is one factor affecting the average number of items retrieved; the precision ratio, which determines the need for output screening and is one factor governing screening costs; the printing method used; and the content and format of the output—for example, how much information is given in a document surrogate. Performance of the presentation subsystem may be evaluated primarily in terms of the ability of the user to distinguish relevant from irrelevant documents on the basis of the surrogate provided. Note that a performance measure for one subsystem may be a factor affecting the cost of another. Thus, the precision ratio is a

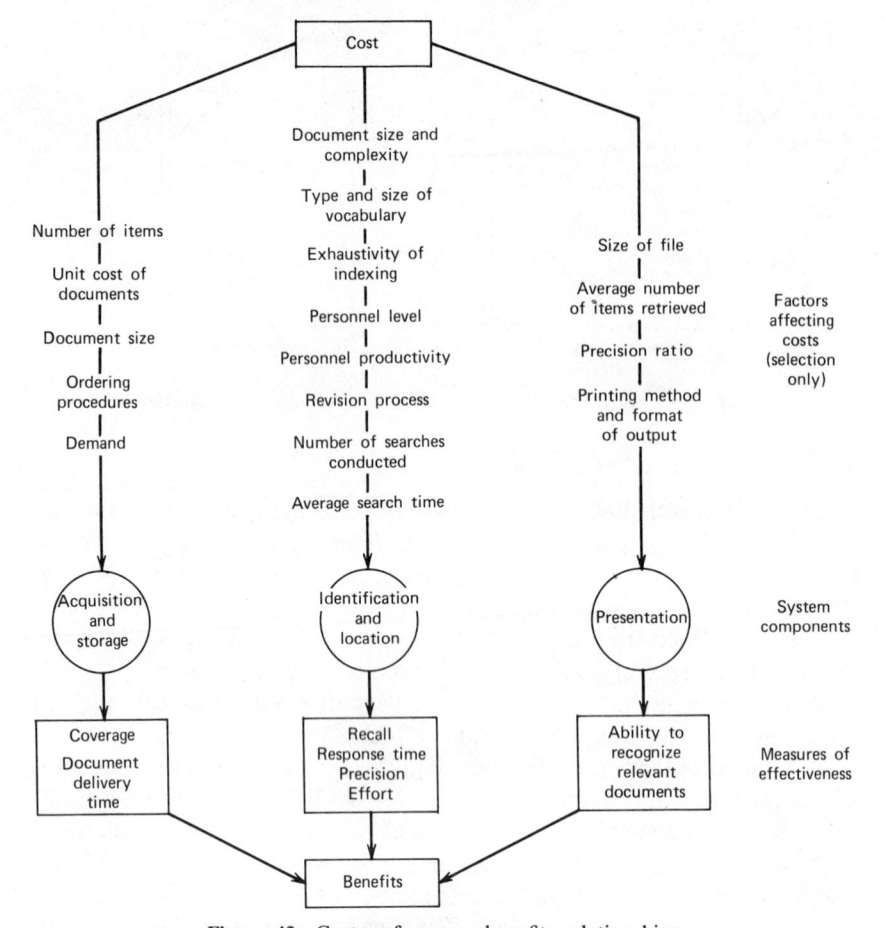

222 Cost-Effectiveness and Cost-Benefit Evaluation

Figure 43 Cost-performance-benefits relationships.

measure of the effectiveness of identification and location and is a factor affecting the costs of presentation.

COST-EFFECTIVENESS ASPECTS OF THE DATA BASE

Two of the most important phenomena in the information services area, from the viewpoint of cost-effectiveness analysis, are the law of obsolescence and the "empirical hyperbolic distribution," exemplified in Bradford's law of scatter and in the principle of least effort as enunciated by Zipf (1949). An excellent review of the subject of obsolescence has been prepared by Line and Sandison (1974) and an equally excellent review of the Bradford-Zipf phenomenon by Fairthorne (1969).

The important law of scattering, first discovered by Bradford, has been discussed, refined, and applied by many later writers. The Bradford law relates to the distribution of periodical articles over the sources, that is, periodicals, in which they are published. If a comprehensive literature search is conducted on some subject, covering a specified period of time, it will be found that the literature is scattered over a very large number of sources. When these sources (journals) are arranged in descending order of productivity, the journal yielding most articles at the top of the list and the journals yielding the fewest at the bottom, it is possible to divide the list of sources into a number of "zones" such that each zone contains approximately the same number of articles. Although the number of articles in each zone is approximately the same, the number of sources yielding these articles varies quite considerably. The first zone, or "nucleus," contains a small number of highly productive journals, and the last zone contains a very large number of journals, each one yielding a very small number of papers in the specified period. The zones thus identified form an approximately geometric series in the form

$$1 : a : a^2 : \ldots a^n$$

where 1 represents the number of journals in the nucleus and a is a multiplier.

For example, a literature search might reveal that in a particular year 375 articles are published on some subject and that they are dispersed over 155 journals. If the journals are divided into three zones, each contributing 125 articles, the first zone (nucleus) may be found to contain 5 journals, the second zone 25, that is, 5×5, and the third 125, that is, 5×5^2. In the third zone each journal contributes only a single paper to the subject.

When the results of a scatter analysis of this type are presented graphically as the cumulative percentage of articles plotted against that of journals yielding them, a curve of the type shown in Figure 44 results. This distribution is similar to that of the occurrence of words in printed text as first described by Zipf. Indeed, this type of distribution is frequently referred to as "Zipfian." The distribution has been shown to apply to a number of phenomena of interest to managers of information centers, including the distribution of use of a document collection and the distribution of sources requested through interlibrary loan procedures.

The cost-effectiveness significance of the Bradford-Zipf distribution in the operation of information services should be rather obvious. A very large number of sources are needed to yield 100% of the literature on

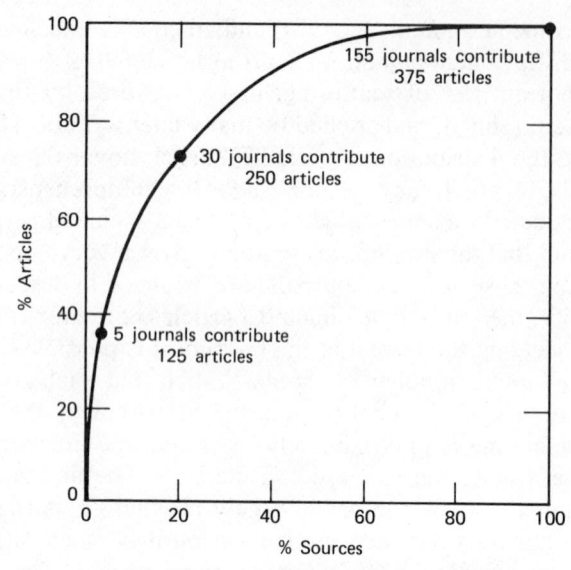

224 Cost-Effectiveness and Cost-Benefit Evaluation

Figure 44 Bradford distribution of 375 articles published in 155 journals.

some subject, but a relatively high yield may come from quite a small number of sources. A Bradford type of analysis has great value in indicating how the financial resources of an information center may be allocated most efficiently in the acquisition of materials. Coupled with the "law of obsolescence," mentioned later, the Bradford distribution also has value in decisions relating to the optimum allocation of available storage space, the documents likely to be most used being in the most accessible areas.

The plot in Figure 44 suggests two possible acquisition strategies. Suppose one were building an information center in some subject field, say, superconductivity. Given that there is a budget of $x available for acquisition of journals, the obvious strategy would be one in which journals are purchased in order of their expected yield of relevant papers until the available budget has been used up. In the example in Figure 44, as few as 30 journals can be expected to yield as much as 66% of the relevant literature, whereas over 100 additional journals would be needed to approach 100% coverage. Another point is worth emphasizing here. The group of high-yield journals will be relatively stable, at least over a short period of time, but the list of journals in the "long tail of the distribution" may be very unstable. The list of journals contributing a single paper each on superconductors in 1976 might be quite different from that contributing one paper each in 1977. For most information centers, 100% coverage of the literature is essentially unattainable. If it were attainable, it would be an unreasonable goal from a cost-effectiveness point of view. To push the coverage from, say, 85% to close to 100% would require a completely disproportionate level of expenditure, since the last 15% of coverage might easily cost as much as, or more than, the first 85%. The alternative purchasing strategy, then, is to establish some realistic goal in coverage, perhaps 85 or 90%, and then use the Bradford distribution, which represents a law of diminishing returns, in order to select those journals which have the highest probability of allowing the goal to be reached.

The problem of optimum allocation of storage space in a library or information center is one to which a similar type of analysis can be applied. Optimum allocation of storage space implies the organization of a collection in such a way that those items most likely to be asked for are kept in the most accessible areas and those least likely to be in demand are kept in the least accessible areas. The problem, obviously, is one of deciding which materials are likely to be in most demand and which in least demand.

The law of obsolescence has great relevance to the subject of optimum allocation of storage space, since, although some conflicting evidence has been produced, it has generally been found that the probability of demand for bibliographic materials declines with their age, especially in science and technology. The Fussler and Simon (1969) study at the University of Chicago, for example, established that it was possible to devise a satisfactory policy for the retirement of books to a secondary storage area on the basis only of language and date of publication. The rate of obsolescence or "aging" of bibliographic materials is now frequently expressed in terms of their "half-life." The half-life of a particular body of literature—for example, on superconductors—is the number of years retrospectively needed to satisfy half of all the requests for literature on this subject or to attract half of all the citations made to it in the current year. Thus, if half of all the citations appearing in the 1977 literature on superconductors is to literature published in the last forty-two months, the half-life of the superconductor literature, measured by bibliographic citation, can be said to be 3½ years. Similarly, if, in a particular physics library, 50% of the requests for superconductor literature are for literature published in the last forty-two months, we could again say that the half-life of this literature, measured in terms of actual demands, is 3½ years. It has frequently been assumed in the past that these two methods of measuring half-life give roughly equivalent results, in other words, that citation patterns can be used to predict patterns of demand for bibliographic materials in libraries. Some doubt has been cast on this assumption by more recent investigators.

The obsolescence principle, coupled with the expected demand for particular journal titles, can be used in the formulation of policies relating to optimum space allocation. Suppose, for example, that a particular information center has enough room on its open-access shelves to store 3000 bound volumes of periodicals. It would be important to allocate this space in such a way that the volumes thus stored would have the greatest probability of being needed by the users of the center. Studies of aging factors can be combined with studies of expected distribution of demand over particular titles (a Bradford-type distribution) in order to determine how this prime space should best be allocated. Journal X, for example, might be retained on open shelves for ten years back, and journal Y need be retained on open shelves only for three years. Studies of this kind are examples of practical cost-effectiveness analysis. If carried out correctly, this type of analysis should indicate that those volumes retained in the most accessible area can be expected to satisfy a specified percentage, say, 85%, of all the demands made by users of the center. When applied to the situation of the machine-readable data base, studies of this kind can be used to determine the optimum set of documents to collect and index, as well as to determine how far back to maintain the data base in its most accessible form—for example, how far back to keep a data base on-line.

Obviously, we would like to be able to make such studies at the design stage, that is, before we actually implement the system. In other words, we need to make cost-effectiveness predictions for various types of materials. This is more difficult than evaluating usage factors in an actual operating system. However, a number of techniques exist that make this type of prediction feasible; for example, by citation counting, analysis of library usage or interlibrary loan traffic, or analysis of subject requests collected from sample user populations and the application of these analyses to predict payoff for various materials.

Wiederkehr (1968) has presented a model that expresses the efficiency of selection policies. For any particular subject area, there is a finite group of documents N published or issued in a particular time period. For a particular group of users in this general subject field, there is a subset of documents M that will be useful in satisfying the information requirements that arise. The perfect selection procedure would select the subset M, and only M, from the general set N. Unfortunately, this is highly unlikely. We cannot precisely define M because we cannot accurately foresee all the demands likely to be made on the system. We can obtain all of M, thus getting 100% coverage of the useful literature, by

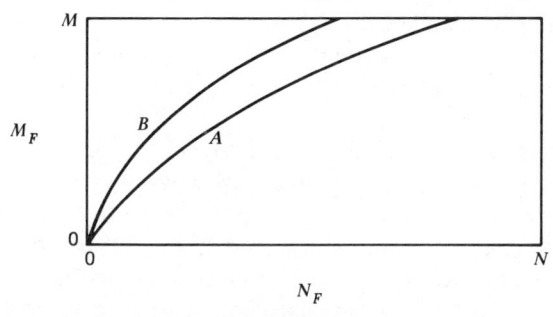

Figure 45 Acquisition characteristic curves.

acquiring all of N, but this is expensive and inefficient because $N - M$, that is, the portion acquired but not used, is likely to be large. An efficient selection procedure acquires the maximum M with the minimum N. If N_F is the subset of documents acquired and processed and M_F is the subset of useful documents that are acquired and processed, the relationship between M_F and N_F for alternative acquisition policies is defined by Wiederkehr as the "acquisition characteristic curve." Figure 45 depicts two curves of this type. The curve B represents a selection policy of greater efficiency than the curve A because M is maximized and N is minimized. We will never be able to define M precisely except by hindsight, based on actual usage records. Nevertheless, studies of usage patterns elsewhere, including citation counts and interlibrary loan records, will help us to predict which part of N is most likely to be the subset M.

COST-EFFECTIVENESS ASPECTS OF INDEXING

There are a number of economic considerations worth investigating in relation to indexing policies and procedures, including

1. The amount of time expended, on the average, in the indexing of a document.
2. The level of exhaustivity adopted in indexing, that is, the number of index terms assigned, on the average, per item.
3. The professional level of personnel used in indexing.
4. The need for an indexing revision procedure.

Probably the most difficult problem relating to indexing policy is to decide the most appropriate level of exhaustivity to adopt, that is, how many index terms to use on the average. The more exhaustive the index-

228 Cost-Effectiveness and Cost-Benefit Evaluation

ing, the greater the recall of the system is likely to be; but the precision is likely to be lower. In a particular unique environment of documents, index language, and requests, there is an optimum level of exhaustivity of indexing. A cost-effectiveness analysis allows us to find this optimum level, that is, the point of diminishing returns after which the addition of further terms is largely unproductive. For example, suppose we index a particular collection of documents at an average level of 15 terms per item, and test the retrieval performance of the system by the use of a representative sample of 50 requests. Using optimum searching strategies, we may find that for this particular group of requests, at the indexing level adopted, the system is operating at 73% recall. By additional indexing experiments in which the requests, search strategies, and index language are held constant, we may find that an increase in exhaustivity to an average of 20 terms would raise the recall performance to 90%; but we would need to raise the average exhaustivity level to 35 terms per article to reach a 95% recall level. Under these conditions, we could establish the average of 20 terms per item as an optimum level to use in this particular environment of documents, requests, and index language. After the 20-term level, in other words, there is evidence of diminishing returns, and we would need to raise the exhaustivity level as high as 35 terms, thus greatly increasing our indexing costs, to achieve a 5% improvement in overall recall. From the results of this type of study, we are able to plot a performance curve of exhaustivity level versus recall ratio. A hypothetical example of such a performance curve is shown in Figure 46. From a plot of this kind we can establish a break-even point for indexing exhaustivity, that is, a point beyond which the addition of further index terms, although adding appreciably to input costs, is not making any highly appreciable difference to the recall potential of the system. If we

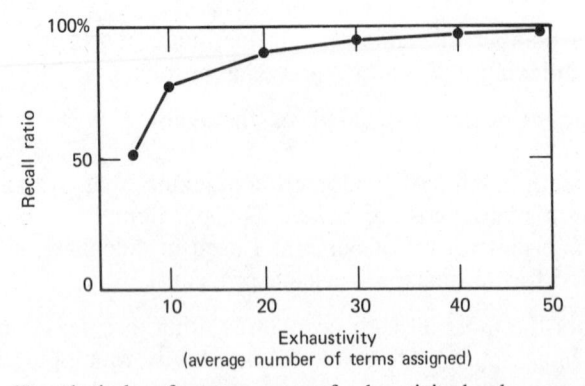

Figure 46 Hypothetical performance curve of exhaustivity level versus recall ratio.

collect a representative sample of subject requests representing actual typical information requirements of potential users and if we can identify certain documents as relevant to the requests, this type of cost-effectiveness analysis can and should be done at the stage of system design.

We can approach what is essentially the same problem from a different direction by studying the effect of varying time expenditures on the indexing operation. The more time we expend in indexing, the more terms we expect to assign on the average. However, there is likely to be a very definite leveling off after a comparatively short expenditure of time—for example, 20 terms in the first ten minutes, 5 additional terms in the next ten minutes, 2 further terms in the next ten minutes. If 90% of the useful* terms are assigned in the first ten minutes of indexing, but an additional thirty minutes is needed to find the extra 10% judged to be useful, we may reasonably conclude that ten minutes per document is an optimum average indexing time, and we can establish our indexing quotas on this basis. Obviously, we can conduct a cost-effectiveness analysis of time expenditure on indexing by experimentation similar to that described in connection with establishing optimum exhaustivity levels. Indeed, because we generally would expect more terms to be assigned as indexing time is increased, we are measuring essentially the same thing.

It is rather more difficult to predict the effect of varying exhaustivity or indexing time on the probable precision of an information retrieval system, but this would be a necessary element in a realistic cost-effectiveness analysis. Such a prediction can in fact be made by means of random sampling procedures. This requires a larger experiment in which, in addition to indexing a set of documents each one of which is known to be relevant to one or more recorded requests, we also index a random sample of additional documents in the same general subject area. When we compare the search strategies for the test requests against the index terms assigned to both relevant and nonrelevant documents, we can measure both recall and precision for the test collection and extrapolate the precision to the entire system data base. This technique has been used successfully by Westat Research, Inc., in the evaluation of experimental retrieval systems at the U.S. Patent Office.

In considering time allowance for indexing, it is necessary to remember that variations in indexing time are likely to affect not only the average exhaustivity of the indexing but also the indexing accuracy. The

---

*By a useful term we mean one that is necessary to allow retrieval of a document in response to a request for which the document is agreed to be relevant. The decision that a particular term should be assigned may be made by a jury of indexers or subject specialists or derived empirically from an analysis of requests and relevance decisions made by system users.

greater the production pressures, the more indexing errors are likely to occur. These errors are of two types: (1) the omission of an important term that should be assigned and (2) the use of an incorrect term. The former, which is likely to be more prevalent, causes recall failures, except in searches involving negations, whereas the latter can lead to both recall and precision failures. A cost-effectiveness analysis relating to indexing time expenditure must take into account the effect of time allowance on accuracy as well as its effect on exhaustivity. In this connection it is important to remember that indexing errors can have a multiplicative effect on recall in postcoordinate retrieval systems. This can be shown by a simple example. Suppose that, in the indexing of a particular document collection, the index term A has been assigned to 90% of the documents to which, by consensus, it should have been assigned, the term B has been assigned to 85% of the documents to which it should have been assigned, and the term C has been assigned to 75% of the documents to which it should have been assigned. When we search on term A alone, we retrieve 90% of the documents that we should retrieve; that is, we achieve 90% recall of the A documents. However, when we search on A *and* B, our recall for this set may drop to 76.5% (90% × 85%), whereas a search on A *and* B *and* C may give us a recall of only 57.4% (90% × 85% × 75%) of documents that properly belong to the ABC set. In considering, from a cost-effectiveness viewpoint, the influence of indexing time on indexing accuracy, we thus need to take into account this multiplicative effect on retrieval performance. This means that we must be able to estimate the average accuracy of assignment of terms throughout the vocabulary of the system and to relate this to the average coordination level used in searches. The effect of various types of indexing error on the effectiveness of postcoordinate searching using various search strategies has been discussed in detail by Bryant, King, and Terragno (1963). King (1965, 1967) has described an application of these techniques and has also developed a useful model for converting data for indexer consistency into data for indexer accuracy, and vice versa.

A very closely related question is that of the necessity for an indexing revision process, that is, the checking of the work of one indexer by a second, usually more experienced, person. Whether or not the revision process is justified on cost-effectiveness grounds depends on

1. The amount of error occurring in unrevised indexing.
2. The amount of error that is corrected by the revision operation.
3. The estimated effect of indexing error, revised and unrevised, on retrieval performance.
4. The cost of revision.

Simple and inexpensive experiments, in which a revision process is conducted and timed on a set of indexed documents, some of which contain known errors, tell us the expected correction rate for the revision operation and its costs. Revisers should be varied to allow determination of average reviser performance and to allow the study of the performance of various types of personnel in this task. Percentage error reduction can then be related to estimated effect on retrieval performance. As a result of this analysis, we should be able to say that a revision operation costing x dollars per year is likely to correct y percent of the indexing errors that occur and that this is likely to have a specified effect on the average recall and precision performance of the system. In passing, it should be noted that a revision operation is more likely to identify and alter incorrect terms than indexer omissions unless these happen to be particularly glaring errors—for example, terms representing concepts occurring in titles.

One further aspect of the indexing process that may be subjected to this type of analysis is the level of personnel required to undertake the indexing. Obviously, indexing costs can be reduced substantially if we can successfully use a less highly educated and thus less highly paid cadre of indexers. At least one large agency has moved successfully from a system in which indexing was done by highly skilled analysts, all with college degrees, to one in which most of the indexing is conducted by personnel without college degrees. Another assumption that is sometimes made is that a good indexer needs to have a formal educational qualification in the subject matter of the documents handled. This has never been proved conclusively, and, in fact, most studies that have been conducted in this area have tended to reveal the opposite. A number of factors determine how senior the indexing staff needs to be, including

1. The complexity of the subject matter handled.
2. The type of index language used. Free key word indexing may require less skilled personnel than use of a classification schedule or a complex scheme of relational indicators.
3. The exhaustivity and specificity of the indexing. The greater the technical detail indexed, the greater the need for subject expertise.
4. The stage of system development. In the early stages of indexing a collection, using a controlled vocabulary, virtually every indexing decision made is intellectual. At a later stage, providing the intellectual decisions have been recorded in an authority file or entry vocabulary, the indexing operation is more likely to be susceptible to delegation to less highly educated personnel who can do much of the work by following decisions made in the past.

5. The quality of the tools provided to aid the indexing process.
6. The quality of the indexing training program.

Certainly a cost-effectiveness analysis of the indexing subsystem would be incomplete without a study of required personnel levels. We should therefore be prepared to experiment by having various document sets indexed by personnel of various levels and comparing the resulting indexing with a standard indexing for the test documents, established by some consensus. Time factors should also be considered. The measured effectiveness of the indexing achieved by these various groups can then be compared with the indexing costs.

COST-EFFECTIVENESS ASPECTS OF INDEX LANGUAGES

Cost-effectiveness analysis is applicable to the design and application of index languages but it is rather more difficult to apply in this area, and the results are more difficult to express in tangible terms. It is expensive to develop and maintain a highly sophisticated index language for vocabulary control in large information retrieval systems. In fact, the more sophisticated the vocabulary, the more expensive it is likely to be to apply and maintain. An important economic consideration is vocabulary size. The more index terms in the vocabulary, that is, the greater the number of document classes that can be uniquely defined, the greater its specificity and the greater the precision capabilities of the system. However, a large, highly specific controlled vocabulary tends to be costly to develop, apply, and update. The specificity of the vocabulary must be related directly to that of the requests made to the system. It is certainly uneconomical and inefficient to develop and use a vocabulary considerably more specific than the level of specificity required by the demands placed on the system. This implies the strong economic necessity of conducting a careful analysis of representative requests at the stage of system design. In considering vocabulary specificity we must, of course, make allowances for growth of the data base and its effect on the average number of citations retrieved per search. A precision of 20% may be tolerable when the average search output is 12 citations, but it may be completely intolerable when the average output is 125 citations.

A closely related consideration is the need for additional precision devices such as links, role indicators, subheadings, and term weighting. These devices are intended to improve system precision by reducing the number of unwanted items retrieved in a search as a result of false coordinations, incorrect term relationships, or highly exhaustive indexing. They are usually costly to apply. Role indicators, in particular, are likely to add substantially to indexing and search formulating costs, and they may add to actual search processing costs. Because they increase specificity of the vocabulary, they almost invariably cause reduced consistency of indexing. Frequently they have a devastating effect on recall. Subheadings, which may function simultaneously as links and roles, also add to indexing costs and reduce indexer consistency. However, they tend to have a less drastic effect than the use of role indicators. In mechanized and semimechanized retrospective search systems, these devices serve to reduce the number of irrelevant citations one must examine to find each relevant one. Obviously they can be justified economically only if they prove cheaper than alternative methods of achieving the same results for the end user. Role indicators, for example, reduce or possibly eliminate one particular type of unwanted retrieval, namely, the incorrect term relationship—the situation, in postcoordinate systems, in which the terms causing retrieval are related but not in the way that the requester wants them related. A cost-effectiveness analysis may well reveal that it is more economical not to use role indicators, thereby saving indexing and searching time, to allow some incorrect term relations to occur, and to eliminate the irrelevant citations thus retrieved through a postsearch screening operation conducted by a member of the information staff.

A very important but usually sadly neglected component of an index language is the entry vocabulary, that is, a vocabulary of natural-language expressions, occurring in documents or requests, that map onto the controlled vocabulary of the system. Usually, the entry vocabulary comprises terms that, for indexing and retrieval purposes, are either considered synonymous with controlled vocabulary terms or are more specific than controlled vocabulary terms—for example, HELIARC WELDING use SHIELDED ARC WELDING. Although an extensive entry vocabulary may be relatively expensive to construct and update, it can have a significant effect on improving performance, by reducing recall failures, particularly of large retrieval systems. It can also have significant long-term benefits to the cost effectiveness of the system by reducing the intellectual burden on both indexers and searchers. An entry vocabulary is really a collection of records of intellectual decisions made primarily by indexers. Unless an intellectual decision made by an indexer—topic X index under term Y—is recorded, the decision will have to be made again—not necessarily with the same mapping results, hence inconsistency—by other indexers or the same indexer at a later date. Moreover, the system searchers also will have to make intellectual decisions, not necessarily agreeing with the indexers, when they come to search for literature on topic X. The larger the entry vocabulary, the fewer current intellectual decisions need to be made by indexers and searchers, thus reducing indexing and search time; the greater the consistency in indexing; the better the recall of the system; and, possibly, the lower the professional level of the staff now needed in the indexing operation.

COST-EFFECTIVENESS ASPECTS OF SEARCHING PROCEDURES

There is a possible tradeoff between effort spent in the creation of a search strategy, for machine retrieval purposes, and that spent in the screening of search output. If we invest a great deal of time in the creation of a carefully constructed, tight search strategy, we can, depending on the capabilities of the system vocabulary, expect to achieve a high-precision search output that requires little or no postediting. An alternative approach would be to search more broadly and remove obvious irrelevancy by the screening of search output. Providing the searcher can examine the output and make relevance predictions that match reasonably well the actual relevance decisions that would be made by the end user, the latter approach may be more effective in terms of achieving high recall at a tolerable precision. It may also be more cost-effective.

Assuming a reasonable agreement between relevance decisions made by screener and end user, we must still determine whether or not a screening operation is worthwhile economically. By evaluation procedures we must determine what proportion of the irrelevant citations, appearing in a search printout, can be eliminated in the screening operation, what proportion of the relevant citations are eliminated at the same time, and how much the screening operation costs, in staff time, per irrelevant citation deleted. From this analysis we can determine how much it costs to use postsearch screening as a means of raising average search precision by, say, 10% and what the average drop in recall is likely to be for a precision increase of this dimension. In a study of the effectiveness of screening in a large mechanized retrieval system—approximately half a million documents—the author discovered that a search analyst, working from a machine printout of document titles only, was able to raise the average search precision from approximately 45 to about 75%. At the same time there was an average recall loss of about 10%. The screening rate was between three and four citations per minute. Figures such as these yield realistic cost figures for the screening operation and allow us to balance the screening costs against the screening effectiveness.

A cost-effectiveness analysis of the searching operation should include a breakdown of the various components in the cost of conducting a search so that any areas of seeming inefficiency may be identified. In the system just mentioned, the search analysts' time was spent roughly as follows in the conduct of searches (time is in average minutes per search):

Discussing requirements with the requester	8
Conceptualization of search strategy	20
Completing search input forms	19
Screening search output	30
Total	77

From these data it was possible to identify an obvious source of inefficiency. Almost as much time was being spent in completing an input form as in deciding which combinations of terms to search. The input form was a fairly complex data processing form requiring the presentation of the strategy in a prescribed manner that demanded great accuracy in spelling, punctuation, and spacing. The searchers were spending valuable time in what was essentially a clerical function—reducing the intellectual strategy to machinable format—that should be a part of the data processing subsystem rather than the search subsystem. In this situation obvious searching economies are possible if the machine input procedures and requirements can be simplified. In considering the various components of searching costs, it is important to distinguish between the costs that are relatively constant with the size of data base and those which tend to increase with the size of the data base. In the example, all time factors are relatively constant except that for screening. As the data base grows, we do not expect that this will necessarily increase the time involved in initial request negotiation, conceptualization of the strategy, or actual search input procedures. On the other hand, growth in the data base causes an increase in the average number of citations retrieved in a search—in fact average search output may grow almost linearly with the growth of the file—and thus screening costs also increase. In considering cost effectiveness of screening, therefore, we must make projections as to what our screening costs are likely to be some years from now.

Just as in indexing, a cost-effectiveness analysis of the search process must evaluate the professional level of personnel required. Obviously, significant economies are possible if the professional level can be reduced. Possibly this might be achieved by the production of improved searching aids that would take some of the intellectual burden off the searcher's shoulders. A further consideration would be the desirable degree of specialization among analysts. It is usually desirable that indexer and searcher be the same person. However, we must also concern ourselves with the cost aspects of amalgamation of the two functions. It may be more economical to form a combined staff, spending part of its time indexing and part of its time searching; on the other hand, it may not. Indexing tends to be more of a production-line operation than searching, and overall productivity may drop when the two functions are combined.

Another factor susceptible to cost-effectiveness analysis is the amount of interaction occurring between the search analyst and the requester. Such interaction takes place to ensure that the request statement, for which the search strategy is constructed, is an accurate reflection of the precise information requirements of the requester. The more interaction that takes place, for the purpose of clarifying a request, the better the end results are likely to be, in terms of recall or precision. However, once more there are possible tradeoffs; for example, between the amount of effort spent in interaction with the requester before the search and that expended in output screening. Moreover, there are various stages at which the interaction could take place: at the request stage; the search formulation stage—presenting the proposed strategy to the requester for his approval or modification—and the output stage—an iterative search procedure by which preliminary search results are evaluated by the requester and a new strategy is constructed, manually or automatically, on the basis of his relevance assessments on retrieved items. The later the interaction takes place in the total retrieval process, the better it is likely to be. Lesk and Salton (1969) discovered, in their evaluation of searches in the SMART system, that postsearch interaction is usually better than presearch interaction. There usually is an optimum set of interaction procedures in a particular environment, and some modes of interaction may actually degrade rather than improve search performance. For example, in the MEDLARS evaluation (Lancaster, 1968a) it was found that face-to-face interviews, between requesters and search analysts or requesters and medical librarians, did not necessarily improve the quality of requests and in some cases actually caused request distortion. It appears to be more effective to have the requester write out his request, in his own natural-language terms, and then to interact to clarify his request statement, than to have the requester discuss his need with an information specialist, the request statement being an outcome of this interview process.

From the cost-effectiveness point of view, the user-system interaction process may be the single most critical area in an information system. If a user makes a poor request, that is, one that does not accurately reflect his actual information need, the search is almost certainly doomed to failure—however efficient the indexing, vocabulary, and search strategies are—and subsequent search effort largely is wasted. To avoid senseless waste in the construction of search strategies, the processing of the search, and the screening of output, techniques used to improve the quality of requests are usually easy to justify economically. A considerable improvement may result, for example, from a well-structured form designed to help the user put the best possible request to the system. The completion of such a form may require more effort on his part initially but results in an improved search product and saves time in the long run—for example, it saves screening time of user or search analyst.

The various possible modes of interaction certainly can be tested for effectiveness and subjected to comparative cost analyses.

TRADEOFFS IN INFORMATION SYSTEMS

It should be obvious from the preceding discussion that there are many possible ways of operating an information system in such a way that it produces acceptable results—for example, retrospective searches that yield an acceptable recall at a tolerable precision to the end user. In other words, there are a number of possible tradeoffs between various processes—for example, indexing and vocabulary effort versus searching effort or search strategy effort versus screening effort. A cost-effectiveness analysis of a complete system compares these possible tradeoffs and determines which is the most efficient combination of procedures for obtaining a particular level of performance, that is, which combination is most effective in relation to the cost variables.

The major tradeoff to be considered is the very general one between input and output costs. Almost invariably, economies in input procedures result in an increased burden on output processes and thus increased output costs. Conversely, greater care in input processing, which usually implies increased input costs, can be expected to improve efficiency and reduce output costs. Some possible tradeoffs are enumerated in the following paragraphs:

1. A carefully controlled and structured index language versus free use of uncontrolled key words. The controlled vocabulary requires effort in construction and maintenance and is more expensive to apply in indexing. It takes longer, on the whole, to select terms from a controlled vocabulary, which may involve a lookup operation, than it does to assign key words freely; moreover, key word indexing may

require less qualified personnel than the use of a more sophisticated controlled vocabulary. The controlled vocabulary, however, saves time and effort at the time of output. Natural-language or key word searching, without the benefit of a controlled vocabulary with classificatory structure, puts increased burden on the searcher, who is virtually forced into the position of constructing a segment of a controlled vocabulary each time he prepares a search strategy—for example, he thinks of all possible ways in which petrochemicals or textile industry could be expressed by key words or in natural-language text. Likewise, the uncontrolled use of key words may lead to reduced average search precision and thus may require additional effort and cost in output screening.

2. Rigid quality control of indexing—for example, by a revision operation—versus indexing without any review procedure. Again, the review increases the indexing costs but presumably saves output costs by reducing screening time necessary to weed out obvious irrelevancy. Whether the input review is justified economically can be determined only by an evaluation of the number of indexing errors occurring and the number of these that could be corrected by a checking operation.

3. A highly specific, controlled vocabulary versus a relatively more broad, controlled vocabulary. The former is generally more expensive to create, maintain, and apply. The more specific the vocabulary, the more difficult it becomes to achieve indexing consistency and the higher the level of the personnel that may be needed to apply it. On the other hand, a highly specific vocabulary may allow high search precision and thus save on output screening time. A particular form of specificity is achieved by role or relational indicators, and these comments apply equally to the use of such devices.

These are merely three examples of possible tradeoffs between input and output effort. Many other possibilities exist. Table 8 presents a tradeoff comparison of two hypothetical information systems. In system A great care and expense is put into the input operation with a resulting economy in output effort and costs. In system B, on the other hand, deliberate policies designed to economize on input costs are in effect with the inevitable result that output effort and costs are increased. System A is not necessarily more efficient than system B, and vice versa. The approach taken in system B may be more cost-effective than that in system A if we can show that it achieves an acceptable level of performance for the end user with overall costs less than those associated with system A.

Table 8 Tradeoff Comparison of Two Hypothetical Information Systems

System A	System B
Input characteristics:	Input characteristics:
A large, carefully controlled vocabulary	A small controlled vocabulary supplemented by the free use of key words
Indexing of medium exhaustivity (an average of 10 terms per document)	Low exhaustivity of indexing (5 terms per document)
Highly trained indexers at a high salary level	Less highly trained indexers without college degrees
An indexing revision process	No indexing revision
Average indexer productivity of 40 items per day	Average indexer productivity of 100–125 items per day
High input costs	Low input costs
Relatively long delay between publication and actual input to system	Fast throughput
Output characteristics:	Output characteristics:
Reduced burden on the searcher in preparation of strategies	Greater burden on the searcher in the preparation of strategies
High precision of raw output	Low precision of raw output
Tolerable recall	Tolerable recall
No screening needed	Screening of raw output needed to raise precision to tolerable level for end user
Fast response time	Delayed response
Relatively low search costs	Relatively high search costs

Many different factors enter into the decision as to whether to put emphasis on the input or output processes of an information system. The most important considerations are probably the following:

1. *Volume.* The volumes of concern are the volumes of documents indexed and the volumes of requests processed annually. In the extreme situation of many documents indexed but comparatively few requests handled, it would be rational, all other things being equal, to economize on input costs and put an additional load on the output function. In the reverse situation—comparatively few documents

input but many requests handled—the opposite would be true, and savings would be best effected at the output stage.
2. *Required Input Speed.* In certain situations it is imperative that documents get into the system as rapidly as possible. This is certainly true, for example, in the situation in which the information system serves a dissemination (current awareness) function, as in certain intelligence situations. Under these circumstances it is likely that required speed of input would outweigh other considerations and that indexing economies would be adopted.
3. *Required Output Speed.* In other situations, rapid and accurate response may be vital—for example, the case of the Poison Information Center—and no economies at input are justified if they are likely to result in delayed response or reduced accuracy of output.
4. *By-products.* Under certain conditions it may be possible to obtain a searchable data base very inexpensively. For example, we may be able to acquire a machine-readable data base, perhaps in natural-language form, that is a by-product of some other operation—for example, publishing or report preparation—or has been made available by some other information center. Even though the input format and quality may not be ideal for our requirements, from the cost-effectiveness viewpoint, if the data base is available at nominal cost, it might be desirable to make use of it, possibly with some slight modifications, and to expend greater effort on the searching operation.

Earlier, we discussed some cost-effectiveness factors relative to the various subsystems of a complete information system: indexing, index language, searching, and user-system interaction. In fact, in the analysis of cost effectiveness, just as in the evaluation of effectiveness, it is unrealistic and dangerous to consider any one of the subsystems in isolation. All these components are very closely related, and a significant change in one will almost certainly cause repercussions throughout the system as a whole. We must be aware of this, and, in any cost-effectiveness analysis, we must be sure to consider the long-term, indirect effects of any system changes as well as the immediate, direct effects. For example, suppose we make the decision to move away from a carefully controlled, sophisticated index language to something much simpler. We can expect the immediate effects to be

1. A reduction in vocabulary control and maintenance costs.
2. A reduction in indexing time.
3. Improved throughput time.

There will also be some long-term, less direct effects:

1. The time required to prepare search strategies may increase, resulting in a rise in searching costs.
2. Search precision may be reduced, and we may find we need an output screening operation.
3. If we now need output screening, we may also need to improve the quality of the document surrogates in the system. Perhaps we will need to include abstracts when they were previously unnecessary.

A similar phenomenon may occur if we increase the average exhaustivity of indexing. As immediate effects we would expect an increase in indexing time and costs, an increase in the average number of documents retrieved per search, an improvement in recall, and a drop in average precision. Again, the long-term effects may be that we need an output screening operation to keep precision, to the end user, at a tolerable level and that we may need improved document surrogates to effect the screening operation. An information system is a complex organism, and we must not expect any change to have only local effects.

COST ANALYSIS FACTORS

One barrier to the application of cost-effectiveness or cost-benefit analysis to information systems is that realistic costing procedures for information products and services are generally lacking. At least, if cost data are available from various services, they are rarely published. We must cost the operations of a system in some meaningful way if we are to be able to measure economic improvements in tangible terms. We can readily measure certain savings—for example, reduction in indexing costs by elimination of certain materials or by reducing exhaustivity of indexing—but how do we measure the cost effectiveness of raising the system performance, for example, from 60% recall at 50% precision to 75% recall at 50% precision?

The problems of costing information systems have been discussed by Marron (1969), who concludes that standard cost accounting procedures, as used in conventional business applications, cannot be applied totally to information center services. A document collection or file is not analogous to machinery or equipment, especially with regard to depreciation. The problem of cost allocation is particularly difficult when a number of different products—for example, abstracts journal, title announcement bulletin, retrospective search, SDI—are generated from the same data base. It is relatively easy to calculate direct output costs, but how do we allocate input costs over the various products and services? Marron addresses this problem but does not present a solution that is entirely satisfactory.

Assuming that we can allocate our input costs in some realistic manner, we should be able to arrive at a series of unit costs for various bibliographic products and services. Typical unit costs might be cost per retrospective search conducted, citation retrieved, citation printed, page printed, or item disseminated. Unfortunately, this type of unit cost is very sensitive to changes in volume but is not at all reflective of changes in performance level. For example, consider the cost per citation retrieved, which has been used as a unit by the National Library of Medicine in the costing of retrospective searches. This unit cost is very sensitive to changes in volume but is not at all reflective of improvements in performance. For example, suppose it is calculated that the unit cost per citation retrieved is 74 cents. Obviously, this unit cost fluctuates with volume of output. Suppose we change our search strategies so that we retrieve, on the average, twice as many citations per search as we did before. The unit cost per citation is also cut approximately in half to about 37 cents, implying greater efficiency. In fact, the change in search strategies may have caused a drastic degradation in performance; broadening of the search strategies causes only additional irrelevancy, and the average search precision drops from 50 to 25%.

Clearly, for cost-effectiveness purposes, we need unit costs that are sensitive to changes in the effectiveness of the system. One such unit cost is the unit cost per relevant citation retrieved C_R. Suppose we have a system that operates at an average of about 50% precision, with a cost per relevant citation retrieved of about $1.48. Obviously, when we make changes to the system that raise its average recall or precision performance, they reduce the cost per relevant citation retrieved. Thus, C_R is a useful unit by which we may express improvements in the cost effectiveness of information systems.

This unit may be used to compare alternative operating modes in a system or the cost effectiveness of two or more essentially different systems. Thus, we can use this measure to assess the economic effects of making changes to our indexing procedures, vocabulary, searching strategies, or mode of interaction with the user. Raising the average indexing exhaustivity, for example, may result in a substantial improvement in recall, and, allowing for increased indexing costs, this in fact may mean a significant reduction in the cost per relevant citation retrieved.

Westat Research, Inc., used the cost per relevant document (patent) retrieved as a unit for measuring the cost effectiveness of six experimental coordinate indexing systems at the U.S. Patent Office and as a means of comparing the retrieval effectiveness of the systems with that of conventional manual searching in classified patent files. The principal component in the unit cost was the average time expended by a patent examiner in finding a patent sufficiently relevant for him to cite against a claim. On this unit-cost basis, most of the experimental systems were not justifiable when compared with manual searching; that is, the cost per relevant patent found was less in manual searching than it was in using the peek-a-boo systems.

Cost per relevant citation is also a unit that can be used to assess the efficiency of printed indexes or abstracts journals or that of a nondelegated search in an on-line system. In this case, the relevant unit cost is the user time required to find a relevant citation. Assume a printed index, say, *Index Medicus* or *Engineering Index,* and assume two users of the index, A and B. Let us also assume that, in an annual cumulation of the index, there are 25 papers of potential interest to user A and 30 papers of potential interest to user B. In consulting the index, A is able to find 20 relevant papers, that is, a recall of 20/25, or 80%, with a total time expenditure of two hours; whereas B is able to find 28 papers, a recall of 93%, in a search taking one hour. Neither is able to achieve 100% recall, because either some potentially relevant items are hidden away under headings that the searchers do not think to consult or they are unable to identify all relevant items from the surrogate (title or abstract) provided. The unit cost, in time, per relevant citation retrieved is six minutes per paper for user A and two minutes per paper for user B. Assuming that both A and B have searched intelligently, the index performed more efficiently for B's search than for A's, probably because the vocabulary of the index matched B's requirements better than it did A's. Obviously, a user judges a printed index by the ease with which he can find relevant citations, that is, the cost per relevant citation retrieved, and the effectiveness of the index to the end user can be improved if we can reduce the average search time of index users. This might be done in a number of different ways: increasing the exhaustivity of the indexing, that is, increasing the number of access points provided; increasing the specificity of the vocabulary, that is, reducing the number of citations listed under each heading; improving the cross-reference structure, so that the user is assisted in the creation of a productive heuristic strategy; or increasing the amount of detail provided in order to improve relevance assessments. The costs of making changes of this type can be calculated, and the results, in terms of average search effectiveness, can also be measured.

Cost effectiveness of these various alternatives can be evaluated by comparing production costs with search effectiveness in terms of average user search time per relevant citation retrieved.

Another possible cost-effectiveness study relates to the optimum allocation of the financial resources of an institution over all the services provided. The object here is to determine if a different distribution of resources will result in better services to the users. The major problem is establishing user preferences and priorities for various services so that the allocation of the budget can be made to correspond to the user priorities. A very useful technique for achieving this was described by Raffel and Shishko (1969). In brief, it involves the use of a type of "management game" played with samples of the user population. The users are given a list of possible services and several possible budgets one of which is the existing budget of the institution. They are also given a list of likely outcomes (benefits and penalties) if changes are made to patterns of service, and the allocation of the budget over these services. The users are asked to allocate the budget available over the various service options in order to reflect their own preferences and needs. The allocation of resources in this way gives the information service a better idea of the needs of users, better than simply asking the users for their preferences in a more abstract way, and different sets of priorities among different segments of the user community can be identified.

Most of the types of study mentioned so far in this chapter are concerned with various manifestations of "diminishing returns." These studies seek to identify some level of service that can be reached efficiently and economically, a level beyond which it is impossible to go without dramatic and disproportionate increases in expenditure. This phenomenon of diminishing returns, applied to library and information services, is referred to by Bourne (1965) in terms of the "90 percent library." It is usually unrealistic, and frequently economically infeasible, to expect an information service to satisfy 100% of all the needs of users. But it is possible to establish a lesser goal—85, 90, or even 95%—that can be achieved efficiently and economically. The types of analysis mentioned in this chapter can be used to determine what level of service is economically feasible and to identify procedures or policies by which it can be provided in the most efficient manner possible.

BENEFIT AND COST-BENEFIT STUDIES

A cost-benefit study is concerned with the relationship between the cost of providing a service and the benefits of having it available. The service is justified if the benefits are judged to exceed the costs. Unfortunately, although the principle of cost-benefit analysis sounds simple, studies of this kind are not at all easy to carry out because of the difficulties of measuring the benefits of information services and, more particularly, putting some monetary value on them. Some possible criteria for establishing a cost-benefit ratio for information services include

1. Cost savings through the use of the service as compared with the costs of obtaining needed information or documents from other sources.
2. Avoidance of loss of productivity—for example, of students, faculty, research workers—that would result if information sources were not readily available.
3. Improved decision making or reduction in the level of personnel required to make decisions.
4. Avoidance of duplication or waste of research and development effort on projects which either have been done before or have been proved infeasible by earlier investigators.
5. Stimulation of invention or productivity by making available the literature on current developments in a particular field.

Mason (1972) and Magson (1973) have both presented techniques that might be used to evaluate the benefits of information services. They attempt to arrive at a "benefit" figure for a particular activity by comparing the cost of the activity with an alternative approach to achieving the same results. One alternative could involve elimination of a certain activity, with library users having to obtain the particular service elsewhere. The measure of "benefit" is the savings associated with the present service as compared with the costs of the alternative method of achieving the same results. Rosenberg (1969) also attempted a cost-benefit analysis of an industrial library through the measurement of the time saved by engineers because of the existence of the library's services. A rather complete analysis of possible approaches to cost-effectiveness and cost-benefit evaluation of information services has been prepared by Flowerdew and Whitehead (1974).

Because of the great difficulties involved in measuring the benefits of information service in tangible terms, most attempts at assessing benefits are content with asking a sample of users their opinions about the benefits of the services provided. There is nothing wrong with this approach, because "user satisfaction" is a major concern of managers of information services, and it may be the only feasible approach to the evaluation of benefits in many circumstances. A careful user study, conducted through interviews or mailed questionnaires, can produce many data to indicate user satisfaction with the services provided by an information center as well as user perceptions of the benefits of having the service available.

It is probably true to say, in fact, that studies of effectiveness and cost effectiveness can be completely objective, but benefit and cost-benefit studies always involve some subjective judgment. For example, it is possible to calculate the costs of three alternative approaches to providing a service with a specified level of effectiveness—for example, an 85% rate of success in document delivery—and to determine that approach A, which costs $32,000 a year, is the most cost-effective. This is a completely objective analysis. But a cost-benefit analysis of the situation is unlikely to be completely objective. Ultimately some individual or organization must decide if it is worth spending $32,000 a year on a document delivery service satisfying 85% of all demands made. This is likely to be a somewhat subjective decision because, as stated earlier, it is rather unlikely that the benefits of the document delivery service can be quantified in any satisfactory way.

The objective of a benefit evaluation is to assess the impact of the information service on the behavior and performance of its users. For reasons discussed earlier, the use of questionnaires or interviews with a sample of the users, institutional or personal, is likely to be the most practical way to conduct a benefit study of this kind. The technique is probably best illustrated through examples.

Two studies of the benefits of information services will be used as examples. The first is the UNESCO "appraisal" of the AGRIS program of FAO, as reported by Badran et al. (1977), and the second is a survey of two current awareness publications in the neurosciences, as reported by Lancaster (1974b).

Although there were several facets to the AGRIS study, the major purpose was to determine what impact the program has had on the dissemination of agricultural information worldwide and what appears to be its potential for the future. The study was conducted in the period October 1976 to March 1977. The major constraints of the evaluation were as follows:

1. It was to be conducted by a four-man international team, including two specialists in agriculture and two in information services.
2. The whole study, including preparation of the report, had to be completed in a period of six months.
3. Funds available for completion of the study were relatively modest—a total of about $50,000.
4. The study was begun at a time when AGRIS had been fully operational for less than two years. The data base was by no means comprehensive, and there was great variation in the extent to which

member nations of FAO were contributing to the data base: some national centers were more or less complete in indexing their national agricultural literature, some were covering a relatively small proportion of the national literature—in some cases, about 20%—and some nations were providing no direct input.

Because the major emphasis was the identification of present and prospective benefits of AGRIS, and, as previously mentioned, the determination of benefits tends to be subjective rather than objective, the AGRIS study was essentially a subjective appraisal made by an independent evaluation team. The team made its report to UNESCO, which, in turn, presented the results to FAO. To ensure that the conclusions and recommendations of the team should benefit from the informed opinion of organizations in many different countries—developed and developing countries, countries participating in AGRIS input at various levels, and some countries not actively participating—it was decided that the time of the team members would most effectively be spent in visiting as many as possible of these countries in the time available for the study.

In order to ensure that the opinions of national representatives were obtained in a consistent manner, the same questions being addressed in each country, an interview guide or questionnaire was prepared by members of the team. This interview guide, in English, French, and Spanish versions (the official languages of FAO), was, wherever possible, distributed to the organizations to be visited in advance of the visits by the team members. Each team member visited a different group of countries. During each visit an interview was conducted with representatives of organizations whose responsibilities are related to AGRIS—AGRIS input centers, liaison offices, and government agencies in the agricultural field. Frequently the interviews were group interviews, gathering the opinions of a group of individuals. The interview guide was regarded as a point of departure only. The interviewees were encouraged to express their opinions on AGRIS-related matters not directly addressed in the interview guide, and these opinions too were recorded by the interviewer (a member of the evaluation team). FAO member nations not selected for a visit were sent a copy of the same questionnaire and asked to complete it and return it by mail. In toto, interviews were conducted in 24 different countries, and mailed questionnaires were received from an additional 11 countries.

The questionnaire and interview guide for the AGRIS study are reproduced in Appendix 1. This is not necessarily presented as an "ideal" questionnaire for a study of this type, and, clearly, it cannot be used intact for studies of the benefit or impact of other information programs. Nevertheless, it may be useful as an example of the types of questions to be addressed in such a benefit study. From an examination of Appendix 1 it can be seen that data or opinions were gathered on each of the following:

1. The extent to which AGRIS products—the printed *Agrindex* and the magnetic tapes—are used in the country, including services provided from them.
2. The value of the products in comparison with other products and services, in printed or tape form, in the provision of agricultural information.
3. Perceived deficiencies in the AGRIS products and ways in which they might be improved.
4. The present level of personnel allocated to AGRIS input operations in each country and the level that would be needed for 100% coverage of the national literature.
5. Difficulties encountered in the provision of AGRIS input.
6. The extent to which AGRIS products have been promoted in the country.
7. The perceived value of AGRIS in the provision of agricultural information services and the impact of the program on the demand for agricultural information.
8. What services AGRIS should concentrate on in its further development.

Completing an evaluation of this kind is rather like completing a jigsaw puzzle—each interview or each questionnaire contributes another part to the puzzle. When all these parts are assembled, an overall picture of the impact, limitations, and problems of the program results. The survey instruments of the AGRIS study proved capable of yielding a body of data, opinion, and insights from which the evaluation team could draw their own conclusions on the impact and benefits of the program. The conclusions of the team, and their recommendations to FAO, are included in Appendix 2 as an example of the type of conclusions and recommendations that can result from a study of this kind.

The second example of a study of the benefits or impact of information services is an evaluation of two current awareness publications in the field of the neurosciences. The publications, *Parkinson's Disease and Related Disorders: Citations from the Literature* and *Biogenic Amines and Transmitters in the Nervous System,* were products of the Neurological Information Network of the National Institute of Neurological Diseases and Stroke (NINDS). The former, PD, is a computer-produced bulletin, generated from the MEDLARS data base of the National Library of Medicine. The latter, BA, is a manually prepared bulletin produced by the Brain Information Service of the University of California at Los Angeles. In 1972, when the study was conducted, PD was distributed free on a worldwide basis, and BA was sold to an international audience at an annual subscription of $12 in the United States and $18 elsewhere. The object of the evaluations was to determine who uses each publication, how much, for what purpose, and with what degree of success. The major purpose was to discover how valuable the publications are to users and what impact they have had on their own research or professional practice as well as their information-seeking behavior.

Because of the wide geographic distribution of the recipients of these publications, the only practical way to conduct the study was through the use of mailed questionnaires. Questionnaires were mailed to all individual recipients, that is, excluding institutional recipients, of each publication: 949 to recipients of PD and 734 to recipients of BA. The questionnaires were sent out with an accompanying letter, on NINDS letterhead, requesting the cooperation of the users. Follow-up postcards were sent out as necessary to procure a high level of response. Both questionnaires were pretested before being used in the final survey. A response rate of 51% was achieved in the PD survey and 69% in the BA survey.

One of the questionnaires is reproduced in Appendix 3 as an example of the types of question that seem important to a study of this kind. It can be seen from this appendix that the questions asked relate to the following types of information:

1. The field of specialization and professional responsibility of the recipient.
2. The degree to which the subject matter of the bulletin is central to his or her professional interests.
3. The information-gathering behavior of the recipient and the importance of the bulletin as a source of information in comparison with other sources.
4. The amount and type of use made of the bulletin.
5. The recipient's judgment on its value, relevance, and completeness.
6. The impact of the bulletin on the recipient's awareness of the literature covered and on his own information-gathering behavior.
7. Use made of specific features of the bulletin and suggestions as to how the bulletin might be made more useful.

As in the case of the AGRIS interview guide, this questionnaire is not necessarily put forward as an "ideal" model. Nevertheless, examples of survey instruments that have been used successfully in earlier studies have value in suggesting the types of questions that might be asked in future studies of this type. The instruments illustrated in Appendixes 1 and 3 are considered useful, therefore, in providing a base on which other studies of the impact or benefits of information services can be built.

Chapter Seventeen

Evaluation of a National Information System

A national information system may embrace a number of separate institutions, each with a special role to play in the provision of information service, and it may make many types of information service available: literature searching, including SDI; factual reference service; document delivery; the publication of indexing or abstracting services; translation facilities or indexes to available translations; a referral center; information analysis centers; consulting and advising services offered through extension officers; and so on. One possible criterion for the evaluation of a national system would be the extent to which all the services identified in Chapter 7 as necessary components of such a system exist in some form in a particular country. Other levels of evaluation would be concerned with effectiveness, cost effectiveness, benefit, and cost benefit aspects of the services provided.

The evaluation of the effectiveness of the literature searching components in a national system does not differ from that of other literature searching situations, as discussed in earlier chapters. But the fact that we are dealing with a rather complex system, incorporating a number of distinct components each with a special function to perform, may create some special problems in the evaluation of both effectiveness and cost effectiveness. The evaluation of a complete system can be regarded as more than the sum of that of its component parts. The relationships existing among these parts is also important. An assessment of the efficiency of the complete system must consider not only the efficiency of the individual components but also their functional interdependence. It is particularly important to identify activities in one component that are rendered less efficient by policies and procedures in existence elsewhere in the system—for example, inconsistencies in formats, incompatibility of communication media, and irregular patterns of flow from one center to another. In other words, it is important to view the national system as a coordinated whole as well as looking at its individual components. One obvious example of interdependency is between literature searching and document delivery services. Technological advances in the former have tended to outpace those in the latter. It is already technologically and economically feasible to bring machine literature searching capabilities into countries that can be considered "less developed" industrially and scientifically. But these services can be expected to create demands on other elements in the national system that are likely to be less well developed, including document delivery services, translation services, and services designed to interpret scientific and technical literature and repackage it for consumption and exploitation in industry, agriculture, public health, and other sectors of society.

The benefits of a national system may be assessed by a survey of the reactions and opinions of a representative sample of institutional and individual users of the service provided. The survey instrument used in the AGRIS study, as illustrated in Appendix 1, illustrates a possible approach to this type of study. Clearly, this cannot be applied intact to the evaluation of any other system. It may, however, suggest types of questions that should be asked in other evaluation studies. It can be modified for use in other applications.

It is possible, too, that the impact of a national system, once it has been fully developed, can be assessed in other ways than the conduct of a user survey. Statistical indicators of the "health" of a national information system are extremely important for planning and management purposes. It is essential for a national government, or some research organization to which this function is delegated, to collect on a regular basis the data needed to monitor the activities of the "information transfer cycle" (see Figure 1) as it applies to the country as a whole.

The health of the communication system in a country can be monitored by the collection, on an annual basis, of data that reflect volume, cost, and time factors related to the various activities depicted in Figure 1. These data constitute the "statistical indicators" of communication. The most important are probably those relating to scientific and technical communication, and this restriction is assumed in the following discussion.

It is important for a country to know at least the following in order to monitor the health of its own communication functions in the field of science and technology:

1. How much of the world output of primary literature in science and technology is acquired and made available through the "formal information system" of the country. These data should preferably be divided according to subject field.
2. How much of the national output of primary literature in science and technology is acquired and made available through the formal information system of the country.
3. The relative proportion of the national output to the world output in the various subject fields.
4. How much of the national output of primary literature is organized and controlled in secondary publications, including national bibliographies and indexing and abstracting services (national and international).
5. How much of the world's secondary literature, in printed and/or machine-readable form, is acquired and made available in the country.
6. How much secondary distribution occurs, as measured by the use of document delivery, reference, literature searching, and other services provided by libraries and other information centers.
7. How much assimilation of the published literature occurs in the country.
8. Time factors associated with the communication cycle, especially the time elapsing between publication of science literature and its availability in the country, on the one hand, and its assimilation by the professional community on the other.
9. Cost factors affecting the communication cycle, including the effect of publication costs on the availability of the literature, the adequacy of the budgets of formal information services for making the literature available, the cost of the organization and control of the literature that is nationally produced, and the cost of information services to the user.

A national system of indicators of this type should be regarded as an important monitoring activity. The importance of these indicators lies not so much in their absolute values as in the changes in these values over time, since such changes will reveal improving or worsening situations in terms of the availability of scientific, technical, and other information resources in a country. Only the larger and more fully developed countries may have as a goal the acquisition and availability of the total world literature in science and technology, but it would be important for all countries to know approximately what proportion of the world literature is acquired and made available year by year. A situation in which progressively less and less of the scientific and technical literature is acquired and made accessible, through the formal information systems of a country, could have serious consequences for its scientific, industrial, and economic development, and the situation in which proportionally more is made accessible each year would indicate the improved health of the national information system.

Some further points are worth emphasis in this connection. First, a country should be concerned not only with gross indicators of how much of the total world literature in science and technology is acquired and made readily accessible but also with more refined indicators in particular subject areas. In some countries, for example, agricultural information may be of extreme importance, and information on nuclear energy may be of quite minor concern. To carry this further, if the economy of a country is very heavily dependent on a single commodity, or a small group of commodities, it would be quite important to develop an indicator of the extent to which the world literature on the commodity is readily accessible in the country. Second, a country should be concerned not only with the extent to which the literature is acquired and made accessible but also that to which it is used, as reflected in data on the use of literature searching, reference, document delivery, and other services provided by the components of the national information system. Increased use of these resources would presumably indicate a healthy situation, and decreased use would indicate the reverse. Ultimately, a country should be concerned with the extent to which the world's scientific and technical literature is assimilated by its own professional community. Unfortunately, the assimilation of the literature is exceedingly difficult to measure. The most likely indicator of assimilation is the extent to which the literature is cited, but this indicator has two obvious limitations: it assumes that the contents of a document cited have in fact been assimilated, which may not always be true, and, more important, it indicates only assimilation of the literature by those who write, which is only a small segment of the total user community and perhaps an infinitesimally small segment in the case of a developing country.

The third point that must be emphasized is that all countries should be concerned with the extent to which their own primary literature is organized, controlled, and made available, since this should be regarded as a prime responsibility of each national information system. Thus, although most countries need not be directly concerned with the extent to which the world literature is organized and controlled by the major secondary services, since they have no direct control over this, every country should be concerned with the extent to which its own primary literature is organized and controlled by both its own national bibliographies and indexes and the international data bases.

The statistical indicators of most concern at the national level, then, vary from country to country. Only the countries that have assumed major responsibilities for indexing and abstracting the world literature of science and technology, such as the United States, France, and the Soviet Union, need be directly concerned with the proportion of the literature that is covered in their secondary services. But the Scandinavian countries, for example, should certainly be concerned with indicators of the extent to which the scientific and technical literature of Scandinavia is indexed and abstracted in the international data bases or those generated in Scandinavia itself.

Moreover, the more advanced developing countries may be concerned with special types of indicators relating to their own rate of science progress. A country such as Brazil is likely to have legitimate interest in the extent to which its own scientists report the results of their research in Portuguese in national journals as opposed to using other languages and the journals of other countries. It will also be interested in the extent to which Brazilian journals are indexed and abstracted in the international services. Presumably, as a country progresses scientifically, its own national channels of communication assume greater importance, in terms of both the proportion of the national research output that is first reported in these channels and the degree to which these channels are recognized in the international services.

In summary, a national information system must be concerned with all the activities depicted in Figure 1, and an important element in evaluation, at the national level, is the collection of statistical indicators of the health of the complete communication cycle in the country.

Apart from the impressive compilation of data for the United States by King et al. (1976), some of the most relevant studies toward the development of statistical indicators of the type outlined have been conducted in Mexico by Armando Sandoval and his colleagues at the Centro de Información Cientifica y Humanistica, Universidad Nacional Autónoma de México. This work is summarized in four papers by Sandoval et al. (1976a, b), Büttenklepper et al. (1976) and Pérez-Guinjoán et al. (1976). The bibliometric studies conducted in Mexico examine the quantity and distribution of articles on Latin America published in non-Latin American journals, including the proportion of the total contributed by Latin American authors, and the extent to which scientific and humanistic research conducted in Latin America is reported in journals of world prestige published outside Latin America. The contribution of individual countries to this literature, the contribution of individual institutions in these countries, and the distribution of the literature over about 4000 journals are also examined. The studies conducted in Mexico can be regarded as useful models of what can be done in the development of indicators of communication, in science, technology, and other fields, that may be of direct concern to policy makers at national levels. The Mexican studies were conducted as one-time surveys, but it is obvious that data of this type are of greatest value if collected, perhaps on a sampling basis, over a period of years, reflecting changing patterns in national and international communication. Ten years ago this type of continuous monitoring would have been difficult to contemplate. Now, however, almost all the world's literature is recorded in machine-readable data bases, and it has become feasible to monitor many important communication phenomena, of the type investigated in the Mexican studies, through the use of "national interest profiles" that can be matched against one or more data bases at regular intervals.

Chapter Eighteen

Pertinence and Relevance

In the earlier chapters we have used the term "relevance" to express the idea of the appropriateness of a document for a particular user. But relevance is not a precise term. Far from it. In this chapter we attempt to draw a meaningful distinction between "pertinence" and relevance, two terms that have been used in the literature of information science to express a relationship between some document and (1) some request for information, (2) some need for information, or (3) some individual who requests or needs information. Thus, it might be said that a particular document is relevant, or pertinent, to a particular request, information need, or individual who requests information on a particular subject. The relationship implied by these terms is extremely important to the evaluation of information services. Unfortunately the two terms have been used rather loosely in the literature, and a considerable amount of controversy seems to exist on what the two terms actually mean and whether or not relevance is in fact relevant to the evaluation of information services. Rees and Saracevic (1966), for example, raise the following questions:

1. Is relevance an adequate criterion for measures (of the performance of a retrieval system); is it a criterion?
2. If relevance is an adequate criterion, what does it represent?

3. Can relevance be used at all in practice; is it measurable; under what conditions (restriction, constraints) can it be employed?

We now try to clarify the issues and the terminology, to present our own views on the subject and those of other writers, and to mention some major research projects relating to the relevance concept.

The concept of relevance needs to be viewed in the broader context of a person needing information and coming to an information retrieval system to seek the information. As mentioned already in Chapter 10, it is quite important to distinguish among information needs, their recognition, and their expression. Information retrieval systems cannot respond to information needs of individuals as such but only to expressions of the needs; that is, an individual who needs information must recognize the need and must, presumably, be sufficiently aroused to take some steps to satisfy it. Only after he recognizes his need and is sufficiently aroused (motivated) will he express it in the form of a request to an information center. The degree to which he is able to recognize the exact nature of his information need and the degree to which his need is accurately reflected in his expression of it, that is, in the request statement, very largely determine how successful the information service is in attempting to satisfy the user. The information service can operate only on the basis of the stated request (expressed need) and, clearly, cannot respond to unrecognized needs or even to recognized needs that are unexpressed. As pointed out elsewhere by Lancaster (1968b), one of the major problems faced by any information service operated in a delegated search mode is to ensure that expressed needs accurately reflect recognized needs. It is not always easy for the person who needs information to express his need clearly and unequivocally to the person who is to search for the information.

Let us assume, then, that some person needs information and he comes to an information center to seek it. Let us also assume that his need is not of a factual data type—for example, the tensile strength of a particular steel—but of the type in which he needs to see documents that describe or discuss a particular subject area—for example, the treatment of disease X with drug Y. The user tries to make his need known to the staff of the center by means of a request statement. An information specialist on the staff of the center converts the request into a search strategy that is then matched against one or more data bases. We assume that the search is conducted in a computer-based system and the output of the search is a printout of representations—for example, bibliographic references—of documents that match the search strategy, that is, documents indexed in such a way that they satisfy the logical and termi-

258   Pertinence and Relevance

nological requirements of the strategy. We now have a whole set of possible relationships to contend with, as depicted in Figure 47.

We can be fairly sure that the document representations match the search strategy; otherwise they would not have been retrieved. We can be less sure that the documents themselves match the search strategy. Some may have been indexed incorrectly. In other cases the terms that caused the document to be retrieved may be essentially unrelated in the document (a false coordination) or related in a different way from that wanted by the searcher (an incorrect term relationship). Some of the retrieved documents may match the search strategy but not the request statement (expressed need of requester). This would happen, for example, if the search strategy includes some terms that are inappropriate to the request or the search is conducted at a higher generic level than that specified in the request.

Some retrieved documents may match the request statement but not the recognized need of the user. This would occur in cases in which the request statement does not completely and accurately represent the recognized need of the requester. Finally, it is conceivable that some of the documents match neither the request statement nor the recognized need but, completely fortuitously, match the actual information need. This

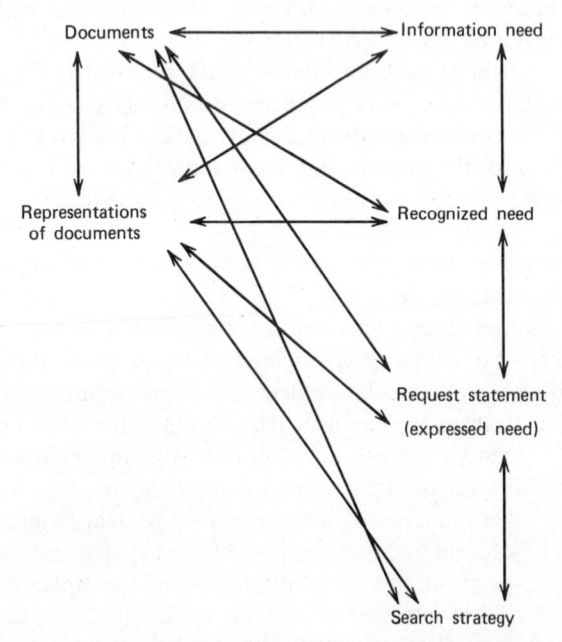

Figure 47   Some relationships important in the evaluation of information retrieval systems.

would imply that the system has retrieved some items that the requester, when he sees them, recognizes to be exactly what he needs to meet his present information requirement. These documents were outside the scope of his request statement because he was unaware that they existed. Consequently he could not, in his own mind, formulate his recognized need with sufficient clarity to allow this type of document to be encompassed by his request statement.

It is clear, then, that fairly complex relationships exist among the variables of information need, recognized need, expressed need, searching strategy, documents, and document representations. The whole situation is further complicated by the fact that some of the relationships are not constant over time. Both recognized needs and actual needs are quite likely to change. Thus, a document may match the recognized need of a requester one day but no longer on the following day. His perception of his need has changed in the intervening period.

Note that in the preceding discussion we have deliberately used the rather innocuous word "match" to refer to various relationships among requests, information needs, documents, and document representations. We now need to discuss what types of matches are involved, who can decide whether or not a match of a particular type has occurred, and what these matches might be called. The information specialist who conducts the search, or some other information specialist associated with the system, is probably in the best position to decide whether or not the document representation matches the search strategy. Match is really a very appropriate term for this relationship: a document representation matches if it contains a certain term, or combination of terms, included in the strategy. Anyone, in fact, who can read and understand the logic of the strategy can decide whether or not such a match has occurred.

Whether or not a particular document matches a search strategy is also best determined by the person constructing the strategy, although it could possibly be decided by another information specialist. This situation is a little more complicated than the one previously mentioned, in two respects:

1. We are concerned with more than a simple term or word match. Now we are concerned with relationships among terms or words, that is, syntactic relationships.
2. The match we are concerned with is, in a sense, between a document and an intended strategy. It is for this reason that the person formulating the search strategy is in the best position to judge whether or not the intended match has occurred.

This situation is perhaps best illustrated by a very simple example. Consider the case in which the searcher uses the strategy READING and EPILEPSY; that is, he asks for documents that contain both words or have been indexed under both terms. Several document representations containing the terms or words are retrieved; that is, they all match the strategy. The "system" has retrieved what it was asked to retrieve, and the search programs have behaved perfectly. But when the searcher looks at the set of documents corresponding to the retrieved representations, he discovers that they are of two types:

1. A large group of documents discussing epilepsy caused by reading, that is, a kind of photic epilepsy.
2. A small group of documents discussing the reading abilities of epileptic children.

It is the first group only that he intended to retrieve. The second group he did not want and, perhaps, did not expect.

In this case we can say that all the representations retrieved match the search strategy but that a few of the documents referred to do not match the intended strategy. The fault here is not with the search programs, or with the searcher's interpretation of the requester's needs, but with the indexing procedures and the indexing vocabulary of the system. If the indexing procedures were such that relationships among terms could be specified precisely—for example, by the use of role indicators—or if the vocabulary was more specific—for example, if the term READING EPILEPSY existed in the thesaurus—these unwanted items would have been avoided. We could hypothesize another situation in which a document representation contains the index term READING and the index term EPILEPSY, that is, it correctly matches the search strategy, but refers to a document which, on examination, is determined to deal not with reading epilepsy but with some other form of the disease. The indexer misinterpreted the document and indexed it incorrectly. In this case the representation, as it stands, matches the strategy, but the representation is incorrect because of an indexing error.

These relationships, between a document representation and a search strategy, are, in a sense, internal to the information system, and decisions as to whether or not appropriate matches have occurred need not involve either system users, that is, requesters, or other subject specialists. In fact, in some cases at least, individuals not directly involved with the system may not understand why a particular failure occurred or even why a particular item was retrieved. It is probably best if we use neither the word relevance nor the word pertinence for these relationships but simply refer to document representations "matching a search strategy" and documents "matching an intended strategy."

RELEVANCE

As mentioned earlier, however, we are concerned not only with matches between documents, or their representations, and searching strategies. We are also concerned with relationships between documents and request statements and between documents and the information needs of users. After an information retrieval system has operated, and retrieved a set of document representations in response to a particular request, it would be possible to retrieve the documents referred to and to decide which match the request and which do not. Who is qualified to make such decisions? We could ask information specialists associated with the system, we could ask the requester, or we could ask one or more independent subject specialists to make these decisions. Clearly, the person making such a decision must know enough about the subject matter that he is able to agree that certain documents are "legitimate responses" to the request and others are not. Legitimate response is admittedly rather vague. The person making the assessment presumably judges a document to be a legitimate response if he feels that the subject matter of the document is sufficiently close to the subject matter requested that the system was "correct" in retrieving it. Unfortunately, these relationships are not very exact. How close is sufficiently close? Closeness of a document to a request cannot be measured precisely; the relationship is subjective and equivocal rather than objective and unequivocal; that is, different judges may make different decisions on the degree of association between a document and a request. It is also quite possible that the same judge may make different decisions on a particular request-document pair at different times. Interjudge and intrajudge consistency, then, may both be somewhat low. Be that as it may, it seems reasonable to refer to this relationship as relevance. In other words, if a judge decides that a certain document is sufficiently close in subject matter to a particular request that the system was "correct" in retrieving it, it seems reasonable to say that he has judged the document to be relevant to the request.

Although other terminology could conceivably be used, we propose to adopt the term relevance to indicate a relationship existing between a document and a request statement in the eyes of a particular judge. It would be wrong to assume that relevance represents a precise, invariant relationship; it does not. In fact, rather than saying that a document is relevant to a request, it would be better to say that the document has been judged relevant to the request by a particular individual or group of individuals.

Since relevance decisions of this type are subjective and quite likely to be inconsistent, it may be dangerous to use a single set of relevance decisions, that is, made by one individual, as the basis for an evaluation of the performance of a retrieval system. For a particular request for which a search has been conducted in the system, one individual may judge 60% of the retrieved items to be relevant, and a second may judge 45% to be relevant, and a third 50%. If we are interested in evaluating the performance of a retrieval system solely on the basis of the document–request statement relationship, it would certainly seem desirable to involve a group of judges and try to arrive at some group consensus as to which documents are relevant to which requests. Use of several judges, working independently in making relevance decisions, would at least give us a ranking of documents in terms of "relevance consensus." We could then express the results of a particular search in the following form:

1. Thirty-five percent of the documents retrieved were judged relevant by all five judges.
2. Forty-three percent were judged relevant by at least four of the five judges.
3. Sixty-two percent were judged relevant by at least three of the judges, and so on.

PERTINENCE

It should be quite clear, however, that relevance decisions made on the basis of the relationship between documents and request statements have only limited use in the evaluation of operating information services. Such relevance decisions tell us nothing about the degree of success achieved in meeting the information needs of users, whether we consider "actual" needs or "recognized" needs, and the service exists, presumably, to meet such needs. It is quite possible for a document to be judged of relevance to a particular request statement by all members of a panel of judges but for the requester himself to decide that the document is of no value in satisfying the information need that prompted his request to the system. If all the documents retrieved by a search are judged of no value by the requester, that is, they do not contribute to the satisfaction of his information need, he will consider the search a failure however many judges we may get to agree that the documents are relevant to the request statement.

Significant differences between document–request relevance judgments made by a panel of judges and document–information need value judgments made by the requester himself would indicate, of course, that the request statement (expressed need) on which the system operated was an imperfect representation of the actual information need. We should not be too surprised, in fact, if these two sets of decisions should differ widely in some searches because it is frequently quite difficult for even a sophisticated requester to make his actual information needs known to an information center. To mention but one example, reported by Lancaster (1968a) in his evaluation of MEDLARS, a search conducted on the basis of the request statement of Cancer in the fetus or newborn infant retrieved 1167 journal articles, most of which would be judged relevant to the request statement by any panel of medical practitioners. But the requester himself made an inexcusably bad request to the system, one much more general than his actual information need. He was really interested in the relationship between teratogenesis and oncogenesis at the cellular level, a highly specific topic, and he judged only one of the 1167 documents of value in contributing to the satisfaction of his information need.

Some people would argue, and have in fact argued in the literature, that a system should be judged only on the basis of the request-document relationship and that it can be expected to do only what it was asked to do. If, for example, a system is asked to retrieve documents on cancer in the fetus or newborn infant and does so, in the estimation of a panel of judges, it has behaved properly whatever the requester may think of the result. This is a very narrow philosophy, one that completely ignores the fact that it is the responsibility of the system to ensure, as far as possible, that the requests received accurately reflect the information needs of system users. A system that accepts all requests at face value, and judges its own performance in terms of how well it responds to them, is almost certainly doomed to failure.

If we are interested in evaluating a "real" information service, that is, one with real users making real requests based on real information needs, it is imperative that we evaluate it in terms of how well it satisfies the information needs of its users. Clearly, only the requester can decide whether or not a particular document contributes to the satisfaction of his information need, since only he knows what his need is. We could refer to these decisions as relevance decisions also. They are "relevance to an information need" decisions rather than "relevance to a request" decisions. However, it might be more appropriate to use the term pertinence in this case; that is, we could use relevance to refer to a relationship between a document and a request, based on the subjective decision of one or more individuals, and pertinence to refer to a relationship between a document and an information need, the decision in this case being made exclusively by the person having the information need. Frankly, the terms we choose to use are quite unimportant. It is important, however, that we recognize the distinction between the two relationships—request and document and information need and document—that we recognize who is qualified to make the decisions in each case, and that we consistently use whatever terminology we choose. To achieve this consistency we use the term pertinence to refer to a relationship between a document and an information need and the term relevance to refer to a relationship between a document and a request statement. This is an arbitrary decision made purely for the sake of convenience. It is our preference to think of these relationships as relevance to a request and relevance to an information need, discarding the term pertinence completely.

As defined above, pertinence decisions are value judgments made by requesters. The decisions reflect the value of a document, at a particular time, in contributing to the satisfaction of an information need. A particular set of such value judgments is "true" only at a particular point in time, that is, the time at which the decisions are made, because information needs, unlike request statements, are unstable—they change, sometimes kaleidoscopically. Thus, a user may come to an information service and make a request based on a recognized information need. Suppose that the system is able to respond virtually immediately, as it might if it is based on printed indexes or on-line services, and retrieves 25 documents. The moment he sees the first document, the requester's perception of his need may change, and this inevitably influences the remainder of his pertinence decisions. This first document may be exactly what he needs; it satisfies his information requirement completely. He may judge the sixth document he sees as of no value because it essentially duplicates the first; the information is redundant. Yet, had he seen the sixth document first, he might well have judged it of value (pertinent) and the first document, coming later in the sequence, of no value. If, instead of receiving the search results on the day of his request, the results are delivered some days later, the requester's perception of his need will have been influenced by all that he has learned in the intervening period. The value judgments he makes on the 25 documents on day 10 will not necessarily be the same as those he would have made on day 1, and both of these may differ somewhat from the judgments he would have made on day 5.

Pertinence decisions, then, are very transient, much more so than relevance decisions. They are influenced by both the passage of time and the sequence in which the decisions are made. This does not make the operation of information services any easier, but it is a fact of life that designers, managers, operators, and evaluators must recognize and be able to adapt to.

By way of summary, the various relationships we have discussed are shown in Table 9, along with a statement as to who is qualified to judge whether or not the relationship holds, and the reasons why we might want

Table 9 Some Relationships of Importance in Information Retrieval

Relationship	Question to be asked	Terminology	Person qualified to answer question	Reasons for wanting answer to question
1. Between search strategy and document representation	Do the terms included in the representation satisfy the logic of the strategy?	Match between strategy and document representation	Any information specialist who understands the system in use	To determine if the search programs or procedures are working correctly
2. Between document and search strategy	Is this document the type of document, in terms of subject matter, that the searcher wanted to retrieve?	Match between document and intended strategy	The person preparing the search strategy; other individuals knowledgeable on the subject matter and the system	To identify the problems listed in No. 1 above; to identify cases of misindexing; to identify syntactic (relational) problems in the system and other problems relating to its vocabulary; to identify errors in the search strategy
3. Between document and request statement	Is this document a correct response to the request made to the system? (Is its subject matter the subject matter requested?)	Relevance of the document to the request	Someone knowledgeable in the subject matter or a jury of people knowledgeable in the subject	To identify the problems listed in No. 2 and to identify problems of misinterpretation of the request by the searcher
4. Between document and information need	Does the document contribute to satisfying the information need of the requester?	Pertinence of the document to the information need	Only the requester himself	To identify the problems listed in No. 3 and to identify problems of user–system interaction leading to discrepancies between the recognized information need and the expressed need (request statement)

to determine whether or not it holds. The four relationships are listed in order of complexity. In terms of their value in system evaluation, the data reflecting the relationships may be considered cumulative. This statement can be explained as follows:

1. If we know which document representations retrieved by a particular search actually match the search strategy used, we can identify problems in the search programs. This is actually a trivial case: we would expect no failures of this type in any but a grossly inefficient system.

We do not learn anything, at this level of evaluation, about the quality of the indexing, vocabulary, or search strategies.
2. If we know which documents, corresponding to the representations retrieved by the search, satisfy the intended strategy of the searcher, we can identify problems in the search programs, if any exist, plus other system problems relating to indexing, vocabulary, or search strategies, as identified in Table 9. We do not, however, learn anything about the quality of the search strategy as a representation of the request statement.
3. If we know which documents, corresponding to the representations retrieved by the search, are judged relevant to the request statement, by, say, a jury of subject specialists, we can identify problems in the search programs, indexing, vocabulary, and search strategies. We can also identify cases in which the search strategy does not completely or accurately reflect the content of the request statement. We still do not know anything about how well the retrieved documents satisfy the information needs of the user and thus have no ability to identify inadequate or misleading request statements due to imperfect user-system interaction.
4. If we know which of the retrieved documents are judged by the requester to contribute to the satisfaction of his information need, that is, pertinent documents, and if we also know the reasons why he judges the other documents to be nonpertinent, we can distinguish the relevance of the search results from their pertinence. In this situation, through appropriate analysis techniques, we can identify all types of problems that might occur in the retrieval system, be they problems of search programs, indexing, vocabulary, search strategy, interpretation of the request by the searcher, or user-system interaction. The use of this type of diagnostic analysis is exemplified in the evaluation of MEDLARS.

It is important to note, however, that the levels of evaluation mentioned in Table 9 are based only on the documents that the system retrieves and not on those which it does not; that is, we have not identified

Documents whose representations match the search strategy but were not retrieved

Documents that match the intended strategy but were not retrieved

Documents that are relevant to the request statement but were not retrieved

Documents that are pertinent to the information need but were not retrieved

To make these determinations we must have some method of estimating how many matching, relevant, or pertinent documents the system failed to retrieve, and we need to be able to identify some of them at least. Some possible procedures for doing this were described in Chapter 9.

THE LITERATURE ON RELEVANCE

So far we have restricted ourselves to presenting our own position on this subject but have made very little reference to the work or opinions of others. In the remainder of this chapter we mention some other literature that has addressed the problems of pertinence and relevance. This is not intended to be a complete survey but merely to refer the reader to further literature that may help to clarify some of the distinctions made earlier and to give a more complete picture of the factors that influence relevance or pertinence decisions.

Kemp (1974) and Foskett (1970, 1972) both adopt the distinction between relevance and pertinence that has been used in this chapter. Kemp points out, as we implied earlier, that for some purposes of system evaluation, relevance decisions suffice; for other purposes, however, it is necessary to obtain pertinence decisions. Kemp refers to relevance decisions as being public and objective, whereas pertinence decisions are private and subjective. We are not fully in agreement with this. Relevance is not objective. If it were, there should be perfect agreement among a group of judges on the relevance of various documents to various requests. Complete agreement of this kind is unlikely to occur. Kemp also draws analogies between the relationship of pertinence and relevance, on the one hand, and that implied in alternative pairs of terms derived from other fields: denotation and connotation, semantics and pragmatics, formal and informal communication, and public and private knowledge. Foskett makes the same distinction between relevance and pertinence that has been made in this chapter. He defines a relevant document as one

... belonging to the field/subject/universe of discourse delimited by the terms of the request, as established by the consensus of workers in that field. ...

and a pertinent document as one

... adding new information to the store already in the mind of the user, which is useful to him in the work that prompted the request.

Foskett notes that frequently, but not always, pertinent documents are also relevant, and vice versa.

Cooper (1971) discusses the subject of relevance at considerable length. Essentially he draws the same distinctions that we have. However, he uses the term "logical relevance" (or "topicality") where we have used "relevance," and the term "utility" where we have used "pertinence." Elsewhere Cooper (1973) has argued that information retrieval systems must be evaluated on the basis of the "utility" of their results:

> It is really documents of high utility, and not merely relevant documents, that the user wants to see.

We are, of course, in full agreement with Cooper on this.

Goffman (1964) fails to distinguish between relevance and pertinence. He defines relevance as "a measure of information conveyed by a document relative to a query," which is comparable to the position taken by Foskett, Kemp, and ourselves, and equivalent to Cooper's "logical relevance." Goffman goes on to say, however, that

> Any measure of information must depend on what is already known: a fact which must be recognized in any assessment of the relevance of a document with respect to a query.

This statement is somewhat confusing because the expression "what is already known" suggests the pertinence relationship rather than the relevance relationship. Goffman's point is that relevance cannot be determined for every document-request pair independently, but that a decision on the relevance of one document, with respect to a request, must be made in relation to decisions on other documents with respect to the same request. We would agree with this only to the extent that we agree that relevance is relative and capable of being judged on some type of scale; that is, it should be possible to ask our relevance judges to divide up a set of documents into at least three sets: (1) clearly relevant to a particular request statement, (2) relevant to the request statement but less relevant than the first documents, and (3) not relevant. In this sense the relevance decisions are relative, since they group or separate documents on the basis of "extent" of relevance. We cannot, however, agree with Goffman if his statement implies that the sequence with which documents are presented to the judge influences relevance decisions and that the judge might decide that a particular document is irrelevant because it duplicates one seen earlier. This type of decision would not be a relevance decision but a pertinence decision, a value judgment made on a document in relation to an information need. Unfortunately it is not clear what Goffman really means because he fails to distinguish between relevance and pertinence and between actual information needs and expressed needs.

Wilson (1973) has introduced the term "situational relevance," which he defines as

... relevance to a particular individual's situation—but to the situation as he sees it, not as others see it or as it "really is." . . .

He goes on further to state that situational relevance is related to concern and not merely to interest. A person might be interested in a particular object or activity without being concerned about it, that is, caring about its condition. Wilson views items of information as situationally relevant if they "answer, or help answer, questions of concern." The notion of situational relevance is compatible with the set of relationships we identified at the beginning of this chapter. Although Wilson places many more restrictions on the definition of the term, situational relevance relates to the relationship between information and perceived information need rather than to that between information and actual need or expressed need.

Belzer (1973) uses relevance where we have used pertinence:

Upon completion of reading the document the user would know, precisely, whether it was relevant to him or not. This is irrespective of the query posed to the system.

The second sentence indicates that Belzer recognizes the distinction between relevance to request and pertinence to information need. He chooses, however, to ignore the former.

O'Connor has discussed the subject of relevance in a series of articles. In one of them (1967) he analyzes, in some detail, the request-document relationship and the effect of the clarity of the request, or lack of it, on relevance judgments. Elsewhere (1969) he has reported on an empirical study of agreements and disagreements in deciding whether or not a particular document "answers" a particular question. O'Connor, although he never explicitly says so, seems to imply that relevance decisions are acceptable bases for system evaluation but that pertinence decisions are not. At least, he is quite critical of those who claim that a system must be evaluated in terms of user needs, mainly on the grounds that "satisfaction of a user's need" is rarely defined precisely. Although we might agree with O'Connor on the last point, we cannot agree that the concept of satisfaction of a user's need is in any way obscure or that it is not susceptible to definition. These points have been argued in the literature by O'Connor (1968a, b) and Lancaster (1968c) to the satisfaction of neither of them.

Various investigators have explored the effect that different forms of document surrogate have on relevance decisions. Typically these studies compare relevance or pertinence decisions made by the same judge, or group of judges, when given various levels of information about a particular group of documents. For example, the judges may first be asked to make relevance predictions on the basis of titles, then on titles plus abstracts or titles plus selected paragraphs of text. Finally, they are asked to judge the relevance of the documents themselves. The results are then compared to determine how much agreement there is between the relevance predictions made on the basis of the various forms of surrogate and the actual relevance decisions based on the documents. Studies of this general type have been reported by Saracevic (1969), Rath et al. (1961), Resnick (1961), Belzer (1973), Kent et al. (1967), Dym (1967b), Shirey and Kurfeerst (1967), and Marcus et al. (1971), among others. As might be expected, relevance predictions generally improve, in the sense that the surrogate-based predictions agree with the document-based decisions, as more information is made available to the judge. Marcus et al. (1971) refer to the quality of a surrogate, in terms of its value in making correct relevance predictions, as its indicativity. They point out that, in general, the indicativity of a record varies directly with its length in number of words.

Two major series of studies have investigated the factors that influence relevance decisions. One of these, conducted by the System Development Corporation (SDC), has been reported by Cuadra and Katter (1967a, b) and by Cuadra et al. (1967). The second, conducted by Western Reserve University, has been reported by Rees (1966) and Rees and Schultz (1967).

Many variables influencing relevance judgments were identified and investigated in the SDC studies; pertinence to information needs, however, was really not considered. Cuadra and Katter (1967b) summarize as follows:

> The studies offer clear evidence that relevance judgments can be influenced by the skills and attitudes of the particular judges, the documents and document sets used, the particular information requirement statements, the instructions and setting in which the judgments take place, the concepts and definitions of relevance employed in the judgments, and the type of rating scale or other medium used to express the judgments. These findings cast serious doubt on the wisdom of treating relevance scores, as usually obtained, as fully adequate criteria for system or subsystem evaluation.

The Western Reserve studies took into account four major variables influencing relevance decisions: stage of research, documents, document representations, and relevance judges. Again, relevance rather than pertinence was investigated. As in the SDC studies, the Western Reserve investigators were able to show that many variables affect the decision as to whether or not a particular document is relevant to a particular request. For example, the degree of the judge's subject knowledge influences his relevance decisions and the consistency with which such decisions are made by a group of judges. Likewise, somewhat different relevance judgments may be made, for a particular set of documents in relation to a particular request statement, at different stages of a research project; that is, the documents judged most relevant by an investigator when he is just beginning a research project may not be judged most relevant toward the end of his project when he is analyzing his own research results.

The most complete discussion of the relevance question is given in a doctoral dissertation by Saracevic (1970a). Saracevic has also prepared a very useful, concise summary of the major findings of various investigators working in relevance experimentation over a ten-year period (1970b).

Because so many factors influencing relevance judgments have been identified, particularly in the SDC and Western Reserve investigations, it is hardly surprising that serious doubts have been voiced on the wisdom of basing system evaluations on relevance decisions. It has to be recognized, however, that, although some of the work on relevance decisions applies equally to pertinence decisions—for example, the influence of the research stage and the indicativity of a surrogate—much is not directly related. In particular, many of the variables investigated relate to interjudge consistency and do not necessarily affect pertinence decisions, which are highly individualistic. In pertinence decisions, which, as stated earlier, are essential to the evaluation of operating information services, we are concerned with factors influencing intrajudge consistency but not directly with those influencing interjudge consistency. Stated in more concrete terms, when we conduct a search in a retrieval system for a particular user, we should be very much concerned with his evaluation of the retrieved items in terms of their pertinence to his information needs. We should also be concerned with the factors influencing his pertinence decisions. But we need not be directly concerned with the fact that a group of subject specialists, when presented with the documents retrieved and the user's request statement, may not agree among themselves as to which documents are relevant to the request. We need be even less concerned with the factors influencing their decisions. Such a study may have academic interest, but it is not directly related to the evaluation of this particular information service. Much interesting and valuable work has been done on the relevance problem that has little direct application to the pertinence problem. Indeed, most of the investigations could not contribute directly to our understanding of the pertinence problem because they were conducted in controlled, experimental settings. Studies of pertinence can be done only in the context of a particular information system serving real users who have real information needs. This situation cannot be simulated successfully in any laboratory setting.

This is not to imply that the relevance problem is not worth investigating or that the studies of factors influencing relevance decisions have no value. Relevance is worth investigating, and the studies do have considerable value. As pointed out earlier, for some purposes of evaluation we may want relevance decisions rather than pertinence decisions. There is a danger, however, in assuming that research on relevance has direct applicability to pertinence and, more particularly, that the large number of variables affecting the consistency with which relevance judgments are made are directly related to the factors influencing pertinence decisions—they are not, or, at least, not necessarily. Clearly, many factors influence the decision of a user as to whether or not a particular item is pertinent to his information needs. These may not be the same factors that would influence his decision were he asked, somewhat artificially, to judge if the same item is relevant to his request statement. The fact is that, although much work has been done on relevance, the more important problem of pertinence has largely been ignored by investigators, perhaps for the very reason that it is not amenable to controlled, experimental study.

There is another point worth emphasis. Although we may get disagreement among a group of judges as to which documents are relevant to a particular request statement, these variations in relevance judgment do not necessarily invalidate certain types of evaluation. Lesk and Salton (1968), for example, have shown quite clearly that inconsistency among relevance judges may have no effect on certain internal aspects of system evaluation. For example, if we wish to compare three different ways of conducting searches in a particular system, we may arrive at the same relative ranking of the performance of these alternatives whichever of, say, five judges makes the relevance decisions; that is, we could get inconsistency among the judges without necessarily changing the relative rankings of the search techniques. In fact, the Lesk and Salton study revealed that even "large scale differences in the relevance assessments" did not produce "significant variations in average recall and precision" for various searching options.

In conclusion we would reiterate that, for certain evaluation purposes, we need relevance decisions and, for others, pertinence decisions are essential. Much work has been done on factors influencing relevance but very little on those influencing pertinence. Both are subjective and equivocal. This does not make them any the less important in system evaluation.

Chapter Nineteen

A Brief History of Evaluation

The literature on evaluation of information systems is voluminous and still growing. The major bibliography, by Henderson (1967), incorporating reports up to 1966, contains 324 items. A second bibliography, covering the period 1967 to 1972, has been issued by Krevitt and Griffith (1973). More recent evaluation studies are reviewed regularly in the *Annual Review of Information Science and Technology*. Although the literature is now extensive, almost all is of recent origin. Of the 324 items in Henderson's bibliography only 36 were published earlier than 1960, the earliest publication being dated 1953. Although the literature of library science is full of system comparisons—for example, dictionary versus classified catalog, Decimal Classification versus Library of Congress—virtually no objective evaluation of systems was conducted before the 1950s.

Probably the first evaluation study of any note was that conducted by Documentation Inc. in 1953 and reported later by Gull (1956). This was a comparison between the Uniterm system and an alphabetical subject catalog prepared by ASTIA (Armed Services Technical Information

Agency). The study was based on a corpus of 15,000 documents indexed using both procedures and tested on the basis of 98 requests submitted by ASTIA users. The results were completely inconclusive: retrieved documents were never submitted to the actual requesters for assessment, and the evaluation team could not agree in their own judgments of relevance of documents to requests. Cleverdon and Thorne (1954) conducted a small test of the Uniterm system that, although not particularly conclusive in itself, laid foundations for the very significant Cranfield studies that were to follow. Swanson (1960) reported a comparison of conventional subject indexing with computer searching of full document texts. The investigation was based on 100 articles in nuclear physics and 50 requests. In the same year, Schuller (1960), at the Netherlands Ministry of Defense, reported a test in which the efficiency of the Uniterm system was compared with that of UDC. No significant difference was found between the performance of the two systems.

The first really major evaluation study was the well-known Cranfield Project, the initial phase of which (Cranfield I) was begun in 1957 and fully reported by Cleverdon (1962). Cranfield I attempted to compare the performance of four index languages: UDC, alphabetical subject catalog, Uniterms, and a special faceted classification. The study was large, involving 18,000 documents and 1200 search topics. The twin measures of recall ratio and precision ratio, originally called a relevance ratio, previously mentioned by Kent et al. (1955), assumed major significance for the first time in the Cranfield experiments. In the comparison of the four systems, many other performance variables were studied, including type of document, indexing time, qualifications of the indexers, and the number of index terms assigned. The results of Cranfield I indicated surprisingly little difference in the performance of the four systems tested. Human errors in indexing and searching were more serious than errors due to file organization. It was concluded that file organization is relatively unimportant in the performance of information retrieval systems. The specificity of the vocabulary and the exhaustivity of the indexing are much more important factors affecting performance. The results of the Cranfield experiments stimulated much discussion and controversy, including critical reviews by Swanson (1965) and Richmond (1963).

Cranfield I was an extremely important study on two counts. First, it showed clearly which factors importantly affect the performance of retrieval systems and which do not. Second, it developed for the first time methodologies that could be applied successfully to evaluation of experimental, prototype, and fully operating information systems.

The techniques of system evaluation developed at Cranfield were applied by the research team to evaluate an operating retrieval system at the English Electric Company. Later, more refined techniques were applied to compare the performance of a manual index, based on a faceted classification, with that of an early computer-based retrieval system, the Index of Metallurgical Literature developed by Western Reserve University for the American Society for Metals. In this study, as reported by Aitchison and Cleverdon (1963), the technique of failure analysis was fully developed for the first time.

Johanningsmeir and Lancaster (1964) applied the Cranfield type of techniques to the evaluation of a prototype retrieval system, SHARP, at the Bureau of Ships. This study cast serious doubts on the cost effectiveness of role indicators in information retrieval systems. These devices were found to improve precision but generally caused a drastic recall loss and added significantly to system costs. Similar findings were made in evaluations conducted by Sinnett (1964) (Air Force Materials Laboratory), Montague (1965) (du Pont), and Mullison et al. (1969).

The National Science Foundation, which funded the Cranfield studies, supported two investigations of criteria for evaluation of information retrieval systems, one conducted by Bourne et al. (1961) and the other by Arthur Andersen & Co. (1962). NSF also, in 1964, sponsored an important conference "to review the work on testing and evaluation of document searching systems and procedures and to consider promising directions for future work in this area." A study by Snyder et al. (1966), also sponsored by NSF, critically reviewed previous experimental designs in evaluation studies and made recommendations as to how the designs could be improved in the future.

The second stage of the Cranfield studies began in 1963 and was fully reported by Cleverdon et al. (1966). The major objective of Cranfield II was to investigate the components of index languages and their effects on the performance of retrieval systems. In Cranfield II the various index language devices were each evaluated in terms of their effect on the recall and precision of a retrieval system. Altogether 29 index languages, consisting of various combinations of the several devices, were evaluated, using a test collection of 1400 documents, mainly in the field of aerodynamics, and 221 test searches. The results of Cranfield II were rather unexpected because, taking both recall and precision into account, the index languages performing best used uncontrolled single words, that is, they were natural-language systems, such as Uniterms, based on words occurring in document texts.

Extensive investigations of mechanized and semimechanized systems have been conducted by Westat Research Inc. for the U.S. Patent Office, one of the most interesting being a study of an indexing system at the file development stage, reported by King and McDonnell (1966). Salton

(1968) has fully evaluated the various searching options offered by SMART, a system based on the processing of abstracts in natural-language form. A limited comparison of SMART with MEDLARS has also been conducted (Salton, 1969, 1972). At the Cambridge Language Research Unit, Sparck-Jones and Jackson (1967) have conducted evaluations of the retrieval performance of a system based on term classes ("clumps") automatically generated on the basis of statistical associations between terms. Other studies of systems based on statistical term associations have been reported by Giuliano and Jones (1966) and Vaswani and Cameron (1970).

The Comparative Systems Laboratory at Case Western Reserve University (1968), established in 1963, has conducted a series of experiments on various indexing procedures, vocabularies, and searching strategies.

The Central Information Reference and Control (CIRC) system operated by the Foreign Technology Division, Wright-Patterson Air Force Base, was evaluated by Taulbee et al. (1967). By far the largest evaluation of an operating system was performed by Lancaster (1968a) on MEDLARS in the period 1966–1968. The study involved the derivation of performance figures and conduct of detailed failure analyses for a sample of 300 real searches conducted in 1966–1967.

The studies mentioned so far are a selection of evaluations of retrospective search systems conducted in the period 1953–1970. The survey is not complete, but the major investigations at least have been highlighted. Some evaluation work, using similar procedures, has also been conducted on systems for the selective dissemination of information (SDI). In fact, it is probably true to say that the evaluation of SDI services has attracted much more attention since 1970 than the evaluation of retrospective search services. Notable examples of studies of this kind include those of Leggate et al. (1973a, b), at the Experimental Information Unit, Oxford University, and of Veal and Wyatt (1974) and Barker et al. (1972a, b), at the United Kingdom Chemical Information Service.

Evaluations of systems, or system components, in laboratory (experimental) settings have continued over the years. Aitchison and Tracy (1969) and Aitchison et al. (1970a), for example, conducted a comparative evaluation of five index languages with a view to selecting the most promising approach in the implementation of the INSPEC system at the Institution of Electrical Engineers. Another comparative evaluation of index languages, this time in the field of information science, is reported by Keen and Digger (1972).

As might be expected, considerable interest has been shown in the evaluation of on-line systems in the past seven years. However, although many user reaction studies have been done, actual evaluations of the performance of on-line systems have been very few so far.

Lancaster (1973) has reported a small-scale evaluation of searches conducted in a predecessor of MEDLINE, and Lancaster et al. (1972) discuss the evaluation of the Epilepsy Abstracts Retrieval System. Recently, Cleverdon (1977) has presented a more detailed evaluation of on-line searching in the system of the European Space Agency.

Evaluations of the benefits or impact of information services have also been rather rare. Perhaps the most significant study of this kind was the evaluation of AGRIS, mentioned in Chapter 16, as reported by Badran et al. (1977). This study was more a political evaluation than an assessment of the actual performance of the program.

As discussed in the preceding chapter, in the evaluation of an information system we must obtain relevance assessments on various documents in relation to various information demands of users. This fact has caused considerable discussion and controversy on the meaning of relevance, who should judge relevance, and the factors affecting relevance judgments. Cuadra and Katter (1967a, b) and Cuadra et al. (1967) studied relevance judgment as a preferential discriminatory response and attempted to identify factors that introduce significant variations in this discriminatory response. The variables studied were people (judges), documents, request statements, judgment conditions, form of system response, and judgmental attitudes (toward intended use of documents). The investigators concluded that relevance scores assigned by judges to documents can be manipulated by giving different instructions to the judges. For example, it is possible to raise or lower scores by telling judges how documents are to be used. Relevance scores are artifacts of particular environments and should not be viewed as absolute numbers. Although this does not invalidate studies in which a given group of judges makes relevance decisions for a specific system, it does cast doubt on the validity of comparative evaluations of systems or subsystems in which the attitudes of the judges are not carefully controlled.

Rees and Schultz (1967) conducted a somewhat similar study in which, in a particular research environment, four independent variables affecting relevance decisions were investigated: the judgmental groups, the stages of a research project, the documents themselves, and representations of them. Perhaps the most interesting finding of this study was that, although the judgmental groups—medical experts, medical scientists, medical students, medical librarians—differed greatly in the absolute relevance values assigned to documents, on an 11-point scale, there was a high correlation among the groups as to the relative positioning, that is, ranking, of the documents. A similar finding was made by Lesk and

Salton (1968). In their study, conducted in the environment of Salton's SMART system, four sets of judgments were compared. A series of 48 requests was searched against a file of 1268 abstracts, in documentation and library science, using the various search options that the SMART system allows. Although the overall consistency of relevance agreement among the groups was not particularly high, the relative performance of the various retrieval methods was unaffected by changes in the relevance decisions; that is, all four sets of decisions caused the same ranking of alternative search procedures.

The application of evaluation procedures to printed indexes and abstracts journals has been somewhat neglected. Only the aspects of coverage and overlap (duplication) have received general attention. Studies of the *Bibliography of Agriculture,* undertaken by Bourne (1969a, b) are good examples of this type of investigation. A rather complete study of overlap among 14 indexing and abstracting services in science and technology has recently been published by Bearman and Kunberger (1977). Martyn and Slater (1964) have conducted one of the very few studies of printed indexes that go beyond the factor of coverage to consider the "findability" (recall) of citations. There is now evidence of renewed interest in evaluation of printed indexes, with relevant contributions being made by Davison and Matthews (1969), Jahoda and Stursa (1969), Virgo (1970), Carroll (1969), and Aitchison et al. (1970b), among others.

The widespread interest in evaluation of information retrieval systems, particularly mechanized systems, appears to have stimulated a concern for the evaluation of library services in general, another area sadly neglected before the 1960s. There is now increasing evidence of the application to library service of evaluation techniques and quantitative procedures derived primarily from the fields of operations research and industrial engineering. Morse (1968) evaluates the effectiveness of library functions, including such problems as estimation of circulation demand, book retirement, and book duplication policies. The final report of a study on the evaluation of the operations of Army Technical Libraries, published by Wessel and Moore (1969), concentrates particularly on the application of management techniques, correlation analysis, and use analysis to library problems. Another major study on the objective testing and measurement of library service was conducted by Orr et al. (1968). The Orr methodologic tools have been applied to the evaluation of the document delivery capabilities of libraries, interlibrary loan service, and basic reference service and to the preparation of inventories of library service. A complete review of the evaluation of library services is presented in another book by Lancaster (1977).

Chapter Twenty

Natural Language in Information Retrieval

An information retrieval system without vocabulary control may be referred to as a "natural-language" or, sometimes, as a "free text" system. The Uniterm system was a natural-language system in which index terms were extracted from documents by human indexers. With the application of computers to information retrieval, natural-language systems became both more prevalent and more feasible. One of the major problems of the Uniterm system, that of the physical manipulation of long lists of words, is trivial in a mechanized system. The terminology relating to natural-language systems is a little confusing—at least, it is used in a rather imprecise way. The following scheme may clarify the possibilities somewhat:

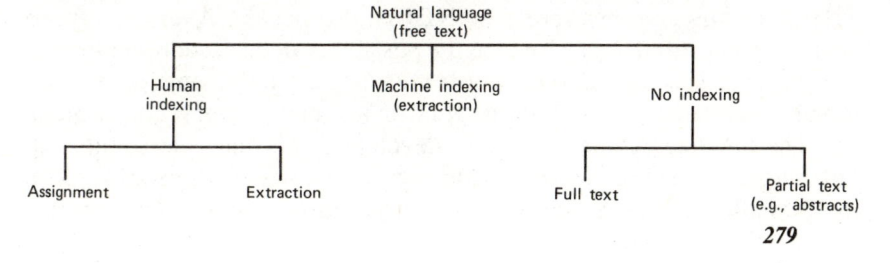

```
                    Natural language
                      (free text)
         ┌───────────────┼───────────────┐
       Human         Machine indexing   No indexing
     indexing         (extraction)
   ┌─────┴─────┐                     ┌──────┴──────┐
Assignment  Extraction            Full text    Partial text
                                              (e.g., abstracts)
```

Human indexers may extract words from a document to represent its subject matter. Alternatively they may assign terms to represent the subject matter without extracting them from the document and without drawing them from a controlled vocabulary. This would be a somewhat unlikely mode of operation, but it is possible. A computer can also extract words from text (machine indexing). On the other hand, a natural-language system may not be based on indexing, in the conventional sense, at all. Instead it may be based on a data base in which the complete text of a corpus of documents is stored or on a data base of partial text—for example, abstracts or titles only. All these may be regarded as natural-language systems. Although much of the following discussion may be equally relevant to all these types, particular emphasis is placed on systems that do not involve indexing by humans or machines, that is, full or partial text systems.

The pioneering work in the application of computers to natural-language searching was conducted in the legal field, specifically by Horty and his associates at the Health Law Center of the University of Pittsburgh. This work has been described by Horty (1960, 1961a, b), Kehl (1962), and Kehl et al. (1961). A brief but graphic account of the capabilities of the system appeared later in a booklet from the Pittsburgh University (1968). The Pittsburgh system was set up to search on inverted files of words occurring in text. Once the syntactic (nonsubstantive) words are eliminated through the use of a machine-stored stop list, all the remaining words are searchable in any combination. There is only one major difference between the inverted files of a full text system of this kind and those which may be established for humanly assigned key words or descriptors selected from a thesaurus. In the latter case the files usually point only to documents, that is, the file consists of document numbers only; whereas in the former the file is likely to point to the exact location, or locations, of each word in each document: document number, paragraph number, sentence number, and exact position in the sentence. In the Pittsburgh system the set of inverted files thus created was referred to as a "concordance." The existence of this type of file allows the conduct of searches incorporating word proximity as a selection criterion. Thus it is possible to request the retrieval of any document in which the word CHILD occurs and the word ABANDON also occurs. Alternatively, to be more precise and thus to reduce the possibility of false coordinations, it is possible to specify that both words must appear in the same paragraph, in the same sentence, or even with no more than x intervening words.

The text-searching system, developed at the University of Pittsburgh, was subsequently transferred to a commercial operation, with the formation of the Aspen Systems Corporation. The system was also adopted by the Department of Defense and put into operation as Project LITE (Legal Information through Electronics). In the 1960s an on-line full-text-searching system, known as Data Central, was developed and made available by a subsidiary of the Mead Corporation. The Data Central system placed emphasis on the legal field, and a large-scale application was made for the Ohio Bar Association (the so-called OBAR system). A much larger Data Central system, known as LEXIS, is now available. Data Central has been described by Giering (1972), and an application in medicine was evaluated by Lancaster et al. (1972). The entire subject of the application of computers to information retrieval in law has been well reviewed by Myers (1973).

In the last ten years a considerable number of machine-readable data bases, mostly in science and technology, have become available as the direct result of the application of computers in the publication and printing of indexing and abstracting services. Since some of the data bases are natural-language files, a considerable amount of additional experience has been accumulated in the searching of text in fields other than law. In particular, the so-called "scientific information dissemination centers" have made extensive use of natural-language searching in the provision of SDI services. A good example of this type of application is given by Williams (1972). In most of these SDI applications inverted files have not been used. Instead, an entire file in magnetic tape form—for example, one month of input to an abstracting publication—is scanned sequentially by computer in order to locate combinations of words that match the requirements of a particular user interest profile. Some very fast and efficient methods have been developed for the serial searching of text in this way. One such procedure, known as the "least common bigram" method, has been described by Onderisin (1971).

Although the computer avoids completely one of the problems faced by the human searcher of a natural-language system in manual form—the difficulty of manipulating long lists of words—it does not contribute directly to solving the intellectual problems of natural-language searching. The thesaurus, or other vocabulary control device, offers many aids to the searcher, including the control of synonyms and near synonyms, the separation of homographs, the use of precoordination to avoid at least some of the problems of false coordination and incorrect term relationships, and the linking together of terms related paradigmatically or syntagmatically. A natural-language system does not in itself incorporate any of these valuable aids. Somewhat comparable aids may, however, be built into the system, or somewhat equivalent results can be achieved by various forms of searching technique. For example, if one facet of a search involves the concept of children, it would be necessary for the searcher to use all the words that might indicate this topic, including CHILD, CHILD'S, CHILDREN, BOY, GIRL, INFANT, BABY, and so on. It may not be at all easy for the searcher to think of all these variants, which are likely to be controlled in a system based on a thesaurus or classification scheme, and it puts a burden on the searcher to expect him to do so. It is perfectly possible to build a type of natural-language thesaurus to control synonymous or semantically related words in a natural-language system, and, in fact, the Pittsburgh system incorporated such an aid. This type of "thesaurus" differs from the more conventional type mentioned earlier in two major respects:

1. It is merely a searching aid and does not normalize the vocabulary at the time of input.
2. It is likely to be quite loosely structured. A thesaurus group may incorporate synonyms, near synonyms, syntactic variants, hierarchically related words, and words related semantically in other ways.

Such a thesaurus probably needs to be humanly constructed, but machine-aided thesaurus construction is also possible.

Even if the searching thesaurus is created entirely by human cerebral effort, the work is likely to be well worthwhile. Otherwise, the same thesaurus, that is, conceptual, groups will be "built" time and time again by different searchers as they interrogate the system—a great waste of intellectual effort—and there is no assurance that a particular searcher will be able to think of all the words needed for a comprehensive search on a particular topic. In fact, a reasonable way to build such a natural-language thesaurus is simply to let the system be used for some months without such an aid and to have the computer store the strategies developed by individual searchers. The strategies are later broken into their components and analyzed. From this analysis is derived the nucleus of a machine-stored natural-language thesaurus. Any string of words that has been used by a searcher in an OR relationship, that is, words considered to be logically substitutable by the searcher, becomes a good candidate to form a thesaurus group. It is quite likely that, for some topics, different searchers will develop somewhat different strategies and that a fairly complete thesaurus group could be formed from the sum of the strategies. Once the basic thesaurus has been developed in this way the thesaurus groups may be incorporated intact into future searching strategies, or they may be augmented by subsequent searchers. Newly developed strategies can also be captured for later analysis. Thus, the thesaurus grows continuously by the incorporation of concept groups actually found useful in the conduct of various searches. The idea of a "growing thesaurus" of this kind has been proposed by Reisner (1963, 1966) and Higgins and Smith (1969).

A natural-language thesaurus, by controlling synonyms and linking related terms, fulfills some of the same functions as the more conventional thesaurus. The problems of ambiguous and spurious relationships among words can be reduced by using word proximity indicators (metric operators), as indicated earlier. The homograph problem is really not serious because character strings that may be ambiguous on their own are likely not to be when used in conjunction with other strings. For example, the word CELL has a number of possible meanings and might therefore be considered ambiguous, but when combined with the word MEMBRANE in a search strategy it loses its ambiguity. In the context of a document in which both words occur, and especially if they occur close to each other, the word CELL is much more likely to refer to a biological cell than to a prison cell or any other type.

Even where no natural-language thesaurus exists to bring related terms together, it is frequently possible to achieve something of the same effect by the intelligent use of truncation in searching. Truncation, which is an extremely important feature of natural-language searching systems, refers to the ability to search on word fragments in place of complete words. "Right truncation" refers to the ability to search on the initial string of characters in a word. Thus a search on the root EPILEP . . . brings in the words EPILEPSY, EPILEPSIES, EPILEPTIC, EPILEPTICS, EPILEPTIFORM, and so on. "Left truncation" refers to the ability to search on the terminal string. If used intelligently, at least in certain scientific fields, left truncation can be used to bring in an entire class of related words. Thus, a search on . . . MYCIN retrieves a whole group of words representing antibiotics, and . . . OTOMY and . . . ECTOMY retrieve a large group of surgical procedures. "Infix truncation" allows the searcher to specify how a word should begin and how it should end, leaving the middle of the word unspecified. Infix truncation is particularly useful in searching on names of chemicals, as in the example TRI . . . COBALTATE. A tape-oriented sequential search system may allow all these types of truncation and simultaneous left and right truncation, that is, it allows the searching of any word fragment. A natural-language system based on inverted files, however, is likely to allow only right truncation because of the way that the files are structured. The use of truncation in natural-language searching is well illustrated in an article by Williams (1972). Even when no search thesaurus exists, it is quite common for natural-language systems to provide at least a list of all the words occurring in the data base with, alongside each, the frequency with which the word appears. Such a list may be printed or displayed on-line. As an aid to truncation, some centers go so far as to print a so-called KLIC index (key letter in context) to show the exact content in which any letter occurs in the data base.

Finally, in a system in which the complete text of documents is stored, it may be necessary to specify that a search should retrieve only those documents in which a particular topic is discussed in some detail rather than merely in passing. A few searching systems give the ability to specify how many times a word, or a word root, should occur in a document before the document is retrieved. A document in which the root EPILEP occurs 10 times, for example, is presumably more likely to deal substantially with epilepsy than one in which the root occurs only once. Another possible approach to improving the relevance of search output is to give increased weight to a word when it occurs in certain key parts of the document—for example, the title, the summary, the conclusions.

COMPARISON OF NATURAL-LANGUAGE AND CONTROLLED VOCABULARY SYSTEMS

The application of computers to information retrieval has greatly increased the feasibility of natural-language searching. It is appropriate, then, to consider the relative merits of basing a mechanized system on natural language or a controlled vocabulary. The controlled vocabulary system has, on the surface, a number of obvious advantages: it controls synonyms and near synonyms and brings semantically related terms together. Because of these aids, the controlled vocabulary system is much easier to search than the natural-language system, that is, it requires less effort on the part of the searcher. Moreover, the controlled vocabulary, if properly constructed, avoids many problems of false coordination or incorrect term relationship. The advantages, however, are not all on the side of the controlled vocabulary. A natural-language system has the major advantage that it is completely specific. Indeed, it is not possible to envision a system in which the language used to represent documents, and to conduct searches, could be more specific than the language used by their authors. In contrast, a controlled vocabulary system is, by definition, not fully specific. Instead of using all the terms occurring in the literature of a particular subject field, the controlled vocabulary uses a selection only, presumably the terms that were considered most important by those who constructed the vocabulary. A thesaurus may be very specific, but it will never be as specific as natural language. It might, for example, allow us to search on JORDAN, but it is unlikely to allow us to search specifically on AMMAN, HUSSEIN, FEDAYEEN, or any of countless other words that might occur in Jordan documents. If we want to conduct a highly specific search, the natural-language system is likely to be much more useful than the controlled vocabulary system.

Natural language has another obvious advantage. It is the language of the discourse of a particular subject field, the language in which its practitioners write or otherwise communicate. As on-line retrieval systems continue to grow, and they undoubtedly will, it is quite likely that we will see more use being made of these systems by the practitioners in various subject fields rather than by information specialists. The subject specialist is much more likely to feel comfortable with the natural language of his own field than with the use of some controlled vocabulary. Indeed, the controlled vocabulary is essentially an artificial language, one in which the terms have assumed special meanings by the way they have been used in indexing. It may take an information specialist some months of training to become thoroughly familiar with the nuances of a large controlled vocabulary. It is unrealistic to expect the subject specialist to learn the policies and protocols that lie behind the use of a controlled language, especially if he is a relatively infrequent user of the system, and many of the nuances may seem to him to be idiosyncratic. It seems reasonable to suppose, then, that natural-language systems favor the subject specialist and controlled vocabularies the information specialist.

The economic aspects of the comparison must also be considered. The human indexing of documents, and its conversion into machine-readable records, is a costly undertaking. It is quite likely to be cheaper to put abstracts or partial text—for example, summary or conclusions—into machine-readable form for searching purposes. The subsequent machine costs are dependent on the length of the record stored and the number of access points for which inverted files are built. A long abstract may be more costly to store and search, but, then, we are buying more access for our money. The economic considerations swing more obviously in favor of natural language, however, if a machine-readable record of text must be created for some other purpose—for example, the printing of an abstracting publication. If a machine-readable abstract must be created for publication purposes, it seems extremely unlikely that the additional human indexing of this item can be economically justified, at least for the purposes of machine-based information retrieval. Economic considerations apply also to the output side of the retrieval operation. Lack of vocabulary control places an increased burden on the searcher and thus increases searching costs. If, however, some form of natural-language search thesaurus, of the type mentioned earlier, is provided, the cost-effectiveness consideration may no longer favor the controlled vocabulary system even at the output side of the operation because it may be cheaper to maintain the less formal, less highly structured natural-language thesaurus than a highly controlled vocabulary.

There are four possible approaches to handling the vocabulary used to represent documents, and to conduct searches, in a retrieval system, as follows:

1. Control of vocabulary at input and output. This is a precontrolled vocabulary as exemplified by use of a conventional thesaurus.
2. No control of any kind at input or output. This is a pure natural-language system.
3. Control of vocabulary at input but no control at output; that is, searchers can use any terms they choose to, and these are "mapped" by computer, by table lookup or some other procedure, to the controlled terms of the system.
4. No control at input but loose control at output through the use of a "search-only" thesaurus. This can be referred to as a postcontrolled vocabulary.

The first two of these alternatives have been discussed already. The third would presumably apply only to a situation in which an organization wished to provide a natural-language interface with an existing controlled vocabulary system. On a limited scale something of this kind already exists in the MEDLINE system of the National Library of Medicine. In MEDLINE it is possible for the searcher to use certain entry vocabulary terms that are converted by table lookup to the controlled terms of the system. But, clearly, it would require an extremely large entry vocabulary to create a high probability that the natural-language terms a searcher uses would in fact be recognized by the system.

The fourth alternative, the postcontrolled vocabulary, seems to have much to commend it for the purposes of computer-based information retrieval. If implemented properly, this approach combines the advantages of natural language with many of the advantages of the more conventional controlled vocabulary. Thus, a search can be conducted at a highly specific level on text words—for example, we can search on Hussein or Varig—or it can be conducted more generically by use of the word groups of the search thesaurus—for example, on the Jordan group or the airline group. In other words, with this approach the specificity is there if the searcher needs to use it, but the capability for various levels of generic search also exists. In the conventional approach to vocabulary control, however, the searcher is entirely limited by the specificity of the terms of the controlled vocabulary, and this may mean that a search for references to King Hussein must retrieve everything indexed under Jordan, much of which may not be relevant. One approach to the postcontrolled vocabulary has been described by Lefever et al. (1972).

It seems very likely that we will see increased emphasis on the use of natural language in information retrieval in the future. This claim seems justified by the following factors:

1. The continued growth in the availability of machine-readable data bases many of which will be in natural-language form.
2. The continued expansion of on-line systems, which is likely, eventually, to put terminals in the offices and homes of scientists and other professionals. Bibliographic searching will be one of many possible applications of these terminals, and a natural-language mode of searching seems imperative in this type of application.
3. A number of evaluation studies have indicated that natural language may offer several advantages over controlled vocabularies in many retrieval situations. This was demonstrated most clearly by the second group of Cranfield studies, as reported by Cleverdon et al. (1966). The investigations of Aitchison et al. (1969–1970) and Lancaster et al. (1972), among others, also tend to confirm this.
4. Natural-language systems have been shown to work, and to work well, in the legal field, the scientific information dissemination centers, the defense and intelligence communities, and elsewhere.
5. New developments in computer storage devices will make the storage of very large text files increasingly feasible.

Even some of the former bastions of the conventional controlled vocabulary have seemingly changed their philosophies in recent years. Klingbiel (1969), of the Defense Documentation Center, for example, has stated categorically that

> Highly structured controlled vocabularies are obsolete for indexing and retrieval (*and that*) the natural language of scientific prose is fully adequate for indexing and retrieval.

Cleverdon has also asserted, on a number of occasions, that performance with natural language can never be lower than that with controlled language.

There is one other vocabulary control possibility, frequently overlooked, that should be mentioned here, namely, the hybrid vocabulary, one that combines a controlled vocabulary with natural language. Typically, in this situation, a relatively broad controlled vocabulary of perhaps several hundred terms provides a kind of overall superstructure for the system. Documents are indexed by one or more of these broad descriptors and also by natural-language terms extracted from title or text or

288   Natural Language in Information Retrieval

both. The natural-language words allow specificity in searching. The broad controlled terms provide for generic search and give context to the natural-language terms. The word STRIKE, for example, implies something quite different when it is combined with a descriptor or code representing labor than when it is combined with a descriptor or code representing military operations. The joint use of a limited controlled vocabulary and an uncontrolled natural-language vocabulary offers powerful retrieval capabilities and has been shown to operate very effectively in a number of applications. One example of the hybrid approach has been described by Uhlmann (1967). A number of mechanized systems now offer some limited capability for hybrid searching, usually by allowing a title word "scan" to supplement a search on the controlled terms of the system. Suppose that a user wants to search for literature on head injuries to football players. The controlled terms of the system do not permit a search at this level of specificity. They do, however, permit a search on the combination HEAD INJURIES and ATHLETIC INJURIES, thus narrowing the search down to head injuries in athletics. It might then be possible to ask the system to narrow the search further by scanning the titles of the retrieved articles and selecting only those in which the word football occurs.

Not all natural-language systems are based on Boolean search logic. Some use weighted term logic, and others use a combination of Boolean logic and term weighting. A few systems allow the user to interrogate by means of a request in English sentence form. This type of system is discussed in the next chapter. It is also possible to search a retrieval system by inputting a string of words, without connecting logic, that represent some information need. The system then looks for pieces of text that best match the input string. Thus, if the original string consists of five words, and some document in the data base contains all five, the document gets the maximum possible weight and is ranked at the top of the list of items retrieved. This technique, referred to by Cleverdon and Harding (1971) as "coordination level search" and by Heaps and Sorenson (1968) as "fractional search," is rarely used, although experiments have shown it to be very efficient.

NATURAL-LANGUAGE SEARCHING

The searching of natural-language data bases on-line is quite similar, in many ways, to the searching of other data bases. The search greatly benefits from a logical conceptual analysis, as illustrated in Chapter 11. A major difference, of course, is that the conceptual analysis is not translated into a particular set of controlled terms. Instead, the searcher must decide which words or phrases are likely to distinguish the documents of probable relevance from those which are unlikely to be relevant. Another major difference is that a search of a natural-language system is likely to be based on combinations of individual words. The word is the major unit of search. In some respects the searching of natural language is more difficult than that of a controlled vocabulary. In other ways, however, natural-language searching offers a number of benefits.

The most obvious advantage of natural language is that it permits the conduct of searches of unlimited specificity. Thus, it is possible to look for documents in which individual companies, products, processes, or even persons are named. The use of Berger equations in vibration analysis, the NASA-Langley solar energy project, grinding machines produced by Schneider Maschinenbau GMBH, and the design and construction of the Bosporus Bridge are all good examples of information needs that might be satisfied very rapidly in a natural-language system. It would be possible to conduct these searches in a controlled vocabulary system, also, but it is likely to be rather more difficult to do so.

The principle of seeking the "least common factor" in a search is even more important in the use of natural-language systems. The first request mentioned above, for example, could probably be handled very effectively simply by searching on the single word BERGER. It is quite likely that the use of the word will narrow down a search to a handful of references that can be displayed on-line in order to determine if any deal with Berger equations applied in vibration analysis. It is not even necessary to think of compound names in their complete form. The word GRINDING combined with the word SCHNEIDER, for example, may well be adequate for handling the third request mentioned above.

Even when searching on other than names, a search in a natural-language data base may frequently be reduced to a few "key" words (the least common factors). Some examples are given below. The subject of an information need is stated and, alongside it, a possible reduction of the need to some word combinations that might be sufficiently discriminating to handle the search on-line:

1. Floating concrete terminal for use in the Arctic   FLOATING and ARCTIC
2. The hot isostatic pressing process   ISOSTATIC
3. Machining metals with a neodymium laser   NEODYMIUM
4. Effect of antioxidants on refined palm oil   PALM and ANTIOXIDANT

290 Natural Language in Information Retrieval

The point we are trying to make is that it is frequently possible to "zero in" on a search through the choice of only one or two key words. The searcher should always be looking for the simplest and most direct approach to retrieval of relevent references. This usually means selecting the essential word that is likely to apply to the smallest number of items in the file. HOT or PRESSING may apply to a large number of items, but ISOSTATIC probably applies to a few only. Therefore, this word is the obvious one to use as a first approach to retrieval of references on hot isostatic pressing.

Not all searches, of course, are as easy to handle as those used in these examples. The less specific the subject of a search, the more difficult it is to handle through the use of natural language. The problem is identifying all the words that might represent some general facet of the request. The approach illustrated in Chapter 11, of analyzing an information need into its component facets and then selecting the terms that best represent each facet, is just as important in natural-language searching. The only essential difference is that, in natural-language searching, we may have no thesaurus, with cross-reference structure, to help us to select all the appropriate terms. In the natural-language system more depends on the ingenuity of the individual searcher.

An illustration will help to clarify the situation. Suppose we are looking for information on mercury levels in water:

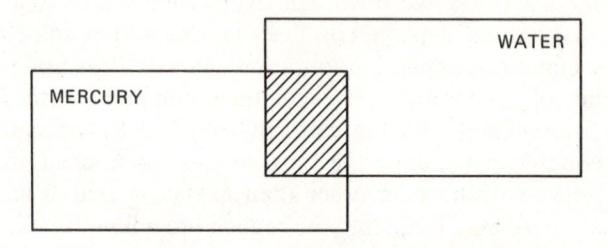

The mercury facet reduces to the words MERCURY and MERCURIC, but it will be completely inadequate to search on the single term WATER. There are many ways in which this facet might be represented in documents: WATER, SEA, OCEAN, STREAM, LAKE, RIVER, and so on. If we want a comprehensive search on this subject, we must ourselves think of all the terms that might represent the water facet in the data base we are using. This is not an insuperable task, but it may be rather more difficult than in a controlled vocabulary system, in which we might reasonably expect all the terms representing bodies of water to be linked by some form of cross-reference.

In some ways, however, natural-language searching may be easier than the search in a controlled vocabulary system. Because we are dealing at the word level, it is usually possible to reduce a search to a smaller number of elements than in the controlled vocabulary search. The request for information on odor control in the paper industry, used as an example in Chapter 11, could probably be reduced simply to

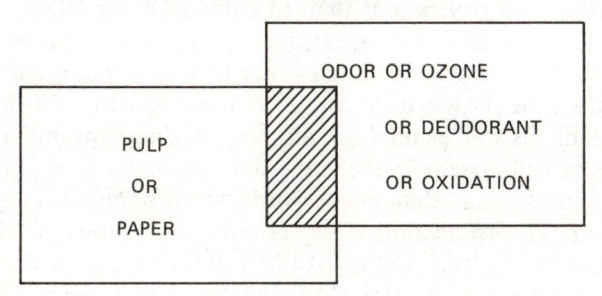

```
              ┌──────────────────────────────┐
        ┌─────┼──────┐  ODOR OR OZONE        │
        │     │▓▓▓▓▓▓│                       │
        │PULP │▓▓▓▓▓▓│  OR DEODORANT         │
        │ OR  │▓▓▓▓▓▓│                       │
        │PAPER│▓▓▓▓▓▓│  OR OXIDATION         │
        └─────┼──────┘                       │
              └──────────────────────────────┘
```

It is very important to recognize that, although a word may be ambiguous or imprecise on its own, this ambiguity or imprecision is likely to disappear almost completely when the word is combined with other words. The word BEAM in electronics means something quite different from the word BEAM in structural engineering. But the combination BEAM and CRACK or CRACKING is more likely to retrieve documents discussing structural beams than electron beams. Likewise, the word GRAIN and the word MIGRATION both have several possible contexts. But when the words are combined in an *and* relationship, they are very likely to retrieve items on grain migration in metals. Used in conjunction with other words in a search strategy, a word that may seem quite general or vague on its own can have quite a high degree of discrimination.

Although we have spoken of the word as the basic unit in the searching of natural-language data bases, this is really an oversimplification. It is probably better to think of a search strategy in terms of both words and word fragments. It is possible to search on parts of words by the principle of truncation. As mentioned earlier, four types of truncation can be recognized:

1. Right truncation, that is, ignoring the ending of a word. The truncation CRACK: will, for example, retrieve documents containing CRACK, CRACKS, CRACKING, and CRACKED.
2. Left truncation, that is, ignoring the beginning of a word. The truncation: MYCIN, for example, is likely to retrieve documents discussing a large group of antibiotics.
3. Simultaneous left and right truncation.
4. Infix truncation, that is, specifying the beginning and end of a word but leaving the middle unspecified.

Right truncation is the most useful for most applications, and it is a powerful device for searching on large groups of related words. Truncation is a useful time-saver, for it avoids the need to enter separately a list of terms all having the same stem. It is even useful for handling many singular-plural situations. It is quicker, for example, to enter DOG: (where : indicates a truncation) than to enter DOG or DOGS.

One must recognize, however, that the use of truncation may also bring in some words that have no relevance to a particular request. It must be used with care. DOG: may cause retrieval of items on doggerel or Dogwood Bank, as well as on dogs, although it is perhaps unlikely that all these subjects will appear in the same data base. As stated previously, however, we must avoid thinking of words or word fragments as standing on their own. The truncation CAT: is quite ambiguous (CATS, CAT, CATERPILLAR, CATALYSIS, CATASTROPHE, CATAMARAN). So is the truncation CRACK: But CAT: AND CRACK: may prove quite precise in the retrieval of documents on catalytic cracking.

It may, of course, be possible to use some command in an on-line system to generate a display of all the words in a data base, for which inverted files have been built, that are alphabetically "close" to some word of interest. It is then possible to select words from this list, by identifying number, in the same way that words are selected from the display of a controlled vocabulary.

In the case of an organization that is developing its own data base, in natural-language form, it may be desirable, as suggested earlier, to create tables of synonyms or words and word fragments that somehow represent the same "concept." These tables, representing concepts frequently referred to in searches, may be stored in the system and displayed on command. A water table, for example, may look like

WATER

WATER: OR LAKE: OR RIVER: OR SEA: OR OCEAN: OR STREAM: OR POND:

(where : indicates a truncation)

The existence of such tables can make the search process more effective and more efficient. They save the time of the searcher and make it less likely that he will overlook some words that would be needed to carry out a comprehensive search. If tables are given unique identifying numbers or names, they can be incorporated intact into an on-line search strategy. Multilingual concept tables, containing equivalent words in a number of languages, can also be built and stored.

Chapter Twenty-One

Automatic Systems

As stated earlier in the book, in "conventional" computerized systems most, if not all, the intellectual processing is conducted by humans, and the computer merely acts as a giant matching device. Over the years, however, some consideration has been given to the possibility of developing more fully automatic retrieval systems, in which human intellectual processing is reduced to a minimum or even eliminated entirely. Computers can, in fact, be used to index documents; to prepare abstracts, or at least extracts, of documents; to automatically elaborate on a searching strategy; or to develop links among semantically related terms, thereby creating a form of searching aid (a kind of machine-constructed thesaurus). Much of the experimentation with "automatic indexing," and related techniques, was conducted in the 1960s, and now we have a handful of systems that are, to a greater or lesser extent, automatic. A fully automatic system would be one in which indexing is conducted by computer, an internally generated thesaurus is prepared, and search strategies are developed automatically from a natural-language statement of information need.

The most common form of automatic indexing is by extraction, that is, words are extracted from text, and this technique was pioneered by

Luhn (1957) and Baxendale (1958), both of IBM. The simplest form of extraction indexing uses word frequency as the basis of its extraction procedures; that is, the computer is used to count the words or phrases that occur most frequently in a document, which obviously must be in machine-readable form, and the extraction programs select, to represent the subject matter of the document, the words or phrases that occur most frequently. A stop list is first used to eliminate from consideration the common, nonsubstantive words. Extraction indexing of this type has been shown to be relatively effective, and the words or phrases selected by machine are quite similar to those which would be extracted by a human indexer.

A less common approach uses relative frequency in place of absolute frequency. In the relative frequency approach, which is rather more complicated, a word is extracted if it occurs more frequently than expected in a particular corpus. Thus, in an aerodynamics document the word AIRCRAFT and the word WING might be rejected, even though they are the most frequently occurring words in the document, and the word FLUTTER might be selected even though, in absolute terms, it is not a high-frequency word.

Other approaches to automatic indexing use other types of extraction criteria in place of, or along with, the statistical criteria. Word position in the document, word type, or even the emphasis placed on words in printing—for example, boldface or italics—may all be used as the basis of selection.

The alternative to extraction indexing is "assignment indexing." In this form of automatic indexing, computer programs attempt to assign to a document one or more terms from some controlled vocabulary. In essence, assignment indexing is just an extension of extraction indexing, for the same type of criteria is used to recognize the most "significant" words in text. In assignment indexing we must develop for each "controlled term" a word profile, that is, a list of words that, if they occur in a document, are likely to indicate that a particular controlled term is relevant and should be assigned. The computer is used to recognize the significant words in a document, using statistical and other criteria. Once the words are identified, they are matched against the word lists or "profiles" associated with each term in the controlled vocabulary. Those controlled terms whose profiles best match the words extracted from the document are then assigned by computer. Automatic assignment indexing is much more difficult than extraction indexing, and it has never been very successful. Except possibly for the production of printed indexes, it is not worth doing anyway, for if you are going to index by machine, you might just as well use the words that appear in documents themselves.

Automatic abstracting is very similar to automatic indexing. In its simplest form, as developed by Luhn, the high-frequency substantive words in a document are identified, and the sentences that contain the highest concentration of high-frequency words are selected and printed out in sequence to form the abstract. The abstract thus created—it is really an extract and the process is best referred to as "automatic extracting"—does not necessarily look like a humanly prepared abstract, but, nevertheless, it usually does give a fairly good indication of what the document is about.

It is also possible to use computer procedures to group text words, or assigned index terms, together in various ways in order to form classes of words or terms that may be useful for retrieval purposes. By the use of these techniques of automatic term classification it is possible to construct a vocabulary that may be regarded as a form of controlled vocabulary. At least, it is a vocabulary in which related terms are brought together to form a class or are linked in some way. Research on automatic term classification has been completely reviewed by Sparck Jones (1974).

The automatic classification of terms is achieved on the basis of statistics on the frequency with which the terms cooccur in documents or index records. The assumption is that the more frequently two words occur together in documents, or the more frequently two terms are used together in indexing, the more likely they are to be related in some way. To carry this to its logical extreme, if word A always occurs with word Q, and Q always occurs with A, the two words are completely substitutable in searching, for the same set of documents will be retrieved whichever of the two words is used. Such absolute correlation is not likely to occur very often, but, in general, it is true that words that are highly correlated statistically are also likely to be semantically related.

In fact, various levels of statistical association can be used in the grouping or linking of words. A first-level statistical association is likely to bring together terms that might be linked by the BT-NT and the RT structure of a conventional thesaurus, but it might also bring in some terms that might not be explicitly linked in the conventional thesaurus. Thus, the word TUBERCULOSIS might be shown to be highly correlated with LUNG, PULMONARY, STREPTOMYCIN, and so on. Variant word forms might also be highly correlated. The word WELD, for example, might occur very frequently with WELDING and WELDED. A class of words formed on the basis of frequency of cooccurrence is thus likely to contain a mixture of words related in various ways. It is unlikely to resemble closely a more conventional term class formed in the construction of a thesaurus by humans. Nevertheless, the class formed automatically in this way may indeed be useful for purposes of information retrieval.

Second-level statistical associations might also be useful in information retrieval. A second-level association is indirect. For example, if the word A occurs very frequently with P, and B also occurs very frequently with P, but A and B occur very infrequently together, there is nevertheless a strong possibility that A and B are directly related. They might, in fact, be synonyms or near synonyms. To give one example, in an aerodynamics collection the word DELTA may never occur without the word WING, and the word TRIANGULAR might never occur without the word WING; but TRIANGULAR and DELTA never occur together or very rarely cooccur. Nevertheless, in this context, the two words are synonymous, for they both describe an identical aerodynamic configuration. These two words are unlikely to be highly correlated in the literature, because a writer who uses the expression delta wing is unlikely to use triangular wing in the same report, and vice versa for the writer who uses triangular wing. These two words can, however, be linked through statistical association procedures, since they share a strong connection with the word WING.

Basically, statistical associations among words or index terms can be used in two different ways in the implementation of retrieval systems. One way is to calculate the various "strengths of association" among all the words or terms occurring in a data base and to store the associations in a type of association matrix. When a particular group of terms is input by a searcher, the system can elaborate on this initial strategy in order to pull in additional terms automatically that are statistically associated with these "starting terms." Both first- and second-level associations can be used. This application, which has been referred to as "associative indexing" or as "associative retrieval," is exemplified by the work of Stiles (1961), Salisbury and Stiles (1969), Spiegel et al. (1962), and Giuliano and Jones (1963).

The second approach entails the a priori formation of classes of terms or words that are highly associated on the basis of cooccurrence statistics. The classes are stored in the system in much the same way that a conventional thesaurus hierarchy is stored. The classes may be incorporated into a search automatically, or, alternatively, their use may be under the control of the searcher; that is, a searcher may ask that one or more terms that he uses in his strategy be expanded into the class to which the term belongs. Major research on this mode of application was conducted by Needham (1961) at the Cambridge Language Research Unit. More recently the work has been carried further by Sparck Jones (1971).

All the systems that have been mentioned so far assume the construction of searching strategies by human analysts, through the use of terms in various logical combinations. It is also possible to design a more "automatic" system, one in which the user may enter a natural-language statement, describing his information need, in the form of one or more sentences. We have the possibility of at least three variations on this basic approach: (1) we can keep the text relatively intact, form inverted files for searching purposes, and search the data base by natural-language queries in the form of English sentences; (2) we can reduce the complete text by certain machine processes (essentially techniques for automatic indexing by extraction) so that we store, for searching purposes, only extracts that are likely to have a high information-bearing content, and again interrogate in sentence form; and (3) we can retain the complete text but apply machine procedures by which words are weighted and grouped together in various ways that may assist the searching process—again, we may interrogate the data base in sentence form.

The first of these variations is exemplified by BROWSER (Browsing On-Line with Selective Retrieval), an IBM system developed by Williams (1969). This is a relatively unsophisticated system based on inverted files of words or, more precisely, word roots (Williams calls them rootwords). Each word in the corpus, however, is given an information value (I value) that is inversely proportional to the frequency with which it occurs in the data base; the least frequent and, therefore, most discriminating, words or roots are given highest I values. An English sentence query can be accommodated by the system: documents are retrieved and displayed in a ranked order, the ranking being based on a composite weight that is the sum of the weights (I values) matching between rootwords occurring in a document and those in the query.

The second variation is exemplified by the LEADERMART system, as described by Kasarda and Hillman (1972), in which documents are reduced to noun phrases for searching purposes. The English language request is matched against the noun phrase store, and those phrases which best match the request are displayed for the searcher's examination. Phrases, and the documents associated with them, can be presented in ranked order according to the degree to which they match the search statement. The phrases that best match the search statement are associated with documents that are most likely to be relevant to the user.

The third variation is exemplified by the SMART system, as described by Salton (1971). SMART is the most sophisticated of the automatic systems. Like BROWSER, Salton's system weights words or word roots to reflect their power of discrimination in searching. In addition, however, the SMART system groups words together in various ways that are designed to optimize the searching process. SMART has an internally stored controlled vocabulary—in the sense that related terms are grouped together by machine* or manual procedures or a combination

---

*Any type of procedure for automatic term classification could be used to construct a machine-stored "transparent thesaurus" of this type.

of the two—that is transparent to the user. SMART, like BROWSER and LEADERMART, searches on an English language request statement and ranks documents in order of the degree to which they match the statement, using the term weights and term groupings as a means of optimizing the matching and ranking process.

Systems of this kind raise at least two questions that are of critical importance to the whole subject of information retrieval. These questions may be stated as follows:

1. Should systems be designed to be interrogated by means of English sentence search statements rather than the translation of an information need into a formal Boolean strategy?
2. Is the performance of systems of this general type sufficiently better than that of simpler natural-language systems—inverted files of text words with Boolean search strategies—so that the additional text processing steps are justified?

These are questions that we cannot yet answer in any definitive way. The idea of being able to interrogate a file by means of an English sentence request is certainly appealing, especially for on-line systems used directly by scientists and other professionals. Clearly, the success of this form of system is heavily dependent not only on the efficiency of the internal ranking algorithms but on the quality of the request statement itself, which needs to be a complete and accurate description of the user's information need. It is also clear that on-line facilities are not being used to their best advantage unless there is positive interaction between user and system. In a system in which all the workings are transparent, that is, unseen by the user, and the user does not participate at all in the search process once his request has been entered, the terminal is being used merely as a data entry device.

Whether systems of the SMART, BROWSER, and LEADERMART type perform substantially better than more "straightforward" text searching systems of the Data Central type is also unclear at the present time, and more comparative evaluations need to be done, holding data base, requests, and relevance assessments constant. The same can be said of the comparison of these systems with precontrolled vocabulary systems and of natural-language systems in general with precontrolled vocabulary systems in an on-line environment. Results presented by Salton (1972) certainly suggest that SMART may perform as well as MEDLARS when both systems are operating in an off-line mode. But would an on-line SMART perform as well as, or better than, MEDLINE, based on a precontrolled vocabulary, and how would either perform in comparison with a system of the Data Central type used with abstracts of medical articles? Such questions have yet to be answered in any definitive way, although Lancaster et al. (1972) did show that an on-line natural-language system in the field of epilepsy, based on abstracts and the Data Central software, performed much better than the same system could have performed on the set of index terms associated with this data base. Such comparisons have so far not been conclusive, and we really need to compare the best examples of one type of system with those of an alternative, competing system. Making this kind of comparison has been difficult to do in the past, but it is now becoming increasingly feasible. LEADERMART, for example, has been applied to several large commercially available data bases, some of the same data bases that are being offered in a more conventional precontrolled vocabulary mode by such organizations as Lockheed and the System Development Corporation (SDC). It would be perfectly possible, therefore, to compare the LEADERMART performance against a more conventional Boolean search approach using SDC's ORBIT software or the DIALOG system of Lockheed, and keeping data bases, requests, and relevance assessments constant. Although comparisons of this type are obviously needed, nothing is being done in this area, and very little interest in such studies has been expressed by those responsible for developing national or international information programs.

Chapter Twenty-Two

The Role of Informal Communication

So far in this text emphasis has been placed on the formal channels of communication and the role of information centers in the formal communication process. It is also necessary to give some consideration to the informal channels of communication. It is obvious that informal communication is much older than formal communication because men communicated with each other informally long before any type of formal communication channels were set up. Oral communication, too, is very much older than written communication. In fact, in the entire history of communication, the written form has assumed major importance only in quite recent times. Many people, of course, communicate only through informal channels. They do not write, do not attend conferences, and perhaps do not read the writings of others. In professional communities, however, and especially in scientific and academic communities, information is transferred through both formal and informal channels. Both are of importance. They complement each other.

It is only in the last twenty years or so, however, that the informal channels of professional communication have been seriously studied and their great importance has become widely recognized. An interesting phenomenon has been observed in science and other fields in which true research is carried out. When a scientist becomes reasonably well established in a field, through conducting research and reporting his research results in professional journals or at scientific conferences, he tends to become "integrated" in a professional communication network; that is, he gets to know other scientists working in the same or related areas. An informal communication network evolves among those scientists, working on similar problems, who know each other or at least know of each other's work. They communicate with each other rather effectively through the telephone, correspondence, and conversations at professional meetings. They inform each other of their research results, discuss the results among themselves, and, perhaps most important, discuss the research they plan to carry out in the immediate future. Both written and oral communication occur in these networks. Drafts of research proposals may be circulated, for review and comment, in such a community. A scientist may also send other types of documents to other scientists either for their critical review or simply for information purposes. Such documents include drafts of papers to be presented at conferences or published in science journals, printed copies of papers before they are actually presented at a conference—these are known as "preprints"—and printed copies of papers that have actually been published in science journals or the proceedings of conferences ("reprints").

The informal networks also serve as a useful source for specific problem-solving information because one scientist is likely to contact another in the network, for advice or information, when he knows that he may be able to help him.

It would be wrong to assume that all scientists working in a specific area of research are integrated into such a communication network. In the first place, it takes time before a scientist becomes well integrated. First he must become known through his research and writing. Thus, the scientists who are best integrated tend to be the senior people who have been working in the field for some time. Second, although there are no real geographic barriers to such networks, geographic, linguistic, political, and economic considerations all tend to influence the composition of the network. Thus, if most research in a particular area is conducted in the United States, the scientists in this country tend to be better integrated in the network as a whole than those working in other countries. In this case, the extent to which the other scientists are included in the network depends on where they were educated, where they have conducted research in the past, the degree to which they attend international meetings, the extent to which they publish, and their familiarity with the English language. It is quite likely that scientists working on similar problems in a particular country may form their own subnetwork, which is then linked, through one or more members, with the subnetworks in other countries.

Finally, there are some scientists who, for one reason or another, prefer to work in comparative isolation and not to communicate with their fellow scientists through these informal channels. All the scientists who, for any reason, are not integrated in an informal communication network are referred to as "isolates."

An example of an informal communication network, derived from Crawford (1971), is given in Figure 48. This represents a network of physicians, physiologists, biochemists, and others interested in the phenomenon of sleep. The complete network is actually composed of a series of subnetworks, enclosed in dotted lines in the diagram, but all the subnetworks are linked together. Notice also, in the top left-hand corner of the diagram, there are two scientists, 47 and 35, who communicate with each other but with no one else, and a further group of three scientists who communicate with each other but with no one else. There are also many isolates in the sleep research community, but they do not appear in the diagram.

A study of how information is transferred in a community of this sort is known as a "sociometric analysis," and the diagram showing the connections between the members is a "sociogram." Figure 48 is a sociogram for the sleep research community. The informal communication network existing in a professional field is frequently referred to as an "invisible college." Figure 48 depicts the invisible college of sleep research.

Invisible colleges tend to be "held together" by certain central scientists. These central scientists are the "sociometric stars." Other scientists cluster around them, and communication converges on them rather like the spokes of a wheel. The sociometric stars of sleep research are somewhat difficult to recognize in Figure 48, because of the great detail of the diagram, but they are there. Figure 49, which is derived from Figure 48, shows only the sociometric stars of the sleep research community. Notice how these stars or central scientists are linked together by communication paths. Most of the communication, represented by solid lines in the diagram, is from one central scientist directly to another, but, in a few cases, two central scientists are linked by a noncentral scientist (broken lines in the diagram). In the sleep community scientist 37 seems to be a "superstar" who is virtually holding the entire communication network together.

It has been shown that the sociometric stars of a research community

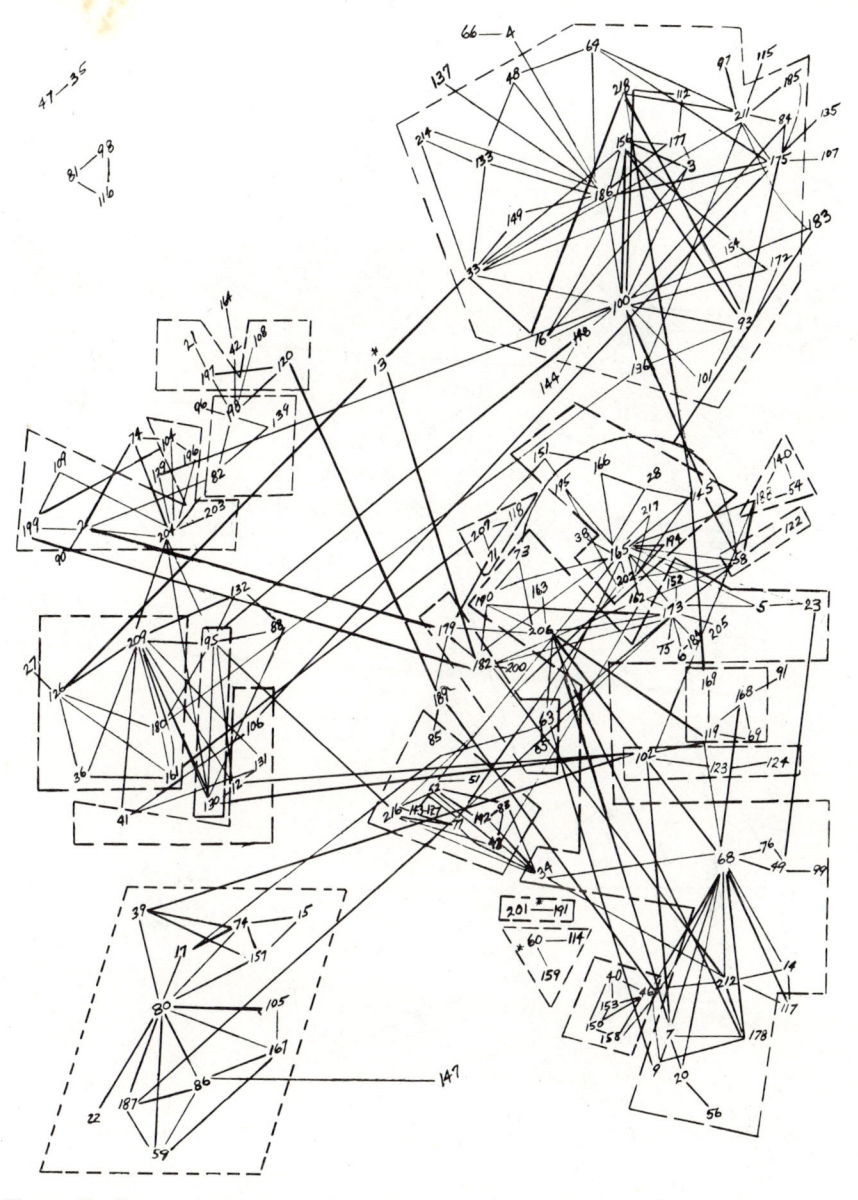

Figure 48 Communication network among scientists involved in sleep research. Reproduced from Crawford (1971).

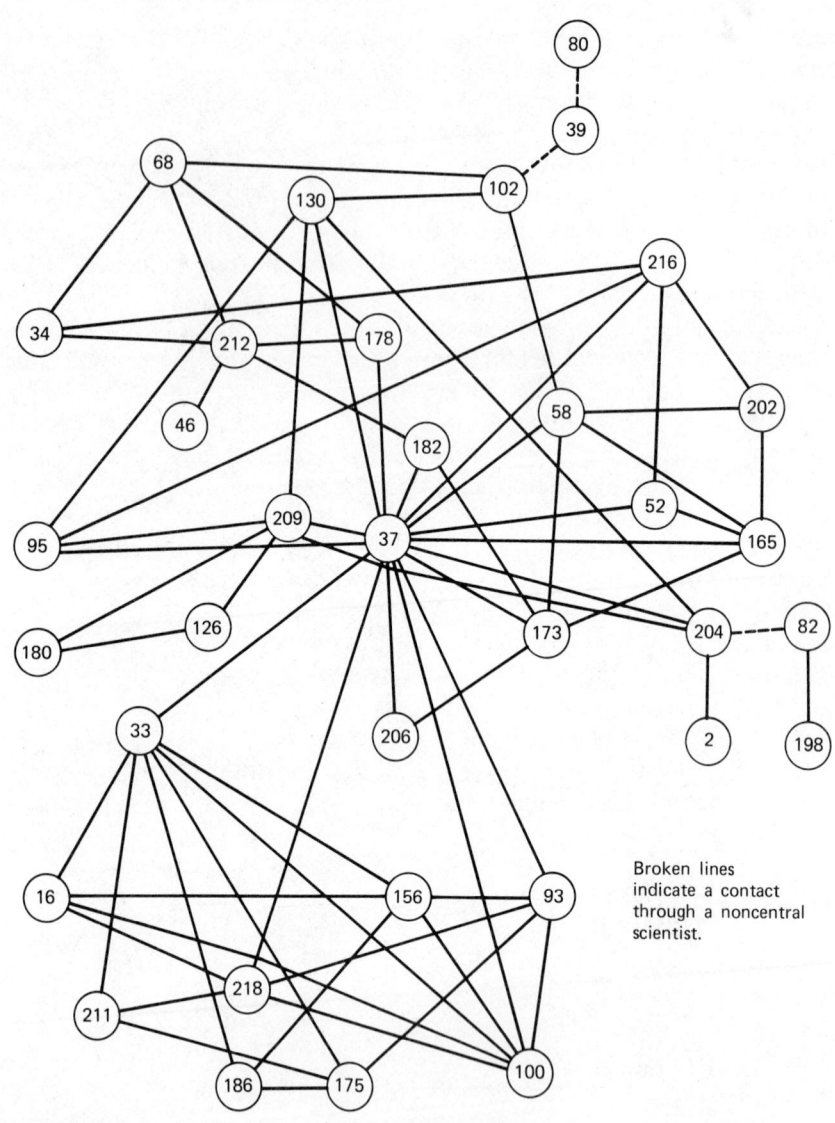

Figure 49 The stars or central scientists of sleep research. Reproduced from Crawford (1971).

are the leaders in more than communication. They also tend to be the research leaders of the field, the most productive members, and perhaps the most influential. They are likely, in addition to being the individuals most contacted by others, to write the most, read the most, and be cited the most in the writing of others. The stars play a key role in the exchange of information in a community. Because they are foci for a large number of professional contacts, they are in a position to be able to supply information to many other scientists. They are also very influential in the diffusion of information on innovations occurring in a field.

These informal communication networks are extremely important in scientific and technical fields. They are in many ways a very effective form of information transfer. In fact, information reaching such an invisible college is likely to travel very rapidly throughout the network. Information on the results of current research spreads through the invisible college network long before the research is reported in the more formal channels of communication, such as the science journal.

Those who are well integrated in an invisible college structure are in a highly favored position in comparison with those not so integrated. They tend to be much more current in their field, and they are the first to adopt, and benefit from, scientific and technological innovations. In contrast, the isolates tend to be less well informed on new developments in their field and adopt innovations at a much later time.

The informal channels through which professionals communicate are of great importance to scientific progress. Communication networks of the type described, although they may be most clearly identifiable in science, also exist in the social sciences and other fields. Informal networks of communication are also present in everyday life. We imply such a network when we say, "I learned of it through the grapevine." In a large company, for example, the secretaries may have their own information network. Information on happenings in the company spreads rapidly through the network. The secretaries who are well integrated in the network may learn of the happenings long before their more isolated colleagues. They may also know about certain company decisions before the professionals for whom they work. Similar phenomena occur in all social organizations. The more sociable, and therefore better integrated, students in a school or university are likely to be better informed on academic or other policies than those who do not mix so much with their colleagues.

It should be fairly obvious, too, that informal channels of communication are also important in industry. A company that is relatively isolated, in that it does not have efficient contacts with the outside world, is likely to find itself lagging behind its competitors. It does not learn very quickly about new materials, equipment, and production techniques. Consequently, it is not in a position to be able continuously to improve its production capacity, reduce costs, develop new products, and so on.

Fortunately it has been found, at least in the United States, that many industrial organizations have their own informal channels of communication. In a particular company there probably exists one or more individuals who are sociometric stars. These are engineers or scientists whom other people in the organization go to when the need for information arises. The sociometric stars of industry have been termed "information gatekeepers," or, sometimes, "technological gatekeepers." These individuals make it their business to inform themselves of new developments of concern to the company, by both reading current literature in the field and maintaining extensive contacts with other individuals in other organizations. Although this may not be his officially designated function in the company, the information gatekeeper plays a key role in industrial progress by bringing information into the organization through both formal and informal channels. A similar phenomenon has been shown to exist at national levels. In some countries international technological gatekeepers have been identified. They are scientists, or other professionals, who keep up to date with new scientific or technological developments abroad, by both reading the literature and maintaining extensive professional contacts with individuals and organizations elsewhere. In a sense they deal with the import and export of information. For obvious reasons, they would play a particularly valuable role in importing to a developing country the technology developed in the more industrially advanced nations.

Informal channels of communication play a major role in the diffusion of information on new developments in a field, that is, on "innovations." A considerable amount of research has been conducted on the "diffusion of innovation," particularly in the fields of agriculture and of medicine. The speed with which an innovation is adopted in a community is dependent on the efficiency and quality of the communication channels and on the attitudes of the members of the community toward the innovation, that is, their tendency to adopt or reject the innovation. Five stages that an individual may go through in the "adoption" process have been identified:

1. Awareness
2. Interest
3. Trial
4. Adoption
5. Confirmation

The awareness stage is largely passive. An individual learns of an innovation because he receives news of it without actively seeking it. The interest stage is more active. When his interest is aroused, the individual seeks more complete information on the innovation and how to adopt it. Sometimes an evaluation stage is separately identified but such a stage is not clearly distinguishable because evaluation of the innovation is, in some sense, likely to occur throughout the entire process.

There are those who adopt an innovation early and those who adopt it late. In fact, in studying the diffusion of innovations, five categories of individuals have been identified: the innovators, the early adopters, the early majority, the late majority, and the laggards. In general, the innovators and the early adopters are likely to be most active in a particular community, well integrated in the informal channels of communication. At one time the diffusion of innovation was thought to be largely a two-step process, with information going first to "opinion leaders" (sociometric stars) and from them directly to other individuals whose actions and attitudes they are able to influence. More recently it has been recognized that the diffusion process is more complicated than suggested in this two-step "model." It is in fact a multistep process, with opinion leaders influencing other opinion leaders and they, in turn, influencing members of their own immediate "community."

The significance of informal communication networks in science and other fields cannot be overemphasized. Coleman et al. (1966), for example, clearly demonstrated the great value of a network of medical practitioners in the diffusion of drug information. When doctors in the network were compared with those not so integrated, differences in time of adoption led to the conclusion that the communication network had a very important effect on the early adoption of new drugs. At the frontiers of a fast-moving field, a scientist integrated in a communication network of this kind is at a great advantage over his nonintegrated colleagues in receiving new information.

Besides dividing human communication into formal and informal, it is possible to use an alternative division into written and oral. A telephone conversation is an oral act of communication in which one individual transmits a message to another, using the telephone circuit as the channel of communication. Under other circumstances a person may prefer to communicate with others by writing a letter, an article in a periodical or newspaper, or perhaps a book. Letters, periodicals, and books are all important channels of communication.

Oral channels of communication have certain advantages over written channels, and written channels have certain advantages over oral channels. They serve different purposes. One is more convenient or efficient under certain circumstances than the other. One obvious advantage of oral communication is that it is interactive and two-way. In a conversation between two people, by telephone or face-to-face, the individuals interact with each other. Sometimes one acts as communication source, and the other as destination; sometimes the roles are reversed. If we have not understood the speaker, that is, received the message, we can ask him to repeat it or to phrase it in a different way. Written communication, on the other hand, is mostly noninteractive. Most people who read articles or books do not respond to the author. The communication is largely one-way. Correspondence is in a somewhat different category. Correspondence may be two-way communication, but the interaction tends to be so slow that much of its true interactive value is lost.

The major disadvantage of oral communication is that it is not a very efficient means of transmitting the same message to a large number of people at the same time. Under certain conditions we may be able to transmit the same message orally to several hundred people—for example, by presenting a paper at a large conference—but usually we can communicate orally only with single individuals or small groups. Radio and television, of course, permit oral communication with millions of individuals, but not everyone has access to such channels of communication, and not all messages are entirely suited to the broadcasting medium.

The distinction between formal communication and informal communication is less precise than that between written and oral communication. In general, oral communication is mostly informal, and most written communication is regarded as formal. But these associations are not absolute. A letter from one scientist to another is a written communication, but it is informal in character; and a talk given to a professional meeting is a formal oral communication. There are certain channels that have been formally established and are formally maintained by professional communities in order to facilitate professional communication among the members of the community. Such channels include publishing channels and professional courses, conferences, and meetings. Any communication that takes place through the formal mechanisms of these channels may be regarded as formal communication whereas all other forms of communication may be considered to be informal. The professional conference, or other meeting, is really in a special category. The papers which are formally presented, and which may be published in the proceedings of the meeting, are certainly formal communications. But much informal communication also takes place at such meetings: in hotel rooms, corridors, and restaurants, and this informal communication may be at least as important to the professional community as the papers formally presented.

Oral and written channels are equally applicable to the problem-solving and decision-making information need and the current awareness information need. Under certain circumstances it is more effective to seek information orally, and in other circumstances it may be better or more convenient to receive it in written form. There is no direct correlation between the two types of information need and the two types of communication. If an engineer needs information to solve a specific problem, he may go to published sources, or he may contact another professional who is a specialist in this particular area. There are many factors that influence the decision as to which of these types of source to go to. If we are quite sure that a particular individual has the information we need, it is frequently more efficient to contact him than to seek a solution in the published literature. But, for many information needs, we do not know any specialist who can give us an immediate answer, and it may be better to seek a solution in the literature than to try to identify a specialist who can help us.

It is important to recognize, also, that the two communication channels are quite interdependent. If we call an engineering consultant, to help us with a specific problem, he may give us the solution "out of his head." That he can do this, however, is probably because he is more familiar than we are with the published literature. This is his field of specialization, and he keeps up-to-date in it, as we must try to do in ours. He may give us a solution that is not recorded anywhere in written form, but this is somewhat unlikely. It is quite probable that if we call a specialist for information, he may need to refer to the published literature himself. In fact, his solution to our problem may be to draw our attention to a publication in which the solution appears. He knows the literature in his field of specialization and can refer to it easily. Much of the most relevant literature may be around him in his office.

But the fact that the solutions to many of our problems exist somewhere in published form does not lessen the value of the oral channels of communication. We go to a specialist because he is more familiar with the literature than we are, and can thus find a solution more rapidly, and because he can evaluate the literature and decide which solutions are most applicable to our needs, or which data are most reliable. Finally, we go to the oral source for "interpretation." This is something that the literature itself cannot provide. If we develop a severe pain in the ear, we could visit a large medical library and review much of the world's literature on diseases of the ear. Perhaps we will look at much more of this literature than many specialists have done. But having the literature available in this case does not solve our problem. Unless we are doctors ourselves, we cannot apply this literature. Probably we do not understand much of it. It would certainly be unwise for us to attempt to diagnose and treat our own condition.

In summary, for problem-solving or decision-making purposes, we sometimes use oral sources of information and sometimes written sources. Frequently we may use both. Moreover, as we have seen already, the oral sources are themselves very heavily dependent on the written sources. The two channels are also applicable to the current awareness situation. The scientist or engineer needs to use both if he really wants to be current with new developments in his field. He attempts to familiarize himself with the most relevant of the new literature, but he may also attend continuing education courses and conferences and generally try to keep up-to-date by talking with other professionals. New products, for example, may be brought to the attention of potential users by representatives of the manufacturers of the products. Thus, representatives of pharmaceutical companies visit doctors in their offices, to inform them on newly available drugs, and representatives of equipment manufacturers visit industrial plants to bring their products to the attention of purchasing agents and others who may be likely to use them.

It should be clear from the discussion above that a professional in any field may use a number of different sources of information. He may contact other individuals, some working in his own organization and some outside it, and he needs to use books, journals, technical reports, and other forms of literature. Many individuals maintain their own collections of the literature that they feel are of most interest to them. These personal information files, located in their own offices, are extremely important. They are the sources of information that are most accessible, and they are likely to be the first source that a professional turns to when the need for information arises. But such personal collections cannot be complete; they do not meet all needs. The professional must have a convenient source to go to for a more complete collection of the published literature. This, of course, is the purpose that libraries and other information centers are intended to serve.

Before we leave completely the subject of informal communication, it seems appropriate to mention a series of experiments in which an attempt was made to "formalize" the informal channels of communication. The Information Exchange Group experiments were conducted by the National Institutes of Health in the period 1961–1967. Under the auspices of NIH, seven information exchange groups were established in various specialized areas of the biomedical sciences. A leading scientist in the area was appointed as chairman of each group. It was the responsibility of this chairman to see that all scientists involved in research and development activities in the area of specialization, including scientists outside the United States, were included in the group. NIH provided administrative and secretarial support to facilitate interchange in the group. All communications, however informal or tentative, that a member wished to share with his colleagues were submitted to the group office, duplicated in multiple copies, and distributed to all members of the group. Exchange increased through a "snowball" effect because one communication would stimulate responses from other members. The NIH Information Exchange Groups made a deliberate attempt to widen the invisible college network, bringing in the younger scientists as well as scientists from countries less well developed than those in the West. Although these experiments were controversial and were bitterly attacked by the editors of some leading science journals, there are many who consider this work the most significant yet to be conducted in the field of scientific communication. Cooper (1968) and Heenan and Weeks (1971) have prepared analyses of the benefits of these experiments, and Green (1967) presents the very positive views of one of the chairmen.

The invisible college phenomenon has been investigated by Price and Beaver (1966) and, in greater detail, by Crane (1972), as well as by Crawford (1971). The gatekeeper concept is discussed by Allen (1964, 1968, 1970a, 1970b), Allen and Cohen (1969), and Allen et al. (1968). The international gatekeeper is dealt with by Allen and Cooney (1973), Cooney and Allen (1974), and Allen et al. (1971). The subject of diffusion of innovation is dealt with by Coleman et al. (1966), Katz (1957), Rogers (1962), Rogers and Beal (1958), and Wilkening (1952, 1956), among others. Useful reviews of various aspects of informal communication can be found in Havelock (1969) and Wilkin (1977).

Chapter Twenty-Three

Users and User Needs

Over the years a very considerable number of so-called "user studies" have been conducted. They have ranged from comprehensive surveys of the information-seeking behavior of large communities—for example, physicists, psychologists, research and development personnel in the Department of Defense—to more restricted studies of the users of a particular library or information center, to highly specific investigations of the users of a single service or tool—for example, a journal readership survey or a catalog use study in a particular library. This chapter does not attempt to present an overview of this mass of literature. Nor does it deal with the possible methodologies by which the needs or demands of users of information services may be studied. Instead, it is restricted to some generalizations on information-seeking behavior and "information needs" to the extent that such generalizations can be drawn from the investigations conducted in the last twenty years. Some useful analyses and interpretations of this literature have already been made, notably by Carter et al. (1967), Brittain (1970), Faibisoff and Ely (1976), and Faibisoff et al. (1973).

Perhaps the single most important finding of user studies in general is that accessibility and ease of use seem to be the most important factors that determine whether or not a particular information service is used. Physical, intellectual, and "psychological" accessibility all enter into this picture. Some studies have shown, in fact, that ease of use is ranked ahead of perceived quality in the selection of an information source. This was the finding, for example, of Rosenberg's (1967) questionnaire survey of 96 professionals in industrial and government organizations. A very similar finding was made by Allen and Gerstberger (1967). Their study, which investigated criteria by which engineers select a source of information when faced with a particular problem-solving situation, attempted to establish empirical support for a model of information-seeking behavior proposed earlier by Allen (1966). According to Allen's model, selection of an information source is based almost exclusively on accessibility, the most accessible source (channel) being chosen first; considerations of quality and reliability are secondary, although they are important in influencing the degree to which the user is willing to accept information supplied from a particular source. The Allen and Gerstberger study found empirical support for Allen's model. Specifically, they concluded that

1. Accessibility is the single most important determinant of the overall extent to which an information channel is used.
2. Both accessibility and perceived technical quality influence the choice of first source.
3. Perception of accessibility is influenced by experience. The more experience an engineer has with a channel, the more accessible he perceives it to be.
4. The rate at which ideas are accepted or rejected is related to the perceived quality of the information provided by a channel. Engineers thus use technical quality as the criterion in a filtering process that compensates, in part, for the neglect of technical quality considerations when selecting an information channel.

One of the most complete studies to determine the effect of accessibility on the use of literature was conducted by Soper (1972). It was based on an analysis of citations appearing in samples of recent scholarly articles in science, the social sciences, and the humanities. For each source cited in a particular article, Soper attempted to determine where the source was physically located at the time the article was written, that is, in the author's personal collection, an office or departmental collection, the library of the author's institution, another library in the same town, or available only through a source outside the town in which the author lived and worked. Soper hypothesized that citation patterns would be directly related to the physical accessibility of materials: the more physically accessible a source, the more likely that it would be cited. This hypothesis was supported by the data collected from 178 respondents and 5175 references. Approximately 59% of all references cited in Soper's sample were located in the personal collections of the authors, approximately 26% in their institutional libraries, and approximately 10% in geographically less accessible libraries. In general, the more accessible a source, the greater the likelihood that it would be cited. Respondents indicated that they preferred to use their personal collections rather than university or other libraries, because their personal collections were more accessible and were arranged to reflect their own specific interests. The material that a scholar or research scientist felt was most important to his work was likely to be in his own collection, even though it also may have appeared in a nearby library. Respondents tended to be negative in their attitudes toward libraries, judging them difficult to use and "generally unpleasant to work in." Ninety-eight percent of all Soper's respondents maintained some type of personal collection, and the tendency to maintain such a collection appeared unrelated to the size or excellence of the respondent's institutional library; that is, personal collections were maintained even when the institutional library was highly rated.

The ease of use factor was highlighted by Mooers (1960) in "Mooers' Law":

> An information retrieval system will tend not to be used whenever it is more painful and troublesome for a customer to have information than for him not to have it.

The most complete analysis of ease of use as a factor influencing human behavior in general can be found in the work of Zipf (1949), in which it is discussed in terms of a "principle of least effort."

A second major conclusion, derived from several studies, is that many professionals feel an "information overload." More "information" reaches them than they can possibly handle. They do not want more information from more sources because they are unable to cope with what they now receive. Instead, they emphasize the need for more selectivity in information services. Selective and critical reviews of the literature—for example, annual reviews—are considered of great importance. So are the evaluation, selection, and synthesis functions performed by information analysis centers (see Chapter 7).

Information services need to be more up-to-date, especially in the sciences. There is need for more rapid and efficient dissemination of the results of scientific research. Unfortunately, most formal information services lag years behind the "research front" in all science fields. The science journal itself is more archival than current, since it generally reports on research that was concluded a year or more earlier, and perhaps begun three years previous, and many of the secondary publications, which index or abstract the journal literature, are six months to a year later still. There is increasing need for making scientists aware of current research, work that is going on now. Hence, the great importance of indexes to ongoing research, as exemplified most obviously by the files of the Smithsonian Science Information Exchange.

As pointed out in the preceding chapter, informal channels of communication are considered more important than formal channels for satisfying many types of information need. Personal files have also been shown to have great importance. When the need for information arises, it is quite likely that the individual turns first to his personal files. If these fail him, he is likely to go the informal route, to contact a colleague or consultant in his own organization or outside it. It is only after these sources are exhausted that he is likely to consider approaching a library or other type of information center. "Going to the library" or "consulting the librarian" are actions that are generally ranked low when professionals are asked to list information sources used in a sequence of perceived convenience or perceived value. That personal files and informal channels tend to appear very high in all rankings of information sources is largely due to convenience and ease-of-use factors. Informal channels are also perceived to be more up-to-date than the more formal sources.

Another conclusion emerges rather clearly from many user studies. The education of users and potential users of information services is a sadly neglected area. Surveys of various communities have repeatedly shown that large segments of the population are completely unaware of many information services that are available to them. Others are vaguely aware that a service exists but have not made use of it because they believe that it is designed to "serve others" and have little idea of what it can do for themselves. Still others may make use of some existing service but fail to exploit it fully because they do not recognize or understand its true capabilities. This was touched on in Chapter 10. People are conditioned by their expectations. They tend to ask for what they think the service can provide, which may be somewhat different from what they really want or need. The use of information sources is an area that is very much neglected at all levels of education. Lack of adequate promotion of information services is a related problem area. Frequently, once a service is designed and implemented, the managers are content to sit back and wait for people to flock in. It is perhaps not surprising that such flocking is often absent. The situation relating to promotion is undoubtedly changing, however, as more and more commercial interests assume increasingly important roles in the provision of information service.

The generalizations referred to above are perhaps the most important that can be drawn from the myriad user studies already conducted. There are several additional observations, in some ways less significant, that may be summarized as follows:

1. Scientists and others tend to have well-ingrained habits regarding the gathering of information. Information systems must adapt to these habits rather than expecting potential users to adapt to the system.
2. Different potential users may have quite different information needs, and a single individual's needs may change rather substantially over time. The research members of an academic community are likely to need different materials from those needed by the teaching members; they are also likely to need a much wider range. It has also been shown that different types of information are needed at different stages of a research project and that the sources used may also vary considerably from one stage of a project to another.
3. The "utility" of documents to a particular group of users involves more than a match of subject matter between the documents and the interests of the users. "Suitability" of the materials—for example, in terms of their level of treatment, form, and language—is also very important.
4. Information services must have a "follow-through" capability. The prime example of this is the need for an adequate and convenient document delivery capability to back up citation retrieval services.
5. Information services must instill confidence in their users. They must present some assurance of continuity, and the staff must be able to communicate intelligently with users at an appropriate technical level. Consistency and completeness—for example, an indexing service must cover all issues of a journal, a library should not have unavoidable gaps in its journal holdings—are also important.
6. There is some evidence that many individuals do not recognize that they have information needs at all. If they do recognize a need, they may not be able to explicate it with sufficient precision to convert it into a demand on some formal information service.

In concluding this brief review of the needs and behavior of users of information services, it seems appropriate to mention some failures or limitations of most of the studies that have so far been conducted. One obvious limitation is that they draw conclusions from the stated behavior of users rather than from their observed behavior. In general, it is easier to ask people what they do than it is to observe how they actually behave. Unfortunately, what people say they do is often different, perhaps quite different, from what they really do. Another related limitation of some studies is that they ask users what they do in general rather than focusing on a single "critical incident." This is a defect because users can generally be more exact in their recollection of a single recent incident than about their general behavior. Recollections of general behavior tend to be vague, if not downright inaccurate. Another related limitation is that most actual observations of user behavior are, of necessity, obtrusive rather than unobtrusive. There is a danger that the obtrusiveness of the study technique will interfere with the reliability of the observations: a person who knows he is observed may behave differently from the way he normally does.

The most significant limitation of most user studies was already highlighted in Chapter 10. It is sufficiently important to discuss again here. It is true that user studies of various kinds have told us a great deal about the demands made on information services by those who presently make use of them. But this is a small tip of a very large iceberg. Knowing a lot about the tip, but very little about the submerged mass, can lead designers and managers of information services into decisions based on assumptions that may be inaccurate and even dangerous.

In many situations the manager of an information service has a sound knowledge only of the demands of present users. Little, if anything, is known of the information needs of those members of the community who are presently making no use of the services provided. For certain kinds of information centers at least, the population of actual users may be quite small in comparison with the population of potential users. It is likely, of course, that not all the information needs of the present users are actually converted into demands on the services provided, but we do not have much knowledge on the differences between the needs that are converted into demands and those which are not. We also know little about the factors that determine whether or not an information need is actually converted into a demand for information service. Moreover, although we know something about the demands made by present users, we may not know very much about the needs that lie behind the demands. We tend to assume that the expressed needs of users are coextensive with their actual needs, but there is much evidence to suggest that many expressed needs are only distant approximations of actual needs. The visible tip of the iceberg, then, is very small indeed, since it consists of only the expressed needs, rather than all of the information needs, of those individuals who are presently using our services. Much less visible, if visible at all, are the needs behind the demands of present users, the needs of present users that are never converted into demands, and the needs of those who are presently making no use of our services.

There is, of course, an obvious explanation for this situation. Demands are much easier to identify than needs, and present users are more easily studied than present nonusers. By focusing on that which is most readily observed, however, and drawing conclusions from these observations, we run into some great dangers. There is a strong tendency for managers of information services to do more of the things that their present users are asking them to do. Perhaps the most obvious example is buying more books or periodicals of the type that present users are asking for. Doing this, however, tends to move information services closer to the needs of present users and further away from those of present nonusers. Moreover, such actions may move the services toward the expressed needs of present users and away from (1) the actual needs behind the expressed needs and (2) the needs of present users that are never converted into demands.

The situation, however, may even be worse than this because volume of present demands may be taken into consideration. The decisions of managers of information services tend to be most influenced by those demands of present users which occur most frequently. This leads to a self-reinforcing situation, in which services are continually moved toward the most frequently occurring demands made by that segment of the population which is presently using the services provided. The services thus become increasingly exclusive, ever favoring present users over present nonusers, ever favoring the heavy users at the expense of the light ones.

This phenomenon has actually been encouraged in professional literature by some writers who should really know better. These authors have advocated that the most frequent users of a particular service be identified, that their interest profiles be established, and that the service should then buy more of the things that they use. Clearly, if we pursue this policy to its logical conclusion, we will find ourselves with a service precisely tailored to the needs of a single individual.

The fact is that, despite hundreds of "user studies," we still know rather little about the real information needs of the various communities information services are designed to serve. What knowledge we do have may be more detrimental than beneficial in the design and management of the services. It is time, perhaps, to abandon user studies and to concentrate instead on a more productive area of research—that of nonuses and nonusers of information services.

Useful surveys or bibliographies of user studies can be found in the work of Atkin (1971), the Auerbach Corporation (1965), Barber (1966), Barnes (1965), Bates (1971), Davis and Bailey (1964), DeWeese (1967), Ford (1973), Lancaster (1974a), Slater (1972), Tobin (1974), Weinstock et al. (1966), and Wood (1971).

Chapter Twenty-Four

The Design of Information Services

On a worldwide basis many thousands of information services exist. Presumably each of these services has been "designed" to meet the information needs of a particular community of users. One would expect, therefore, that a considerable body of knowledge must exist on how to go about designing information services. But no such body of knowledge does exist. At least, the literature that actually discusses design principles for information systems or information services is practically nonexistent. Many factors influencing the success or failure of information services have been recognized and discussed in this text. This chapter attempts to pull some of this material together and derive from it some principles that might be used as the basis of a reasonably systematic approach to the design of information services.

There is one cardinal principle that must be borne in mind from the very beginning. An information system is more likely to be accepted and adopted by a user community if the community has been actively involved in the design of the system from the very beginning. However carefully a system has been designed, it is likely to face great apathy or even resistance if members of the population to be served feel that it has been designed and foisted on them by some outside group that cannot possibly understand their own real needs. Although it is very difficult to achieve any significant level of user involvement in the design of certain types of information service—for example, one designed to serve a national or international community of users—it should be perfectly possible to achieve a high level of user involvement in the design of a system to serve a particular organization. The strategy here is to form a design team consisting of information specialists and representative members of the user community. In designing a service for an industrial organization or a government agency, for example, responsible representatives of each branch, division, or other administrative unit to be served should be selected to participate in the design team. It is important to gain the sympathy and cooperation of the managers of the various units to be served. Each manager must select a staff member to represent the interests of his unit. The staff member must be someone who is highly experienced in the work of the unit, sufficiently senior to have authority to speak for the unit's interests on the team, and, above all, sympathetic to the design project. The amount of time spent by the user representatives depends on the size of the project and the duration and intensity of the design effort. It is highly unlikely that they will devote themselves full-time to the design activity. In fact, the design team may meet only once each week or even less frequently at some stages of the project.

It is important to recognize the true function of the user representatives. Although they participate in design decisions, they are unlikely to become involved in detail in the intricacies of the system design. This is the function of the information specialists on the team. The user representatives speak for the interests of their units; they carry back, for discussion in the units, the ideas and concepts generated by the design team, and they participate in the evaluation of the system at each stage of its development.

The major stages involved in the design of the system should be

1. Conceptualization stage, in which a "paper model" of the system is developed.
2. Prototype stage. Here a working prototype is developed on a small scale. This is really an experimental stage. It might, for example, involve the production of a single sample issue of some publication—for example, a printed index or abstracts bulletin—or it might involve a working demonstration of the capabilities of an on-line retrieval system.

3. Evaluation of the prototype. This involves, at the very least, some carefully controlled user reaction studies.
4. Modification or refinement of the design on the basis of the evaluation results.
5. Implementation of the system on a full scale.
6. Implementation of some type of quality control activity, based on feedback from users, to ensure that the system remains responsive to the needs of the population served.

The user representatives must be involved, in at least an advisory capacity, in all these activities.

SOME DESIGN CONSIDERATIONS

It is impossible to go into detail here on all facets of the design of information services. Indeed, the subject merits a volume of its own. Moreover, there are many possible types of information service, each with its own special characteristics. It seems pointless to discuss the pros and cons of various services in a vacuum. The detailed requirements of a particular service can be identified only after a rather thorough analysis of the information needs and present information-gathering behavior of the community to be served. This chapter can deal only in generalities.

Some major design considerations can be derived from the preceding chapter. Clearly, the system must be perceived to be readily accessible and convenient to use. In the contemporary setting this may mean a system with on-line terminals in each user office and a query language that is easy to learn and apply. The system must also adapt to the present behavior and preferences of those to be served. For example, in many organizations personal or office files may be considered the single most important information source. A central system, even if readily accessible and convenient to use, is unlikely to replace these resources completely. The central system must adapt to this situation, perhaps by allowing on-line digital files to be built up by individuals to replace their paper files. The overall system might then be designed to allow symbiosis between the personal or office files and the central files. The individual could then build his own information files at an on-line terminal, indexing them in any way he wishes, and use his on-line terminal to access his personal files, office files, and organization-wide files, perhaps also going beyond into outside information services available through other service centers.

It is clear that some type of user study must be conducted, to identify the most important information needs, before any system can be "conceptualized." For reasons of space, if nothing else, the methodologies for the conduct of such studies are outside the scope of the present text. Nevertheless, we attempt to identify some major decisions that need to be made and suggest some possible approaches through which information may be gathered to allow the decisions to be made intelligently.

For many types of information service some important decisions to be made relate to the questions

1. What is to be included in the data base?
2. How is this data base to be indexed? This involves indexing policy decisions as well as vocabulary control decisions.
3. How is the user to interact with this system?

Since it is extremely unlikely that the collection of materials in some information center, or the data base of sources from which some information service is provided, can ever be complete, an important design consideration is the establishment of an appropriate selection policy. The selection policy might cover, for example, journal titles and report series. There are a number of possible approaches to the determination of which materials are likely to have greatest payoff in terms of the interests of the community to be served. One obvious approach is to incorporate a direct question relating to most valuable journals, report series, and other types of materials in a questionnaire or interview survey of a sample of the user population. Unfortunately, this approach is likely to result in a rather short list of "most obvious" sources, the listings of many respondents looking somewhat similar. This approach is likely to reinforce what the system designer already knows rather then revealing anything radically new. A second possible approach is to take the reports, journal articles, and other publications generated by members of the population to be served, assuming that a significant number of them do in fact publish, and study the lists of sources cited in these publications. There is an obvious danger in this approach when the population to be served is drawn from a single organization: authors are likely to cite the most accessible materials, those already available in the organization, and the most accessible materials do not necessarily coincide exactly with the set of "most useful" materials. Other possible approaches include (1) forming lists of citations from samples of current articles drawn from the literature of the subject field as a whole and (2) determining the sources that are most used in other information centers serving populations with similar subject interests. The latter may be the most effective technique of all. But it is not always possible to identify a comparable information center, and if one can be identified, it may be quite difficult to acquire the needed use information—for example, the information center of one company in the energy field may be unwilling to provide this type of information to a competitor. It is likely, in fact, that a number of different techniques need to be used before a decision can be reached on which sources should form the basis of some dissemination or retrospective search service.

The list of sources, moreover, will not be completely stable. It must change with time to reflect the emergence of new sources, the demise of others, and changing emphases in the interests of the population to be served. Other than purely subject considerations must also be taken into account. The material must be understandable by the users. Thus, it should be at the appropriate technical and intellectual level and in languages that the users can read or for which translations can readily be obtained when the material is recognized to be of sufficient value. As mentioned in Chapter 16, cost-effectiveness considerations also apply. The resources available for acquisition of materials must be allocated to those sources having the greatest probability of use to the community served. This implies the need for a ranking of sources on a usefulness scale.

More difficult, perhaps, than the decision on what to include in the data base are the decisions on how to index the materials. This raises questions on what type of indexing to use, how exhaustively to index, and how specific the system vocabulary needs to be. Such decisions are frequently made on the basis of "educated guesses." But there are perhaps more systematic approaches that might be used to gather the necessary data. A user survey, for example, can collect details of specific information needs occurring in the community to be served. Information on the latest information need of each member of the community (the "critical incident") can contribute not only to our knowledge of needed sources but to our knowledge of how exhaustively and specifically the material needs to be indexed. There are several parts of a user questionnaire that could contribute lists of terms, at the appropriate level of specificity, to be included in the first draft of a thesaurus: the detailed description of the respondent's present professional responsibilities, his own free description of his major subject interests, and one or more "critical incidents" of information needs. Another possible approach, which has been used, for example, by Pickford (1968) and Dym (1967a), is to have potential users underline key words and phrases in representative documents that closely match their subject interests. This technique provides raw material for the development of a controlled vocabulary; it also indicates how exhaustively the documents need to be indexed to allow them to be retrieved in response to the specific demands of the users. As discussed in Chapter 12, an index language should have "user warrant" as well as "literary warrant." A technique that draws terms from the literature has the latter. A technique that draws terms from user questionnaires has the former. A technique in which users draw terms from the literature has both.

Design of system outputs must receive the same level of attention as the decisions relating to system inputs. Although the major input considerations—data base, indexing, vocabulary—remain relatively constant from one information service to another, the output considerations vary widely with the precise nature of the service to be provided. In the case of an on-line retrieval system, for example, it is necessary to determine what capabilities are needed in the searching software. This, in turn, depends partly on some of the input considerations—for example, if a thesaurus is to be used. It is also affected by the question of whether searches are to be conducted by the "end users" or information specialists on their behalf. The requirements for searching software must be based on knowledge of the characteristics of the data bases to be processed as well as how the data bases will be exploited by users. It is necessary to use this knowledge to develop a set of "functional requirements" for the software. This set of functional requirements is then used as requirements levied against the systems analysts and programmers who are to implement the system or as a "shopping list" that can be compared with the characteristics of software packages available for leasing or purchase.

We have restricted this discussion of system design to generalities and some more specific considerations relating to "intellectual" and software decisions. Hardware requirements have been ignored. This is deliberate. The hardware is sometimes a "given," that is, the system must function on facilities already available in the organization. At other times, the hardware requirements can be identified only after the other parameters of the system have been recognized and reduced to a set of functional requirements. Hardware cannot be specified until we know precisely what it is to accomplish. As mentioned earlier in the chapter, it is highly desirable that the entire design process be carried out with the close cooperation of members of the user communities. The system functional requirements constitute a formal "conceptualization" of the system. The conceptualization must be tested against the user community to determine its reaction. The design and implementation of a prototype or "model," on a small scale, should precede the full-scale implementation of a system wherever possible. The prototype, too, must be tested and evaluated by the user community.

Literature directly related to design principles for information services is very sparse. Faibisoff and Ely (1976) have suggested some useful system design "guidelines," derived from our present knowledge of the behavior and needs of users of information services, and Cooper (1970) has attempted to derive some "design equations" from performance measures applicable to retrieval systems. A "systems approach" to the design of information services is presented by Liston and Schoene (1971). Three types of models for the design of information systems are described by Zimmerman (1977). A useful analysis of "user factors" to be taken into account in the design of on-line retrieval systems has been prepared by Martin and Parker (1971).

Chapter Twenty-Five

The Future: Paperless Information Systems

Elsewhere, in another book (Lancaster, 1978), I have discussed in detail some of the problems involved in present methods of disseminating, storing, and retrieving scientific and technical information and have suggested that we are moving rapidly and inevitably toward a paperless system of communication. It seems appropriate, therefore, to conclude the present volume with a brief summary of the major existing problems and a fleeting glimpse of what paperless systems of the future may look like. Whether we like it or not, society is evolving from one whose formal communication has, for centuries, been based on print on paper to one whose formal communication will be largely electronic.

Messages are disseminated as print on paper, because, for most types, there has been no other way in the past of reaching a wide audience. Now, however, it is possible to create a message, perhaps a lengthy document, at one on-line terminal and transmit it to others where it can be read. The recipient can store a message "electronically," and index, augment, or redistribute it without generating paper. An electronic environment makes paper superfluous. It is probable that the great majority of documents distributed now for their information content will be issued electronically in the future, including indexing and abstracting services, handbooks, directories, technical reports, patents, standards, and journals in science and other fields.

Before documents can be disseminated electronically, they must exist in machine-readable form, and the potential audience must be well equipped with on-line terminals. Although these requirements are not yet satisfied, they are likely to be, for a wide range of documents and users, in the future. Moreover, they are already satisfied in some specialized applications, notably the defense and intelligence community, where prototype systems already permit documents to be generated, transmitted, used, stored, indexed, and retransmitted in a paperless mode. Paperless systems are unlikely to be confined to defense and intelligence applications. Indeed, they are almost certain to emerge in virtually all fields.

Consider the formal system through which results of science research are transmitted, as illustrated in Chapter 1. Economic, social, and industrial progress are all dependent on scientific discovery. Discovery, in turn, depends heavily on the ability of the science community to assimilate the results of previous research, since modern science is a social activity with progress achieved through the process of aggregation, one research group building on the work of others. A breakdown in the science communication system could have very serious consequences and, in fact the system already exhibits signs of collapse. Some channels are almost closed, others are beginning to. If the results of scientific research continue to be disseminated as print on paper, their accessibility will progressively decline.

CURRENT PROBLEMS IN SCIENCE COMMUNICATION

The literature of science and technology increases in step with scientific and technical growth and thus at a very rapid pace. This "information explosion" has two dimensions: (1) growth in number of information packages and (2) growth in size of the packages. Best available estimates indicate that there are now about 50,000 journals in science and technology and that this number increases at a compound rate of 2 to 4% annually. The size of each of these "packages" also increases. Sandoval (1976b) has pointed out that *Biochimica et Biophysica Acta*, for example, has grown at an approximately logarithmic rate since its foundation in

1947; it now doubles in size about every 4.6 years. Besides journal growth, there is comparable growth in technical reports, patents, dissertations, films, videotapes, and other documentary forms. Although the literature increases, however, the time anyone has to read it remains more or less constant. A scientist who spends 10% of his day in "keeping up," a proportion that remains steady over the years, finds twice as much published in his field in 1976 as was published in 1966. He must fall further and further behind unless he adopts more efficient methods for keeping current.

Secondary publications increase in number and size at more or less the same rate as primary literature. Ashworth (1974) demonstrated size increase dramatically with data on the number of years it took *Chemical Abstracts* to publish successive millions of abstracts:

First million	32 years (1907–1938)
Second million	18 years
Third million	8 years
Fourth million	4.75 years
Fifth million	3.3 years

Clearly, if the primary literature continues its exponential growth and if *Chemical Abstracts* continues to stay abreast of this growth, this service must soon publish 1 million abstracts annually.

Closely related to growth is the problem of "literature scatter." The more a field grows, the more dispersed its literature is. As shown in Figure 44, there may be 375 papers published on a particular subject in one year. Although a small number of journals, perhaps 5, may contribute about one-third of all these papers, and as few as 30 may contribute two-thirds, the final third may be distributed over as many as 125 titles. A scientist who scans five key journals in this field might at best discover one-third of the papers relevant to his field of specialization. It is no longer possible to remain well informed by scanning a small selection of journals. The only way to do it effectively is through secondary publications, and preferably by participating in a current awareness service in which a computer is used to search this secondary literature.

Another problem is that there may be a delay of many months between completion of a project and submission of a paper for publication, with a further substantial delay before it appears in print. As publishing space becomes more scarce, because publishers restrict growth to minimize price increases, publication delays extend. According to Roistacher (1978), *Sociometry* received 550 manuscripts in 1974 but had space to publish only 39 of them. Today's science journal is more archival than current, reporting research terminated many months ago. Information from this research was long ago disseminated to those well integrated socially in the science community. Those who would be at the forefront of their field cannot rely on the journal alone but must also use other documents—for example, technical reports—and, more important, turn to informal information channels.

Publication costs have been increasing rapidly because of rising costs of labor, materials, and facilities. Costs would accelerate if the amount published remained constant. When amount published and production costs both grow, price increases become alarming. In 1940, *Chemical Abstracts* could be purchased for $12 annually; in 1977, it cost $3500. The average United States subscription price for a chemistry or physics journal went from $18.42 in 1965 to $65.57 in 1975, and further substantial increases are forecast. De Gennaro (1977) mentions that *Inorganica Chimica Acta* was available to libraries for $26 in 1970 but cost $235 in 1975, a leap of 804%.

Prices of some science publications increased several hundred percent in a period when the general rate of inflation, measured by the Wholesale Price Index, was only 60%. *Psychological Abstracts*, to take one example, rose from $20 in 1963 to $190 in 1973. This reduces its accessibility to the psychology community unless salaries of psychologists increased a comparable 850% in this decade, which is clearly not the case. The trend is unambiguous. Secondary publications have largely priced themselves beyond the pocket of the individual and are available only in libraries. Ever-increasing costs are now putting some beyond the reach of the smaller institutions. Thus, they become available only in the larger libraries. The same fate is in store for the science journal. The ratio of institutional to individual subscribers is changing, slowly but surely, in favor of the former. Soon the primary literature will be available only in libraries; later, the more expensive journals will be found only in the larger libraries. If science publication continues as at present, it seems inevitable that primary journals will continue to move to the institutional subscriber, and secondary services will move increasingly out of the reach of the poorer libraries. Accessibility of information thereby declines continuously.

Publication costs outstrip inflation as a whole because publishing is still a labor-intensive industry, which, unlike others, has not yet raised productivity substantially through automation. The Industrial Production Index shows that, between 1967 and 1974, United States industry improved productivity by 24.8%, the rubber and plastics component by 64.4%, but printing and publishing by only 12.3%.

Libraries, largely dependent on this labor-intensive industry, are labor-intensive themselves. Budgets therefore increase rapidly but dwindle in purchasing power relative to total expenditures. Figures from Dunn et al. (1972) indicate that between 1965 and 1972, mean expenditures of 58 major research libraries increased 103%, mean expenditures for materials and binding by 78%, but volume of new additions by only 35%. Baumol and Marcus (1973) have shown that operating expenses of libraries increase rapidly even in periods of economic stability.

The only long-term solution to these problems appears to lie in greatly increased automation throughout the complete system by which research results are disseminated, stored, retrieved, and used; it lies in paperless systems.

THE ACHIEVEMENTS OF AUTOMATION

As described in Chapters 4 and 5, automation has already brought major improvements in access to information sources, notably through the phenomenal growth of machine-readable data bases and on-line systems to make them accessible. Cost of access has also declined dramatically. In 1970, a one-hour demonstration of on-line searching in Illinois was estimated to cost about $50, of which $3 to $5 was computer time and the remainder the cost of a telephone connection to California. Now, through TELENET, the communication cost of this demonstration is a mere $3. In 1977, Bibliographic Retrieval Services was quoting on-line connect costs as low as $10 per hour for high volume users. For data bases without royalty charges, the cost of a typical on-line search can be as little as $2.50 to $3.50, exclusive of terminal rental or purchase (minimal when amortized over many searches), the time of the searcher, and cost of printing citations off-line. Even with a royalty charge of $15 per connect hour, total on-line search costs could be as low as $5.75 to $8.50.

On-line access to many data bases is already cheaper than purchase of printed access. It costs $4000 a year, without storage and handling, to make *Chemical Abstracts* accessible on library shelves. An on-line search of this data base, however, might be conducted at an access cost of $10 or less and is likely to be much more effective than a search of the printed version. A library must do 400 searches a year of the printed source to make access cost per search comparable with access cost of the on-line data base. Machine-readable data bases and on-line technology change the entire economics of access to information sources. Access to a printed data base requires capital investment in subscription, storage, and handling costs, which can be justified only if the annual volume of use is sufficient to reduce the cost per search to a reasonable level. In contrast, on-line services make data bases accessible in a "pay as you go" mode, and their costs are much less volume-dependent. They make data bases available to libraries that cannot afford access to printed equivalents.

In summary, machine-readable data bases and on-line access have improved availability of information sources, reduced distance as a barrier to communication, made information sources as accessible in small communities as in major cities, and significantly cut access costs. The accessibility of information resources in electronic form is improving as rapidly as their accessibility in printed form is declining, and cost of the former is falling as rapidly as cost of the latter is rising. Moreover, cost and accessibility through electronics will improve, and cost and accessibility through print on paper can only deteriorate further.

Other achievements, although less impressive, have occurred in automation of acquisitions, cataloging, circulation, and other library activities. Automation has so far had little impact on production, distribution, and use of primary literature. Further major improvements in the dissemination and exploitation of information will come only when automation is applied to every step of the communication cycle (Figure 1) from composition of a document to its distribution and use. Such completely paperless systems seem inevitable.

A SCENARIO FOR THE FUTURE

Some basic assumptions underlying any discussion of a paperless future are that computers will continue to increase in power and decline in cost, methods of data transmission will become cheaper and more efficient, new storage devices will permit vast quantities of text to be held in a readily accessible form, and terminals will fall in price to a point at which every scientist will have one in his office and, perhaps, in his home. These developments, highly probable, will produce the communication "structure" to permit the substitution of electronics for many activities and institutions now operating largely through print on paper.

The scientist of the year 2000 will use a terminal in many different ways: to receive, transmit, compose, and search for text, seek answers to factual questions, build files, and converse with colleagues. The terminal provides a single entry to a wide range of capabilities that will substitute, wholly or in part, for many activities now handled in different ways.

Scientists will use terminals as electronic notebooks in which results from ongoing research can be entered at any time. Research reports, derived from these notes, will be written at the terminal. Text editing programs will simplify the making of corrections and alterations. On-line reference tools, including dictionaries and various data banks, will make accurate reporting much easier. An author can copy into a report quotations, tables, or references from earlier reports in machine-readable files.

When satisfied with a draft, a scientist may have it informally reviewed by submitting it to a few colleagues. The text is copied from his secure personal files into some limited-access file. A message, addressed to the colleagues selected, enters the communication system. It asks them to examine the draft and provides information needed to access it. The next time each uses a terminal in a "mail scan" mode, he will receive the message and, when convenient, examine the text.

The author may modify his report after receiving comments from these reviewers. It may then be transmitted electronically to a sponsoring agency or the publisher of some electronic journal. Primary publication may be a direct electronic analog of the present system. Descriptions of ongoing research projects will enter files similar to those now maintained by the Smithsonian Science Information Exchange. Patents, dissertations, standards, and other forms will all go into electronic files. Unrefereed reports will appear in data bases of government agencies and other sponsors of research.

Science "journals" will continue to be published by societies and commercial enterprises. They will build data bases comparable with the present journal packages: an applied physics file, a heat transfer file, and so on. Refereeing will continue, all communication among referees, authors, and editors taking place electronically. On-line directories of referees, automatic scheduling and follow-up procedures, and profile matching algorithms will all assist the efficient allocation of reports to referees. Acceptance into a public data base implies that an article has satisfied the refereeing process and received the "endorsement" of the publisher. Space considerations will not constrain publishing decisions, resulting in greatly reduced publication delays. The refereeing process, as Roistacher (1978) suggests, may allocate a numerical score to a document. All articles achieving some minimum score will be published, the score being carried with the document. A form of "public refereeing" is also possible. Monitors will record amount of use an item receives, readers can assign standard weights to it, and they can place comments, anonymous or signed, into a public comment file.

A paperless system will force rather sweeping changes in the way that literature is distributed and paid for. Some form of SDI service will inform a user of any new document, added to any accessible data base, that matches his interest profile. National and international on-line SDI services, based on discipline-oriented and mission-oriented secondary data bases, will emerge.

The user will pay for the amount of SDI service received. Costs will be low because of the great size of the population served. The SDI services, besides using citations or abstracts to bring documents to the attention of users, will tell them how to access the full text and how much this will cost. In the paperless system, an individual pays for just as much as he chooses to use.

Secondary publishers will continue to index and abstract primary literature, all processing being done on-line. The "scope" of a secondary data base need no longer be defined by a list of sources covered. Instead, interest profiles of secondary publishers may be matched against updates of primary data bases, matching items being disseminated to these secondary services rapidly and automatically. The customers of the secondary publishers, or of information centers, would in turn have their interest profiles matched regularly against the data bases of these institutions. This, of course, is just one possible "model" for a dissemination system of the future. It may seem a rather radical departure from present practice, but, in an electronic age, radical departures from tradition will be inevitable.

The electronic dissemination system will be one in which the scientist can reasonably expect to receive a few things each day in the mail. Any item he has no use for can be disposed of immediately by pushing a button. Items of immediate interest can be pursued at once. Other citations may be read off into private files for later action. An item viewed in its entirety can also be copied into private files in much the same way that an article may be placed in paper files. The private electronic file can be indexed in any way, each item with as many access points as the user wishes. Its search capabilities will greatly exceed those of paper files, and it will occupy virtually no space.

The terminal gives the scientist access to personal files and files maintained by colleagues or by his department. When these fail him, it will provide entry to limitless on-line resources: electronic equivalents of printed handbooks, directories, dictionaries, encyclopedias, almanacs and other reference tools, and indexes to primary text. Scientists will seek information by a "widening horizons" approach, going from personal files to institutional to national and international resources. Any data or text thus found can easily be transferred to personal files.

On-line dialogue, "real time" or delayed, can occur with consultants, colleagues, and specialists located at information centers. "Computer conferencing" will replace the mails for much professional correspondence. The distinction between formal and informal communication will be much less sharp, and attempts to meld the two forms will be more practicable than they are in the present environment.

I predict that a fully developed electronic system, having most if not all of these features, will exist by the year 2000, if not earlier. It will be achieved by combining many separate services, activities, and experiments already in existence. Major steps toward the system have already occurred. Data bases will continue to proliferate in social sciences and the humanities as well as in science, and accessibility will continue to improve through further implementation of on-line networks. Primary text will become available in machine-readable form as more and more publishers convert to computerized operations. The "editorial processing center," as described by Bamford (1973), may allow even small publishers to automate. Further improvements in computer and communications technologies will result in greatly reduced costs for storage, transmission, and exploitation of large volumes of text.

Computer text editing was already quite advanced when Van Dam and Rice (1971) reviewed the state of the art, and many improvements have occurred since then. In the business world, "word processing" is replacing "typing," and the paperless office (see, for example, Yasaki, 1975) is emerging. Computer conferencing, as described by Price (1975), is developing rapidly, and some organizations already use this, rather than the mails, for intracompany correspondence. A few experimental "journals" in electronic form have appeared, and on-line systems to support personal files are available at several universities. Without exaggeration, all features of the model described could be implemented today if these various technologies and experiments were amalgamated in a new science communication system. Technological, intellectual, and social obstacles still exist (see Lancaster, 1978); although some problems are difficult, none is insoluble.

CONCLUSION

We are moving rapidly and inevitably toward a paperless society. Advances in computer science and communications technology allow the conceptualization of a global system in which research reports are composed, published, disseminated, and used in a completely electronic mode. Paper need never exist in this environment. We are presently in an interim stage in the natural evolution from print on paper to electronics: the computer is used to print, and the resulting publications are mailed as print on paper. Machine-readable data bases exist side by side with printed versions but have not yet replaced them. This situation will undoubtedly change. When the great majority of potential users of a publication have ready access to terminals and when the number of users is great enough to support machine-readable files completely, the transition to electronic distribution and use of information sources will be made.

Appendix One

Interview Guide Used in Evaluation of AGRIS

AGRIS APPRAISAL STUDY

This questionnaire is being sent to AGRIS Liaison Officers and to AGRINDEX Input Centres.

It covers aspects both of the AGRIS programme as a whole and of AGRINDEX specifically. It is important that the whole questionnaire be answered as completely and accurately as possible. However, if any particular question is not applicable to your situation, it may be omitted. If a report or other document is available which supports the answer to any specific question, please attach a copy. If any answer is an estimate, please note the fact. You are encouraged to explain or elaborate on your answers wherever appropriate.

The completed questionnaire should be returned by air mail as soon as possible, and no later than February 21st, to:

> John Martyn
> Aslib R&D Department
> 36 Bedford Row
> London WC1R 4JH
> UNITED KINGDOM

Reproduced from Badran et al. (1977) by permission of UNESCO.

Appendix One

1. Do you receive AGRINDEX tapes?
   ☐ YES   ☐ NO   ☐ NO, but intend to receive in future

2. If you receive AGRINDEX tapes, does any further duplication of the tapes, completely or partially, occur?
   ☐ YES Please give details   ☐ NO

3. If you receive, or will receive, AGRINDEX tapes, what use is or is proposed to be made of these tapes? (Please check all applicable boxes)

   a. Providing a current awareness service ☐

   b. Retrospective searching ☐

   c. Selecting documents for acquisition ☐

   d. For other purposes (please explain) ☐

   e. No use to be made of the tapes (please explain why, below) ☐

4. If AGRINDEX products (in printed or tape form) form the basis of a *current awareness* service offered by your centre, how many individuals receive such service?

5. If AGRINDEX products (in printed or tape form) form the basis of a *retrospective search* service offered by your centre, approximately how many searches were conducted in 1976?

6. Please list the indexing and/or abstracting services that you consider (upon consultation, if appropriate, with a sample of users of agricultural information) to be most useful in the provision of agricultural information within your country. Rank in order of usefulness (most useful first):

Printed versions	*In magnetic tape form* (if used in the country)
1.	1.
2.	2.
3.	3.
4.	4.
5.	5.

7. If AGRINDEX (in printed or tape form) is not listed in the first position in the ranking, please explain why the preferred source(s) is/are found to be more useful:

8. In what ways could AGRINDEX (in printed or tape form) be improved in order to make it more useful in the provision of agricultural information services in your country? (Check all applicable boxes)

   a. Improved coverage of journal literature ☐

   b. Improved coverage of non-journal literature ☐

   c. Inclusion of more popular literature from technical or trade sources ☐

   d. Restrict coverage (indicate nature of restriction) ☐

   e. Make the categorisation scheme more specific ☐

   f. More extensive cross-referencing among categories ☐

   g. Provide more specific subject indexes ☐

   h. Provide subject indexing based on the use of an agricultural thesaurus ☐

   i. Provide better control of the quality of the bibliographic entries ☐

   j. Provide more detailed information on how each document could be obtained ☐

   k. Other means of improvement (please specify) ☐

9. Of the needed improvements you have selected in the preceding question, please circle the two that you feel should receive greatest priority.

10. What is your best estimate of the total number of articles and reports within the scope of AGRINDEX produced in your country each year?

338   Appendix One

11. With regard to your own input into AGRINDEX can you estimate how complete is your coverage of your national literature in agriculture:

	Up to 25% cover	26–50% cover	51–75% cover	76–90% cover	Over 90% cover
a. In journal form	☐	☐	☐	☐	☐
b. In other form	☐	☐	☐	☐	☐

12. What would you estimate to be the total effort in man-years needed to achieve complete coverage in input each year?

13. What are the present manpower resources devoted to this activity in your country?

14. In what areas do you encounter difficulties in providing national input to AGRIS? (Check all applicable boxes)

    a. Locating candidate documents for inclusion ☐

    b. Deciding whether a particular document should be included or not ☐

    c. Conforming to AGRIS guidelines ☐

    d. Getting sufficient resources (personnel, equipment or funds) to process the national output of agricultural literature (please explain) ☐

    e. Other problems (please explain) ☐

15. How many of the copies of AGRINDEX distributed by FAO to the national input centre or liaison officer (usually 3) are retained at the point of receipt?

16. What use is made of these retained copies? (Check all applicable boxes)

    a. In providing a current awareness service ☐

    b. In retrospective searching ☐

c. In selecting documents for acquisition ☐

d. Used for other purposes (please explain below) ☐

17. Please list the institutions to which any copies *not retained* at point of receipt are distributed.

18. For any copies not retained at point of receipt, for what purposes are these used? (Check all applicable boxes)

    a. General reference ☐

    b. Agricultural research ☐

    c. Agricultural training ☐

    d. Agricultural extension workers (either directly or through one of the preceding uses) ☐

    e. Other categories of use (please explain) ☐

19. A certain number of additional copies have been provided free of charge to your government. Please provide any information available on the distribution and use of these copies (as in questions 15–18).

20. Have steps been taken to promote the awareness and use of AGRINDEX in your country (please give details)?
    YES ☐   NO ☐

21. Is the provision of agricultural information within your country likely to be adversely affected by:

                                                                      YES   NO

    a. The recent increase from $60 to $250 in the annual subscription price of AGRINDEX? ☐ ☐

    b. The recent reduction in the number of copies distributed free of charge to your government? ☐ ☐

340   Appendix One

22. Do you consider that the participation of your country in AGRIS has led to improved identification (bibliographic control) of your national agricultural literature:

	YES	NO
a. From journal sources	☐	☐
b. From non-journal sources	☐	☐

23. Do you consider that the participation of your country in AGRIS has led to improvements in collecting your national agricultural literature:

	YES	NO
a. From journal sources	☐	☐
b. From non-journal sources	☐	☐

24. Do you consider that the AGRIS programme has improved your national awareness of, or access to, the agricultural literature of other countries?

	YES	NO
a. Awareness of the literature	☐	☐
b. Access to the literature	☐	☐

25. If the answer to questions 22, 23 or 24 was NO, are there any ways in which the AGRIS programme could offer help with these problems?

    ☐ YES   Please explain   ☐ NO

26. Is there any evidence that the existence of AGRIS has stimulated an increased demand for agricultural documents in your country?

    ☐ YES   Please give details   ☐ NO

27. Is AGRINDEX increasing the demand for the translation of foreign agricultural literature in your country?

    ☐ YES   ☐ NO

Have any special provisions been made for translation as a result?

☐ YES Please explain   ☐ NO

28. Since initiation of AGRINDEX, is there any evidence of increased demand from other countries for your national agricultural literature?

    ☐ YES   ☐ NO

29. Has the AGRIS programme had any influence in improving cooperation

	YES	NO
a. Among organisations concerned with agricultural information within the country (please give details below)?	☐	☐
b. Between national organisations and organisations in other countries (please give details below)?	☐	☐

30. What do you consider to be the major objectives of the AGRIS programme?

31. Below is given a list of possible developments that might arise from the expansion of the AGRIS programme (AGRIS Level 2). Please indicate by checking the appropriate box in the right-hand columns the importance of each development to the improvement of accessibility and use of agricultural information in your country.

	Very necessary	Desirable	Unimportant	No opinion
a. Creation of new specialised information centres devoted to specific agricultural topics	☐	☐	☐	☐

b. A greater level of coordination or cooperation among existing specialised information centres ☐ ☐ ☐ ☐

c. Production of review articles on specific agricultural topics ☐ ☐ ☐ ☐

d. Production of reports of recent achievements in agricultural research and development, written for the non-scientist ☐ ☐ ☐ ☐

e. Providing tools for the location of available translations of agricultural documents ☐ ☐ ☐ ☐

f. Production of multilingual glossaries in agriculture ☐ ☐ ☐ ☐

g. Providing facilities for education/training of users of agricultural information ☐ ☐ ☐ ☐

h. Creation of machine-readable files of numerical, statistical or other types of data of possible utility to the agricultural community ☐ ☐ ☐ ☐

i. Improved mechanisms for access to literature notified by AGRINDEX ☐ ☐ ☐ ☐

j. Please assess the importance of multilingualism and multilingual services within the above developments ☐ ☐ ☐ ☐

k. Other developments (please specify) ☐ ☐ ☐ ☐

32. Do you consider that the AGRIS programme has contributed in your country to the establishment or strengthening of any elements of a national information system for agriculture, such as a

national agricultural library, specialised information centres, training programmes for agricultural specialists etc.?

☐ YES ☐ NO

If the answer to this question is YES please give details or supply supporting documentation describing the AGRIS impact.

33. Do you consider that benefits of participation in AGRIS outweigh the costs of national involvement in the programme?

    ☐ YES ☐ NO

34. What impact has the AGRIS programme had on the planning and implementation of information services covering aspects of science and technology other than agriculture in your country?

35. Record any additional comments or criticisms you would like to make concerning the AGRIS programme.

The information below is requested for statistical purposes only and will not be used in the final assessment of AGRIS.

Name of person completing questionnaire ⎯⎯⎯⎯⎯⎯⎯⎯⎯⎯⎯⎯⎯⎯⎯⎯⎯⎯

Title or position ⎯⎯⎯⎯⎯⎯⎯⎯⎯⎯⎯⎯⎯⎯⎯⎯⎯⎯

Organisation ⎯⎯⎯⎯⎯⎯⎯⎯⎯⎯⎯⎯⎯⎯⎯⎯⎯⎯

Country ⎯⎯⎯⎯⎯⎯⎯⎯⎯⎯⎯⎯⎯⎯⎯⎯⎯⎯

Appendix Two

Conclusions and Recommendations from the AGRIS Evaluation

REPORT ON THE INDEPENDENT APPRAISAL OF AGRIS

Introduction

In accordance with the wish of the Conference of the Food and Agriculture Organization of the United Nations (Report of the 17th Session, paragraph 259(h)), an independent appraisal of AGRIS was organised by UNESCO. A Study Team of two agricultural experts and two information system specialists was appointed in December 1976 to carry out the appraisal. Members of the Study Team conducted interviews in twenty-four countries and regional centres, and a postal questionnaire was distributed to other participating countries. A questionnaire survey of the use of AGRINDEX was carried out, and further information was obtained by study visits to the AGRIS Coordinating Centre in the Food and Agriculture Organization of the United Nations, and to the AGRIS Input Unit in Vienna. A study was also made of the content and composition of AGRIN-

Reproduced from Badran et al. (1977) by permission of UNESCO.

DEX. The principal findings and recommendations of the Study Team are summarised below.

Findings

1. The major achievements of AGRIS so far are related more to its promise than to its actual performance, and many of the views expressed to the Study Team, particularly by developing countries, relate to its perceived potential. The value of Level 1 as the major means of increasing the control and use of agricultural information world-wide has not yet been realised, largely because of its novelty and incomplete coverage. Nevertheless, there is much evidence that AGRIS has contributed significantly to the development of national capabilities for the transfer and management of agricultural information, more particularly in countries without fully-developed systems devoted to this end, by facilitating the development or creation of units or cooperative systems for collecting and processing agricultural documents, by training input personnel and by making national agricultural literature more generally available than was previously the case.

It has also operated to create a climate of opinion within which such developments, particularly within a framework of international cooperation, are possible, and it is explicitly seen in a number of countries as being a logical manifestation of the UNISIST concept. In a majority of the countries submitting input to AGRIS Level 1, it is considered that the benefits of involvement in AGRIS outweigh the costs, with respondents in additional countries considering that benefits will outweigh costs in the future. There are strong indications that the benefits assignable to AGRIS will increase.

2. There are four principal reasons why AGRIS Level 1 has not yet gained full acceptance: the incomplete coverage as yet of agricultural documentation, the relatively short existence of the data-base, the lack of wide accessibility (because the printed versions are not yet widely disseminated throughout the user community, software for tape manipulation is not generally available and the service is not universally available on-line) and the lack of adequate promotion.

3. It is the feeling of the Study Team that the value of the AGRIS programme, and especially of Level 1, lies not only in its promise for the increased exploitation of agricultural information but also in its character as an internationally visible symbol of the mandate of the Food and Agriculture Organization of the United Nations. The programme is recognised to be potentially of great importance in the transfer of agricultural technology between developed and develop-

ing countries, a view which is shared in the majority of the countries participating in the programme. In view of this, it is felt that the level of financial and policy commitment to the programme by the Food and Agriculture Organization of the United Nations has been insufficient to allow its full development. In addition, the effectiveness of the programme has been diluted by attempts to develop Levels 1 and 2 concurrently; a greater proportion of the resources available should have been devoted initially to strengthening and hastening the development of Level 1.

4. A further significant barrier to the realisation of the potential of AGRIS is the uneven level of commitment to the programme by the Food and Agriculture Organization of the United Nations member nations, some countries being fully committed to securing full national input to Level 1, some making token input only, and others essentially providing no input. A guarantee of the continued existence of AGRIS, coupled with a more positive commitment on the part of the Food and Agriculture Organization of the United Nations, would undoubtedly increase the extent of participation.

5. The most significant failing of AGRIS so far has been its inability to secure comprehensive input from the United States. The United States has not thus far provided a level of commitment consonant with its role as a prime mover in the AGRIS programme and the Food and Agriculture Organization of the United Nations itself has not given highest priority to the resolution of this problem.

6. The Food and Agriculture Organization of the United Nations has so far placed most emphasis on securing and organising inputs to AGRIS, and not enough effort has been given to the provision of training, guidance and support (including software support) for the exploitation of the data base in printed and machine-readable forms. As a result, there is a danger that there will be loss of impetus in the development of the programme, and possibly a loss of credibility in the utility of the system.

7. Because AGRINDEX is so new a tool, and because it has not been very effectively promoted, its use worldwide has been limited, although there is evidence that where it is available and known, it is used. Because of its limited availability and use so far, the recent substantial price increase is expected to have minimal short-term effects on the provision of agricultural information. However, it is felt to be unfortunate that the Food and Agriculture Organization of the United Nations was obliged to accede to a new pricing policy at a time when active promotion of more widespread accessibility of the index through subscription channels should have taken place.

8. In some countries, a significant barrier to increased AGRIS participation is the lack of available resources to translate from the vernacular into the carrier language, English.

9. It is widely felt that the approach to indexing presently used in AGRIS is inadequate for searching the database in printed and machine-readable form. In addition, cumulative indexes are needed to make the printed version useful as a retrospective search tool.

10. Improved facilities for securing access to material notified by AGRIS are needed.

11. We would point out to the Food and Agriculture Organization of the United Nations or to the FAO designated publishers that citations obtained from sources 'in the public domain' cannot be copyrighted and that therefore AGRINDEX copyright statements cannot be applied to these citations.

12. In the opinion of the Study Team, outright suspension of AGRIS or holding its development at the present pace would significantly impede the developing countries' access to information of a practical nature which could be of immediate utility to them.

13. Should the programme not be allowed to develop to its full potential, the Food and Agriculture Organization of the United Nations investment to date, and the considerable resources allocated to its support by other agencies and by member countries, will be largely wasted. In addition, a serious danger would exist that the Food and Agriculture Organization of the United Nations and other agencies of the United Nations would face a lack of credibility in the initiation of any further international cooperative undertakings.

Recommendations

1. The Study Team endorses the AGRIS concept and recommends that the Food and Agriculture Organization of the United Nations, other interested bodies and Member Nations commit the necessary level of resources required to develop Level 1 into a single comprehensive data base covering both the conventional and the non-conventional literature of the agricultural sciences, available in printed, machine-readable and on-line modes, and, as this is achieved, to effect the implementation of Agris Level 2 in keeping with the perceived priorities of member nations. Level 1 is the seedbed from which the Level 2 developments grow. Advances desired in Level 2 should be considered as the responsibility not only of the AGRIS Coordinating Centre but of the Food and Agriculture Organization of the United Nations as a whole and of other

interested bodies. In this respect the Food and Agriculture Organization of the United Nations should re-examine the conceptual interdependence of Level 1 and Level 2.

2. As a top priority, failing a more complete commitment of resources on the part of the United States, the Food and Agriculture Organization of the United Nations should support the development of a conversion program which will allow the transformation of National Agricultural Library formats into formats approved by the International Organisation for Standardisation. The incorporation of full input for the United States is essential to the continued survival and success of AGRIS.

3. While continuing to secure maximum coverage in the data base, the Food and Agriculture Organization of the United Nations should devote increasing attention to outputs and services. While not supplying services directly itself, it should, in cooperation with other bodies, promote the development and availability of software for the exploitation of the data base; it should encourage networks and commercial enterprises to make the data base accessible on-line; and it should devote resources to training personnel (both information staff and potential users) in Member Nations in the efficient exploitation of the data bases, in machine-readable and printed form, for the provision of services to the agricultural community.

4. As the data base is expanded, the Food and Agriculture Organization of the United Nations must introduce a more refined approach to categorisation and indexing to optimise the accessibility of the contents. A more detailed study of approaches to the problem of vocabulary is needed. Further, we recommend that the printed version be supplied with appropriate cumulative indexes to increase its utility as a retrospective search tool.

5. While we recommend specific changes to AGRIS Level 1 to improve its utility, we urge that changes must be made after due consultation with those organisations that have already developed software for the exploitation of the data base, in order that these refinements should cause the minimum disruption in existing services and that they can be effected with the minimum cost throughout the system.

6. We recognise that the language barrier impedes the provision of input from some countries, but at present see no clear way of solving this problem. However, we urge that the Food and Agriculture Organization of the United Nations itself and other interested bodies

should devote resources to an investigation of possible means of ameliorating this situation, including the possibility of developing multilingual glossaries, of devoting increased attention to this problem in training programmes, and of assessing the feasibility of applying limited machine-aided translation capabilities.

7. As soon as Level 1 is firmly established in terms of comprehensiveness, further study should be carried out to decide the optimum means of supplying documents which are notified in the data base.

8. We recommend that the AGRIS Coordinating Centre undertake more sensitive monitoring, quantitatively and qualitatively, of the input from participating countries, in order that those centres that are encountering difficulties in maintaining the necessary standards and levels of productivity can be given the necessary advice and assistance. A further evaluation of internal efficiency should be carried out after three years, but the continued existence of AGRIS should not under any circumstances be made dependent on the outcome of such an evaluation.

9. To improve communication and a sense of community among input centres and between these centres and the Coordinating Centre, the implementation of an AGRIS newsletter is recommended. Such a newsletter would carry news from individual centres, notices of change or improvement effected by the Coordinating Centre, and occasional statistical analyses of input by region, language, country or whatever other breakdown appears to be of interest.

10. We recommend that the Food and Agriculture Organization of the United Nations and/or the publishers of AGRINDEX should adopt a more aggressive approach to the marketing and promotion of the AGRIS data base in machine-readable and printed forms.

11. In view of the importance of adequate and regular consultation among the active components of the system, we recommend that regular, possibly annual, meetings of AGRIS liaison officers be held.

Note

For the guidance of users of this report, the Study Team has allocated priorities to their recommendations as follows:

First priority	Recommendations 1 and 2
Second priority	Recommendations 3, 9, 10 and 11
Third priority	Recommendations 4, 5, 6, 7 and 8

Appendix Two

The priorities assigned should not be interpreted as meaning that recommendations classed as of lower priority can be considered as unimportant. All are necessary. It is acknowledged that not all recommendations can be implemented within the present budget, but it must be recognised that the level of resources committed to a full implementation differs from the level committed to the experimental or prototype phase. If a full policy commitment to the programme is accepted, increased financial commitment is implied.

Appendix Three

Questionnaire Used in the Evaluation of a Current Awareness Publication

DEPARTMENT OF HEALTH, EDUCATION, AND WELFARE
PUBLIC HEALTH SERVICE
NATIONAL INSTITUTES OF HEALTH
BETHESDA, MARYLAND 20014

December 8, 1972

Dear Colleague:

Nobody likes to complete questionnaires. Unfortunately, though, this is the only feasible method we can employ to study the degree of use, mode of use and value of the bibliography, <u>Parkinson's Disease and Related Disorders: Citations from the Literature</u>.

We are assuming that any recipient who has found the bibliography of positive value will consent to spend a few minutes on its evaluation. When such a bibliography is produced and distributed free to a large population, it is mandatory to review its use and value periodically. Professor F. W. Lancaster has contracted to work with the National Institute of Neurological Diseases and Stroke on the evaluation.

We are also required by the Joint Congressional Committee on Printing to edit the mailing list regularly. We ask you, therefore, to check your name and address on the enclosed card and return this to us with the questionnaire. If you do not return the card, we must interpret this as an indication of lack of interest; we will, accordingly, remove non-respondents from the mailing list.

Please take a few moments to answer the questions posed and return the questionnaire and the address card in the envelope provided.

Sincerely yours,
Neurological Information Network
National Institute of Neurological
Diseases and Stroke

NIH-T138
11-72

Questionnaire of a Current Awareness Publication 353

O.M.B. No. 68-S72157
Approval Expires 2-28-73

STUDY OF USE
PARKINSON'S DISEASE AND RELATED DISORDERS: CITATIONS FROM THE LITERATURE

INSTRUCTIONS:
1. Where appropriate, identify correct response by entering number in box provided.
2. Check your mailing address on the card. If it is incorrect, make corrections **ON THE CARD**.
3. Staple address card to questionnaire.
4. Mail to address shown below. (Self-addressed envelope provided.)

1. NAME AND ADDRESS

   PLEASE STAPLE ADDRESS CARD TO QUESTIONNAIRE AND RETURN TO

   PROFESSOR F. W. LANCASTER
   GRADUATE SCHOOL OF LIBRARY SCIENCE
   UNIVERSITY OF ILLINOIS
   URBANA, ILLINOIS 61801

2a. PROFESSIONAL IDENTITY

   1 = NEUROSURGEON   4 = NONCLINICAL RESEARCH SCIENTIST
   2 = NEUROLOGIST   5 = OTHER (Specify)
   3 = RESIDENT

2b. IF A NONCLINICAL RESEARCH SCIENTIST, PLEASE INDICATE DISCIPLINE

   1 = ANATOMY   3 = PHYSIOLOGY
   2 = BIOCHEMISTRY   4 = OTHER (Specify)

3. INDICATE THE PERCENTAGE OF YOUR TIME SPENT IN EACH OF THE FOLLOWING PROFESSIONAL ACTIVITIES. CHECK ALL BOXES. TOTAL SHOULD EQUAL 100%.

   % TEACHING   % RESEARCH   % CLINICAL

   % ADMINIS-   % OTHER (Specify)
     TRATION

4a. ARE YOU CURRENTLY AFFILIATED WITH SOME HOSPITAL

   1 = YES
   2 = NO

4b. IF "YES", INDICATE TYPE OF HOSPITAL (Enter "0" in boxes that are not applicable; enter "X" in boxes that are.)

   1 = UNIVERSITY   2 = NON-UNIV.   3 = NON-TEACHING PRIVATE   4 = VA   5 = UN-AFFILIATED   6 = OTHER (Specify)

NOTE: Throughout this questionnaire "the bibliography" refers to PARKINSON'S DISEASE AND RELATED DISORDERS: CITATIONS FROM THE LITERATURE

Appendix Three

5a. ARE YOU PRESENTLY AFFILIATED WITH A UNIVERSITY OR COLLEGE

    1 = YES
    2 = NO

5b. IF "YES," PLEASE INDICATE YOUR ACADEMIC RANK

    1 = PROFESSOR   4 = INSTRUCTOR   7 = OTHER (Specify)
    2 = ASSOCIATE PROFESSOR   5 = RESEARCH ASSOCIATE
    3 = ASSISTANT PROFESSOR   6 = POSTDOCTORAL TRAINEE

6. IS THE LITERATURE ON PARKINSON'S DISEASE AND RELATED DISORDERS

    1 = CENTRAL TO YOUR PROFESSIONAL INTERESTS
    2 = PERIPHERAL TO YOUR PROFESSIONAL INTERESTS
    3 = OF NO DIRECT INTEREST AT PRESENT

7. APPROXIMATELY HOW MANY SCIENTIFIC JOURNALS DO YOU REGULARLY READ OR SCAN (Enter number.)

8. SINCE YOU BEGAN RECEIVING THIS BIBLIOGRAPHY, HAS THERE BEEN ANY QUANTITATIVE CHANGE IN YOUR OWN DIRECT SCANNING OF JOURNALS OR READING OF ARTICLES

    a. SCANNING JOURNALS   b. READING ARTICLES

    1 = SCAN FEWER JOURNALS THAN BEFORE   1 = READ FEWER ARTICLES THAN BEFORE
    2 = SCAN MORE JOURNALS THAN BEFORE   2 = READ MORE ARTICLES THAN BEFORE
    3 = SCAN ABOUT THE SAME NUMBER AS BEFORE 3 = READ ABOUT THE SAME NUMBER AS BEFORE

9. INDICATE YOUR USE OR NON-USE OF THE FOLLOWING INDEXES

    a. INDEX MEDICUS   b. ABRIDGED INDEX MEDICUS

    1 = USE FREQUENTLY   1 = USE FREQUENTLY
    2 = USE OCCASIONALLY   2 = USE OCCASIONALLY
    3 = NEVER USE   3 = NEVER USE

10. LIST IN ORDER OF IMPORTANCE UP TO FIVE PUBLICATIONS THAT ARE MOST USEFUL IN KEEPING YOU INFORMED OF NEW LITERATURE RELEVANT TO YOUR CURRENT PROFESSIONAL INTERESTS. NAME SPECIFIC PUBLICATIONS, NOT TYPES OF PUBLICATIONS (e.g., "indexes," "reviews.")

(1) _____

(2) _____

(3) _____

(4) _____

(5) _____

11a. DO YOU USE ANY SERVICES OTHER THAN PUBLICATIONS TO KEEP YOU INFORMED OF NEW LITERATURE (e.g., services for selective dissemination of information (SDI)).

    1 = YES
    2 = NO

Questionnaire of a Current Awareness Publication

11b.   IF "YES," PLEASE LIST SPECIFIC SERVICES, NOT JUST TYPES OF SERVICES

   (1) _____

   (2) _____

   (3) _____

   (4) _____

   (5) _____

12a.   WHO USES THE COPY OF THE BIBLIOGRAPHY YOU RECEIVE

   1 = YOURSELF EXCLUSIVELY
   2 = SHARE WITH COLLEAGUES
   3 = MAKE NO USE YOURSELF BUT PASS IT ON

12b.   IF ANSWER IS "3", WHOM DO YOU PASS IT ON TO

   1 = A COLLEAGUE
   2 = A LIBRARY

12c.   INCLUDING YOURSELF, APPROXIMATELY HOW MANY PEOPLE USE THIS COPY

13.   WHICH OF THESE STATEMENTS BEST DESCRIBES YOUR USE OF THE BIBLIOGRAPHY AS A TOOL FOR KEEPING INFORMED OF NEW LITERATURE

   1 = REGULARLY SCAN EACH ISSUE
   2 = SCAN IRREGULARLY AS TIME PERMITS
   3 = SELDOM SCAN ANY ISSUES (Indicate specific reasons why not)

14.   WHEN YOU EXAMINE THE BIBLIOGRAPHY DO YOU

   1 = SCAN THE ENTIRE ISSUE
   2 = SCAN CITATIONS UNDER CERTAIN HEADINGS ONLY
   3 = MAKE OTHER USE OF IT (Please specify)

15.   AS A TOOL FOR KEEPING YOU INFORMED OF NEW LITERATURE RELEVANT TO YOUR CURRENT PROFESSIONAL INTERESTS, HOW WOULD YOU RATE THIS BIBLIOGRAPHY

   1 = OF MAJOR VALUE
   2 = OF CONSIDERABLE VALUE
   3 = OF MINOR VALUE
   4 = OF NO VALUE

Appendix Three

16. HAS THE BIBLIOGRAPHY HAD ANY IMPACT ON THE AMOUNT OF TIME YOU SPEND IN KEEPING CURRENT WITH SCIENTIFIC LITERATURE OF DIRECT CONCERN TO YOU

    1 = INCREASED THE AMOUNT OF TIME SPENT
    2 = GREATLY REDUCED THE AMOUNT OF TIME SPENT
    3 = SLIGHTLY REDUCED THE AMOUNT OF TIME SPENT
    4 = HAD NO REAL EFFECT ON THE AMOUNT OF TIME SPENT

17. HAS THE BIBLIOGRAPHY HAD ANY IMPACT ON YOUR AWARENESS OF NEW SCIENTIFIC LITERATURE OF DIRECT CONCERN TO YOU

    1 = FEEL MUCH BETTER INFORMED
    2 = FEEL SOMEWHAT BETTER INFORMED
    3 = FEEL NO BETTER INFORMED THAN BEFORE RECEIVING IT, BUT FEEL MORE CERTAIN THAT YOU ARE NOT MISSING ANY PAPERS OF DIRECT CONCERN TO YOU
    4 = NO REAL IMPACT EITHER IN IMPROVING AWARENESS OF THE LITERATURE OR AS AN INSURANCE AGAINST MISSING PAPERS OF POTENTIAL IMPORTANCE.

18. IN A TYPICAL ISSUE OF THE BIBLIOGRAPHY APPROXIMATELY HOW MANY REFERENCES DO YOU FIND THAT ARE DIRECTLY RELEVANT TO YOUR INTERESTS

    1 = LESS THAN 2   4 = 11-15
    2 = 2-5   5 = 16-20
    3 = 6-10   6 = OVER 20

19. APPROXIMATELY WHAT PROPORTION OF RELEVANT REFERENCES ARE NEW TO YOU (i.e., brought to your attention for the first time by this bibliography)

    1 = LESS THAN 25%   3 = 51% to 75%
    2 = 25% to 50%   4 = OVER 75%

20. BASED ON YOUR OWN KNOWLEDGE OF THE LITERATURE OF PARKINSONISM AND RELATED DISORDERS, DO YOU FEEL THAT THE COVERAGE OF THIS BIBLIOGRAPHY IS

    1 = LESS THAN 50% COMPLETE   3 = 75%-90% COMPLETE
    2 = 50%-75% COMPLETE   4 = OVER 90% COMPLETE

21. HAS THIS BIBLIOGRAPHY BROUGHT TO YOUR ATTENTION INFORMATION THAT DID ANY OF THE FOLLOWING
    1 = YES
    2 = NO

    a. PREVENTED THE DUPLICATION OF RESEARCH EFFORT CONDUCTED ELSEWHERE

    b. SAVED A SIGNIFICANT AMOUNT OF TIME IN YOUR OWN RESEARCH EFFORT

    c. SIGNIFICANTLY CHANGED THE DIRECTION OR EMPHASIS OF A RESEARCH EFFORT

    d. CONTRIBUTED DIRECTLY TO A PROBLEM OF PATIENT CARE

    e. LED TO THE CONSIDERATION OF A NEW VIEWPOINT ON A RESEARCH PROJECT

f. ☐ SUGGESTED A DIFFERENT INTERPRETATION OF SOME RESEARCH DATA THAN THE INTERPRETATION PREVIOUSLY CONSIDERED

22a. DO YOU KEEP BACK ISSUES OF THE BIBLIOGRAPHY FOR REFERENCE PURPOSES

☐ 1 = YES
2 = NO

22b. IF "YES", APPROXIMATELY HOW MANY TIMES HAVE YOU CONSULTED BACK ISSUES TO FIND ARTICLES ON A PARTICULAR SUBJECT IN THE PAST 12 MONTHS

☐

22c. HOW MANY TIMES HAVE YOU CONSULTED BACK ISSUES TO FIND ARTICLES BY A PARTICULAR AUTHOR IN THE PAST 12 MONTHS

☐

23a. IF THIS BIBLIOGRAPHY WERE NO LONGER PUBLISHED ARE THERE OTHER SOURCES YOU WOULD USE TO KEEP UP WITH THE LITERATURE ON THIS SUBJECT

☐ 1 = YES
2 = NO

23b. IF "YES", PLEASE LIST SOURCES. NAME SPECIFIC PUBLICATIONS NOT CATEGORIES OF PUBLICATIONS SUCH AS "INDEXES" OR ""REVIEWS".

(1) _____

(2) _____

(3) _____

(4) _____

(5) _____

24a. WOULD YOU SUBSCRIBE IF A NOMINAL FEE (for example $2.50) WERE CHARGED SHOULD FREE DISTRIBUTION BE DISCONTINUED   b.   IF IT IS NECESSARY TO INCREASE THE FEE, HOW MUCH ARE YOU WILLING TO PAY

☐ 1 = YES
2 = NO

☐ 1 = UP TO $20.00 PER YEAR
2 = UP TO $30.00 PER YEAR
3 = UP TO $50.00 PER YEAR

25. DO YOU USE THE AUTHOR INDEX IN THIS BIBLIOGRAPHY

☐ 1 = FREQUENTLY
2 = OCCASIONALLY
3 = NEVER

Appendix Three

26. WOULD THE BIBLIOGRAPHY BE LESS USEFUL IF THE AUTHOR INDEX WERE OMITTED

    1 = MUCH LESS
    2 = A LITTLE LESS
    3 = NO LESS

27. UNDER EACH PAPER LISTED IN THE BIBLIOGRAPHY APPEARS A LIST OF HEADINGS REPRESENTING THE SUBJECT MATTER OF THAT PAPER. DO YOU USE THIS LIST.

    1 = FREQUENTLY
    2 = OCCASIONALLY
    3 = NEVER

    PLEASE INDICATE FOR WHAT PURPOSE YOU USE THESE HEADINGS

28. IF THE LIST OF SUBJECT HEADINGS UNDER EACH CITATION WERE OMITTED, WOULD THE BIBLIOGRAPHY BE OF LESS VALUE

    1 = MUCH LESS
    2 = SLIGHTLY LESS
    3 = NO REDUCTION

29a. COULD THE FORMAT AND/OR ORGANIZATION OF THE BIBLIOGRAPHY BE IMPROVED TO MAKE IT MORE USEFUL TO YOU

    1 = YES
    2 = NO

29b. IF "YES", HOW MIGHT IT BE IMPROVED

30a. WOULD A SIMILAR PUBLICATION COVERING ANOTHER DISEASE BE OF VALUE TO YOU

    1 = YES
    2 = NO

30b. IF "YES", PLEASE INDICATE THE DISEASES YOU WOULD LIKE TO HAVE COVERED

31. DO YOU WISH TO CONTINUE RECEIVING THIS PUBLICATION

    1 = YES
    2 = NO

    IF "YES", PLEASE RETURN THE ADDRESS CARD WITH THE QUESTIONNAIRE WITHIN 30 DAYS. FAILURE TO RETURN THE ADDRESS CARD WILL RESULT IN REMOVAL OF YOUR NAME FROM THE MAILING LIST

32. IF YOU HAVE ANY ADDITIONAL FAVORABLE OR UNFAVORABLE COMMENTS ABOUT THIS BIBLIOGRAPHY, PLEASE RECORD THEM BELOW

Bibliography

Aitchison, J. B., and C. W. Cleverdon (1963). *A Report on a Test of the Index of Metallurgical Literature of Western Reserve University.* Cranfield, England: College of Aeronautics.

Aitchison, T. M., and J. M. Tracy (1969). *Comparative Evaluation of Index Languages. Part I. Design.* London: The Institution of Electrical Engineers. Report R 70/1.

Aitchison, T. M., et al. (1970a). *Comparative Evaluation of Index Languages. Part II. Results.* London: The Institution of Electrical Engineers. Report R 70/2.

Aitchison, T. M., et al. (1970b). *Laboratory Evaluation of Printed Subject Indexes. Part I. Design and Methodology.* London: The Institution of Electrical Engineers. Report R 70/5.

Allen, T. J. (1964). *The Use of Informational Channels in Research and Development Proposal Preparation.* Cambridge: Massachusetts Institute of Technology, Sloan School of Management, Paper 97-64.

Allen, T. J. (1966). *Managing the Flow of Scientific and Technological Information.* Cambridge: Massachusetts Institute of Technology, Sloan School of Management, PB 174 440.

Allen, T. J. (1968). "Organizational Aspects of Information Flow in Technology." *ASLIB Proceedings*, **20**, 433–454.

Allen, T. J. (1970a). "Roles in Technical Communication Networks." In *Com-*

munication among Scientists and Engineers, C. E. Nelson and D. K. Pollock, Eds. Lexington, Mass.: Heath Lexington Books, pp. 191–208.

Allen, T. J. (1970b). "Communication Networks in R&D Laboratories." *R&D Management*, **1**, 14–21.

Allen, T. J., and S. I. Cohen (1969). "Information Flow in Research and Development Laboratories." *Administrative Science Quarterly*, **14**, 12–19.

Allen, T. J., and S. Cooney (1973). "Institutional Roles in Technology Transfer: The Situation in One Small Country." *R&D Management*, **4**, 41–51.

Allen, T. J., and P. G. Gerstberger (1967). *Criteria for Selection of an Information Source*. Cambridge: Massachusetts Institute of Technology, Sloan School of Management. Another version appears in *Journal of Applied Psychology*, **52**, 272–279 (1968).

Allen, T. J., et al. (1968). *The Problem of Internal Consulting in Research and Development Organizations*. Cambridge: Massachusetts Institute of Technology, Sloan School of Management, Paper 319-68.

Allen, T. J., et al. (1971). "The International Technological Gatekeeper." *Technology Review*, **73**, 36–43.

Arthur Andersen & Co. (1962). *Research Study of Criteria and Procedures for Evaluating Scientific Information Systems*. New York.

Ashmole, R. F., et al. (1973). "Cost Effectiveness of Current Awareness Services in the Pharmaceutical Industry." *Journal of the American Society for Information Science*, **24**, 29–39.

Ashworth, W. (1974). "The Information Explosion." *Library Association Record*, **76**, 63–68, 71.

Atkin, P. (1971). *Bibliography on Use Studies of Public and Academic Libraries 1950–November 1970*. London: The Library Association Library and Information Bulletin, no. 14.

Auerbach Corporation (1965). *DOD User Needs Study—Phase 1*. Philadelphia. Tech. Mem. 1151-TR-3.

Badran, O. A., et al. (1977). *Report on the Independent Appraisal of AGRIS*. Paris: UNESCO. SC/77/WS/20. English, French, and Spanish versions.

Bagg, T. C., and M. E. Stevens (1961). *Information Selection Systems Retrieving Replica Copies: A State-of-the-Art Report*. Washington, D.C.: National Bureau of Standards.

Bamford, H., Jr. (1973). "The Editorial Processing Center." *IEEE Transactions on Professional Communication*, PC-16, pp. 82–83.

Barber, A. S. (1966). "A Critical Review of the Survey of Scientists' Use of Libraries." In *The Provision and Use of Library and Documentation Services*, W. L. Sanders, Ed. Oxford: Pergamon, pp. 145–179.

Barker, F. H., et al. (1972a). "Comparative Efficiency of Searching Titles, Abstracts, and Index Terms in a Free-Text Data Base." *Journal of Documentation*, **28**, 22–36.

Barker, F. H., et al. (1972b). "Report on the Evaluation of an Experimental Computer-Based Current Awareness Service for Chemists." *Journal of the American Society for Information Science*, **23**, 85–99.

Barnes, R. C. M. (1965). "Information Use Studies. Part II. Comparison of Some Recent Surveys." *Journal of Documentation*, **21**, 169–176.

Bibliography 361

Barry, S. G. (1976). *Indexes to Expertise: An Examination of Practical Systems.* Final Report to The British Library Research and Development Department. London: School of Librarianship, Polytechnic of North London.

Bates, M. (1971). *User Studies: A Review for Librarians and Information Scientists.* Washington, D.C.: Office of Education. ED 047 738.

Baumol, W. J., and M. Marcus (1973). *Economics of Academic Libraries.* Washington, D.C.: American Council on Education.

Baxendale, P. B. (1958). "Machine-Made Index for Technical Literature—An Experiment." *IBM Journal of Research and Development*, **2**, 354–361.

Bearman, T. C., and W. A. Kunberger (1977). *A Study of Coverage Overlap among Fourteen Major Science and Technology Abstracting and Indexing Services.* Philadelphia: National Federation of Abstracting and Indexing Services, Report no. NFAIS-77/1.

Belzer, J. (1973). "Information Theory as a Measure of Information Content." *Journal of the American Society for Information Science*, **24**, 300–304.

Bourne, C. P. (1963). *Methods of Information Handling.* New York: Wiley.

Bourne, C. P. (1965). "Some User Requirements Stated Quantitatively in Terms of the 90 Percent Library." In *Electronic Information Handling*, A. Kent and O. E. Taulbee, Eds. Washington, D.C.: Spartan Books, pp. 93–110.

Bourne, C. P. (1969a). *Characteristics of Coverage by the Bibliography of Agriculture of the Literature Relating to Agricultural Research and Development.* Palo Alto, Calif.: Information General Corporation, June, 1969, PB 185 425.

Bourne, C. P. (1969b). *Overlapping Coverage of Bibliography of Agriculture by 15 Other Secondary Services.* Palo Alto, Calif.: Information General Corp. PB 185 069.

Bourne, C. P., et al. (1961). *Requirements, Criteria and Measures of Performance of Information Storage and Retrieval Systems.* Menlo Park, Calif.: Stanford Research Institute.

Brittain, J. M. (1970). *Information and Its Users.* Bath: Bath University Press.

Bryant, E. C., D. W. King, and P. J. Terragno (1963). *Some Technical Notes on Coding Errors.* Bethesda, Md.: Westat Research, Inc. PB 166 487.

Büttenklepper, A., et al. (1976). "Research at Latin American Institutions of Higher Education: A Bibliometric Approach." Paper presented at the 38th World Congress of FID, Mexico City.

Campey, L. H. (1972). *Generating and Printing Indexes by Computer.* London: ASLIB. ASLIB Occasional Paper 11.

Campey, L. H. (1973). "Survey of Index Generation Programs." *Information Storage and Retrieval*, **9**, 441–448.

Carroll, K. H. (1969). "An Analytical Survey of Virology Literature Reported in Two Announcement Journals." *American Documentation*, **20**, 234–237.

Carter, L. F., et al. (1967). *National Document Handling Systems for Science and Technology.* New York: Wiley.

Case Western Reserve University, Center for Documentation and Communication Research (1968). *An Inquiry into Testing of Information Retrieval Systems*, Final Report, 3 parts, Cleveland, Ohio.

Casey, R. S., et al. Eds. (1958). *Punched Cards: Their Applications to Science and Industry.* 2nd ed. New York: Reinhold.

Cleverdon, C. W. (1962). *Report on Testing and Analysis of an Investigation into the Comparative Efficiency of Indexing Systems.* Cranfield, England: College of Aeronautics.

Cleverdon, C. W. (1977). *A Comparative Evaluation of Searching by Controlled Language and Natural Language in an Experimental NASA Data Base.* European Space Agency, Space Documentation Service. Draft Report.

Cleverdon, C. W., and P. Harding (1971). *Interim Report on an Investigation on Mechanised Information Retrieval Service in a Specialised Subject Area.* Cranfield, England: Cranfield Institute of Technology.

Cleverdon, C. W., and R. G. Thorne (1954). *A Brief Experiment with the Uniterm System of Coordinate Indexing for the Cataloging of Structural Data.* Farnborough, England: Royal Aircraft Establishment. RAE Library Memorandum no. 7, AD 35004.

Cleverdon, C. W., et al. (1966). *Factors Determining the Performance of Index Languages.* Cranfield, England: College of Aeronautics, 3 vols.

Coates, E. J. (1960). *Subject Catalogues: Headings and Structure.* London: The Library Association.

Coleman, J. S., et al. (1966). *Medical Innovation: A Diffusion Study.* Indianapolis: Bobbs-Merrill.

Cooney, S., and T. J. Allen (1974). "The Technological Gatekeeper and Policies for National and International Transfer of Information." *R & D Management*, **5**, 29–33.

Cooper, M. (1968). "Current Information Dissemination: Ideas and Practices." *Journal of Chemical Documentation*, **8**, 207–218.

Cooper, W. S. (1969). "Is Interindexer Consistency a Hobgoblin?" *American Documentation*, **20**, 268–278.

Cooper, W. S. (1970). "On Deriving Design Equations for Information Retrieval Systems." *Journal of the American Society for Information Science*, **21**, 385–395.

Cooper, W. S. (1971). "A Definition of Relevance for Information Retrieval." *Information Storage and Retrieval*, **7**, 19–37.

Cooper, W. S. (1973). "On Selecting a Measure of Retrieval Effectiveness." *Journal of the American Society for Information Science*, **24**, 87–100.

Costigan, D. M. (1975). *Micrographic Systems.* Silver Spring, Md.: National Micrographics Association.

Courtot, M. (1975). *Microform Indexing and Retrieval Systems.* Silver Spring, Md.: National Microfilm Association.

Crane, D. (1972). *Invisible Colleges: Diffusion of Knowledge in Scientific Communities.* Chicago: University of Chicago Press.

Crawford, S. (1971). "Informal Communications among Scientists in Sleep Research." *Journal of the American Society for Information Science*, **22**, 301–310.

Cuadra, C. A., and R. V. Katter (1967a). "Opening the Black Box of 'Relevance.'" *Journal of Documentation*, **23**, 291–303.

Cuadra, C. A., and R. V. Katter (1967b). "The Relevance of Relevance Assessment." *Proceedings of the American Documentation Institute*, **4**, 95–99.

Cuadra, C. A., et al. (1967). *Experimental Studies of Relevance Judgments: Final Report*. Santa Monica, Calif.: System Development Corporation, 3 vols.

Cummings, M. M. (1967). "Needs in the Health Sciences." In *Electronic Handling of Information: Testing and Evaluation*, A. Kent et al. Eds. Washington, D. C.: Thompson, pp. 13–23.

Davis, R. A., and C. A. Bailey (1964). *A Bibliography of Use Studies*. Philadelphia: Drexel Institute of Technology.

Davison, P. S., and D. A. R. Matthews (1969). "Assessment of Information Services." *ASLIB Proceedings*, **21**, 280–283.

DeGennaro, R. (1977). "Escalating Journal Prices: Time to Fight Back." *American Libraries*, **8**, 69–74.

De Weese, L. C. (1967). "A Bibliography of Library Use Studies." In *Report on a Statistical Study of Book Use*, by A. K. Jain. Lafayette, Ind.: Purdue University.

Doyle, L. B. (1975). *Information Retrieval and Processing*. Los Angeles: Melville (Wiley).

Dunn, O. C., et al. (1972). *The Past and Likely Future of 58 Research Libraries, 1951–1980: A Statistical Study of Growth and Change*. 1970–71 ed. Lafayette, Ind.: Purdue University.

Dym, E. D. (1967a). "A New Approach to the Development of a Technical Thesaurus." *Proceedings of the American Documentation Institute*, **4**, 126–131.

Dym, E. D. (1967b). "Relevance Predictability: I. Investigation Background and Procedures." In *Electronic Handling of Information: Testing and Evaluation*, A. Kent et al., Ed. Washington, D.C.: Thompson Book Co., pp. 175–185.

Faibisoff, S. G., and D. P. Ely (1976). "Information and Information Needs." *Information Reports and Bibliographies*, **5**(5), 2–16.

Faibisoff, S. G., et al. (1973). *An Introduction to Information and Information Needs: Comments and Readings*. Syracuse, N.Y.: Syracuse University, Center for the Study of Information and Education.

Fairthorne, R. A. (1965). Personal communication.

Fairthorne, R. A. (1969). "Empirical Hyperbolic Distributions (Bradford-Zipf-Mandelbrot) for Bibliometric Description & Prediction." *Journal of Documentation*, **25**, 319–343.

Flowerdew, A. D. J., and C. M. E. Whitehead (1974). *Cost-Effectiveness and Cost Benefit Analysis in Information Science*. London: London School of Economics and Political Science. OSTI Report No. 5206.

Ford, G. (1973). "Progress in Documentation: Research in User Behaviour in University Libraries." *Journal of Documentation*, **29**, 85–106.

Foskett, A. C. (1970). *A Guide to Personal Indexes Using Edge-Notched, Uniterm and Peek-a-boo Cards*. 2nd ed. Hamden, Conn.: Archon Books.

Foskett, A. C. (1977). *The Subject Approach to Information*. 3rd ed. Hamden, Conn.: Linnet Books.

Foskett, D. J. (1970). "Classification and Indexing in the Social Sciences." *ASLIB Proceedings*, **22**, 90–100.

Foskett, D. J. (1972). "A Note on the Concept of 'Relevance.'" *Information Storage and Retrieval*, **8**, 77–78.

Fussler, H. H., and J. L. Simon (1969). *Patterns in the Use of Books in Large Research Libraries.* Chicago: University of Chicago Press.

Gardin, J. C. (1965). *Syntol.* New Brunswick, N.J.: Rutgers, the State University.

Giering, R. H. (1972). *This Is Data Central (1972 Technical Specifications).* Dayton, Ohio: Data Corporation, DTN-72-2.

Giuliano, V. E., and P. E. Jones, Jr. (1963). "Linear Associative Information Retrieval." In *Vistas in Information Handling.* Vol. 1. P. W. Howerton and D. C. Weeks, Eds. Washington, D. C.: Spartan, pp. 30–54.

Giuliano, V. E., and P. E. Jones, Jr. (1966). *Study and Test of a Methodology for Laboratory Evaluation of Message Retrieval Systems,* Cambridge, Mass.: A. D. Little.

Goffman, W. (1964). "On Relevance as a Measure." *Information Storage and Retrieval*, **2**, 201–203.

Goffman, W., and V. A. Newill (1964). *Methodology for Test and Evaluation of Information Retrieval Systems.* Cleveland, Ohio: Western Reserve University, Center for Documentation and Communication Research.

Green, D. (1967). "Death of an Experiment." *International Science and Technology*, **65**, 82–88.

Gull, C. D. (1956). "Seven Years of Work on the Organization of Materials in the Special Library." *American Documentation*, **7**, 320–329.

Havelock, R. G. (1969). *A Comparative Study of the Literature on the Dissemination and Utilization of Scientific Knowledge.* Washington, D.C.: Department of Health, Education and Welfare. ED 029 171.

Heaps, D. M., and P. Sorenson (1968). "An On-Line Personal Documentation System." *Proceedings of the American Society for Information Science*, **5**, 201–207.

Heenan, W. F., and D. C. Weeks (1971). *Informal Communication Among Scientists.* George Washington University, Biological Sciences Communication Project.

Henderson, M. M. (1967). *Evaluation of Information Systems: A Selected Bibliography with Informative Abstracts.* NBS Techical Note 297. Washington, D.C.: National Bureau of Standards.

Herner, S., and M. J. Vellucci (1972). *Selected Federal Computer-Based Information Systems.* Washington, D.C.: Information Resources Press.

Hersey, D. F. (1978). "Information Systems on Research in Progress." In *Annual Review of Information Science and Technology,* Vol. 13. White Plains, N.Y.: Knowledge Industry Publications Inc., in press.

Higgins, L. D., and F. J. Smith (1969). "On-Line Subject Indexing and Retrieval." *Program: News of Computers in Libraries*, **3**, 147–156.

Hitch, C. J., and R. McKean (1960). *The Economics of Defense in the Nuclear Age.* Cambridge, Mass.: Harvard University Press.

Hoey, P. O. (1972). "Systematic Utilization of Human Resources as an Integral Part of Information Science Work." *Journal of the American Society for Information Science*, **23**, 384–391.

Horty, J. F. (1960). "Experience with the Application of Electronic Data Processing Systems in General Law." *Modern Uses of Logic in Law*, **60D**, 158–168.

Horty, J. F. (1961a). "Electronic Data Retrieval of Law." *Current Business Studies*, **36**, 35–46.

Horty, J. F. (1961b). "Legal Research Using Electronic Techniques." *5th Biennial A.A.L.L. Institute of Law Librarians Proceedings*, pp. 56–68.

Hulme, E. W. (1911). "Principles of Book Classification." *Library Association Record*, **13**, 354–58, 389–94, 444–49.

Jahoda, G. (1970). *Information Storage and Retrieval Systems for Individual Researchers*. New York: Wiley-Interscience.

Jahoda, G., and M. L. Stursa (1969). "A Comparison of a Keyword from Title Index with a Single Access Point per Document Alphabetic Subject Index." *American Documentation*, **20**, 377–380.

Johanningsmeier, W. F., and F. W. Lancaster (1964). *Project SHARP (Ships Analysis and Retrieval Project) Information Storage and Retrieval System: Evaluation of Indexing Procedures and Retrieval Effectiveness*. Washington, D.C.: Bureau of Ships, Department of the Navy, NAVSHIPS 250-210-3.

Kasarda, A. J., and D. J. Hillman (1972). "The LEADERMART System and Service." *Proc. of the Annual Conference of the Association for Computing Machinery*, pp. 469–477.

Katz, E. (1957). "The Two-Step Flow of Communication: An Up-to-Date Report on an Hypothesis." *Public Opinion Quarterly*, **21**, 61–78.

Keen, E. M. (1966). *Measures and Averaging Methods Used in Performance Testing of Indexing Systems*. Cranfield, England: ASLIB Cranfield Research Project.

Keen, E. M. (1971). "Evaluation Parameters." *The SMART Retrieval System: Experiments in Automatic Document Processing*, G. Salton, Ed. Englewood Cliffs, N.J.: Prentice-Hall, pp. 74–111.

Keen, E. M., and J. A. Digger (1972). *Report of an Information Science Index Languages Test*. 2 vols. Aberystwyth: College of Librarianship Wales, Department of Information Retrieval Studies. OSTI Report 5120.

Kehl, W. B. (1962). "Communication between Computer and User in Information Searching." *Information Retrieval Management*, L. H. Hattery and E. M. McCormick, Eds. Detroit, Mich.: American Data Processing, pp. 83–91.

Kehl, W. B., et al. (1961). "An Information Retrieval Language for Legal Studies." *Association for Computing Machinery Communications*, **4**, 380–89.

Kemp, D. A. (1974). "Relevance, Pertinence and Information System Development." *Information Storage and Retrieval*, **10**, 37–47.

Kent, A. (1967). "Centralization, Decentralization, and Specialization—A Problem in Resource Allocation." In *Electronic Handling of Information: Testing and Evaluation*, A. Kent et al., Eds. Washington, D.C.: Thompson, pp. 25–40.

Kent, A., et al. (1955). "Machine Literature Searching. VIII. Operational Criteria for Designing Information Retrieval Systems." *American Documentation*, **6**, 93-101.

Kent, A., et al. (1967). "Relevance Predictability in Information Retrieval Systems." *Methods of Information in Medicine*, **6**, 45-51.

King, D. W. (1965). "Evaluation of Coordinate Index Systems during File Development." *Journal of Chemical Documentation*, **5**, 96-99.

King, D. W. (1967). *Comments on the Meaning and Interpretation of Consistency Measures for Evaluating Indexing Processes.* Memorandum to U.S. Patent Office. Bethesda, Md.: Westat Research, Inc.

King, D. W., and E. C. Bryant (1971). *The Evaluation of Information Services and Products.* Washington, D.C.: Information Resources Press.

King, D. W., and P. M. McDonnell (1966). "Evaluation of Coordinate Index Systems during File Development. Part II." *Journal of Chemical Documentation*, **6**, 235-240.

King, D. W., F. W. Lancaster, D. D. McDonald, N. K. Roderer, and B. L. Wood (1976). *Statistical Indicators of Scientific and Technical Communication (1960-1980).* Rockville, Md.: King Research, Inc., vol. 2.

Klingbiel, P. H. (1969). *Machine-Aided Indexing.* Alexandria, Va.: Defense Documentation Center. AD 696 200.

Kochen, M. (1975). "Organizing Knowledge for Coping With Needs." Paper presented at the Third International Study Conference on Classification Research, Bombay, India, January, 1975.

Krevitt, B. I., and B. C. Griffith (1973). "Evaluation of Information Systems: A Bibliography, 1967-1972." *Information Reports and Bibliographies*, 2(6), 1-34.

Lancaster, F. W. (1968a). *Evaluation of the MEDLARS Demand Search Service.* Bethesda, Md.: National Library of Medicine.

Lancaster, F. W. (1968b). "Interaction between Requesters and a Large Mechanized Retrieval System." *Information Storage and Retrieval*, **4**, 239-252.

Lancaster, F. W. (1968c). Letter to the Editor. *American Documentation*, **19**, 206.

Lancaster, F. W. (1968d). "On the Need for Role Indicators in Postcoordinate Retrieval Systems," *American Documentation*, **19**, 42-46.

Lancaster, F. W. (1971). "Aftermath of an Evaluation." *Journal of Documentation*, **27**, 1-10.

Lancaster, F. W. (1972). *Vocabulary Control for Information Retrieval.* Washington, D.C.: Information Resources Press.

Lancaster, F. W. (1973). *Evaluation of On-line Searching in MEDLARS (AIM-TWX) by Biomedical Practitioners.* Urbana, Ill.: Graduate School of Library Science, University of Illinois. ED 062 989.

Lancaster, F. W. (1974a). "Assessment of the Technical Information Requirements of Users." In *Contemporary Problems in Technical Library and Information Center Management: A State of the Art,* Ed. A. Rees, Washington, D.C.: American Society for Information Science, pp. 59-85.

Lancaster, F. W. (1974b). "A Study of Current Awareness Publications in the Neurosciences." *Journal of Documentation*, **30**, 255-72.

Lancaster, F. W. (1977). *The Measurement and Evaluation of Library Services.* Washington, D.C.: Information Resources Press.

Lancaster, F. W. (1978). *Toward Paperless Information Systems.* New York: Academic Press.

Lancaster, F. W., and E. G. Fayen (1973). *Information Retrieval On-Line.* Los Angeles: Melville (Wiley).

Lancaster, F. W., et al. (1972). "Evaluating the Effectiveness of an On-line, Natural Language Retrieval System." *Information Storage and Retrieval*, **8**, 223–245.

Lefever, M., et al. (1972). "Managing an Uncontrolled Vocabulary Ex-post Facto." *Journal of the American Society for Information Science*, **23**, 339–342.

Lefkovitz, D. (1969). *File Structures for On-Line Systems.* New York: Spartan.

Leggate, P. (1975). "Computer-Based Current Awareness Services." *Journal of Documentation*, **31**, 93–115.

Leggate, P., et al. (1973a). "Evaluation of an SDI Service Based on the *Index Chemicus* Registry System." *Journal of Chemical Documentation*, **13**, 192–203.

Leggate, P., et al. (1973b). *The BA Previews Project: The Development and Evaluation of a Mechanised SDI Service for Biologists.* Oxford: Oxford University, Experimental Information Unit. OSTI Report no. 5140.

Leonard, L. E. (1975). *Inter-indexer Consistency and Retrieval Effectiveness: Measurement of Relationships.* Ph.D. dissertation. Urbana: University of Illinois.

Lesk, M. E., and G. Salton (1968). "Relevance Assessments and Retrieval System Evaluation." *Information Storage and Retrieval*, **4**, 343–359.

Lesk, M. E., and G. Salton (1969). "Interactive Search and Retrieval Methods Using Automatic Information Displays." *AFIPS Conference Proceedings, 1969 Spring Joint Computer Conference*, **34**, 435–439.

Line, M. B. (1973). "The Ability of a University Library to Provide Books Wanted by Researchers." *Journal of Librarianship*, **5**, 37–51.

Line, M. B., and A. Sandison (1974). " 'Obsolescence' and Changes in the Use of Literature with Time." *Journal of Documentation*, **30**, 283–350.

Liston, D. M., and M. L. Schoene (1971). "A Systems Approach to the Design of Information Systems." *Journal of the American Society for Information Science*, **22**, 115–122.

Luhn, H. P. (1957). "A Statistical Approach to Mechanized Encoding and Searching of Literary Information." *IBM Journal of Research and Development*, **1**, 309–317.

Luhn, H. P. (1958). "A Business Intelligence System." *IBM Journal of Research and Development*, **2**(4), 314–319.

Magson, M. S. (1973). "Techniques for the Measurement of Cost-Benefit in Information Centres." *ASLIB Proceedings*, **25**, 164–185.

Mandersloot, W. G. B. et al. (1970). "Thesaurus Control—the Selection, Grouping, and Cross-Referencing of Terms for Inclusion in a Coordinate Index Word List." *Journal of the American Society for Information Science*, **21**, 49–57.

Marcus, R. S., et al. (1971). "The User Interface for the Intrex Retrieval System." In *Interactive Bibliographic Search: The User/Computer Interface*, Montvale, N.J.: AFIPS Press, pp. 159–201.

Marron, H. (1969). "On Costing Information Services." *Proceedings of the American Society for Information Science*, **6**, 515–520.

Martin, T. H. (1974). *A Feature Analysis of Interactive Retrieval Systems*. Stanford: Stanford University, Institute for Communication Research. PB 235 952.

Martin, T. H., and E. B. Parker (1971). "Designing for User Acceptance of an Interactive Bibliographic Search Facility." In *Interactive Bibliographic Search: The User/Computer Interface*, Montvale, N.J.: AFIPS Press, pp. 45–52.

Martyn, J. (1964). "Unintentional Duplication of Research." *New Scientist*, **21**, 338.

Martyn, J. (1967). "Tests on Abstracts Journals: Coverage, Overlap and Indexing." *Journal of Documentation*, **23**, 45–70.

Martyn, J., and M. Slater (1964). "Tests on Abstracts Journals." *Journal of Documentation*, **20**, 212–235.

Mason, D. (1972). "PPBS: Application to an Industrial Information and Library Service." *Journal of Librarianship*, **4**, 91–105.

Mathies, M. L., and P. G. Watson (1973). *Computer-Based Reference Service*. Chicago: American Library Association.

Mauerhoff, G. R. (1974). "Selective Dissemination of Information." *Advances in Librarianship*, **4**, 25–62.

Mills, J. (1960). *A Modern Outline of Library Classification*. London: Chapman & Hall.

Montague, B. A. (1965). "Testing, Comparison and Evaluation of Recall, Relevance and Cost of Coordinate Indexing with Links and Roles." *American Documentation*, **16**, 201–208.

Montgomery, R. R. (1973). "An Indexing Coverage Study of Toxicological Literature." *Journal of Chemical Documentation*, **13**, 41–44.

Mooers, C. N. (1960). "Mooers' Law or Why Some Retrieval Systems Are Used and Others Are Not." *American Documentation*, **11**(3), ii.

Morse, P. M. (1968). *Library Effectiveness: A Systems Approach*. Cambridge, Mass.: M.I.T. Press.

Mullison, W. R., et al. (1969). "Comparing Indexing Efficiency, Effectiveness, and Consistency with or without the Use of Roles." *Proceedings of the American Society for Information Science*, **6**, 301–310.

Myers, J. M. (1973). "Computers and the Searching of Law Texts in England and North America: A Review of the State of the Art." *Journal of Documentation*, **29**, 212–228.

Needham, R. M. (1961). *Research on Information Retrieval, Classification and Grouping, 1957–61*. Cambridge, England: Cambridge Language Research Unit.

O'Connor, J. (1967). "Relevance Disagreements and Unclear Request Forms." *American Documentation*, **18**, 165–177.

O'Connor, J. (1968a). "Some Questions Concerning 'Information Need.'" *American Documentation*, **19**, 200–203.

O'Connor, J. (1968b). Letter to the Editor. *American Documentation*, **19**, 416–417.

O'Connor, J. (1969). "Some Independent Agreements and Resolved Disagreements about Answer-Providing Documents." *American Documentation*, **20**, 311–319.

O'Donohue, C. H. (1973). "Comparison of Service Centers and Document Data Bases—A User's View." *Journal of Chemical Documentation*, **13**, 27–29.

Oliver, L. H. et al. (1966). *An Investigation of the Basic Processes Involved in the Manual Indexing of Scientific Documents.* Bethesda, Md.: General Electric Co., Information Systems Operation. PB 169 415.

Onderisin, E. M. (1971). "The Least Common Bigram: A Dictionary Arrangement Technique for Computerized Natural-Language Text Searching." *Association for Computing Machinery Proceedings*, pp. 82–96.

Orr, R., et al. (1968). "Development of Methodologic Tools for Planning and Managing Library Services." *Bulletin of the Medical Library Association*, **56**(3 and 4) (3 parts).

Pérez-Guinjoán, A. (1976). "Research in Latin America: A Bibliometric Approach." Paper presented at the 38th World Congress of FID, Mexico City.

Perry, J. W., and A. Kent (1957). *Documentation and Information Retrieval: An Introduction to Basic Principles and Cost Analysis.* Cleveland, Ohio: Western Reserve University Press.

Pickford, A. G. A. (1968). "An Objective Method for the Generation of an Information Retrieval Language." *Information Scientist*, **2**, 17–37.

Pittsburgh, University (1968). *Searching Law by Computer: How it Works.* Pittsburgh, Pa.

Price, C. R. (1975). "Conferencing via Computer: Cost Effective Communication for the Era of Forced Choice." H. A. Linston and M. Turoff, Eds., *The Delphi Method: Techniques and Applications.* Reading, Mass.: Addison-Wesley, pp. 497–516.

Price, D. J. de Solla and D. deB. Beaver (1966). "Collaboration in an Invisible College." *American Psychologist*, **21**, 1011–1018.

Quade, E. S. (1966). *Systems Analysis Techniques for Planning-Programming-Budgeting.* Santa Monica, Ca.: The Rand Corporation. P-3322.

Raffel, J. S., and R. Shishko (1969). *Systematic Analysis of University Libraries.* Cambridge, Mass.: M.I.T. Press.

Rath, G. J., et al. (1961). "Comparison of Four Types of Lexical Indicators of Content." *American Documentation*, **12**, 126–130.

Rees, A. M. (1966). "The Relevance of Relevance to the Testing and Evaluation of Document Retrieval Systems." *ASLIB Proceedings*, **18**, 316–326.

Rees, A. M., and T. Saracevic (1966). "The Measurability of Relevance." *Proceedings of the American Documentation Institute*, **3**, 225–234.

Rees, A. M., and D. G. Schultz (1967). *A Field Experimental Approach to the Study of Relevance Assessments in Relation to Document Searching: Final Report.* Cleveland, Ohio: Case Western Reserve University, 2 vols.

Reisner, P. (1963). "Construction of a Growing Thesaurus by Conversational Interaction in a Man-Machine System." *American Documentation Institute Short Papers*, Part 1, pp. 99–100.

Reisner, P. (1966). *Evaluation of a "Growing" Thesaurus.* Yorktown Heights, N.Y.: IBM, Thomas Watson Research Center. Research Paper RD-1662.

Resnick, A. (1961). "Relative Effectiveness of Document Titles and Abstracts for Determining Relevance of Documents." *Science*, 134, 1004–1006.

Richmond, P. A. (1963). "Review of the Cranfield Project." *American Documentation*, 14, 307–311.

Robertson, S. E. (1969). "The Parametric Description of Retrieval Tests." *Journal of Documentation*, 25(1), 1–27; (2), 93–107.

Rogers, E. M. (1962). *Diffusion of Innovations.* New York: Free Press.

Rogers, E. M., and G. M. Beal (1958). "The Importance of Personal Influence in the Adoption of Technological Changes." *Social Forces*, 36, 329–335.

Roistacher, R. C. (1978). "The Virtual Journal." *Computer Networks*, 2, 18–24.

Rosenberg, K. C. (1969). "Evaluation of an Industrial Library: A Simple-Minded Technique." *Special Libraries*, 60, 635–638.

Rosenberg, V. (1967). "Factors Affecting the Preferences of Industrial Personnel for Information Gathering Methods." *Information Storage and Retrieval*, 3, 119–127.

Salisbury, B. A., Jr., and H. E. Stiles (1969). "The Use of the B-Coefficient in Information Retrieval." *American Society for Information Science Proceedings*, 6, 265–268.

Salton, G. (1968). *Automatic Information Organization and Retrieval.* New York: McGraw-Hill.

Salton, G. (1969). "A Comparison between Manual and Automatic Indexing Methods." *American Documentation*, 20, 61–71.

Salton, G. (1971). *The SMART Retrieval System: Experiments in Automatic Document Processing.* Englewood Cliffs, N.J.: Prentice-Hall.

Salton, G. (1972). "A New Comparison between Conventional Indexing (MEDLARS) and Automatic Text Processing (SMART)." *Journal of the American Society for Information Science*, 23, 75–84.

Sandoval, A. M., et al. (1976a). "A Current Latin American Bibliography Compiled from Non-Latin American Journals: A Bibliometric Study." Paper presented at the 38th World Congress of FID, Mexico City.

Sandoval, A. M., et al. (1976b). "The Vehicles of the Results of Latin American Research: A Bibliometric Approach." Paper presented at the 38th World Congress of FID, Mexico City.

Saracevic, T. (1969). "Comparative Effects of Titles, Abstracts and Full Texts on Relevance Judgements." *Proceedings of the American Society for Information Science*, 6, 293–299.

Saracevic, T. (1970a). "On the Concept of Relevance in Information Science," Ph.D. dissertation. Cleveland, Ohio: Case Western Reserve University.

Saracevic, T. (1970b). "Ten Years of Relevance Experimentation—A Summary and Synthesis of Conclusions." *Proceedings of the American Society for Information Science*, 7, 33–36.

Schuller, J. A. (1960). "Experience with Indexing and Retrieving by UDC and Uniterms." *ASLIB Proceedings,* **12,** 373–389.

Sharp, J. R. (1966). "The SLIC Index." *American Documentation,* **17,** 41–44.

Shirey, D. L., and M. Kurfeerst (1967). "Relevance Predictability-Data Reduction." In *Electronic Handling of Information: Testing and Evaluation,* A. Kent et al., Eds. Washington, D.C.: Thompson Book Co., pp. 187–198.

Simonton, W., Ed. (1963). *Information Retrieval Today.* Minneapolis: University of Minnesota Library School.

Sinnett, J. D. (1964). *An Evaluation of Links and Roles Used in Information Retrieval.* Dayton, Ohio: Air Force Materials Laboratory, Wright Patterson Air Force Base.

Slater, M. (1972). "User and Library Surveys." In *British Librarianship and Information Science, 1966–1970,* H. W. Whatley, Ed. London: The Library Association, pp. 232–256.

Smith, S. W. (1976). "Venn Diagramming for On-Line Searching." *Special Libraries,* **67,** 510–517.

Snyder, M. B., et al. (1966). *Methodology for Test and Evaluation of Document Retrieval Systems: A Critical Review and Recommendations.* McLean, Va.: Human Sciences Research Inc.

Soergel, D. (1974). *Indexing Languages and Thesauri: Construction and Maintenance.* Los Angeles: Melville (Wiley).

Sommar, H. G., and D. E. Dennis (1969). "A New Method of Weighted Term Searching with a Highly Structured Thesaurus." *Proceedings of the American Society for Information Science,* **6,** 193–198.

Soper, M. E. (1972). "The Relationships between Personal Collections and the Selection of Cited References," Ph.D. dissertation. Urbana, Ill.: Graduate School of Library Science, University of Illinois.

Sparck-Jones, K. (1971). *Automatic Keyword Classification for Information Retrieval.* Hamden, Conn.: Archon Books.

Sparck-Jones, K. (1974). *Automatic Indexing 1974: A State of the Art Review.* Cambridge, England: Computer Laboratory, University of Cambridge. OSTI Report 5193.

Sparck-Jones, K., and D. M. Jackson (1967). *The Use of the Theory of Clumps for Information Retrieval.* Cambridge, England: Cambridge Language Research Unit. OSTI Report 5014.

Spiegel, J., et al. (1962). *Statistical Association Procedures for Message Content Analysis.* Bedford, Mass.: Mitre Corporation.

Stiles, H. E. (1961). "Machine Retrieval Using the Association Factor." In *Machine Indexing, Progress and Problems.* Washington, D.C.: American University.

Swanson, D. R. (1960). *An Experiment in Automatic Text Searching, Word Correlation and Automatic Indexing.* Phase 1, Final Report, Report No. C82-OU4. Canoga Park, Calif.: Thompson Ramo Wooldridge Inc.

Swanson, D. R. (1965). "The Evidence Underlying the Cranfield Results." *Library Quarterly,* **35,** 1–20.

Swets, J. A. (1963). "Information Retrieval Systems." *Science,* **141,** 245–250.

Taulbee, O. E., et al. (1967). *Testing and Evaluation of the FTD CIRC System.* New York: Research and Technology Division, Rome Air Development Center.

Tobin, J. C. (1974). "A Study of Library 'Use Studies.'" *Information Storage and Retrieval,* **10,** 101–113.

Tocatlian, J. (1975). "International Information Systems." *Advances in Librarianship,* **5,** 1–60.

Tomberg, A. (1977). "European Information Networks." In *Annual Review of Information Science and Technology,* Vol. 12. White Plains, N.Y.: Knowledge Industry Publications Inc., pp. 219–246.

Uhlmann, W. (1967). "A Thesaurus *Nuclear Science and Technology*: Principles of Design." *Teknisk Vetenskaplig Forskning* (TVF), **38,** 46–52.

Van Dam, A., and D. C. Rice (1971). "On-Line Text Editing: A Survey." *Computing Surveys,* **3,** 93–114.

Vaswani, P. K. T., and J. B. Cameron (1970). *The National Physical Laboratory Experiments in Statistical Word Associations and Their Use in Document Indexing and Retrieval.* Teddington, Middlesex, England: National Physical Laboratory.

Veal, D. C., and B. K. Wyatt (1974). "The Application of a Measure of Cost Effectiveness to an Evaluation of an Operational Computer-Based Information Retrieval Service." In *EURIM: A European Conference on Research into the Management of Information Services and Libraries.* London: ASLIB, pp. 125–133.

Vickery, B. C. (1960). *Faceted Classification: A Guide to Construction and Use of Special Schemes.* London: ASLIB.

Virgo, J. A. (1970). "An Evaluation of Index Medicus and MEDLARS in the Field of Ophthalmology." *Journal of the American Society for Information Science,* **21,** 254–263.

Weinstock, M. J., et al. (1966). "User Practices Based on a Review of User Studies." In *A Recommended Design for the United States Medical Library and Information System,* Vol. 2. Washington, D.C.: Herner and Company, section V, pp. 1–56.

Weisman, H. M. (1972). *Information Systems, Services, and Centers.* New York: Becker and Hayes.

Wessel, C. J., and K. L. Moore (1969). *Criteria for Evaluating the Effectiveness of Library Operations and Services.* Washington, D.C.: John I. Thompson & Co. ATLIS Report No. 21.

Wiederkehr, R. R. V. (1968). "A Net Benefit Model for Evaluating Elementary Document Retrieval Systems." In *Westat Research, Inc., Evaluation of Document Retrieval Systems: Literature Perspective, Measurement, Technical Papers.* Bethesda, Md.: Westat Research, Inc. PB 182 710.

Wilkening, E. A. (1952). "Informal Leaders and Innovators in Farm Practices." *Rural Sociology,* **17,** 272–275.

Wilkening, E. A. (1956). "Roles of Communicating Agents in Technological Changes in Agriculture." *Social Forces,* **34,** 361–367.

Wilkin, A. (1977). "Personal Roles and Barriers in Information Transfer." *Advances in Librarianship,* **7,** 257–297.

Williams, J. H., Jr. (1969). *BROWSER: An Automatic Indexing On-Line Text Retrieval System.* Annual Progress Report. Gaithersburg, Md.: IBM Federal Systems Division. AD 693 143.

Williams, M. E. (1972). "Experiences of IIT Research Institute in Operating a Computerized Retrieval System for Searching a Variety of Data Bases." *Information Storage and Retrieval,* **8,** 57–75.

Williams, M. E., and K. MacLaury (1977). "Mapping of Chemical Data Bases Using a Relational Data Base Structure." In *Computers in Chemical Education and Research,* E. V. Ludeña et al., Eds. New York, Plenum.

Williams, M. E., and S. H. Rouse (1976). *Computer Readable Bibliographic Data Bases: A Directory and Data Sourcebook.* Washington, D.C.: American Society for Information Science.

Wilson, P. (1973). "Situational Relevance." *Information Storage and Retrieval,* **9,** 457–471.

Wood, D. M. (1971). "User Studies: A Review of the Literature from 1966–1970." *ASLIB Proceedings,* **23,** 11–23.

Yasaki, E. K. (1975). "Toward the Automated Office," *Datamation,* 21(2), 59–62.

Zimmerman, P. J. (1977). "Principles of Design for Information Systems." *Journal of the American Society for Information Science,* **28,** 183–191.

Zipf, G. K. (1949). *Human Behavior and the Principle of Least Effort.* Cambridge, Mass.: Addison-Wesley.

Index

Accessibility of information services, 86-87, 312-314, 321, 330-331
Accuracy of indexing, 196-197, 210, 229-231
Achievements of automation, 330-331
Activities of information retrieval systems, 7-13
Advantages of computer-based systems, 67-68
AGRIS, 106
  evaluation of, 246-248, 277, 335-350
Aitchison, J. B., 275, 359
Aitchison, T. M., 276, 278, 287, 359
Allen, T. J., 311, 313, 359, 360, 362
Ambiguous and spurious relationships, 183-184, 190, 232-233
Analyticosynthetic classification, 21-22
Armed Services Technical Information Agency, 35-36, 273-274. *See also* Defense Documentation Center
Arthur Andersen & Co., 275, 360
Ashmole, R. F., 217, 360
Ashworth, W., 328, 360
Aspen Systems Corporation, 280
Assignment indexing, 294
Assimilation of information, 3, 253
Atkin, P., 318, 360
Auerbach Corporation, 318, 360
Automatic abstracting, 294-295
Automatic classification, 295
Automatic indexing, 293-294
Automatic systems, 293, 299
Automation, achievements of, 330-331

Badran, O. A., 246, 277, 335, 344, 360
Bagg, T. C., 94, 360
Bailey, C. A., 318, 363
Bamford, H., Jr., 334, 360

Barber, A. S., 318, 360
Barker, F. H., 276, 360
Barnes, R. C. M., 318, 360
Barry, S. G., 96, 361
BASIS, 77
Bates, M., 318, 361
Batten system, 24
Baumol, W. J., 330, 361
Baxendale, P. B., 294, 361
Beal, G. M., 311, 370
Bearman, T. C., 278, 361
Beaver, D. deB., 311, 369
Belzer, J., 269, 270, 361
Benefit analysis, 121-122, 219, 244-249
Bibliographic Retrieval Services, 82-83
Bibliographic warrant, 188
Bibliography of Agriculture, 208, 278
Bibliometric studies, 208, 222-226, 254-255
Boolean logic, 50-60
Bourne, C. P., 30, 94, 208, 244, 275, 278, 361
Bradford's law, 222-225
Brittain, J. M., 312, 361
BROWSER, 297
Bryant, E. C., 122, 230, 361, 365
Büttenklepper, A., 255, 361

Cambridge Language Research Unit, 276, 296
Cameron, J. B., 276, 372
Campey, L. H., 22, 361
Carroll, K. H., 278, 361
Carter, L. F., 312, 361
Case Western Reserve University, 276, 361. *See also* Western Reserve University
Casey, R. S., 30, 362
Chain indexing, 21-22
Chemical Abstracts, growth of, 328

Cleverdon, C. W., 118, 119, 274-275, 277, 287, 288, 359, 362
Clumps, 295-296
Coates, E. J., 21, 362
Cohen, S. I., 311, 360
Coleman, J. S., 307, 311, 362
Combination, 20-22
Communication networks, 300-311
Components of information, retrieval systems, 13-14
Conceptual analysis, 9, 10, 39-40, 48, 192-193
Concordance, 280
Conferences, 308
Consistency of indexing, 197-198, 210
Controlled vocabularies, compared with natural language, 284-288
Cooney, S., 311, 360, 362
Cooper, M., 311, 362
Cooper, W. S., 198, 267-268, 325, 362
Coordination level search, 288
Cordonnier, G., 24
Cost, of information services, 218-219
  input versus output, 237-240
  of on-line searches, 82-83, 87-88, 330-331
  of publications, 329
  per relevant citation, 242-244
Cost analysis, 241-244
Cost-benefit analysis, 109-110, 121-122, 244-249
Cost criteria, 109-110, 205-207
Cost-effectiveness, 109-110, 120-122, 218-244
  of indexing, 227-232
  of index languages, 232-234
  of search procedures, 234-237
  of selection procedures, 222-227
Costigan, D. M., 94, 362
Courtot, M., 94, 362
Coverage, 119-120, 133, 207-209
Crane, D., 311, 362
Cranfield Project, 274, 287
Crawford, S., 302-305, 311, 362
Criteria for evaluation, 108-120
Critical incident technique, 316-317
Cuadra, C. A., 270, 277, 362, 363
Cummings, M. M., 87, 363

Cumulated Index Medicus, 36, 45
Current awareness needs, 6-7, 309-310
  services, evaluation of, 248-249, 351-358
  see also Selective Dissemination of Information

Data banks, 79
Data bases, 78-89
  cost-effectiveness aspects, 222-227
  evaluation of, 204-211
  factors affecting performance of information services, 14, 33-34
  selection of, 154-156
Data Central, 77, 281, 298-299
Data retrieval, 13
Davis, R. A., 318, 363
Davison, P. S., 208, 278, 363
Decision making needs, 6-7, 309-310
Defense Documentation Center, 35-36, 101, 287. *See also* Armed Services Technical Information Agency
De Gennaro, R., 329, 363
Delays in publication, 328-329
Delegated search, 10
Demands, 140-153, 317-318
Demand searches, 7, 45, 48, 50-62
Dennis, D. E., 175, 371
Design of information services, 319-325
De Weese, L. C., 318, 363
DIALOG, 76
Diffusion of information, 306-307
Digger, J. A., 276, 365
Documentation Inc., 273-274
Document delivery, 6, 11, 209
  via microforms, 91-93
Document-term matrix, 30-34, 65-66
Doyle, L. B., 94, 363
Dunn, O. C., 330, 363
Duplication of index entries, 19
Dym, E. D., 270, 323, 363

Ease of use, 312-314
Eastman Kodak Co., 92
Economics of information services, 82-83, 87-88
Edge-notched cards, 27-28
Educational Resources Information Center, 68, 104-105

Education of users, 315
Effectiveness evaluation, 108-109, 121-139
Effort, 117, 312-314
Ely, D. P., 312, 324, 363
Entry vocabulary, 188-190, 233-234
ESANET, 85
EURONET, 85-86
European Space Agency, 77, 80, 85
Evaluation, 108-139, 199-278
    criteria, 108-120
    of data bases, 204-211
    history, 273-278
    of service centers, 211-217
    see also Cost-benefit analysis; Cost effectiveness
Exhaustivity, of indexing, 193-196, 210, 227-230, 324
    of search strategies, 157-164
Expressed needs, 140-153
Extraction indexing, 293-294

Factors affecting performance of information systems, 14, 33-34, 137-139, 176-177, 185-191
Faibisoff, S. G., 312, 324, 363
Failure analysis, 126, 137
Fairthorne, R. A., 118, 223, 363
Fallout, 118
False coordinations, 183-184
Fayen, E. G., 71, 75, 367
File structure of on-line systems, 73-75
Flowerdew, A. D. J., 245, 363
Food and Agriculture Organisation, 106, 246-248. *See also* AGRIS
Ford, G., 318, 363
Foskett, A. C., 22, 30, 363
Foskett, D. J., 267, 364
Fractional search, 288
Free text, *see* Natural language
Functions of information retrieval systems, 1-14
Fussler, H. H., 225, 364
Future of information system, 326-334

Gardin, J. C., 180, 364
Gatekeepers, 306
Generality, 119
Gerstberger, P. G., 313, 360

Giering, R. H., 281, 364
Giuliano, V. E., 276, 296, 364
Goffman, W., 118, 268, 364
Green, D., 311, 364
Griffith, B. C., 273, 365
Group SDI, 66-67
Growing thesaurus, 282-283
Growth of literature, 327-328
Gull, C. D., 273-274, 364

Half life, 225-226
Harding, P., 288, 362
Havelock, R. G., 311, 364
Heaps, D. M., 288, 364
Heenan, W. F., 311, 364
Henderson, M. M., 273, 364
Herner, S., 107, 364
Hersey, D. F., 99, 364
Higgins, L. D., 283, 364
Hillman, D. J., 297, 365
History, of evaluation, 273-278
    of information retrieval, 15-16
    of on-line systems, 76-77
Hitch, C. J., 220, 364
Hoey, P. O., 96, 365
Homographs, 180
Horty, J. F., 280, 365
Hulme, E. W., 188, 365
Hybrid vocabularies, 287-288

Image Systems Inc., 92
Improving an information service, 199-203
Incorrect term relationships, 183-184
Indexing, 9, 192-198, 210, 323-324
    cost-effectiveness aspects, 227-232
    forms, 40, 42-43, 46-47
    for MEDLARS, 37-44
    personnel, 231-232
    revision of, 230-231
    specificity, 41
    time expenditures, 229-230
Index languages, 178-191, 323-324
    cost-effectiveness aspects, 232-234
    see also Natural language
Index Medicus, 36-45
Indicators of communication, 251-255
Informal communication, 300-311, 315
Information analysis centers, 102-104

Information Bank of *New York Times*, 77, 79, 81
Information centers, 95-107
Information Exchange Group experiments, 310-311
Information explosion, 327-328
Information needs, 6-7, 140-153, 312-318
Information overload, 314
Information retrieval, defined, 11-12
Information services librarians, 84, 88-89
Information transfer cycle, 1-4, 251-255
Innovation, 306-307
Input costs versus output costs, 237-240
INQUIRE, 77
INSPEC, 276
Interface role of information services, 4-6
International Atomic Energy Agency, 106
International information services, 105-107
International Nuclear Information System (INIS), 106
Inverted files, 27-34, 73-75, 280
Invisible colleges, 301-305
Item entry systems, 27-34

Jackson, D. M., 276, 371
Jahoda, G., 30, 278, 365
Johanningsmeir, W. F., 275, 365
Jones, P. E., Jr., 276, 296, 364

Kasarda, A. J., 297, 365
Katter, R. V., 270, 277, 362, 363
Katz, E., 311, 365
Keen, E. M., 119, 365
Kehl, W. B., 280, 365
Kemp, D. A., 267, 365
Kent, A., 104, 118, 270, 274, 365, 369
Kessler, M. M., 76
King, D. W., 122, 230, 254, 275, 361, 365
KLIC index, 284
Klingbiel, P. H., 287, 365
Known item need, 6
Kochen, M., 141, 365
Krevitt, B. I., 273, 365
Kunberger, W. A., 278, 361
Kurfeerst, M., 270, 371

Lancaster, F. W., 22, 71, 75, 123, 130, 137, 147, 188, 190, 200, 236, 246, 257,
263, 269, 275, 276, 277, 278, 281, 287, 299, 318, 326, 334, 365, 366, 367
Latent needs, 140-153
Law, *see* Legal retrieval
LEADER, 297
Leasing of data bases, 80
Least common bigram, 281
Least common factor in searching, 61, 172, 289-290
Lefever, M., 287, 367
Lefkovitz, D., 75, 367
Legal retrieval, 280-281
Leggate, P., 68, 276, 367
Leonard, L. E., 198, 367
Lesk, M. E., 236, 272, 277-278, 367
LEXIS, 77, 281
Limitations of precoordinate systems, 16-22
Line, M. B., 141, 223, 367
Links, 184
Liston, D. M., 235, 367
LITE, 281
Literary warrant, 188, 323-324
Lockheed Missiles and Space Company, 76, 156
Luhn, H. P., 64-65, 294-295, 367

McDonald, D. D., 365
McDonnell, P. M., 275, 365
Machine-readable data bases, 78-89
  evaluation of, 204-211
McKean, R., 220, 364
MacLaury, K., 156, 373
Macroevaluation, 122
Magson, M. S., 245, 367
Mandersloot, W. G. B., 180, 367
Marcus, M., 330, 361
Marcus, R. S., 270, 368
Marron, H., 241-242, 368
Martin, T. H., 75, 325, 368
Martyn, J., 133, 208, 278, 368
Mason, D., 245, 368
Match, between search strategy and documents, 258-260, 265-266
Matching subsystem, 15-34
Mathies, M. L., 68, 173, 368
Matthews, D. A. R., 208, 278, 363
Mauerhoff, G. R., 68, 368

Medical Literature Analysis and Retrieval
 System (MEDLARS), 38-62, 66-67,
 78-80, 86-87, 104, 105
 evaluation of, 123-124, 137-139, 147,
 200, 276
Medical Subject Headings, 39
MEDLINE, 77, 80-81
MENTOR, 92
Mexico, 254-255
Microevaluation, 122
Microform Data Systems Inc., 92
Microform retrieval systems, 90-94
Microstar, 92
Mills, J., 22, 368
Montague, B. A., 275, 368
Montgomery, R. R., 208-209, 368
Mooers, C. N., 27-28, 314, 368
Mooers' Law, 314
Moore, K. L., 278, 372
Morse, P. M., 278, 368
Mullison, W. R., 275, 368
Multidimensionality of subject matter, 16-24
Myers, J. M., 281, 368

National Aeronautics and Space Administration, 36, 66, 76-77, 80, 101
National information systems, components of, 95-107
 evaluation of, 250-255
National Institute of Neurological Diseases and Stroke, 248-249
National Institutes of Health, 310-311
National Library of Medicine, 36-62, 66-67, 80-81. *See also* Medical Literature Analysis and Retrieval System ; MEDLINE
National Referral Center, 96
National Technical Information Service, 66, 101-102
Natural language, 279-292
 compared with controlled vocabularies, 284-288
Near synonyms, 179-180
Need, *see* Information needs
Needham, R. M., 296, 368
Networks, 79, 85-86, 104-105. *See also* Communication networks

Newill, V. A., 118, 364
Ninety percent library, 244
Notched cards, 27-28
Novelty, 120, 132-133

Obsolescence, 222-223, 225-226
O'Connor, J., 269, 368, 369
O'Donohue, C. H., 213-214, 216-217, 369
Off-line systems, 35-68
Ohio Bar Automated Research (OBAR), 77, 281
Oliver, L. H., 198, 369
Onderisin, E. M., 281, 369
Ongoing research, 96-99, 314-315
On-line service centers, 81-83
On-line systems, 69-77, 80-89
 costs, 82-83
 history, 76-77
Optical coincidence, 24-25
Optimization of search procedures, 61-62
Oracle, 94
Oral communication, 307-310
ORBIT, 72, 77
Orr, R., 278, 369
Output costs versus input costs, 237-240

Paperless information systems, 326-334
Paradigmatic relations, 180
Parker, E. B., 325, 368
Passage retrieval, 13
Patent Office, 30, 242-243
Peek-a-boo, 24-25
Perez-Guinjoán, A., 255, 369
Performance measures, 108-120
Permutation, 20-22
Perry, J. W., 369
Personal files, 315, 321
Pertinence, 256-272
Photocomposition, 36, 45
Pickford, A. G. A., 323, 369
Pittsburgh University, 280, 369
Postcontrolled vocabulary, 281-283, 286-287, 292
Postcoordinate systems, 22-30, 40
Precision, 111-117, 127-139
Precoordinate systems, 16-22
Price, C. R., 334, 369
Price, D. J. de Solla, 311, 369

Index

Principle of least effort, 222, 312-314
Printed indexes, evaluation, 278
  production, 44-45
Problem solving needs, 6-7, 309-310
Problems of science communication, 327-330
Punched cards, 30

Quade, E. S., 220, 369
Quality criteria, 109-120, 207-211
Quality of indexing, 196-197, 210, 229-231
Quasi-synonyms, 180
Question answering, 12

Raffel, J. S., 244, 369
Ranked output, 57-58, 118-119
Rapid Selector, 93-94
Rath, G. J., 270, 369
Real time, 71-72
Recall, 111-117, 127-139
RECON, 76-77, 80
Recurring bibliographies, 66-67
Rees, A. M., 256-257, 270-271, 277, 369
Referral activities, 96
Referral data base, 155-156
Regional information centers, 83-85
Reisner, P., 283, 370
Relevance, 256-272, 277-278
Relevance assessments, 128-129
Requests, 10, 147-153, 236-237, 261-267
Resnick, A., 270, 370
Retrospective searching, 7, 45, 48, 50-62
Revision of indexing, 230-231
Rice, D. C., 334, 372
Richmond, P. A., 274, 370
Robertson, S. E., 119, 370
Roderer, N. K., 365
Rogers, E. M., 311, 370
Roistacher, R. C., 328, 332, 370
Role indicators, 184, 232-233, 275
Rosenberg, K. C., 245, 370
Rosenberg, V., 313, 370
Rouse, S. H., 79, 373

Salisbury, B. A., Jr., 296, 370
Salton, G., 119, 236, 272, 275-276, 277-278, 297-298, 367, 370
Sandison, A., 223, 367

Sandoval, A. M., 254-255, 327, 370
Saracevic, T., 256-257, 270, 271, 369, 370
SCANNET, 85
Scanning in indexing, 39
Scatter of literature, 222-225, 328
Scenario for future system, 331-334
Schoene, M. L., 325, 367
Schuller, J. A., 274, 371
Schultz, D. G., 270-271, 277, 369
Scientific information dissemination centers, 80
Screening of output, 175, 234-235
SDI, *see* Selective Dissemination of Information
Search procedures, 10, 32-33, 48, 50-62, 156-175
  cost-effectiveness aspects, 234-237
  in natural language, 288-292
  in on-line systems, 72-73, 164-173
Selected Current Aerospace Notices, 66
Selected Listing in Combination (SLIC), 21
Selected Research in Microfiche, 66, 101
Selecting data base, 154-156
Selection procedures, 322-323
  cost-effectiveness aspects, 222-227
Selective Dissemination of Information (SDI), 63-67. See also Group SDI
Service center evaluation, 211-217
Sharp, J. R., 21, 371
Shirey, D. L., 270, 371
Shishko, R., 244, 369
Simon, J. L., 225, 364
Simonton, W., 30, 371
Sinnett, J. D., 275, 371
Slater, M., 133, 208, 278, 318, 368, 371
SLIC index, 21
SMART, 276, 277-278, 297-298
Smith, F. J., 283, 364
Smith, S. W., 169, 371
Smithsonian Science Information Exchange, 97-99, 315
Snyder, M. B., 275, 371
Sociograms, 302-305
Sociometric analysis, 302-305
Soergel, D., 188, 371
Sommar, H. G., 175, 371
Soper, M. E., 313-314, 371
Sorenson, P., 288, 364

Sparck Jones, K., 276, 295, 296, 371
Specificity, in indexing, 41
  in searching, 157-164
  in vocabularies, 185-190, 210, 232
Spiegel, J., 296, 371
STAIRS, 77
Statistical associations, 295-296
Stevens, M. E., 94, 360
Stiles, H. E., 296, 370, 371
Stringsearch, 172
Structure of vocabulary, 190-191
Stursa, M. L., 278, 365
Subheadings, 40-41, 184
Subject needs, 6-7
Subsearches, 57-58
Swanson, D. R., 274, 371
Swets, J. A., 118, 371
Synonym control, 179-180
Syntagmatic relations, 180-181
Synthesis in indexing, 19-20
System Development Corporation, 72, 77, 270

Taube, M., 25-27
Taulbee, O. E., 276, 372
Telenet, 77, 82-83
Term entry systems, 27-34
Terminals, 70-71
Terragno, P. J., 230, 361
Thesauri, 181-182, 282-283
Thorne, R. G., 274, 362
Time criteria, 109-110, 117, 209-210
Time-shared communications networks, 77
Time sharing, 71
TIP System, 76
Tobin, J. C., 218, 372
Tocatlian, J., 107, 372
Tomberg, A., 86, 372
Tracy, J. M., 276, 359
Tradeoffs in information systems, 237-241
Translations centers, 102
Translation step of indexing, 9, 193
Truncation, 283, 291-292
Tymshare, 77

Uhlmann, W., 288, 372

Ultramicrofiche, 92
UNESCO, 106-107
Ungerer, H., 86
UNISIST, 106-107
Uniterm system, 25-26, 273-274, 279
User, interest profiles, 63-67
  involvement in system design, 319-321
  studies, 312-318, 321-323
  warrant, 188, 323-324
User-system interaction, 147-153, 236-237

Van Dam, A., 334, 372
Vaswani, P. K. T., 276, 372
Veal, D. C., 276, 372
Vellucci, M. J., 107, 364
Vickery, B. C., 22, 372
Virgo, J. A., 278, 372
Vocabulary control, 178-191, 284-288

Watson, P. G., 68, 173, 368
Weeks, D. C., 311, 364
Weighted indexing, 172-173
Weighted term searching, 173-175
Weinstock, M. J., 318, 372
Weisman, H. M., 107, 372
Wessel, C. J., 278, 372
Westat Research Inc., 242-243, 275
Western Reserve University, 35, 270-271, 275. *See also* Case Western Reserve University
Whitehead, C. M. E., 245, 363
Wiederkehr, R. R. V., 226-227, 372
Wilkening, E. A., 311, 372
Wilkin, A., 311, 372
Williams, J. H., Jr., 297, 373
Williams, M. E., 79, 156, 281, 283, 373
Wilson, P., 269, 373
Wood, B. L., 365
Wood, D. M., 318, 373
Written communication, 307-310
Wyatt, B. K., 276, 372

Yasaki, E. K., 334, 373

Zator system, 27-28
Zimmerman, P. J., 325, 373
Zipf, G. K., 222, 223, 314, 373